The World's Story

IN
FOURTEEN VOLUMES
WITH ILLUSTRATIONS
VOLUME II

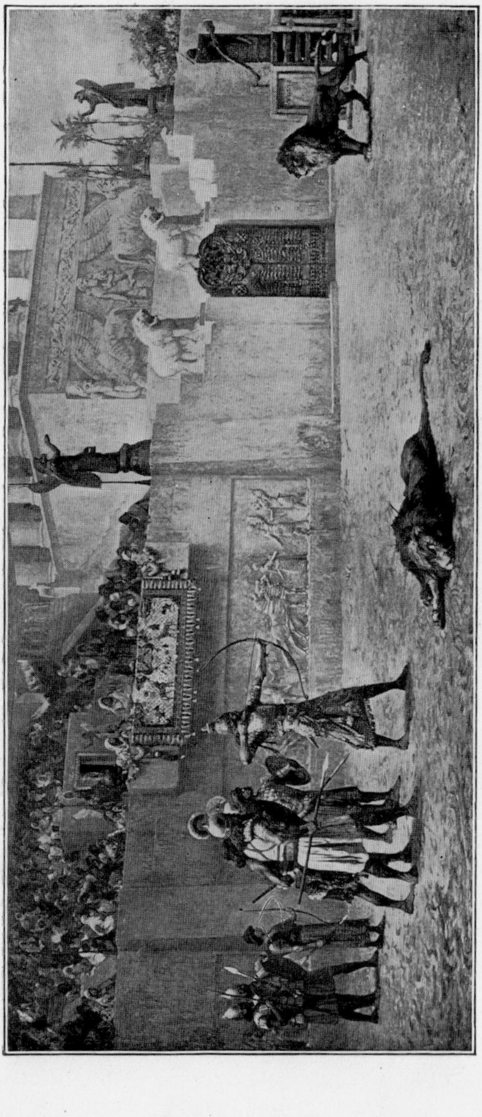

THE PASTIMES OF AN ASSYRIAN KING

BY FREDERICK ARTHUR BRIDGMAN

(*American painter.* 1847)

THE Assyrians were a cruel race. Their captives were tortured in fashions too horrible to relate. Even their amusements were hardly less cruel than their war-making, for their one great delight was the chase; or, as here shown, even in a descent into the arena to slaughter wild animals that had been captured and driven out of their cages to afford marks for the archery of the king.

The favorite Assyrian form of decoration was a sharp and clear-cut bas-relief. This bas-relief was used in great degree as a form of historical composition, and there were court sculptors who made a business of immortalizing in this way the royal exploits in hunting and warfare, and such peaceful scenes as the king dining with his queen in the palace garden. The sculptor also carved mammoth bulls and lions to terrify the enemy from the gates of the city, but it was in the relief work that he met his greatest success. These reliefs were usually arranged on the walls in long horizontal bands. Generally they were colored. The stone ground was left in its natural tint, but the figures and the hieroglyphics and the draperies were painted in brilliant hues. No knowledge of perspective had the Assyrian artist, but his work, limited as was his domain, did tell a story clearly and interestingly.

THE PASTIMES OF AN ASSYRIAN KING

INDIA PERSIA
MESOPOTAMIA AND PALESTINE

The World's Story
A HISTORY OF THE WORLD
IN STORY SONG AND ART
EDITED BY
EVA MARCH TAPPAN

VOLUME II

BOSTON AND NEW YORK
HOUGHTON MIFFLIN COMPANY
The Riverside Press Cambridge
1914

954
J16L

COPYRIGHT, 1914, BY HOUGHTON MIFFLIN COMPANY

ALL RIGHTS RESERVED

NOTE

ALL rights in material used in this volume are reserved by the holders of the copyright. The publishers and others named in the subjoined list are the proprietors, either in their own right or as agents for the authors, of the selections taken by their permission from the works enumerated, of which the ownership is hereby acknowledged. The Editor takes this opportunity to thank both authors and publishers for the ready generosity with which they have given permission to include these selections in "The World's Story."

"A Brief History of the Indian People," by W. W. Hunter: published in the United States by the Oxford University Press, New York; in Great Britain by the Clarendon Press, Oxford.

"Hindu Literature, or the Ancient Books of India," by Elizabeth A. Reed: copyright, 1890, by S. C. Griggs & Company; used by permission of the publishers, Scott, Foresman & Company, Chicago.

"The Light of Asia," by Sir Edwin Arnold: published by George Routledge & Sons, Ltd., London.

"Karma," by Paul Carus: published by The Open Court Publishing Co., Chicago.

"Laos Folk-Lore of Farther India," by Katherine Neville Fleeson: published by Fleming H. Revell Company, New York.

"Cradle Tales of Hinduism," by Sister Nivedita (Margaret E. Noble): published by Longmans, Green & Company, New York and London.

NOTE

"Behar Proverbs," by John Christian: published by George Routledge & Sons, Ltd., London.

"Plutarch's Lives," corrected and translated by A. H. Clough: published by Little, Brown & Co., Boston.

"Asoka," by Vincent A. Smith: published by The Clarendon Press, Oxford.

"Sakoontala, or the Lost Ring," translated by Sir Monier Monier-Williams: published by Dodd, Mead & Company, New York.

"A Visit to India, China and Japan," by Bayard Taylor: published by G. P. Putnam's Sons, New York.

"Forty-one Years in India," by Lord Roberts: published by Longmans, Green & Company, New York.

"Scenes through the Battle Smoke," by Rev. Arthur Male: reprinted by permission of Mrs. John C. Gostick, holder of the copyright.

"Modern India and the Indians," by Sir Monier Monier-Williams: published by George Routledge & Sons, Ltd., London.

"Ramakrishna, His Life and Sayings," by F. Max Müller: published in the United States by Charles Scribner's Sons, New York; in Great Britain by Longmans, Green & Company, London.

"Peeps at Great Cities: Delphi and the Durbar," by John Finnemore: published by Adam & Charles Black, London.

"Cyrus the Great," by Jacob Abbott: published by Harper & Brothers, New York.

"Stories of the East from Herodotus," by Alfred J. Church: published in the United States by Dodd, Mead & Company, New York; in Great Britain by Seeley, Service & Company, Ltd., London.

NOTE

"Persian Literature, Ancient and Modern," by Elizabeth A. Reed: copyright, 1893, by S. C. Griggs & Company; used by permission of the publishers, Scott, Foresman & Company, Chicago.

"Persian Children of the Royal Family," by Wilfred Sparroy: published by John Lane, New York and London.

"Persia as It is," by C. J. Wills: published by Sampson Low, Marston & Company, Ltd., London.

"Persian Life and Customs," by Rev. S. G. Wilson: published in the United States by Fleming H. Revell Company, New York; in Great Britain by Oliphant, Anderson & Ferrier, Edinburgh and London.

"Persia and the Persians," by S. G. W. Benjamin: published by T. Fisher Unwin, London.

"Social Life among Assyrians and Babylonians," by A. H. Sayce: published by The Religious Tract Society, London.

"Our Young Folks' Josephus," by William Shepard: published by J. B. Lippincott Company, Philadelphia.

"History of France," by Guizot; published by Sampson Low, Marston & Company, Ltd., London.

CONTENTS

INDIA

I. THE COMING OF THE ARYANS

HYMN TO INDRA AND SOMA	*From the Rig-veda*	3
THE PEOPLE WHOM THE ARYANS FOUND IN INDIA	*Sir William Wilson Hunter*	5
From "A Brief History of the Indian Peoples."		
SAVITRI'S CHOICE	*From the Mahabharata*	11
Rewritten by Elizabeth A. Reed.		

II. BUDDHA AND HIS TEACHINGS

THE LIFE OF BUDDHA	*Sir William Wilson Hunter*	27
From "A Brief History of the Indian Peoples."		
STORIES OF BUDDHA	*Sir Edwin Arnold*	
BUDDHA AND THE WOUNDED SWAN		31
HOW BUDDHA WON THE PRINCESS		33
BUDDHA AND THE LAMB		38
HOW BUDDHA COMFORTED THE SORROWING MOTHER . . .		39
THE FIVE RULES OF BUDDHA		41
From "The Light of Asia."		
KARMA, A STORY OF BUDDHIST ETHICS . . .	*Paul Carus*	43

III. A GROUP OF FOLK-LORE STORIES

RIGHT AND MIGHT	*Katherine Neville Fleeson*	67
THE MAN IN THE MOON	*Katherine Neville Fleeson*	69
THE LEGEND OF THE RICE . . .	*Katherine Neville Fleeson*	71
From "Laos Folk-Lore of Farther India."		
THE LORD KRISHNA AND THE LAPWING'S NEST	*Margaret E. Noble*	72
From "Cradle Tales of Hinduism."		
THE PEACOCK AND THE TORTOISE	*John Christian*	73
LET'S SEE ON WHICH SIDE THE CAMEL SITS .	*John Christian*	75
THE WASHERMAN AND THE DONKEY . . .	*John Christian*	76
THE SEVEN WEAVERS AND THE FIELD OF FLAX	*John Christian*	78
SOME INDIAN PROVERBS	*John Christian*	79
From "Behar Proverbs."		

CONTENTS

IV. INDIA IN DAYS OF YORE

ALEXANDER THE GREAT IN INDIA . . . . *Plutarch* 83
From "Plutarch's Lives," corrected and translated by A. H. Clough.
THE ROCK EDICTS OF ASOKA . . . *Asoka, King of Behar* 91
KUNÂLA THE OBEDIENT, SON OF ASOKA . *Vincent A. Smith* 95
From "Asoka, the Buddhist Emperor of India."
POEMS BY KING BHARTRIHARI . . . . *Bhartrihari* 98
From "A Century of Indian Epigrams," translated by Paul Elmer More.
SAKOONTALA, OR THE LOST RING . . . . *Kalidasa* 99
Translated from the Sanskrit by Sir Monier Monier-Williams.

V. THE MOGUL CONQUEST

THE PEACOCK THRONE OF THE GREAT MOGUL, SHAH JEHAN
Jean Baptiste Tavernier 115
From "Tavernier's Travels."
THE TAJ MAHAL, THE MOST BEAUTIFUL TOMB IN THE WORLD
Bayard Taylor 118
From "A Visit to India, China, and Japan."
ON THE MARCH WITH AURUNGZEBE . . . *François Bernier* 128
From "Travels in the Mogul Empire."
THE DECLINE OF THE MOGUL EMPIRE . . *T. B. Macaulay* 143
From "Lord Clive."

VI. INDIA BECOMES A BRITISH PROVINCE

HOW ROBERT CLIVE DEFENDED ARCOT
Thomas Babington Macaulay 151
THE BLACK HOLE OF CALCUTTA . *Thomas Babington Macaulay* 157
From "Lord Clive."
THE IMPEACHMENT OF WARREN HASTINGS
Thomas Babington Macaulay 162
From "Warren Hastings."
INDIAN CUSTOMS AND MANNERS IN 1840
Mountstuart Elphinstone 169
From "History of India."
THE RELIEF OF LUCKNOW . . . *Robert Traill Spence Lowell* 180
WHEN QUEEN VICTORIA BECAME EMPRESS OF INDIA
Field-Marshal Lord Roberts 184
From "Forty-one Years in India."

CONTENTS

VII. THE INDIA OF TO-DAY

WHAT IS CASTE? . . . . *Sir William Wilson Hunter* 193
  From "A Brief History of the Indian Peoples."
THE AMUSEMENTS OF AN EASTERN KING . . . *Anonymous* 196
HOW THE MOHAMMEDANS KEEP THE FESTIVAL OF THE MOHURRIM . . . . *Anonymous* 201
  From "The Private Life of an Eastern King," by a member of the Household of Nussir-u-deen, late King of Oude.
SUNDAY IN THE BRITISH ARMY IN INDIA . *Rev. Arthur Male* 216
  From "Scenes through the Battle Smoke."
CAMP LIFE IN INDIA . . . . . *Sir Monier Monier-Williams* 224
THE TOWERS OF SILENCE . . . *Sir Monier Monier-Williams* 234
  From "Modern India."
FABLES OF RAMAKRISHNA, A BRAHMAN SAINT OF TO-DAY
  Ramakrishna 245
  From "Ramakrishna, his Life and Sayings," by F. Max Müller.
THE CORONATION DURBAR OF 1911 . . . *John Finnemore* 248
  From "Peeps at Great Cities: Delhi and the Durbar."

SIAM

THE RECEPTION OF A WHITE ELEPHANT *Mrs. A. H. Leonowens* 263
  From "The English Governess at the Siamese Court."
THE WHITE ELEPHANT . . . . *Heinrich Heine* 269
  Translated by E. A. Böwring.

AFGHANISTAN

THE HILL OF BONES . . . . *Rev. Arthur Male* 275
  From "Scenes through the Battle Smoke."

PERSIA

I. THE MIGHTY EMPIRE

SOHRAB'S LAST CONTEST . . . . *Matthew Arnold* 285
  From "Sohrab and Rustum."
WHEN CYRUS THE GREAT WAS A BOY . . . . *Xenophon* 294
  From "The Cyropædia, or Instruction of Cyrus."
HOW CYRUS THE GREAT WON THE LAND OF GOLD *Jacob Abbott* 303
  From "Cyrus the Great."

CONTENTS

THE SEVEN SLEEPERS OF EPHESUS IN THE LAND OF LYDIA
                                  Johann Wolfgang von Goethe 329
    Translated by W. E. Aytoun.
KING DARIUS AND THE FLYING SCYTHIANS . . . *Herodotus* 334
    From "Stories of the East from Herodotus," by A. J. Church.
HOW XERXES SET OUT TO CONQUER GREECE . . *Herodotus* 347
    Translated by Henry Carey.

II. DAYS OF DECLINE

THE LAST KING OF PERSIA . . . . *Plutarch* 365
    From "Plutarch's Lives," corrected and translated by A. H. Clough.
DARA . . . . *James Russell Lowell* 378
THE BUILDING OF THE BRIDGE OF TUS . *Elizabeth A. Reed* 381
    From "Persian Literature Ancient and Modern."
LITTLE STORIES FROM SADI . . . . *Sadi* 387
    From "Persian Poetry for English Readers," by S. Robinson.

III. STORIES OF MODERN PERSIA

POE'S TALES AT THE PERSIAN COURT . . . *Wilfrid Sparroy* 393
THE PRINCE WHO LOST HIS BOOK . . . . *Wilfrid Sparroy* 401
THE FOOD OF THE ROYAL TUTOR . . . . *Wilfrid Sparroy* 406
    From "Persian Children of the Royal Family."
A PERSIAN WEDDING . . . . *C. J. Wills* 411
    From "Persia as It is."
THE PERSIAN BAZAARS   *Eustache de Lorey and Douglas Sladen* 421
    From "Queer Things about Persia."
NEW YEAR'S CALLS AND GIFTS . . . . *Samuel G. Wilson* 430
    From "Persian Life and Customs."

IV. HOW THINGS ARE DONE IN PERSIA

HOW THE PERSIANS BUILD A HOUSE . . *S. G. W. Benjamin* 447
THE AUDIENCE CHAMBER OF THE SHAH . *S. G. W. Benjamin* 449
HOW TO MAKE CALLS . . . . *S. G. W. Benjamin* 451
MAKING A PRESENT TO AN OFFICIAL . . *S. G. W. Benjamin* 455
GETTING A GLASS OF MILK . . . . . *S. G. W. Benjamin* 457
    From "Persia and the Persians."
HOW A PERSIAN MOHAMMEDAN SAYS HIS PRAYERS *S. G. Wilson* 458
    From "Persian Life and Customs."

CONTENTS

MESOPOTAMIA

I. THE KINGDOMS OF CHALDÆA AND ASSYRIA

THE CHALDÆANS AND THEIR WAYS . . *Diodorus the Sicilian*	463
From "The Historical Library of Diodorus the Sicilian," translated by G. Booth.	
HOW THE CHALDÆANS WROTE BOOKS . . . . *G. Maspero*	468
From "The Dawn of Civilization, Egypt and Chaldæa."	
THE TOWER OF BABEL . . . . *Sir David Lyndsay*	473
HOW THE ASSYRIANS AND BABYLONIANS LIVED *A. H. Sayce*	475
From "Social Life among the Assyrians and Babylonians."	
THE DESTRUCTION OF SENNACHERIB . . . . . *Lord Byron*	484

II. BABYLON THE MAGNIFICENT

HOW SEMIRAMIS BUILT BABYLON . . . *Diodorus the Sicilian*	489
THE MAKE-BELIEVE ELEPHANTS OF SEMIRAMIS *Diodorus the Sicilian*	495
From "The Historical Library of Diodorus the Sicilian," translated by G. Booth.	
DANIEL THE FEARLESS . . . . *From the Old Testament*	502
BELSHAZZAR . . . . *Heinrich Heine*	509
Translated by C. G. Leland.	
THE FALL OF BABYLON . . . . *Jacob Abbott*	511
From "History of Cyrus the Great."	

PALESTINE

I. IN OLD TESTAMENT TIMES

THE JOURNEY TO THE PROMISED LAND *From the Old Testament*	529
THE SHEPHERD BOY WHO BECAME KING *From the Old Testament*	546
THE STORY OF KING SOLOMON . . *From the Old Testament*	560
STORIES FROM THE TALMUD . . . . *Unknown*	571
From "Selections from the Talmud," translated by H. Polano.	
THE DESTRUCTION OF JERUSALEM . . . . *Flavius Josephus*	579
From "Our Young Folks' Josephus," by William Shepard.	

II. A ROMAN PROVINCE

ON THE MORNING OF CHRIST'S NATIVITY . . . *John Milton*	585
THE BURNING OF THE TEMPLE . . . . . *Flavius Josephus*	596
From "Our Young Folks' Josephus," by William Shepard.	

CONTENTS

III. THE CRUSADES

"God Willeth It!" . . . *François Pierre Guillaume Guizot* 605
From "The History of France."
The Tearing-Down of England's Flag . *Sir Walter Scott* 611
From "The Talisman."
The Children's Crusade . . . . . *Eva March Tappan* 620
From "Old World Hero Stories."
The Children's Crusade . . *Henry Wadsworth Longfellow* 623
St. Louis as a Prisoner . . . . *Joseph François Michaud* 625
From "History of Crusades."

ILLUSTRATIONS

THE PASTIMES OF AN ASSYRIAN KING	*Frederick A. Bridgman*	
		Frontispiece
INTERIOR OF THE TEMPLE OF VIMALA SAH	*Photograph*	90
PRINCE WITH ATTENDANTS IN A GARDEN	*Indian painting*	114
WOMEN OF THE PALACE AT PLAY	*Indian painting*	142
JESSIE'S DREAM	*Frederick Goodall*	180
AN IDOL CAR WITH STONE WHEELS	*Photograph*	200
THE LAST VOYAGE	*Edwin L. Weeks*	244
CRŒSUS SHOWING SOLON HIS TREASURES	*Salomon Koninck*	302
THE FAMILY OF DARIUS AT THE FEET OF ALEXANDER THE GREAT		
	Paul Veronese	368
THE LION HUNT	*Assyrian bas-relief*	474
JEREMIAH AT THE FALL OF JERUSALEM	*Eduard F. Bendemann*	582
THE CRUSADERS BEFORE JERUSALEM	*Wilhelm von Kaulbach*	610

INDIA

I
THE COMING OF THE ARYANS

HISTORICAL NOTE

PERHAPS three thousand years ago and perhaps longer, our ancestors, the Aryans, lived in central Asia. They kept great herds of cattle and drove them from one place to another, wherever the grass was most plentiful. Occasionally they planted grain and waited leisurely for it to grow and ripen. Once in a while a company of the Aryans left their lands and roamed away to some other country. One of these companies made their way to India, overpowering the people that had previously held the land.

These Aryans were by no means an ignorant folk. They knew how to weave, to sew, to use iron, and to tame domestic animals. They pictured their gods as bright, cheerful beings, and were happy in their worship. Many of their hymns of praise have come down to us in an ancient collection known as the "Rig-Veda." Two others of their literary works are of especial interest: the "Mahabharata," a collection of versified legends about the early kings; and the "Ramayana," whose subject is the coming of the Aryans to southern India.

As the centuries passed, the people of India became divided into four classes or orders: priests, warriors, tillers of the soil, and serfs, these last being the descendants of the aborigines. The priests or Brahmans were highest in rank, and were the lawmakers and the literary men of the land.

HYMN TO INDRA AND SOMA

[Between 2000 and 1500 B.C. ?]

FROM THE RIG-VEDA

[This hymn comes from the book called the "Rig-Veda," or *hymn lore*. Indra was worshiped as god of the air, Soma of the moon, and Surya of the sun. The thunderbolt was Indra's weapon against the demons Ahi and Vritra.
The Editor.]

Indra and Soma, great is your greatness!
   Twain gods triumphant, great deeds ye have done.
Victors of Heaven, ye led Surya captive,
   Darkness ye conquered, the Hordes one by one
   Of the Impious slain — this ye Twain have done!

Indra and Soma, Twain gods and mighty;
   Ye lit the Glow and Dawn woke to mirth;
Surya, ye Twain, led forth in his glory,
   Pillared the Sky and outspread mother Earth; —
   Twain gods and mighty, the Day ye gave birth!

Indra and Soma, Twain gods and slayers
   Of Ahi, the dragon — withholder of Rain —
And Vritra, — to ye the Sky made surrender,
   Ye roused the Torrents of Rivers amain
   The Seven Seas flooding, — ye mighty gods Twain.

Indra and Soma, Twain gods and mighty,
   Plenteously fed ye the hungering Kine;

HYMN TO INDRA AND SOMA

Swelling with pearl-tinted milk the lean udders,
  Gathered the far-roving, many-hued Kine; —
  All the Cloud-glories, ye Twain gods are thine!

Indra and Soma, Twain gods and mighty,
  Ye gave the Guerdon by which foes are slain;
Giving, ye mighty gods, heroic Valor
  To men for an Armor, new triumphs to gain; —
  From ye came these Guerdons, ye mighty gods Twain.

THE PEOPLE WHOM THE ARYANS FOUND IN INDIA

BY SIR WILLIAM WILSON HUNTER

THE oldest dwellers in India consisted of many tribes, who, in the absence of a race-name of their own, are called the non-Aryans or Aborigines. They have left no written records; indeed, the use of letters, or of any simplest hieroglyphics, was to them unknown. The sole works of their hands which have come down to us are rude stone circles, and the upright slabs and mounds beneath which, like the primitive peoples of Europe, they buried their dead. From the remains found in these tombs, we only discover that at some far-distant but unfixed period, they knew how to make round pots of hard, thin earthenware, not inelegant in shape; that they fought with iron weapons, and wore ornaments of copper and gold. Earlier remains prove, indeed, that these ancient tomb-builders formed only one link in a chain of primeval races. Before them, India was peopled by tribes unacquainted with the metals, who hunted and warred with polished flint axes and other deftly wrought implements of stone, similar to those found in northern Europe. And even these were the successors of yet ruder beings, who have left their agate knives and rough flint weapons in the Narbada Valley. In front of this far-stretching background of the Early-Metal and Stone Ages, we see the so-called Aborigines being beaten down by the newly arrived Aryan race.

The victorious Aryans called the early tribes Dasyus or "enemies," and Dasas, or "slaves." The Aryans entered India from the colder north, and prided themselves on their fair complexion. Their Sanskrit word for "color" (*varna*) came to mean "race" or "caste." The old Aryan poets, who composed the Veda at least three thousand and perhaps four thousand years ago, praised their bright gods, who, "slaying the Dasyus, protected the Aryan color"; who "subjected the black-skin to the Aryan man." They tell us of their own "stormy deities, who rush on like furious bulls and scatter the black-skins." Moreover, the Aryan, with his finely formed features, loathed the squat Mongolian faces of the Aborigines. One Vedic poet speaks of the non-Aryans as "noseless," or "flat-nosed," while another praises his own "beautiful-nosed" gods. The same unsightly feature was commented on with regard to a non-Aryan Asiatic tribe, by the companions of Alexander the Great on his Indian expedition, at least a thousand years later. But indeed the Vedic hymns abound in scornful epithets for the primitive tribes, as "disturbers of sacrifices," "gross feeders on flesh," "raw eaters," "lawless," "not-sacrificing," "without gods," and "without rites." As time went on, and these rude tribes were driven back into the forest, they were painted in still more hideous shapes, till they became the "monsters" and "demons" of the Aryan poet and priest. Their race-name, Dasyu, or "enemy," thus grew to signify goblin or devil.

Nevertheless all the non-Aryans could not have been savages. We hear of wealthy Dasyus or non-Aryans; and the Vedic hymns speak of their "seven castles" and "ninety forts." The Aryans afterwards made alliance with non-Aryan tribes; and some of the most powerful kingdoms of India were ruled by non-Aryan kings. Nor were the non-Aryans devoid of religious rites or of cravings after a future life. "They adorn," says an ancient Sanskrit book, "the bodies of their dead with gifts, with raiment, with ornaments; imagining that thereby they shall attain the world to come." These ornaments are the bits of bronze, copper, and gold which we now dig up from beneath their rude stone monuments. In the "Ramayana," or Sanskrit epic which narrates the advance of the Aryans into southern India, a non-Aryan chief describes his race as "of fearful swiftness, unyielding in battle, in color like a dark-blue cloud."

In the old Aryan colonies among the Five Rivers of the Punjab, each house-father was a husbandman, warrior, and priest. But by degrees certain gifted families, who composed the Vedic hymns or learned them off by heart, were always chosen by the king to perform the great sacrifices. In this way probably the priestly caste sprang up. As the Aryans conquered more territory, fortunate soldiers received a larger share of the lands than others, and cultivated it not with their own hands, but by means of the vanquished non-Aryan tribes. In this way the Four Castes arose. First, the priests, or Brahmans. Second, the warriors or fighting companions of the king, called Rajputs or Kshattriyas, literally, "of the royal stock." Third, the agricultural settlers, who kept the old name of Vaisyas, from the root *vis*, which in the primitive Vedic period had included the whole people. Fourth, the Sudras, or conquered non-Aryan tribes, who became serfs. The three first castes were of Aryan descent, and were honored by the name of the Twice-born Castes. They could all be present at the sacrifices, and they worshiped the same bright gods. The Sudras were "the slave-bands of black descent" of the Veda. They were distinguished from their "Twice-born" Aryan conquerors as being only "Once-born," and by many contemptuous epithets. They were not allowed to be present at the great national sacrifices or at the feasts which followed them. They could never rise out of their servile condition; and to them was assigned the severest toil in the fields, and all the hard and dirty work of the village community.

The Brahmans, or priests, claimed the highest rank. But they seem to have had a long struggle with the Kshattriya or warrior caste before they won their proud position at the head of the Indian people. They afterwards secured themselves in that position by teaching that it had been given to them by God. At the beginning of the world, they said, the Brahman proceeded from the mouth of the Creator, the Kshattriya from his arms, the Vaisya from his thighs or belly, and the Sudra from his feet. This legend is true so far, that the Brahmans were really the brain-power of the Indian people, the Kshattriyas its armed hands, the Vaisyas the food-growers, the Sudras the downtrodden serfs. At any rate, when the Brahmans had established their power, they made a wise use of it. From the ancient Vedic times they recognized that if they were to exercise spiritual supremacy, they must renounce earthly pomp. In arrogating the priestly function, they gave up all claim to the royal office. They were divinely appointed to be the guides of nations and the counselors of kings, but they could not be kings themselves. As the duty of the Sudra was to serve, of the Vaisya to till the ground and follow middle-class trades or crafts; so the business of the Kshattriya was to fight the public enemy, and of the Brahman to propitiate the national gods.

Each day brought to the Brahmans its routine of ceremonies, studies, and duties. Their whole life was mapped out into four clearly defined stages of discipline. For their existence, in its full religious significance, commenced not at birth, but on being invested at the close of childhood with the sacred thread of the "Twice-born." Their youth and early manhood were to be entirely spent in learning by heart from an older Brahman the inspired scriptures, tending the sacred fire, and serving their preceptor. Having completed his long studies, the Brahman entered on the second stage of his life, as a householder. He married and commenced a course of family duties. When he had reared a family and gained a practical knowledge of the world, he retired into the forest as a recluse, for the third period of his life; feeding on roots or fruits, and practicing his religious duties with increased devotion. The fourth stage was that of the ascetic or religious mendicant, wholly withdrawn from earthly affairs, and striving to attain a condition of mind which, heedless of the joys or pains or wants of the body, is intent only on its final absorption into the deity. The Brahman, in this fourth stage of his life, ate nothing but what was given to him unasked, and abode not more than one day in any village, lest the vanities of the world should find entrance into his heart. Throughout his whole existence he practiced a strict temperance; drinking no wine, using a simple diet, curbing the desires; shut off from the tumults of war, as his business was to pray, not to fight, and having his thoughts ever fixed on study and contemplation. "What is this world?" says a Brahman sage. "It is even as the bough of a tree, on which a bird rests for a night, and in the morning flies away."

SAVITRI'S CHOICE

FROM THE MAHABHARATA; REWRITTEN BY ELIZABETH A. REED

[The "Mahabharata" is one of the famous epics of the Hindus. It is the longest poem in the world, being more than seven times as long as the "Iliad" and the "Odyssey," taken together. The word "Mahabharata" means "the great war of King Bharata"; but only a small portion of the book is given to the tale of the war, and the book is really a mass of story, philosophy, legend, and mythology.

The Editor.]

Long years ago there lived in palace halls the mighty King of Kekaya. Gallant and brave in person, just and beneficent in the administration of the laws of his realm, he was the hero of his people and they rendered to him a loyal obedience.

But King Asva-pati carried a desolate heart amid the magnificence which surrounded him, for the gods had written him childless. Through long years of faithful fasting and penance his prayers had been unanswered. But one glad day the goddess of the sun arose from his sacrificial fire; beautiful and bright she came in the form of glorious womanhood, and rising through the crimson flame stepped into the royal presence, saying: "What wilt thou, mighty Raja, that I shall do for thee? I have listened to thy prayers; I have watched thy penance, and seen the bounty of thine offerings. During all the years of thy reign the poor have found in thee a valued friend, and now, O King! I wait to do thy bidding; tell me now the dearest wish of thy heart." And Asva-pati answered: "Oh, beautiful goddess, 't is for my barren line that I do penance and have performed my vows, lo! these many years. Give me an heir for my throne and kingdom; give me children to grace my royal hearthstone." Then the radiant goddess, smiling, said: "I knew thy wish, O King, and there shall be born a daughter unto thee — not a son, but a fair girl — the loveliest that the stars have ever shone upon"; and, smiling still, the beauteous vision vanished in the sacrificial flame.

Time passed on with flying feet, and erelong a child was given to the royal house, and courtiers brought their praise unto the palace gates, while the streets of the city were ringing with joyous music, and everywhere the glad news went that the queen had borne a daughter — a babe of loveliest mould. The child was named Savitri, and the happy father made a royal birthday feast; the poor were fed and the city was decorated with bright flags and long festoons of flowers. Every porch and pillar was made bright and fragrant with floral vines, and the great vases in front of the palace were filled with branches of orange and mango trees.

The little one who met with such a royal welcome grew more beautiful as the years went by, and when she reached the fair heights of womanhood she was a vision of grace and loveliness. The lithe figure of this Indian maid was like a dream of beauty and grace, and the rosy light of health flashed through the olive shades of her face. The crimson lips smiled over pearly teeth and the great dark eyes were luminous with light and love. But still no raja dared to ask the hand of the princess in marriage. Her loveliness and truth, her queenly independence had awed them into silence.

At last her father gave to her a princess's right to choose for herself a lord, and gave his royal word that the man she chose should be welcomed by her sire. A royal train moved through the provinces and visited every court, for Savitri with her ministers and maidens would take the air and travel for the princess's health. They received everywhere a royal welcome, but she loved best the trees and groves; hence, they wandered through the fragrant woods and gathered fruits and flowers there.

One day they found a hermit, aged and blind, who with his faithful wife sat in the dense shade of a teak tree, whose abundant leaves gleamed in the sunshine above them and protected them from its heat. The gentle princess stayed to give them a few kindly words and enjoy the wild flowers around the hermitage. While she listened to their story a young man came from the thicket bearing the sacred wood to be used in the evening sacrifice. He stopped in wonder and admiration before Savitri, and her eyes rested a moment upon his manly form and honest face. It was Satyavan, the hermit's son, who stayed to serve his aged parents in their banishment. The princess had dawned upon his vision like a dream of heaven, and like a dream she vanished from his woodland home, leaving her memory to haunt his steps and make his loneliness more terrible. In the still hours of the night he heard her voice and saw the lovely face which had become part of his being.

One day the Maha-raja sat in his council hall with the sage Narada. They were talking in low tones of the affairs of state when the king's daughter was announced. With her dark eyes glowing with light and happiness she stepped into the royal presence and bowed meekly before her father, who laid his hand lovingly upon her dark hair, as he bent down and caressed his child. Narada looked in admiration upon the princess and said to the king, "Thy daughter is very fair. Thou shouldst give her in marriage to the raja of some goodly kingdom." "For this purpose she has been abroad," replied the king. Then, turning to his daughter, he said, "My child, hast thou chosen thy lord?" But she answered not. Standing before the sage with her face crimsoned with blushes, her eyes mutely appealed to her father to stay his questions. Reading her wish, he said, "Fear not, my child, to speak before the sage Narada; he is thy father's best and truest friend; but tell me if thou hast found the object of thy search." Then she answered: "Father, I have been long away; I have visited the courts of princes; I have offered sacrifice in the sacred groves, and I have found in one of these the banished King of Chalva, who lost his throne and kingdom because of blindness. An usurper reigns upon his throne, and his faithful queen stays with him in the woodland cot. Their loyal son ministers to their wants; he brings them fruit and game for food; he feeds their sacrificial fire and pulls the sacred kusa grass to make their couch both soft and warm; he brings fresh water from the passing brook and gives them love and tenderness in their daily need. Father, I have chosen him, this banished prince, to be my lord."

Then said Narada, "Not he, my child, — thou canst not choose the banished Satyavan. He is both brave and noble; a grander youth never trod a kingly court, but o'er his head there hangs a fearful fate. He is doomed to die, and in a year the gods decide that he must go." Her blushes fled and her cheeks grew strangely pale as she answered: "Whether he live long or die to-day, whether he be full of grace and wisdom, or graceless stand before me, my heart hath chosen once — it chooseth not again, and I have my father's royal pledge that he will ratify my decision."

Then said the king, "Remember, child, the sad lot of Hindu widowhood and choose again. The noblest raja in the land would gladly call thee wife. Let not this banished youth who has only a year to live take my peerless Indian gem into his rough woodland home."

The dark eyes were raised again to his and in their liquid depths he read her answer even before her lips replied, "A loyal heart can choose but one, and a loyal sire will not revoke his promise."

Then the raja sighed, "As thou wilt, dear child, but for thine own sake I would have had thee make a wiser choice." One quick look of gratitude flashed from the wondrous eyes, then bending her blushing face to kiss her father's hand and reverently bidding the sage farewell, she left the council hall.

Having given his royal sanction to his daughter's choice, the king ordered that preparations should be made for the coming nuptials. Though the bride should dwell in a lonely hermitage, she would still be a king's daughter, and her robes even in the woodland should befit her noble birth. It was an imperial pageant that went forth to the humble dwelling of the hermit; there were the priests and sages and courtiers, and the royal family, mounted upon the war elephants with their costly trappings.

Amid the strains of martial music the train went forth from the palace gates. No courier had been sent to give warning of their coming; therefore the king ordered a halt when near the hermitage, and he himself went forward to hold council with the blind lord of the humble home. Courteous salutations were passed between them, and after extending the modest hospitalities that still were his, the blind king asked what brought the Maharaja to his door. "I have come," said he, "to ask of you that you will ratify my daughter's choice; she hath chosen your son Satyavan to be her lord."

Then answered the banished king, "In the days of my proud position it was my ambition to link my house with yours by ties of blood, O noble king! but now that my kingdom is lost and I am but a dethroned and banished sovereign, I could not take the lovely princess from her palace home to share our humble fate."

But the raja replied, "You and I are both too old to think that happiness is dependent upon luxury. We know that love can hold her sylvan court in humblest bower, and your son is the lady's choice. She has chosen to dwell in modest guise with him she loves rather than share the splendors of another. Shall we deny her wish?"

"Nay, never," said the banished king. "Her gracious wish is mine, and great honor she brings to our fallen house. May the blessings of Indra rest upon her beauteous head!" And calling Satyavan he told him why the raja came. The bewildered prince could scarcely believe the lovely princess had chosen him. His words were few; but his eyes were eloquent with the joy his lips refused to voice.

Then the royal train was ordered into view, and there beneath the massive trees were gathered priest and sage with golden jars filled from the waves of the sacred Ganges. Beyond the great trees where the hermitage stood were thickets of rose laurel, whose fragrance filled the air; on the other side a silver brook was hastening by to find rest on the bosom of a clear lake, beneath the fragrant cups of lotus blossoms and white lilies. Here in Nature's temple, beneath her shining dome and beside her sacred pools, with legal rites the two were bound in holy marriage; and Love stayed by and held his court where the royal lovers pledged their faith.

The raja and his queen bade their child a fond farewell, and when they passed from sight the princess took from her hands and arms the costly jewels that she wore and laid aside her silken robes; then on her delicate form she placed the rough garments that befitted her new station as a hermit's wife. Thus she proved the great love that brought her here; she could not wear a finer robe than he; she could not see her little hands decked with gold and gems while his were roughened with honest toil. She had chosen to share the fortune of the man she loved, and no ray of barbaric splendor should suggest to him that she cared for things he could not furnish. The gray-haired mother looked smilingly on and loved the loyal wife, whose gracious ways and loving words soon won the heart of the banished king as well.

The little family dwelt in their forest home in sweet content and the days went by on silver feet. To Satyavan it seemed that life's ills all were done, and he rested in the heaven of his happiness, feeling that the gods could do no more. But Savitri carried in her loving heart a fearful dread — a counting of the days when the death decree should be fulfilled. When the sun went down in the sea and the soft folds of night cooled the fevered earth, she knew that one day less remained to Satyavan.

At last the days had nearly fled — the little wife grew strangely still; her gentle, loving deeds were still her own, but her songs were hushed in tearful prayers. When the time was nearly come she sat beneath a great tree like a beautiful statue and neither ate nor drank. For three long days and nights she sat thus, mutely imploring the gods to save from death's decree the man she loved. During all the year she had carried the fatal secret in her own faithful heart. She could not pain the others with the weight of her terrible woe, and they wondered now at the severity of her penance; but they thought she craved some great gift of the gods, and they could not deny her wish.

The fateful day dawned at last and found her weak and faint, but she would not taste of food. Only one plea she made — that she might go with Satyavan when he went out into the forest to cut the sacred wood for the evening sacrifice.

Tenderly he remonstrated, "The way is rough and thy little feet are tender; the mother's side is a safer place for thee." But still she pleaded, "I cannot let thee go unless I am with thee"; and Satyavan looked down into the depths of her tearful eyes, that looked back love and tenderness into his own. Then said he, "Surely thou shalt go and make the dark wood glad with thy sweet presence."

Cheerily he set out axe in hand through the wilderness, making a path for the little feet that patiently followed his own. The morning was wondrously bright; flower-laden trees stood here and there along the pathway; gigantic climbers grew in the thickets in great profusion, interlacing the smaller trees and even piling their gorgeous blossoms upon their heads. The sunlight lay upon the surface of the little lake near their home, and bright water-birds hovered above the reeds and rushes, or settled down amidst the white lilies and fragrant lotus cups near the water's edge. Away in the distance the Himalayas lifted their snowy brows into the blue heavens and reflected the sun's rays from their icy peaks. "Is it not beautiful?" said Satyavan, pointing to the landscape around him, or directing her attention to the strange wild flowers springing from the mosses at their feet. And smiling the little wife replied, even while the fearful dread around her heart almost stayed its beating.

Afar from home, they gathered fruits and flowers for the evening sacrifice, and all the while the anxious wife watched with aching heart every look and motion of her lord. He struck the tree to gather sacred wood, and blow after blow of his axe echoed through the forest. At last he reeled in sudden pain and cried, "I cannot work"; then falling at her feet he fainted there. Quickly the beloved head was laid upon her lap, and eagerly she strove by chafing the temples and tired hands to bring the life tide back. She knew it was the day of fate, but still she could not yield.

INDIA

Suddenly at her side she saw a fearful shape, that was neither god nor man — tall and dark with visage grim, he looked down pitilessly upon them both. His garments were crimson as if with blood; his cruel eyes glowed like burning coals in their deep sockets. In one hand he bore a long black noose and bent over Satyavan. As the specter leaned above her husband, the trembling princess laid the head tenderly upon the ground, and springing up reverently folded her hands in supplication, and prayed to know who he was and why he came. He answered, "I am Yama, the god of death, and I am come to bear away the soul of Satyavan." "But," pleaded the wife, "'t is thy messengers that bear away the souls of men. Why is it, mighty chief, that thou hast come?" "Because Prince Satyavan was the grandest, noblest of his race," replied the god, "and none save Yama's self was worthy to bear his soul away." And bending lower still he fitted the dreadful noose and drew out the soul of Satyavan; then silently he strode away toward the southland with his prize, leaving the poor body pale and cold, with life and grace and beauty gone.

But the stricken princess followed him. With her hands folded in supplication she hastened on behind this fearful King of Death. At last he turned. "Go back," said he; "why dost thou follow in my steps? No mortal e'er has dared to come whither I shall go. Go back and perform the funeral rites for thy dead lord."

But she replied: "Wherever my lord is borne, there I shall surely go; he is my life, my all; I cannot leave him, and I must go with thee. By reason of my wifely love thou wilt let me come." And still she followed on until the King of Death himself felt pity for the faithful wife,

SAVITRI'S CHOICE

and turning back he said: "Return, my child, to life and health. Thy wifely love is good, but the kingdom of Yama is not the place for thee. Still, I will grant thee any boon that thou dost crave, except this life that I am bearing away." Then said Savitri, "Let the blind and banished king, my husband's father, have both his sight and throne restored." "It shall be so," returned the god. "I grant thee this because of thy purity and fidelity; but now turn back; our way is long and dark, thy little feet are already weary, and thou wilt die upon the road."

"I am not weary," said Savitri, "I cannot tire while I am near to Satyavan. Wherever he is borne, there the loyal wife must go." And the tireless feet toiled patiently on behind the King of Death until he turned again and said: "Darkness is coming on; soon thou canst not find thy way alone. I will give to thee another boon — anything except this life, and then thou must return." Quickly the princess thought of her own sire, whose only child now followed Death — thought of his lonely home and coming age, and she said, "Give to my father princely sons to bear his royal name. This is the boon I crave, O mighty one." "So shall it be," returned the king; "and now I have granted thy wishes, go back to life and light." But she only answered plaintively, "I cannot go, great king. I cannot leave my lord. Thou hast taken him, and my heart is in thy hand. I must surely come with thee."

Darkness came slowly down in the dense forest, and her tender feet were torn with thorns and cut with the sharp stones of the rugged path. Hungry wolves and jackals pressed around her, while night birds spread their black wings above her and startled the silence with their cries. Trembling with terror and faint with grief and hunger, she still pursued her way. Her tear-blinded eyes could no longer see the terrible shape she followed, but she heard his footfalls and almost felt his fearful strides, for it seemed that every step came down upon her bleeding heart.

At last they came to a cavern, dark and damp as death itself, and here again Yama turned upon the pitiful figure in the darkness behind him, and this time he fiercely demanded, "Art thou still upon my track? If thou wert not so true and good, I would take thee in my arms, and my worms should feed upon thy beauty; but thou art truth itself, and I will give to thee, poor child, one more boon. In pity for thy grief I will give thee anything thou wilt — except this life within my hand." Then answered Savitri, "Give me children — the sons of Satyavan. Let me bear to him brave, loyal heirs of his goodness and his truth."

Death grimly smiled. Should he be conquered yet by this little Hindu wife? But he answered: "Yama hath promised thee, and I must grant thee even this." Then with rapid strides he entered the great vault of the cavern, while the startled bats and owls flapped their dark wings and made the place more hideous with their cries. But still he heard the patter of patient feet behind him, and his burning eyeballs blazed in the darkness upon poor Savitri.

"Go back," he said. "Thou shalt return; I will bear no longer with thy persistent following!" "I would go back, O mighty Yama, if I could," wailed the weary

SAVITRI'S CHOICE

wife, "but in your hands you carry my own life. 'T is only my helpless frame that follows thee, and now I am so weak with grief and fear that I must come nearer to Satyavan"; and the tired head drooped upon the dark cold hand of Death, close to the life she craved. The pitiless king felt the soft touch of tear-wet cheeks and clinging hair, and again his cruel heart was softened by her faithful love. "Thou art innocence itself, and tenderness and truth," said Yama. "Thou hast taught me lessons new of woman's fidelity. Ask any boon thou wilt, and it shall be thine."

Then at his feet she fell in grateful joy and tenderly caressed them. "This time, O King," she cried, "thou hast excepted nothing, and I ask not wealth, nor throne, nor heaven itself. I crave my heart, my life — give me my Satyavan!" The fire in his eyes beamed more softly, and the light in them was almost tender as he said: "Fair queen, thou art the brightest gem of womankind. Here, take thy Satyavan. Saved by his peerless wife, he long shall live and reign with her, and his line shall be upheld by princely sons who shall call thee mother. Go now, my child, time hasteth, and long hast thou been with me." Then turning gloomily away, he went down — down into the darkness of the cavern. But the glad wife, holding her precious treasure close to her heart, retraced her steps back through the darkness of cavern and wood, her torn feet climbing the ascending stairway, fearing nothing, knowing nothing, save that in her arms she carried her beloved.

It was dark in the forest, where the dense foliage almost shut out the light of noontime, but it was lighter here where only little groves of sacred fig trees and thickets of flowering shrubs obscured the vision, and traces of gold and crimson still lingered round the setting sun. Thankful for the light, she hastened to where the body lay, and raising the head pressed it tenderly again to her bosom, and gently wooed the lifetide to heart and pulse. Soft and warm his hand became, and his lips moved to speak a tender word that had died upon them when Yama came. The evening light was gone, and darkness came down with velvet touch around them, but the glorious stars came out and the southern constellations flashed like crown jewels above the living prince and his loyal wife.

II
BUDDHA AND HIS TEACHINGS

HISTORICAL NOTE

ACCORDING to the legends of Buddha, he was a prince who gave up his life of luxury to become a religious recluse, in the hope of thus finding peace of soul. After years of spiritual struggling this finally came to him, and he set out to preach his beliefs. Two of his chief doctrines were metempsychosis and *nirvana*. According to the first, at a man's death his spirit enters at once into some other form, the sum total of his actions, that is, his *karma*, deciding whether it shall be superior or inferior to the one which he has heretofore occupied. According to the second, life is hopelessly unhappy, and the only escape is into *nirvana*, or extinction. Whether this meant extinction of all desires, extinction of the soul, or merely its absorption into the universal soul is a disputed question.

THE LIFE OF BUDDHA

[Born between 562 and 552 B.C.; died between 482 and 472 B.C.]

BY SIR WILLIAM WILSON HUNTER

GAUTAMA, afterwards named Buddha, "The Enlightened," was the only son of the King of Kapilavastu. The king wished to see his son grow up into a warrior like himself; but the young prince shunned the sports of his playmates, and spent his time alone in nooks of the palace garden. When he reached manhood, however, he showed himself brave and skillful with his weapons. He won his wife by a contest at arms over all rival chiefs. For a time he forgot the religious thoughts of his boyhood in the enjoyment of the world. But in his drives through the city he was struck by the sights of old age, disease, and death which met his eye; and he envied the calm of a holy man, who seemed to have raised his soul above the changes and sorrows of this life. After ten years, his wife bore to him an only son; and Gautama, fearing lest this new tie should bind him too closely to the things of earth, retired about the age of thirty to a cave in the jungles. The story is told how he turned away from the door of his wife's lamplit chamber, denying himself even a parting caress of his new-born babe, lest he should wake the sleeping mother, and galloped off into the darkness. After a gloomy night ride, he sent back his one companion, the faithful charioteer, with his horse and jewels to his father. Having cut off his long warrior hair, and exchanged his princely raiment for the rags of a poor passer-by, he went on alone, a homeless beggar. This giving up of princely pomp, and of loved wife and new-born son, is the "Great Renunciation" which forms a favorite theme of the Buddhist scriptures.

For a time Gautama studied under two Brahman hermits. They taught him that the peace of the soul was to be reached only by mortifying the body. He then buried himself deeper in the jungles, and during six years wasted himself by austerities in company with five disciples. But instead of earning peace of mind by fasting and self-torture, he sank into a religious despair, during which the Buddhist scriptures affirm that the enemy of mankind, Mara, wrestled with him in bodily shape. Torn with doubts as to whether all his penance availed anything, the haggard hermit fell senseless to the earth. When he recovered, the mental agony had passed. He felt that the path to salvation lay not in self-torture in mountain jungles or caves, but in preaching a higher life to his fellow-men. He gave up penance. His five disciples, shocked by this, forsook him; and he was left alone in the forest. The Buddhist scriptures depict him as sitting serene under a fig tree, while demons whirled round him with flaming weapons. From this temptation in the wilderness he came forth with his doubts forever laid at rest, seeing his way clear, and henceforth to be known as Buddha, literally "The Enlightened."

Buddha began his public teaching in the Deer Forest, near the great city of Benares. Unlike the Brahmans, he preached, not to one or two disciples of the sacred caste, but to the people. His first converts were common men, and among the earliest were women. After three months he had gathered around him sixty disciples, whom he sent forth to the neighboring countries with

THE LIFE OF BUDDHA

these words: "Go ye now, and preach the most excellent law." Two thirds of each year he spent as a wandering preacher. The remaining four months, or the rainy season, he abode at some fixed place, teaching the people who flocked around his little dwelling in the bamboo grove. His five old disciples, who had forsaken him in the time of his sore temptation in the wilderness, now came back to their master. Princes, merchants, artisans, Brahmans and hermits, husbandmen and serfs, noble ladies and repentant women who had sinned, were added to those who believed. Buddha preached throughout Behar, Oudh, and the adjacent districts in the Northwestern Provinces. He had ridden forth from his father's house as a brilliant young prince. He now returned to it as a wandering preacher, in dingy yellow robes, with shaven head and the begging-bowl in his hand. The old king heard him with reverence. The son whom Buddha had left as a new-born babe was converted to the faith; and his beloved wife, from the threshold of whose chamber he had ridden away into the darkness, became one of the first of Buddhist nuns.

Buddha's Great Renunciation took place in his thirtieth year. After long self-preparation, his public teaching began when he was about thirty-six, and during forty-four years he preached to the people. In foretelling his death, he said to his followers: "Be earnest, be thoughtful, be holy. Keep steadfast watch over your own hearts. He who holds fast to the law and discipline, and faints not, he shall cross the ocean of life and make an end of sorrow. The world is fast bound in fetters," he added; "I now give it deliverance, as a physician who brings heavenly medicine. Keep your mind on my teaching: all other things change, this changes not. No more shall I speak to you. I desire to depart. I desire the eternal rest (*nirvana*)." He spent the night in preaching, and in comforting a weeping disciple. His last words, according to one account, were, "Work out your salvation with diligence." He died calmly, at the age of eighty, under the shadow of a fig tree, according to the commonly received tradition in 543 B.C.; or according to later criticism in 478 B.C.

Buddha taught that the state of a man in this life, in all previous and in all future lives, is the result of his own acts (*karma*). What a man sows, that he must reap. As no evil remains without punishment, and no good deed without reward, it follows that neither priest nor God can prevent each act from bringing about its own consequences. Misery or happiness in this life is the unavoidable result of our conduct in a past life; and our actions here will determine our happiness or misery in the life to come. When any creature dies, he is born again in some higher or lower state of existence, according to his merit or demerit. His merit or demerit consists of the sum total of his actions in all previous lives. A system like this, in which our whole well-being — past, present, and to come — depends upon ourselves, leaves little room for a personal God.

The pious Buddhist strives to reach a state of holy meditation in this world, and looks forward to an eternal calm in a world to come. Buddha taught that this end could only be reached by leading a good life. Instead of the Brahman sacrifices, he laid down three great duties, namely, control over self, kindness to other men, and reverence for the life of all living creatures.

STORIES OF BUDDHA

BY SIR EDWIN ARNOLD

I

BUDDHA AND THE WOUNDED SWAN

In the royal garden on a day of spring,
A flock of wild swans passed, voyaging north
To their nest-places on Himâla's breast.
Calling in love-notes down their snowy line
The bright birds flew, by fond love piloted;
And Devadatta, cousin of the prince,
Pointed his bow, and loosed a willful shaft
Which found the wide wing of the foremost swan
Broad-spread to glide upon the free blue road,
So that it fell, the bitter arrow fixed,
Bright scarlet blood-gouts staining the pure plumes.
Which seeing, Prince Siddârtha took the bird
Tenderly up, rested it in his lap —
Sitting with knees crossed, as Lord Buddha sits —
And, soothing with a touch the wild thing's fright,
Composed its ruffled vans, calmed its quick heart,
Caressed it into peace with light kind palms
As soft as plantain-leaves an hour unrolled;
And while the left hand held, the right hand drew
The cruel steel forth from the wound and laid
Cool leaves and healing honey on the smart.
Yet all so little knew the boy of pain
That curiously into his wrist he pressed

INDIA

The arrow's barb, and winced to feel it sting,
And turned with tears to soothe his bird again.
  Then some one came who said, "My prince hath shot
A swan, which fell among the roses here,
He bids me pray you send it. Will you send?"
"Nay," quoth Siddârtha, "if the bird were dead
To send it to the slayer might be well,
But the swan lives; my cousin hath but killed
The godlike speed which throbbed in this white wing."
And Devadatta answered, "The wild thing,
Living or dead, is his who fetched it down;
'T was no man's in the clouds, but fall'n 't is mine,
Give me my prize, fair Cousin." Then our Lord
Laid the swan's neck beside his own smooth cheek
And gravely spake, "Say no! the bird is mine,
The first of myriad things which shall be mine
By right of mercy and love's lordliness.
For now I know, by what within me stirs,
That I shall teach compassion unto men
And be a speechless world's interpreter,
Abating this accursed flood of woe,
Not man's alone; but, if the prince disputes,
Let him submit this matter to the wise
And we will wait their word." So was it done;
In full divan the business had debate,
And many thought this thing and many that,
Till there arose an unknown priest who said,
"If life be aught, the savior of a life
Owns more the living thing than he can own
Who sought to slay — the slayer spoils and wastes,
The cherisher sustains, give him the bird":
Which judgment all found just; but when the king

STORIES OF BUDDHA

Sought out the sage for honor, he was gone;
And some one saw a hooded snake glide forth, —
The gods come ofttimes thus! So our Lord Buddh
Began his works of mercy.
                      Yet not more
Knew he as yet of grief than that one bird's,
Which, being healed, went joyous to its kind.

II

HOW BUDDHA WON THE PRINCESS

  But they who watched the prince at prize-giving
Saw and heard all, and told the careful king
How sate Siddârtha heedless, till there passed
Great Suprabuddha's child, Yasôdhara;
And how — at sudden sight of her — he changed,
And how she gazed on him and he on her,
And of the jewel-gift, and what beside
Passed in their speaking glance.
                      The fond king smiled:
"Look! we have found a lure; take counsel now
To fetch therewith our falcon from the clouds.
Let messengers be sent to ask the maid
In marriage for my son." But it was law
With Sâkyas, when any asked a maid
Of noble house, fair and desirable,
He must make good his skill in martial arts
Against all suitors who should challenge it;
Nor might this custom break itself for kings.
Therefore her father spake: "Say to the king,
The child is sought by princes far and near;

INDIA

If thy most gentle son can bend the bow,
Sway sword, and back a horse better than they,
Best would he be in all and best to us:
But how shall this be, with his cloistered ways?"
Then the king's heart was sore, for now the prince
Begged sweet Yasôdhara for wife — in vain,
With Devadatta foremost at the bow,
Ardjuna master of all fiery steeds,
And Nanda chief in sword-play; but the prince
Laughed low and said, "These things, too, I have
 learned;
Make proclamation that thy son will meet
All comers at their chosen games. I think
I shall not lose my love for such as these."
So 't was given forth that on the seventh day
The Prince Siddârtha summoned whoso would
To match with him in feats of manliness,
The victor's crown to be Yasôdhara.

Therefore, upon the seventh day, there went
The Sâkya lords and town and country round
Unto the maidân; and the maid went too
Amid her kinsfolk, carried as a bride,
With music, and with litters gayly dight,
And gold-horned oxen, flower-caparisoned.
Whom Devadatta claimed, of royal line,
And Nanda and Ardjuna, noble both,
The flower of all youths there, till the prince came
Riding his white horse Kantaka, which neighed,
Astonished at this great strange world without:
Also Siddârtha gazed with wondering eyes
On all those people born beneath the throne,

STORIES OF BUDDHA

Otherwise housed than kings, otherwise fed,
And yet so like — perchance — in joys and griefs.
But when the prince saw sweet Yasôdhara,
Brightly he smiled, and drew his silken rein,
Leaped to the earth from Kantaka's broad back,
And cried, "He is not worthy of this pearl
Who is not worthiest; let my rivals prove
If I have dared too much in seeking her."
Then Nanda challenged for the arrow-test
And set a brazen drum six gows away,
Ardjuna six and Devadatta eight;
But Prince Siddârtha bade them set his drum
Ten gows from off the line, until it seemed
A cowry-shell for target. Then they loosed,
And Nanda pierced his drum, Ardjuna his,
And Devadatta drove a well-aimed shaft
Through both sides of his mark, so that the crowd
Marveled and cried; and sweet Yasôdhara
Dropped the gold sari o'er her fearful eyes,
Lest she should see her prince's arrow fail.
But he, taking their bow of lacquered cane,
With sinews bound, and strung with silver wire,
Which none but stalwart arms could draw a span,
Thrummed it — low laughing — drew the twisted string
Till the horns kissed, and the thick belly snapped:
"That is for play, not love," he said; "hath none
A bow more fit for Sâkya lords to use?"
And one said, "There is Sinhahânu's bow,
Kept in the temple since we know not when,
Which none can string, nor draw if it be strung."
"Fetch me," he cried, "that weapon of a man!"
They brought the ancient bow, wrought of black steel,

INDIA

Laid with gold tendrils on its branching curves
Like bison-horns; and twice Siddârtha tried
Its strength across his knee, then spake — "Shoot now
With this, my cousins!" but they could not bring
The stubborn arms a hand's-breadth nigher use;
Then the prince, lightly leaning, bent the bow,
Slipped home the eye upon the notch, and twanged
Sharply the cord, which, like an eagle's wing
Thrilling the air, sang forth so clear and loud
That feeble folk at home that day inquired
"What is this sound?" and people answered them,
"It is the sound of Sinhahânu's bow,
Which the king's son has strung and goes to shoot";
Then fitting fair a shaft, he drew and loosed,
And the keen arrow clove the sky, and drave
Right through that farthest drum, nor stayed its flight,
But skimmed the plain beyond, past reach of eye.

Then Devadatta challenged with the sword,
And clove a Talas-tree six fingers thick;
Ardjuna seven; and Nanda cut through nine;
But two such stems together grew, and both
Siddârtha's blade shred at one flashing stroke,
Keen, but so smooth that the straight trunks upstood,
And Nanda cried, "His edge turned!" and the maid
Trembled anew, seeing the trees erect,
Until the Devas of the air, who watched,
Blew light breaths from the south, and both green crowns
Crashed in the sand, clean-felled.
                        Then brought they steeds,
High-mettled, nobly-bred, and three times scoured
Around the maidân, but white Kantaka

STORIES OF BUDDHA

Left even the fleetest far behind — so swift,
That ere the foam fell from his mouth to earth
Twenty spear-lengths he flew; but Nanda said,
"We too might win with such as Kantaka;
Bring an unbroken horse, and let men see
Who best can back him." So the syces brought
A stallion dark as night, led by three chains,
Fierce-eyed, with nostrils wide and tossing mane,
Unshod, unsaddled, for no rider yet
Had crossed him. Three times each young Sâkya
Sprang to his mighty back, but the hot steed
Furiously reared, and flung them to the plain
In dust and shame; only Ardjuna held
His seat awhile, and, bidding loose the chains,
Lashed the black flank, and shook the bit, and held
The proud jaws fast with grasp of master-hand,
So that in storms of wrath and rage and fear
The savage stallion circled once the plain
Half-tamed; but sudden turned with naked teeth,
Gripped by the foot Ardjuna, tore him down,
And would have slain him, but the grooms ran in
Fettering the maddened beast. Then all men cried,
"Let not Siddârtha meddle with this Bhût,
Whose liver is a tempest, and his blood
Red flame"; but the prince said, "Let go the chains,
Give me his forelock only," which he held
With quiet grasp, and, speaking some low word,
Laid his right palm across the stallion's eyes,
And drew it gently down the angry face,
And all along the neck and panting flanks,
Till men astonished saw the night-black horse
Sink his fierce crest and stand subdued and meek,

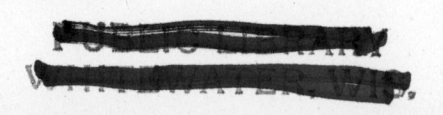

INDIA

As though he knew our Lord and worshiped him.
Nor stirred he while Siddârtha mounted, then
Went soberly to touch of knee and rein
Before all eyes, so that the people said,
"Strive no more, for Siddârtha is the best."
And all the suitors answered "He is best!"

III

BUDDHA AND THE LAMB

          While the Master spake
Blew down the mount the dust of pattering feet,
White goats and black sheep winding slow their way,
With many a lingering nibble at the tufts,
And wanderings from the path, where water gleamed
Or wild figs hung. But always as they strayed
The herdsman cried, or slung his sling, and kept
The silly crowd still moving to the plain.
A ewe with couplets in the flock there was,
Some hurt had lamed one lamb, which toiled behind
Bleeding, while in the front its fellow skipped,
And the vexed dam hither and thither ran,
Fearful to lose this little one or that;
Which when our Lord did mark, full tenderly
He took the limping lamb upon his neck,
Saying, "Poor woolly mother, be at peace!
Whither thou goest I will bear thy care;
'T were all as good to ease one beast of grief
As sit and watch the sorrows of the world
In yonder caverns with the priests who pray."

STORIES OF BUDDHA

IV

HOW BUDDHA COMFORTED THE SORROWING MOTHER

Whom, when they came unto the riverside,
A woman — dove-eyed, young, with tearful face
And lifted hands — saluted, bending low:
"Lord! thou art he," she said, "who yesterday
Had pity on me in the fig grove here,
Where I live lone and reared my child; but he
Straying amid the blossoms found a snake,
Which twined about his wrist, whilst he did laugh
And tease the quick forked tongue and opened mouth
Of that cold playmate. But, alas! ere long
He turned so pale and still, I could not think
Why he should cease to play, and let my breast
Fall from his lips. And one said, 'He is sick
Of poison'; and another, 'He will die.'
But I, who could not lose my precious boy,
Prayed of them physic, which might bring the light
Back to his eyes; it was so very small
That kiss-mark of the serpent, and I think
It could not hate him, gracious as he was,
Nor hurt him in his sport. And some one said,
'There is a holy man upon the hill —
Lo! now he passeth in the yellow robe —
Ask of the Rishi if there be a cure
For that which ails thy son.' Whereon I came
Trembling to thee, whose brow is like a god's,
And wept and drew the face-cloth from my babe,
Praying thee tell what simples might be good.
And thou, great sir! didst spurn me not, but gaze

INDIA

With gentle eyes and touch with patient hand;
Then draw the face-cloth back, saying to me,
'Yea! little sister, there is that might heal
Thee first, and him, if thou couldst fetch the thing;
For they who seek physicians bring to them
What is ordained. Therefore, I pray thee, find
Black mustard-seed, a tola; only mark
Thou take it not from any hand or house
Where father, mother, child, or slave hath died;
It shall be well if thou canst find such seed.'
Thus didst thou speak, my Lord!"

                               The Master smiled
Exceeding tenderly. "Yea! I spake thus,
Dear Kisagôtami! But didst thou find
The seed?"

                 "I went, Lord, clasping to my breast
The babe, grown colder, asking at each hut —
Here in the jungle and towards the town —
'I pray you, give me mustard, of your grace,
A tola — black'; and each who had it gave,
For all the poor are piteous to the poor;
But when I asked, 'In my friend's household here
Hath any peradventure ever died —
Husband or wife, or child, or slave?' they said:
'O Sister! what is this you ask? the dead
Are very many, and the living few!'
So with sad thanks I gave the mustard back,
And prayed of others; but the others said,
'Here is the seed, but we have lost our slave!'
'Here is the seed, but our good man is dead!'
'Here is some seed, but he that sowed it died
Between the rain-time and the harvesting!'

STORIES OF BUDDHA

Ah, sir! I could not find a single house
Where there was mustard-seed and none had died!
Therefore I left my child — who would not suck
Nor smile — beneath the wild-vines by the stream,
To seek thy face and kiss thy feet, and pray
Where I might find this seed and find no death,
If now, indeed, my baby be not dead,
As I do fear, and as they said to me."

"My sister! thou hast found," the Master said,
"Searching for what none finds — that bitter balm
I had to give thee. He thou lovedst slept
Dead on thy bosom yesterday: to-day
Thou know'st the whole wide world weeps with thy woe:
The grief which all hearts share grows less for one.
Lo! I would pour my blood if it could stay
Thy tears and win the secret of that curse
Which makes sweet love our anguish, and which drives
O'er flowers and pastures to the sacrifice —
As these dumb beasts are driven — men their lords.
I seek that secret: bury thou thy child!"

V

THE FIVE RULES OF BUDDHA

Kill not — for Pity's sake — and lest ye slay
The meanest thing upon its upward way.

Give freely and receive, but take from none
By greed, or force or fraud, what is his own.

INDIA

Bear not false witness, slander not, nor lie;
Truth is the speech of inward purity.

Shun drugs and drinks which work the wit abuse
Clear minds, clean bodies, need no Sôma juice.

Touch not thy neighbor's wife, neither commit
Sins of the flesh unlawful and unfit.

KARMA: A STORY OF BUDDHIST ETHICS[1]

BY PAUL CARUS

Commit no evil; but do good
And let thy heart be pure.
That is the gist of Buddhahood,
The lore that will endure.
The Dhammapada.

DÊVALA'S RICE-CART

LONG, long ago in the days of early Buddhism, India was in a most prosperous condition. The Aryan inhabitants of the country were highly civilized, and the great cities were centers of industry, commerce, and learning.

It was in those olden times that Pandu, a wealthy jeweler of the Brahman caste, traveled in a carriage to Bârânasî, which is now called Benares. He was bent on some lucrative banking business, and a slave who attended to the horses accompanied him.

The jeweler was apparently in a hurry to reach his destination, and as the day was exceedingly pleasant, since a heavy thunderstorm had cooled the atmosphere, the horses sped along rapidly.

While proceeding on their journey the travelers overtook a samana, as the Buddhist monks were called, and the jeweler, observing the venerable appearance of the holy man, thought to himself: "This samana looks noble and saintly. Companionship with good men brings luck; should he also be going to Bârânasî, I will invite him to ride with me in my carriage."

Having saluted the samana the jeweler explained

[1] Copyright (U.S.A.) by The Open Court Publishing Company.

whither he was driving and at what inn he intended to stay in Bârânasî. Learning that the samana, whose name was Nârada, also was traveling to Bârânasî, he asked him to accept a seat in his carriage. "I am obliged to you for your kindness," said the samana to the Brahman, "for I am quite worn out by the long journey. As I have no possessions in this world, I cannot repay you in money; but it may happen that I can reward you with some spiritual treasure out of the wealth of the information I have received while following Shâkyamuni, the Blessed One, the Great Buddha, the Teacher of gods and men."

They traveled together in the carriage and Pandu listened with pleasure to the instructive discourse of Nârada. After about an hour's journey, they arrived at a place where the road had been rendered almost impassable by a washout caused by the recent rain, and a farmer's cart heavily laden with rice prevented further progress. The loss of a linchpin had caused one of the wheels to come off, and Dêvala, the owner of the cart, was busily engaged in repairing the damage. He, too, was on his way to Bârânasî to sell his rice, and was anxious to reach the city before the dawn of the next morning. If he was delayed a day or two longer, the rice merchants might have left town or bought all the stock they needed.

When the jeweler saw that he could not proceed on his way unless the farmer's cart was removed, he began to grow angry and ordered Mahâduta, his slave, to push the cart aside, so that his carriage could pass by. The farmer remonstrated because, being so near the slope of the road, it would jeopardize his cargo; but the Brahman

KARMA: A STORY OF BUDDHIST ETHICS

would not listen to the farmer and bade his servant overturn the rice-cart and push it aside. Mahâduta, an unusually strong man, who seemed to take delight in the injury of others, obeyed before the samana could interfere. The rice was thrown on the wayside, and the farmer's plight was worse than before.

The poor farmer began to scold, but when the big, burly Mahâduta raised his fist threateningly, he ceased his remonstrances and only growled his curses in a low undertone.

When Pandu was about to continue his journey the samana jumped out of the carriage and said: "Excuse me, sir, for leaving you here. I am under obligations for your kindness in giving me an hour's ride in your carriage. I was tired when you picked me up on the road, but now, thanks to your courtesy, I am rested, and recognizing in this farmer an incarnation of one of your ancestors, I cannot repay your kindness better than by assisting him in his troubles."

The Brahman jeweler looked at the samana in amazement: "That farmer, you say, is an incarnation of one of my ancestors? That is impossible!"

"I know," replied the samana, "that you are not aware of the numerous important relations which tie your fate to that of the farmer; but sometimes the smartest men are spiritually blind. So I regret that you harm your own interests, and I shall try to protect you against the wounds which you are about to inflict upon yourself."

The wealthy merchant was not accustomed to being reprimanded, and feeling that the words of the samana, although uttered with great kindness, contained a

INDIA

stinging reproach, bade his servant drive on without further delay.

THE JEWELER'S PURSE

The samana saluted Dêvala, the farmer, and began to help him repair his cart and load up the rice, part of which had been thrown out. The work proceeded quickly and Dêvala thought: "This samana must be a holy man; invisible *devas*[1] seem to assist him. I will ask him how I deserved ill-treatment at the hands of the proud Brahman." And he said: "Venerable sir, can you tell me why I suffer an injustice from a man to whom I have never done any harm?"

And the samana said: "My dear friend, you do not suffer an injustice, but only receive in your present state of existence the same treatment which you visited upon the jeweler in a former life. You reap what you have sown, and your fate is the product of your deeds. Your very existence, such as it is now, is but the *karma* of your past lives."

"What is my *karma?*" asked the farmer.

"A man's *karma*," replied the samana, "consists of all the deeds both good and evil that he has done in his present and in any prior existence. Your life is a system of many activities which have originated in the natural process of evolution, and have been transferred from generation to generation. The entire being of every one of us is an accumulation of inherited functions which are modified by new experiences and deeds. Thus we are what we have done. Our *karma* constitutes our nature. We are our own creators."

[1] Spiritual beings, gods or angels.

KARMA: A STORY OF BUDDHIST ETHICS

"That may be as you say," rejoined Dêvala, "but what have I to do with that overbearing Brahman?"

The samana replied: "You are in character quite similar to the Brahman, and the *karma* that has shaped your destiny differs but little from his. If I am not mistaken in reading your thoughts, I should say that you would, even to-day, have done the same unto the jeweler if he had been in your place, and if you had such a strong slave at your command as he has, able to deal with you at his pleasure."

The farmer confessed that if he had had the power, he would have felt little compunction in treating another man, who had happened to impede his way, as he had been treated by the Brahman, but thinking of the retribution attendant upon unkind deeds, he resolved to be in the future more considerate with his fellow-beings.

The rice was loaded and together they pursued their journey to Bârânasî, when suddenly the horse jumped aside. "A snake, a snake!" shouted the farmer; but the samana looked closely at the object at which the horse shuddered, jumped out of the cart, and saw that it was a purse full of gold, and the idea struck him: "This money can belong to no one but the wealthy jeweler."

Nârada took the purse and found that it contained a goodly sum of gold pieces. Then he said to the farmer: "Now is the time for you to teach the proud jeweler a lesson, and it will redound to your well-being both in this and in future lives. No revenge is sweeter than the requital of hatred with deeds of good will. I will give you this purse, and when you come to Bârânasî drive up to the inn which I shall point out to you; ask for

INDIA

Pandu, the Brahman, and deliver to him his gold. He will excuse himself for the rudeness with which he treated you, but tell him that you have forgiven him and wish him success in all his undertakings. For, let me tell you, the more successful he is, the better you will prosper; your fate depends in many respects upon his fate. Should the jeweler demand any explanation, send him to the *vihâra*,[1] where he will find me ready to assist him with advice in case he may feel the need of it."

BUSINESS IN BENARES

To corner the market of the necessities of life is not a modern invention. The Old Testament contains the story of Joseph, the poor Hebrew youth who became minister of state, and succeeded with unscrupulous but clever business tricks in cornering the wheat market, so as to force the starved people to sell all their property, their privileges, and even their lives, to Pharaoh. And we read in the "Jâtaka Tales" that one of the royal treasurers of Kâsî, which is the old name of Bârânasî, made his first great success in life by cornering the grass market of the metropolis on the day of the arrival of a horse dealer with five hundred horses.

When Pandu the jeweler arrived at Bârânasî, it so happened that a bold speculator had brought about a corner in rice, and Mallika, a rich banker and a business friend of Pandu, was in great distress. On meeting the jeweler he said: "I am a ruined man and can do no business with you unless I can buy a cart of the best rice for the king's table. I have a rival banker in Bârânasî who, learning that I had made a contract with the royal

[1] Buddhist monastery.

KARMA: A STORY OF BUDDHIST ETHICS

treasurer to deliver the rice to-morrow morning, and being desirous to bring about my destruction, has bought up all the rice in Bârânasî. The royal treasurer must have received a bribe, for he will not release me from my contract, and to-morrow I shall be a ruined man unless Krishna[1] will send an angel from heaven to help me."

While Mallika was still lamenting the poverty to which his rival would reduce him, Pandu missed his purse. Searching his carriage without being able to find it, he suspected his slave Mahâduta; and calling the police, accused him of theft, and had him bound and cruelly tortured to extort a confession.

The slave in his agonies cried: "I am innocent, let me go, for I cannot stand this pain; I am quite innocent, at least of this crime, and suffer now for other sins. Oh, that I could beg the farmer's pardon whom, for the sake of my master, I wronged without any cause! This torture, I believe, is a punishment for my rudeness."

While the officer was still applying the lash to the back of the slave, the farmer arrived at the inn and, to the great astonishment of all concerned, delivered the purse. The slave was at once released from the hands of his torturer. But being dissatisfied with his master, he secretly left and joined a band of robbers in the mountains, who made him their chief on account of his great strength and courage.

When Mallika heard that the farmer had the best rice to sell, fit for delivery to the royal table, he at once bought the whole cartload for treble the price that the farmer had ever received. Pandu, however, glad at heart

[1] A Brahman god.

to have his money restored, rewarded the honest finder, and hastened at once to the *vihâra* to receive further explanation from Nârada, the samana.

Nârada said: "I might give you an explanation, but knowing that you are unable to understand a spiritual truth, I prefer to remain silent. Yet I shall give you some advice: Treat every man whom you meet as your own self; serve him as you would demand to be served yourself; for our *karma* travels; it walks apace, though, and the journey is often long. But be it good or evil, finally it will come home to us. Therefore it is said: —

> 'Slowly but surely deeds
>   Home to the doer creep.
> Of kindness sow thy seeds,
>   And bliss as harvest reap.'"

"Give me, O samana, the explanation," said the jeweler, "and I shall thereby be better able to follow your advice."

The samana said: "Listen, then; I will give you the key to the mystery. If you do not understand it, have faith in what I say. Self is an illusion, and he whose mind is bent upon following self, follows a will-o'-the-wisp which leads him into the quagmire of sin. The illusion of self is like dust in your eye that blinds your sight and prevents you from recognizing the close relations that obtain between yourself and your fellows, which are even closer than the relations that obtain among the various organs of your body. You must learn to trace the identity of your self in the souls of other beings. Ignorance is the source of sin. There are few who know the truth. Let this motto be your talisman: —

KARMA: A STORY OF BUDDHIST ETHICS

'Who injureth others
Himself hurteth sore;
Who others assisteth
Himself helpeth more.
Let th' illusion of self
From your mind disappear,
And you'll find the way sure;
The path will be clear.'

"To him whose vision is dimmed by the dust of the world, the spiritual life appears to be cut up into innumerable selves. Thus he will be puzzled in many ways concerning the nature of rebirth, and will be incapable of understanding the import of an all-comprehensive loving-kindness toward all living beings."

The jeweler replied: "Your words, O venerable sir, have a deep significance, and I shall bear them in mind. I extended a small kindness, which caused me no expense whatever, to a poor samana on my way to Bârânasî, and lo! how propitious has been the result! I am deeply in your debt, for without you I should not only have lost my purse, but would have been prevented from doing business in Bârânasî which greatly increases my wealth, while if it had been left undone it might have reduced me to a state of wretched poverty. In addition, your thoughtfulness and the arrival of the farmer's rice-cart preserved the prosperity of my friend Mallika, the banker. If all men saw the truth of your maxims, how much better the world would be! Evils would be lessened, and public welfare enhanced."

The samana replied: "Among all the religions there is none like that of the Buddha. It is glorious in the beginning, glorious in the middle, and glorious in the end. It is glorious in the letter and glorious in the spirit. It

INDIA

is the religion of loving-kindness that rids man of the narrowness of egotism and elevates him above his petty self to the bliss of enlightenment which manifests itself in righteousness."

Pandu nodded assent and said: "As I am anxious to let the truth of the Buddha be understood, I shall found a *vihâra* at my native place, Kaushambî, and invite you to visit me, so that I may dedicate the place to the brotherhood of Buddha's disciples."

AMONG THE ROBBERS

Years passed on, and Pandu's *vihâra* at Kaushambî became a place in which wise samanas used to stay and it was renowned as a center of enlightenment for the people of the town.

At that time the king of a neighboring country had heard of the beauty of Pandu's jewelry, and he sent his treasurer to order a royal diadem to be wrought in pure gold and set with the most precious stones of India. Pandu gladly accepted the order and executed a crown of the most exquisite design. When he had finished the work, he started for the residence of the king, and as he expected to transact other profitable business, took with him a great store of gold pieces.

The caravan carrying his goods was protected by a strong escort of armed men, but when they reached the mountains they were attacked by a band of robbers led by Mahâduta, who beat them and took away all the jewelry and the gold, and Pandu escaped with great difficulty. This calamity was a blow to Pandu's prosperity, and as he had suffered some other severe losses his wealth was greatly reduced.

KARMA: A STORY OF BUDDHIST ETHICS

Pandu was much distressed, but he bore his misfortunes without complaint, thinking to himself: "I have deserved these losses for the sins committed during my past existence. In my younger years I was very hard on other people; because I now reap the harvest of my evil deeds I have no reason for complaint."

As he had grown in kindness toward all beings, his misfortunes only served to purify his heart; and his chief regret, when thinking of his reduced means, was that he had become unable to do good and to help his friends in the *vihâra* to spread the truths of religion.

Again years passed on, and it happened that Panthaka, a young samana and disciple of Nârada, was traveling through the mountains of Kaushambî, and he fell among the robbers in the mountains. As he had nothing in his possession, the robber chief beat him severely and let him go.

On the next morning Panthaka, while pursuing his way through the woods, heard a noise as of men quarreling and fighting, and going to the place he saw a number of robbers, all of them in a great rage, and in their midst stood Mahâduta, their chief; and Mahâduta was desperately defending himself against them, like a lion surrounded by hounds, and he slew several of his aggressors with formidable blows, but there were too many for him; at last he succumbed, and fell to the ground as if dead, covered with wounds.

As soon as the robbers had left the place, the young samana approached to see whether he could be of any assistance to the wounded men. He found that all the robbers were dead, and there was but little life left in the chief.

At once Panthaka went down to the little brooklet which was murmuring near by, fetched fresh water in his bowl and brought it to the dying man. Mahâduta opened his eyes and gnashing his teeth, said: "Where are those ungrateful dogs whom I have led to victory and success? Without me as their chief they will soon perish like jackals hunted down by skillful hunters."

"Do not think of your comrades, the companions of your sinful life," said Panthaka, "but think of your own fate, and accept in the last moment the chance of salvation that is offered you. Here is water to drink, and let me dress your wounds; perhaps I may save your life."

"Alas! alas!" replied Mahâduta, "are you not the man whom I beat but yesterday? And now you come to my assistance, to assuage my pain! You bring me fresh water to quench my thirst, and try to save my life! It is useless, honorable sir, I am a doomed man. The churls have wounded me unto death, — the ungrateful cowards! They have dealt me the blow which I taught them."

"You reap what you have sown," continued the samana; "had you taught your comrades acts of kindness, you would have received from them acts of kindness; but having taught them the lesson of slaughter, it is but your own deed that you are slain by their hands."

"True, very true," said the robber chief, "my fate is well deserved; but how sad is my lot, that I must reap the full harvest of all my evil deeds in future existences! Advise me, O holy sir, what I can do to lighten the sins of my life which oppress me like a great rock placed upon my breast, taking away the breath from my lungs."

KARMA: A STORY OF BUDDHIST ETHICS

Said Panthaka: "Root out your sinful desires; destroy all evil passions, and fill your heart with kindness toward all your fellow-beings."

THE SPIDER-WEB

While the charitable samana washed the wounds, the robber chief said: "I have done much evil and no good. How can I extricate myself from the net of sorrow which I have woven out of the evil desires of my own heart? My *karma* will lead me to hell and I shall never be able to walk in the path of salvation."

Said the samana: "Indeed your *karma* will in its future incarnations reap the seeds of evil that you have sown. There is no escape from the consequences of our actions. But there is no cause for despair. The man who is converted and has rooted out the illusion of self, with all its lusts and sinful desires, will be a source of blessing to himself and others.

"As an illustration, I will tell you the story of the great robber Kandata, who died without repentance and was reborn as a demon in hell, where he suffered for his evil deeds the most terrible agonies and pains. He had been in hell several *kalpas*,[1] and was unable to rise out of his wretched condition, when Buddha appeared upon earth and attained to the blessed state of enlightenment. At that memorable moment a ray of light fell down into hell quickening all the demons with life and hope, and the robber Kandata cried aloud: 'O blessed Buddha, have mercy upon me! I suffer greatly, and although I have done evil, I am anxious to walk in the noble path of righteousness. But I can-

[1] A long period of time, an æon.

INDIA

not extricate myself from the net of sorrow. Help me, O Lord; have mercy on me!'

"Now, it is the law of *karma* that evil deeds lead to destruction, for absolute evil is so bad that it cannot exist. Absolute evil involves impossibility of existence. But good deeds lead to life. Thus there is a final end to every deed that is done, but there is no end to the development of good deeds. The least act of goodness bears fruit containing new seeds of goodness, and they continue to grow, they nourish the poor suffering creatures in their repeated wanderings in the eternal round of *samsâra*[1] until they reach the final deliverance from all evil in *nirvâna*.

"When Buddha, the Lord, heard the prayer of the demon suffering in hell, he said: 'Kandata, did you ever perform an act of kindness? It will now return to you and help you to rise again. But you cannot be rescued unless the intense sufferings which you endure as consequences of your evil deeds have dispelled all conceit of selfhood and have purified your soul of vanity, lust, and envy.'

"Kandata remained silent, for he had been a cruel man, but the Tathâgata in his omniscience saw all the deeds done by the poor wretch, and he perceived that once in his life when walking through the woods he had seen a spider crawling on the ground, and he thought to himself, 'I will not step upon the spider, for he is a harmless creature and hurts nobody.'

"Buddha looked with compassion upon the tortures

[1] *Samsâra* is the restlessness of the world and of worldly life, *nirvâna* is the peace of mind of him who has overcome the illusion of self.

KARMA: A STORY OF BUDDHIST ETHICS

of Kandata, and sent down a spider on a cobweb and the spider said: 'Take hold of the web and climb up.'

"Having attached the web at the bottom of hell, the spider withdrew. Kandata eagerly seized the thin thread and made great efforts to climb up. And he succeeded. The web was so strong that it held, and he ascended higher and higher.

"Suddenly he felt the thread trembling and shaking, for behind him some of his fellow-sufferers were beginning to climb up. Kandata became frightened. He saw the thinness of the web, and observed that it was elastic, for under the increased weight it stretched out; yet it still seemed strong enough to carry him. Kandata had heretofore only looked up; he now looked down, and saw following close upon his heels, also climbing up on the cobweb, a numberless mob of the denizens of hell. 'How can this thin thread bear the weight of all?' he thought to himself; and seized with fear he shouted loudly: 'Let go the cobweb. It is mine!'

"At once the cobweb broke, and Kandata fell back into hell.

"The illusion of self was still upon Kandata. He did not know the miraculous power of a sincere longing to rise upwards and enter the noble path of righteousness. It is thin like a cobweb, but it will carry millions of people, and the more there are that climb it, the easier will be the efforts of every one of them. But as soon as the idea arises in a man's heart: 'This is mine; let the bliss of righteousness be mine alone, and let no one else partake of it,' the thread breaks and he will fall back into his old condition of selfhood. For selfhood is dam-

INDIA

nation, and truth is bliss. What is hell? It is nothing but egotism, and *nirvâna* is a life of righteousness."

"Let me take hold of the spider-web," said the dying robber chief, when the samana had finished his story, "and I will pull myself up out of the depths of hell."

THE CONVERSION OF THE ROBBER CHIEF

Mahâduta lay quiet for a while to collect his thoughts, and then he addressed the samana not without effort: —

"Listen, honorable sir, I will make a confession: I was the servant of Pandu, the jeweler of Kaushambî, but when he unjustly had me tortured I ran away and became a chief of robbers. Some time ago when I heard from my spies that Pandu was passing through the mountains, I succeeded in robbing him of a great part of his wealth. Will you now go to him and tell him that I have forgiven from the bottom of my heart the injury which he unjustly inflicted upon me, and ask him, too, to pardon me for having robbed him. While I stayed with him his heart was as hard as flint, and I learned to imitate the selfishness of his character. I have heard that he has become benevolent and is now pointed out as an example of goodness and justice. He has laid up treasures of which no robber can ever deprive him, while I fear that my *karma* will continue to linger in the course of evil deeds; but I do not wish to remain in his debt so long as it is still in my power to pay him. My heart has undergone a complete change. My evil passions are subdued, and the few moments of life left me shall be spent in the endeavor to continue after death in the good *karma* of righteous aspirations. Therefore, inform Pandu that I have kept the gold crown which he wrought

KARMA: A STORY OF BUDDHIST ETHICS

for the king, and all his treasures, and have hidden them in a cave near by. There were only two of the robbers under my command who knew of it, and both are now dead. Let Pandu take a number of armed men and come to the place and take back the property of which I have deprived him. One act of justice will atone for some of my sins; it will help to cleanse my soul of its impurities and give me a start in the right direction on my search for salvation."

Then Mahâduta described the location of the cave and fell back exhausted.

For a while he lay with closed eyes as though sleeping. The pain of his wounds had ceased, and he began to breathe quietly; but his life was slowly ebbing away, and now he seemed to awake as from a pleasant dream.

"Venerable sir," said he, "what a blessing for me that the Buddha came upon earth and taught you and caused our paths to meet and made you comfort me. While I lay dozing I beheld as in a vision the scene of the Tathâgata's final entering into *nirvâna*. In former years I saw a picture of it which made a deep impression on my mind, and the recollection of it is a solace to me in my dying hour."

"Indeed, it is a blessing," replied the samana, "that the Buddha appeared upon earth; he dispelled the darkness begotten by ill will and error, and attained supreme enlightenment. He lived among us as one of us, being subject to the ills of life, pain, disease, and death, not unlike any mortal. Yet he extinguished in himself all selfishness, all lust, all greed for wealth and love of pleasure, all ambition for fame or power, all hankering after things of the world and clinging to anything transitory and illusive. He was bent only on the one aim, to reach the immortal and to actualize in his being that which cannot die. Through the good *karma* of former existences and his own life he reached at last the blessed state of *nirvâna*, and when the end came he passed away in that final passing away which leaves nothing behind but extinguishes all that is transitory and mortal. Oh, that all men could give up clinging and thereby rid themselves of passion, envy, and hatred!"

Mahâduta imbibed the words of the samana with the eagerness of a thirsty man who is refreshed by a drink of water that is pure and cool and sweet. He wanted to speak, but he could scarcely rally strength enough to open his mouth and move his lips. He beckoned assent and showed his anxiety to embrace the doctrine of the Tathâgata.

Panthaka wetted the dying man's lips and soothed his pain, and when the robber chief, unable to speak, silently folded his hands, he spoke for him and gave utterance to such vows as the latter was ready to make. The samana's words were like music to the ears of Mahâduta. Filled with the joy that originates with good resolutions and entranced by the prospect of an advance in the search for a higher and better life, his eyes began to stare and all pain ceased.

So the robber chief died converted in the arms of the samana.

THE CONVERTED ROBBER'S TOMB

As soon as Panthaka, the young samana, had reached Kaushambî, he went to the *vihâra* and inquired for Pandu the jeweler. Being directed to his residence he gave him a full account of his recent adventure in the forest. And Pandu set out with an escort of armed men and secured the treasures which the robber chief had concealed in the cave. Near by they found the remains of the robber chief and his slain comrades, and they gathered the bodies in a heap and burned them with all honors.

The ashes were collected in an urn and buried in a tumulus on which a stone was placed with an inscription written by Panthaka, which contained a brief report of Mahâduta's conversion.

Before Pandu's party returned home, Panthaka held a memorial service at the tumulus in which he explained the significance of *karma*, discoursing on the words of Buddha: —

>"By ourselves is evil done,
>By ourselves we pain endure.
>By ourselves we cease from wrong,
>By ourselves become we pure.
>No one saves us but ourselves,
>No one can and no one may:
>We ourselves must walk the path,
>Buddhas merely teach the way."

"Our *karma*," the samana said, "is not the work of Ishvara, or Brahma, or Indra, or of any one of the gods. Our *karma* is the product of our own actions. My action is the womb that bears me; it is the inheritance which devolves upon me; it is the curse of my misdeeds and the blessing of my righteousness. My action is the resource by which alone I can work out my salvation."

Then the samana paused and added: —

"While every one is the maker of his own *karma*, and we reap what we have sown, we are at the same time co-responsible for the evils of evil-doers. Such is the interrelation of *karma* that the errors of one person are mostly mere echoes of the errors of others. Neither the curse of our failings nor the bliss of our goodness is purely our own. Therefore when we judge the bad, the vicious, the criminal, let us not withhold from them our sympathy, for we are partners of their guilt."

Among the people of the surrounding villages the tumulus became known as "The Converted Robber's Tomb," and in later years a little shrine was built on the spot where wanderers used to rest and invoke the Buddha for the conversion of robbers and thieves.

THE BEQUEST OF A GOOD KARMA

Pandu carried all his treasures back to Kaushambî, and using with discretion the wealth thus unexpectedly regained, he became richer and more powerful than he had ever been before, and when he was dying at an advanced age he had all his sons, and daughters, and grandchildren gathered round him and said unto them: —

"My dear children, do not blame others for your lack of success. Seek the cause of your ills in yourselves. Unless you are blinded by vanity you will discover your fault, and having discovered it you will see the way out of it. The remedy for your ills, too, lies in yourselves. Never let your mental eyes be covered by the dust of selfishness, and remember the words which have proved a talisman in my life: —

> 'Who injureth others
> Himself hurteth sore.
> Who others assisteth
> Himself helpeth more.

KARMA: A STORY OF BUDDHIST ETHICS

      Let th' illusion of self
      From your mind disappear:
      And you'll find the way sure;
      The path will be clear.'

"If you heed my words and obey these injunctions you will, when you come to die, continue to live in the good *karma* that you have stored up, and your souls will be immortalized according to your deeds."

III
A GROUP OF FOLKLORE STORIES

HISTORICAL NOTE

INDIA is of all countries richest in folklore, and has a large collection of stories ascribed to Buddha. It is thought that these come from some ancient source, and that our familiar "Æsop's Fables" have the same origin. After Buddha's death, his disciples cultivated the habit of identifying any specially good character in these ancient tales with their Master himself in some one of his numerous incarnations. India is the homeland of fairy tales, and it has been estimated that more than one third of the common tales of Europe are originally from Indian sources. One characteristic of the Indian tales, which indicates a high degree of enlightenment, is the tender sympathy with animals which is common to them.

RIGHT AND MIGHT

BY KATHERINE NEVILLE FLEESON

While a deer was eating wild fruit, he heard an owl call "Haak, haak" (a spear), and a cricket cry, "Wat" (surrounded), and, frightened, he fled.

In his flight he ran through the trees up into the mountains and into streams. In one of the streams the deer stepped upon a small fish and crushed it almost to death.

Then the fish complained to the court, and the deer, owl, cricket, and fish had a lawsuit. In the trial came out this evidence: —

As the deer fled, he ran into some dry grass, and the seed fell into the eye of a wild chicken, and the pain of the seed in the eye of the chicken caused it to fly up against a nest of red ants. Alarmed, the red ants flew out to do battle, and in their haste, bit a mongoose. The mongoose ran into a vine of wild fruit and shook several pieces of it on the head of a hermit who sat thinking under a tree.

"Why didst thou, O fruit, fall on my head?" cried the hermit.

The fruit answered: "We did not wish to fall; a mongoose ran against our vine and threw us down."

And the hermit asked, "O mongoose, why didst thou throw the fruit?"

The mongoose answered: "I did not wish to throw down the fruit, but the red ants bit me, and I ran against the vine."

INDIA

The hermit asked, "O ants, why did ye bite the mongoose?"

The red ants replied: "The hen flew against our nest and angered us."

The hermit asked: "O hen, why didst thou fly against the red ants' nest?"

And the hen replied: "The seed fell into my eyes and hurt me."

And the hermit asked, "O seed, why didst thou fall into the hen's eyes?"

And the seed replied: "The deer shook me down."

The hermit said unto the deer, "O deer, why didst thou shake down the seed?"

The deer answered: "I did not wish to do it, but the owl called, frightening me, and I ran."

"O owl," asked the hermit, "why didst thou frighten the deer?"

The owl replied: "I called, but as I am accustomed to call — the cricket, too, called."

Having heard the evidence, the judge said, "The cricket must replace the crushed parts of the fish and make it well," as he, the cricket, had called and frightened the deer.

The cricket was smaller and weaker than the owl or the deer, therefore had to bear the penalty.

THE MAN IN THE MOON

BY KATHERINE NEVILLE FLEESON

THERE was a blacksmith once who complained: "I am not well, and my work is too warm. I want to be a stone on the mountain. There it must be cool, for the wind blows and the trees give a shade."

A wise man who had power over all things replied, "Go thou, be a stone." And he was a stone, high up on the mountain-side.

It happened that a stone-cutter came that way for a stone, and when he saw the one that had been the blacksmith, he knew that it was what he sought, and he began to cut it.

The stone cried out: "This hurts. I no longer want to be a stone. A stone-cutter I want to be. That would be pleasant."

The wise man, humoring him, said, "Be a cutter." Thus he became a stone-cutter, and as he went seeking suitable stone, he grew tired, and his feet were sore. He whimpered, "I no longer want to cut stone. I would be the sun; that would be pleasant."

The wise man commanded, "Be the sun." And he was the sun.

But the sun was warmer than the blacksmith, than a stone, than a stone-cutter, and he complained, "I do not like this. I would be the moon. It looks cool."

The wise man spake yet again, "Be the moon." And he was the moon.

INDIA

"This is warmer than being the sun," murmured he, "for the light from the sun shines on me ever. I do not want to be the moon. I would be a smith again. That, verily, is the best life."

But the wise man replied, "I am weary of your changing. You wanted to be the moon; the moon you are, and it you will remain."

And in yon high heaven lives he to this day.

THE LEGEND OF THE RICE

BY KATHERINE NEVILLE FLEESON

In the days when the earth was young and all things were better than they now are, when men and women were stronger and of greater beauty, and the fruit of the trees was larger and sweeter than that which we now eat, rice, the food of the people, was of larger grain. One grain was all a man could eat; and in those early days, such, too, was the merit of the people, they never had to toil gathering the rice, for, when ripe, it fell from the stalks and rolled into the villages, even unto the granaries.

And upon a year when the rice was larger and more plentiful than ever before, a widow said to her daughter, "Our granaries are too small. We will pull them down and build larger."

When the old granaries were pulled down and the new one not yet ready for use, the rice was ripe in the fields. Great haste was made, but the rice came rolling in where the work was going on, and the widow, angered, struck a grain and cried, "Could you not wait in the fields until we were ready? You should not bother us now when you are not wanted."

The rice broke into thousands of pieces and said, "From this time forth, we will wait in the fields until we are wanted," and from that time the rice has been of small grain, and the people of the earth must gather it into the granary from the fields.

THE LORD KRISHNA AND THE LAPWING'S NEST

A FOLKLORE TALE RETOLD BY MARGARET E. NOBLE

It was the battle of Kurukshetra. The white conch-shells were about to sound, the elephants to march forward, and the attack of the archers to commence. The moment was brief and terrible. Banners were flying, and the charioteers preparing for the advance. Suddenly a little lapwing, who had built her nest in the turf of a hillock in the midst of the battlefield, drew the attention of the Lord Krishna by her cries of anxiety and distress for her young. "Poor little mother!" he said tenderly, "let this be thy protection!" And, lifting a great elephant-bell that had fallen near, he placed it over the lapwing's nest. And so, through the eighteen days of raging battle that followed, a lapwing and her nestlings were kept in safety in their nest, by the mercy of the lord, even in the midst of the raging field of Kurukshetra.

THE PEACOCK AND THE TORTOISE

BY JOHN CHRISTIAN

ONCE upon a time a peacock and a tortoise became great friends. The peacock lived on a tree on the banks of the stream in which the tortoise had his home; and daily the peacock after he had a drink of water danced near the stream and displayed his gay plumage for the amusement of his friend. One unfortunate day, a bird-catcher who was on the prowl caught the peacock and was about taking him away to the market. The unhappy bird begged of his captor to allow him to bid his friend the tortoise good-bye, as it would be the last time he would see him. The bird-catcher allowed him his prayer and took him to the tortoise, who was greatly moved to see his friend a captive. The tortoise asked the bird-catcher to let the peacock go; but he laughed at the request, saying that was his means of livelihood. The tortoise then said, "If I make you a handsome present, will you let my friend go?" "Certainly," answered the bird-catcher, "that is all I want." Whereupon the tortoise dived into the water and in a few seconds came up with a handsome pearl, which, to the great astonishment of the bird-catcher, he handed to him. This was beyond his expectations, and he let the peacock go immediately.

A short time after, the avaricious man came back and told the tortoise that he thought he had not paid enough for the release of his friend, and threatened that, unless a match to that pearl was obtained for him, he would again catch the peacock. The tortoise, who had already advised his friend to betake himself to a distant jungle on being set free, was greatly enraged at the greed of this man. "Well," said the tortoise, "if you insist on having another pearl like it, give it to me and I will fish you out an exact match for it." The cupidity of the bird-catcher prevented his reasoning that "one in the hand was equal to two in the bed of the stream," and he speedily gave the pearl to the wily tortoise, who swam out with it saying, "I am no fool to take one and give two!" and forthwith disappeared, leaving the bird-catcher to be sorry ever after for his covetousness.

LET'S SEE ON WHICH SIDE THE CAMEL SITS

BY JOHN CHRISTIAN

[This proverb is the Hindu equivalent of "He laughs best who laughs last."

The Editor.]

Once a greengrocer and a potter jointly hired a camel; and each filled one side of the pannier with his goods. The camel as he went along the road took a mouthful every now and then, as he had a chance, from the greengrocer's bag of vegetables. This provoked a laugh from the potter, who thought he had the best of the bargain. But the time came for the camel to sit, and he naturally sat on the heavier side, bearing down on the pots, and also to have his mouth free to operate on the bag of greens. This caused the pots to break in the bag, and then the greengrocer had all the laugh to himself.

THE WASHERMAN AND THE DONKEY

BY JOHN CHRISTIAN

A STORY is told of an over-credulous washerman who was childless. This preyed upon his mind very much and was a permanent cause of unhappiness. One day, in the course of his work, he went to the house of the town kazi (or magistrate). He heard the kazi reproaching one of his pupils in this wise: "Not long ago you were a jackass; I made a man of you," etc. The washerman did not wait to hear the rest. He hastened home with all speed and told his wife that he had made a discovery which they were to lose no time in utilizing. "The kazi, my dear," said the washerman, "can make a man of a donkey. Why should we fret any longer for a child? Let us take our donkey to him and beg of him to transform him."

The washerman and his wife, with their donkey, were shortly after this conversation on their way to the kazi. Their mission being explained with many supplications, the kazi, quick-sighted, and with an eye to business, accepted the charge, and promised to effect the metamorphosis in a year. The washerman on his part promised to give his services free for that period.

A year passed in waiting and in happy hopes. On the appointed day the washerman and his companion presented themselves before the kazi. The kazi took them aside and pointed out a strong young man among his pupils. "There," he whispered to the washerman,

THE WASHERMAN AND THE DONKEY

"is your donkey. You see the change: now persuade him and take him home." The washerman and his wife flew to their newly created son, and with many endearing terms prepared to embrace him and made other affectionate advances.

Amazed at this unaccountable conduct of these low people, the lad resisted at first, but as they persisted, he grew furious. After receiving many a cuff from the lad, a happy idea struck the washerman's wife: turning to her husband she said, " Go you and fetch his peg, rope, and grain-bag; perhaps they may remind him of what he was once." The washerman in hot haste went home and fetched them. But it seemed to make matters worse. The washerman held up each of these articles to the young man's view, and said, in the most persuasive tone he could command, "Come home, my son. Do you forget the day you were my donkey? This was the peg to which I would tether you, this your tether rope, and this your food-bag; come to your home!" By this time a jeering crowd had gathered round the young man, and this so infuriated him that he turned to and gave the washerman the soundest thrashing he had ever received in his life. The poor dupe of a washerman — the story says — went home thoroughly convinced that what fate had ordained it was useless to fight against, looking upon his punishment as a just return for his presumption.

THE SEVEN WEAVERS AND THE FIELD OF FLAX

BY JOHN CHRISTIAN

[THE weaver is the hero of many tales like the following. *The Editor*.]

SEVEN weavers once started on a moonlight journey. They had not gone very far from their home when they lost the road. After trying to find their way, they came to a field of flax, which they took to be a river, as the field was in flower, and they fancied the blue color of the flower to be that of water. They stripped themselves and began swimming. After hard labor, they got across. To make certain that no one was drowned, they took the precaution of counting themselves before resuming their journey; but they discovered that one of them was missing, as each forgot to count himself. Grieved at the loss of one of their company, they had not the heart to pursue their journey, but returned home.

SOME INDIAN PROVERBS

Self-praise is no praise.

The young crow is wiser than its mother.
What is play to one is death to another.
In a treeless country, the castor-oil plant is a big tree.
A scalded cat dreads cold water.
The washerman never tears his father's clothes.
A fool went to fish, but lost his fishing-basket.
A thief is a thief, whether he steals a diamond or a cucumber.
God takes care of a blind cow.
One who cannot dance blames the floor.

IV
INDIA IN DAYS OF YORE

HISTORICAL NOTE

LITTLE was known of India before the invasion of Alexander the Great, in 327 B.C. This was a daring attempt, and rich in its consequences. After Alexander's death the country fell into the hands of Seleucus Nicator. He was the founder of the Syrian kingdom, which for more than two hundred years took a prominent part in the politics of the world.

For the first thousand years of the Christian era, the history of India is obscure. Several times the country seems to have been invaded by wild tribes of Scythians and Tartars, and fertile provinces wrested from the natives. Authentic history begins in the eleventh century with the coming of the Mohammedans under Sultan Mahmud, a Turk, who invaded India seventeen times and conquered the country to the Ganges. In 1168, his kingdom was overthrown by the Afghans and fell apart into a number of smaller states, which were easily conquered by the Mogul invaders of the sixteenth century.

ALEXANDER THE GREAT IN INDIA[1]

[327 B.C.]

BY PLUTARCH

[ALEXANDER THE GREAT, with his army of Macedonians and Greeks, invaded India in 327 B.C. The Punjab was then ruled by several petty kings so jealous of one another that some of them were inclined to join him if only he would overthrow the others. Porus was one of those who opposed him. The men of Alexander's army were overcome by the intense heat and clamored to leave the country. Therefore Alexander "subjugated no province, but he made alliances, founded cities, and planted Greek garrisons."

The Editor.]

ALEXANDER in his own letters has given us an account of his war with Porus. He says the two armies were separated by the river Hydaspes, on whose opposite bank Porus continually kept his elephants in order of battle, with their heads towards their enemies, to guard the passage; that he, on the other hand, made every day a great noise and clamor in his camp, to dissipate the apprehensions of the barbarians; that one stormy, dark night he passed the river, at a distance from the place where the enemy lay, into a little island, with part of his foot and the best of his horse. Here there fell a most violent storm of rain, accompanied with lightning and whirlwinds, and seeing some of his men burnt and dying with the lightning, he nevertheless quitted the island and made over to the other side. The Hydaspes, he says, now after the storm, was so swollen and grown so rapid

[1] From *Plutarch's Lives*. Corrected and translated by A. H. Clough. Copyright (U.S.A.), 1876., by Little, Brown, and Company.

as to have made a breach in the bank, and a part of the river was now pouring in here, so that when he came across, it was with difficulty he got a footing on the land, which was slippery and unsteady, and exposed to the force of the currents on both sides. This is the occasion when he is related to have said, "O ye Athenians, will ye believe what dangers I incur to merit your praise?" This, however, is Onesicritus's story. Alexander says, here the men left their boats, and passed the breach in their armor, up to the breast in water, and that then he advanced with his horse about twenty furlongs [1] before his foot, concluding that if the enemy charged him with their cavalry, he should be too strong for them; if with their foot, his own would come up time enough to his assistance. Nor did he judge amiss; for being charged by a thousand horse, and sixty armed chariots, which advanced before their main body, he took all the chariots, and killed four hundred horse upon the place. Porus, by this time guessing that Alexander himself had crossed over, came on with his whole army, except a party which he left behind to hold the rest of the Macedonians in play, if they should attempt to pass the river. But he apprehending the multitude of the enemy, and to avoid the shock of their elephants, dividing his forces, attacked their left wing himself, and commanded Cœnus to fall upon the right, which was performed with good success. For by this means both wings being broken, the enemies fell back in their retreat upon the center, and crowded in upon their elephants. There rallying they fought a hand-to-hand battle, and it was the eighth hour of the day before they were entirely de-

[1] Two and a half miles.

feated. This description the conqueror himself has left us in his own epistles.

Almost all the historians agree in relating that Porus was four cubits and a span [1] high, and that when he was upon his elephant, which was of the largest size, his stature and bulk were so answerable, that he appeared to be proportionably mounted, as a horseman on his horse. This elephant, during the whole battle, gave many singular proofs of sagacity and of particular care of the king, whom as long as he was strong and in a condition to fight, he defended with great courage, repelling those who set upon him; and as soon as he perceived him overpowered with his numerous wounds and the multitude of darts that were thrown at him, to prevent his falling off, he softly knelt down and began to draw out the darts with his proboscis. When Porus was taken prisoner, and Alexander asked him how he expected to be used, he answered, "As a king." For that expression, he said, when the same question was put to him a second time, comprehended everything. And Alexander, accordingly, not only suffered him to govern his own kingdom as satrap under himself, but gave him also the additional territory of various independent tribes whom he subdued, a district which, it is said, contained fifteen several nations, and five thousand considerable towns, besides abundance of villages. To another government, three times as large as this, he appointed Philip, one of his friends.

Some little time after the battle with Porus, Bucephalus died, as most of the authorities state, under cure of his wounds, or as Onesicritus says, of fatigue and age,

[1] About six feet, eight inches.

being thirty years old. Alexander was no less concerned at his death than if he had lost an old companion or an intimate friend, and built a city, which he named Bucephalia, in memory of him, on the bank of the river Hydaspes. He also, we are told, built another city, and called it after the name of a favorite dog, Peritas, which he had brought up himself. So Sotion assures us he was informed by Potamon of Lesbos.

But this last combat with Porus took off the edge of the Macedonians' courage, and stayed their further progress into India. For having found it hard enough to defeat an enemy who brought but twenty thousand foot and two thousand horse into the field, they thought they had reason to oppose Alexander's design of leading them on to pass the Ganges too, which they were told was thirty-two furlongs broad and a hundred fathoms deep, and the banks on the farther side covered with multitudes of enemies. For they were told that the kings of the Gandaritans and Præsians expected them there with eighty thousand horse, two hundred thousand foot, eight thousand armed chariots, and six thousand fighting elephants. Nor was this a mere vain report, spread to discourage them. For Androcottus, who not long after reigned in those parts, made a present of five hundred elephants at once to Seleucus, and with an army of six hundred thousand men subdued all India. Alexander at first was so grieved and enraged at his men's reluctancy, that he shut himself up in his tent, and threw himself upon the ground, declaring, if they would not pass the Ganges, he owed them no thanks for anything they had hitherto done, and that to retreat now was plainly to confess himself vanquished. But at last the reasonable persuasions of his friends and the cries and lamentations of his soldiers, who in a suppliant manner crowded about the entrance of his tent, prevailed with him to think of returning. Yet he could not refrain from leaving behind him various deceptive memorials of his expedition, to impose upon after-times, and to exaggerate his glory with posterity, such as arms larger than were really worn, and mangers for horses, with bits of bridles above the usual size, which he set up and distributed in several places. He erected altars, also, to the gods, which the kings of the Præsians even in our time do honor to when they pass the river, and offer sacrifice upon them after the Grecian manner. Androcottus, then a boy, saw Alexander there, and is said often afterwards to have been heard to say, that he missed but little of making himself master of those countries; their king, who then reigned, was so hated and despised for the viciousness of his life and the meanness of his extraction.

Alexander was now eager to see the ocean. To which purpose he caused a great many rowboats and rafts to be built, in which he fell gently down the rivers at his leisure, yet so that his navigation was neither unprofitable nor inactive. For by several descents upon the banks, he made himself master of the fortified towns, and consequently of the country on both sides. But at a siege of a town of the Mallians, who have the repute of being the bravest people of India, he ran in great danger of his life. For having beaten off the defendants with showers of arrows, he was the first man that mounted the wall by a scaling ladder, which, as soon as he was up, broke and left him almost alone, exposed to the darts which the barbarians threw at him in great numbers from below. In this distress, turning himself as well as he could, he leaped down in the midst of his enemies, and had the good fortune to light upon his feet. The brightness and clattering of his armor when he came to the ground made the barbarians think they saw rays of light, or some bright phantom playing before his body, which frightened them so at first, that they ran away and dispersed; till seeing him seconded but by two of his guards, they fell upon him hand to hand, and some, while he bravely defended himself, tried to wound him through his armor with their swords and spears. And one who stood farther off drew a bow with such just strength, that the arrow finding its way through his cuirass, stuck in his ribs under the breast. This stroke was so violent that it made him give back, and set one knee to the ground, upon which the man ran up with his drawn scimitar, thinking to dispatch him, and had done it, if Peucestes and Limnæus had not interposed, who were both wounded, Limnæus mortally, but Peucestes stood his ground, while Alexander killed the barbarian. But this did not free him from danger; for besides many other wounds, at last he received so weighty a stroke of a club upon his neck, that he was forced to lean his body against the wall, still, however, facing the enemy. At this extremity, the Macedonians made their way in and gathered round him. They took him up, just as he was fainting away, having lost all sense of what was done near him, and conveyed him to his tent, upon which it was presently reported all over the camp that he was dead. But when they had with great difficulty and pains sawed off the shaft of the arrow, which was of wood, and so with much trouble got off his

ALEXANDER THE GREAT IN INDIA

cuirass, they came to cut out the head of it, which was three fingers broad and four long, and stuck fast in the bone. During the operation, he was taken with almost mortal swoonings, but when it was out he came to himself again. Yet though all danger was past, he continued very weak, and confined himself a great while to a regular diet and the method of his cure, till one day hearing the Macedonians clamoring outside in their eagerness to see him, he took his cloak and went out. And having sacrificed to the gods, without more delay he went on board again, and as he coasted along, subdued a great deal of the country on both sides, and several considerable cities.

In this voyage, he took ten of the Indian philosophers prisoners, who had been most active in persuading Sabbas to revolt, and had caused the Macedonians a great deal of trouble. These men, called Gymnosophists, were reputed to be extremely ready and succinct in their answers, which he made trial of, by putting difficult questions to them, letting them know that those whose answers were not pertinent, should be put to death, of which he made the eldest of them judge.

The first being asked which he thought most numerous, the dead or the living, answered, "The living, because those who are dead are not at all."

Of the second, he desired to know whether the earth or the sea produced the largest beast; who told him, "The earth, for the sea is but a part of it."

His question to the third was, "Which is the cunningest of beasts?" "That," said he, "which men have not yet found out."

He bade the fourth tell him what argument he used

to Sabbas to persuade him to revolt. "No other," said he, "than that he should either live or die nobly."

Of the fifth he asked, "Which was eldest, night or day?" The philosopher replied, "Day was eldest, by one day at least." But perceiving Alexander not well satisfied with that account, he added that he ought not to wonder if strange questions had as strange answers made to them.

Then he went on and inquired of the next, what a man should do to be exceedingly beloved. "He must be very powerful," said he, "without making himself too much feared."

The answer of the seventh to his question, how a man might become a god, was, "By doing that which was impossible for men to do."

The eighth told him, "Life is stronger than death, because it supports so many miseries."

And the last being asked, how long he thought it decent for a man to live, said, "Till death appeared more desirable than life."

Then Alexander turned to him whom he had made judge, and commanded him to give sentence. "All that I can determine," said he, "is, that they have every one answered worse than another."

"Nay," said the king, "then you shall die first, for giving such a sentence."

"Not so, O king," replied the gymnosophist, "unless you said falsely that he should die first who made the worst answer."

In conclusion he gave them presents and dismissed them.

INTERIOR OF THE TEMPLE OF VIMALA SAH

INTERIOR OF THE TEMPLE OF VIMALA SAH

The history of this temple is thus given by James Fergusson: —

"It was hardly to be wondered at that Mount Abu was early fixed upon by the Hindus and Jains as one of their sacred spots. Rising from the desert as abruptly as an island from the ocean, it presents on almost every side inaccessible scarps five or six thousand feet high, and the summit can only be approached by ravines cut into its sides. When the summit is reached, it opens out into one of the loveliest valleys imaginable, six or seven miles long, by two or three miles in width, cut up everywhere by granite rocks of the most fantastic shapes, and the spaces between them covered with trees and luxuriant vegetation. . . . During the age of Jain supremacy, it was adorned with several temples, two of which are unrivaled for certain qualities by any temples in India. They are built wholly of white marble, though no quarries of that material are known to exist within three hundred miles of the spot, and to transport and carry it uphill to the site of these temples must have added immensely to the expense of the undertaking.

"The more modern of the two was built by the same brothers, Tejpala and Vastupala, who erected the triple temple at Girnar. This one, we learn from the inscription, was erected between the years 1197 and 1247, and for minute delicacy of carving and beauty of detail stands almost unrivaled even in the land of the patient and lavish labor.

"The other, built by another merchant prince, Vimala Sah, apparently about the year A.D. 1032, is simpler and bolder, though still as elaborate as good taste would allow in any purely architectural object."

The exterior of this temple is plain, but within it is elaborately and magnificently ornamented. The ceiling of the cell rises to a lofty, spire-like roof. Surrounding the temple and attached to the building are fifty-five chapels, each containing an image of the saint, for it was considered that a god was honored in proportion to the number of his images.

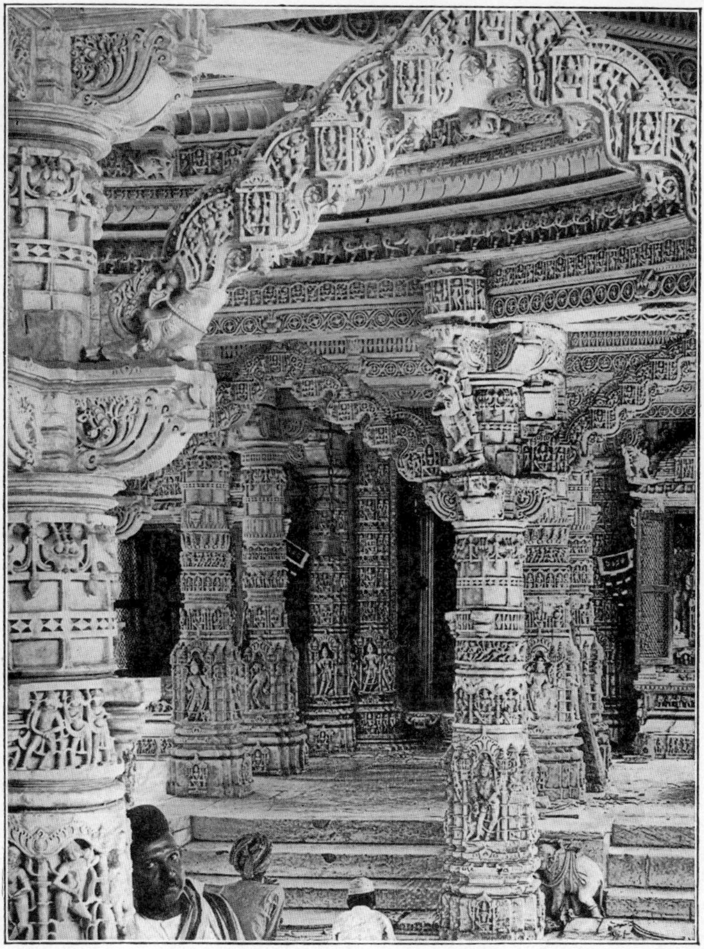

THE ROCK EDICTS OF ASOKA
[About 257 B.C.]

[ASOKA, King of Behar, became a convert to Buddhism about 257 B.C. He was a most zealous missionary, and his little sermons, known as "Edicts," were carved upon the rocks and pillars, and may still be seen. The following are some of them.

The Editor.]

THE FRUIT OF EXERTION

THUS saith His Sacred Majesty: —

For more than two-and-a-half years I was a lay disciple, without, however, exerting myself strenuously. But it is more than a year since I joined the Order, and have exerted myself strenuously.

During that time the gods who were regarded as true all over India have been shown to be untrue.

For this is the fruit of exertion. Nor is this to be attained by a great man only, because even by the small man who chooses to exert himself immense heavenly bliss may be won.

For this purpose has the precept been composed: —

"Let small and great exert themselves."

My neighbors too should learn this lesson; and may such exertion long endure!

And this purpose will grow — yea, it will grow immensely — at least one-and-a-half-fold will it increase in growth.

INDIA

And this purpose must be written on the rocks, both afar off and here; and, wherever there is a stone pillar, it must be written on the stone pillar.

And according to this text, so far as your jurisdiction extends, you must send it out everywhere.

By (me) while on tour was the precept composed. 256 (?) departures from staging-places (or possibly, days spent abroad).

SUMMARY OF THE LAW OF PIETY

Thus saith His Sacred Majesty: —

Father and mother must be hearkened to; similarly, respect for living creatures must be firmly established; truth must be spoken. These are the virtues of the Law of Piety which must be practiced. Similarly, the teacher must be reverenced by the pupil, and towards relations fitting courtesy must be shown.

This is the ancient nature (of piety) — this leads to length of days, and according to this men must act.

Written by Paḍa the scribe.

THE SACREDNESS OF LIFE

This pious edict has been written by command of His Sacred and Gracious Majesty the King.

Here [in the capital] no animal may be slaughtered for sacrifice, nor may the holiday-feast be held, because His Sacred and Gracious Majesty the King sees much offense in the holiday-feast, although in certain places holiday-feasts are excellent in the sight of His Sacred and Gracious Majesty the King.

Formerly, in the kitchen of His Sacred and Gracious Majesty the King each day many hundred thousands of living creatures were slaughtered to make curries. But now, when this pious edict is being written, only three living creatures are slaughtered [daily] for curry, to wit, two peacocks and one antelope — the antelope, however, not invariably. Even those three living creatures henceforth shall not be slaughtered.

THE PROMPT DISPATCH OF BUSINESS

Thus saith His Sacred and Gracious Majesty the King: — For a long time past it has not happened that business has been dispatched and that reports have been received at all hours. Now by me this arrangement has been made that at all hours and in all places — whether I am dining, or in the ladies' apartments, in my bedroom, or in my closet, in my (?) carriage, or in the palace gardens — the official Reporters should report to me on the people's business, and I am ready to do the people's business in all places.

And if, perchance, I personally by word of mouth command that a gift be made or an order executed, or anything urgent is intrusted to the superior officials, and in that business a dispute arises or a fraud occurs among the monastic community, I have commanded that immediate report must be made to me at any hour and in any place, because I never feel full satisfaction in my efforts and dispatch of business. For the welfare of all folk is what I must work for — and the root of that, again, is in effort and the dispatch of business. And whatsoever exertions I make are for the end that I may discharge my debt to animate beings, and that while I make some happy here, they may in the next world gain heaven.

INDIA

For this purpose, have I caused this pious edict to be written, that it may long endure, and that my sons and grandsons may exert themselves for the welfare of all folk. That, however, is a difficult thing save by the utmost exertion.

ASOKA'S VISIT TO THE BIRTHPLACE OF BUDDHA

His Sacred and Gracious Majesty the King, when he had been consecrated twenty years, having come in person, did reverence; and, because "Here Buddha was born, the Sakya sage," a great (?) railing of stone was prepared, and a stone pillar erected.

Because "Here the Venerable One was born" the village of Lummini was made free of religious cesses and declared entitled to the eighth share (of the produce claimed by the Crown).

KUNÂLA THE OBEDIENT, SON OF ASOKA

BY VINCENT A. SMITH

In the seventh century A.D. pilgrims were shown a *stûpa* at Taxila, which was said to have been built by Asoka to mark the spot where the eyes of his beloved son Kunâla were torn out. The story of Kunâla is to the following effect.

After the death of his faithful consort Asandhimitrâ, King Asoka, late in life, married Tishyarakshitâ, a dissolute and unprincipled young woman. In pursuance of a deep-laid scheme for the destruction of him who by his virtue had put her vice to shame, the queen with honied words persuaded the king to depute Kunâla to the government of distant Taxila.

The prince obediently accepted the honorable commission, and when departing was warned by his father to verify orders received, which, if genuine, would be sealed with an impression of the king's teeth. The queen bided her time, with ever-growing hatred. After the lapse of some months she wrote a dispatch, addressed to the viceroy's ministers at Taxila, directing them immediately on receipt of the orders to put out the eyes of the viceroy, Prince Kunâla, to lead him and his wife into the mountains, and to there leave them to perish.

She sealed the dispatch with royal red wax, and, when the king was asleep, furtively stamped the wax with the impression of his teeth, and sent off the orders with all speed to Taxila. The ministers who received the orders knew not what to do. The prince, noticing their confusion, compelled them to explain. The ministers wished to compromise by detaining the prince in custody, pending a reference to the capital. But the prince would not permit of any delay, and said: "My father, if he has ordered my death, must be obeyed; and the seal of his teeth is a sure sign of the correctness of the orders. No mistake is possible." He then commanded an outcast wretch to pluck out his eyes. The order was obeyed, and the prince, accompanied by his faithful wife, wandered forth in sightless misery to beg his bread.

In the course of their weary wanderings they arrived at Pâtaliputra. "Alas," cried the blind man, "what pain I suffer from cold and hunger. I was a prince; I am a beggar. Would that I could make myself known, and get redress for the false accusations brought against me." He managed to penetrate into an inner court of the palace, where he lifted up his voice and wept, and, to the sound of a lute, sang a song full of sadness.

The king in an upper chamber heard the strains, and, thinking that he recognized the voice and touch as those of his son, sent for the minstrel. The king, when he beheld his sightless son, was overwhelmed with grief, and inquired by whose contrivance all this misery had come about. The prince humbly replied: "In truth, for lack of filial piety I have thus been punished by Heaven. On such and such a day suddenly came a loving order, and I, having no means of excusing myself, dared not shrink from the punishment."

The king, knowing in his heart that Queen Tishya-

KUNÂLA THE OBEDIENT, SON OF ASOKA

rakshitâ was guilty of the crime, without further inquiry caused her to be burnt alive, and visited with condign punishment every person, high or low, who had any share in the outrage. The officials were some dismissed, some banished, some executed. The common people were, according to one account, massacred, and, according to another, transported across the Himâlayas to the deserts of Khotan.

In those days a great saint named Ghosha dwelt in the monastery by the holy tree of Mahâbodhi. To him the king brought Kunâla, and prayed that his son might receive his sight. The saint commanded that on the morrow a great congregation should assemble to hear his preaching of the Law, and that each person should bring a vessel to receive his tears. A vast multitude of men and women assembled, and there was not one of those who heard the sermon but was moved to tears, which fell into the vessels provided.

The saint collected the tears in a golden vase, and said these words: "The doctrine which I have expounded is the most mysterious of Buddha's teaching; if that exposition is not true, if there is error in what I have said, then let things remain as they are; but, if what I have said is true and free from error, let this man, after washing his eyes with these tears, receive his sight."

Whereupon Kunâla washed in the tears and received his sight.

POEMS BY KING BHARTRIHARI

[Early in the Christian era]

TRANSLATED BY PAUL ELMER MORE

[BHARTRIHARI was a ruler who lived at some time early in the Christian era. He abandoned the luxuries of his throne and made his home in the forest, where he could meditate at his will and be free from the honors and temptations of life in a palace.

The Editor.]

I

ONE law there is: no deed perform
To others that to thee were harm;
And this is all, all laws beside
With circumstances alter or abide.

II

Like as our outworn garments we discard,
And other new ones don;
So doth the Soul these bodies doff when marred,
And others new put on.

Fire doth not kindle It, nor sword divides,
Nor winds nor waters harm;
Eternal and unchanged the One abides,
And smiles at all alarm.

III

Like as a goldsmith beateth out his gold
To other fashions fairer than the old,
So may the Spirit, learning ever more,
In ever nobler forms his life infold.

SAKOONTALA, OR THE LOST RING

[Third century, A.D.]

TRANSLATED FROM THE SANSKRIT OF KALIDASA BY SIR MONIER MONIER-WILLIAMS

[IN *Sakoontala*, the most famous of the Indian dramas, the heroine, from whom the play is named, has been brought up as his own daughter by the chief of a group of hermits. The king visits the hermitage, woos her, and wins her for his queen. He is obliged to return to his capital; but he leaves with Sakoontala his signet ring as a token of his love. After a time, she goes to the royal palace, but the king declares that he never saw her. She raises her hand to show him the ring, but it has disappeared; it has slipped from her finger while she was bathing in the Ganges. He has entirely forgotten her, but neither she nor the king knows that this is because a curse has been laid upon him. At length a fisherman brings in the ring, which he has found in a fish. At once the curse is removed, and the king remembers his bride. But she has vanished, and her husband is broken-hearted. Some time after this, the king, when on a visit to a sacred grove, sees a young boy playing fearlessly with the cub of a lion, and feels a remarkable interest in the child. Then follows the closing act of the play.

The Editor.]

KING [*taking the child by the hand*]

I MARVEL that the touch of this strange child
Should thrill me with delight; if so it be,
How must the fond caresses of a son
Transport the father's soul who gave him being!

ATTENDANT [*looking at them both*]

Wonderful! Prodigious!

INDIA

KING

What excites your surprise, my good woman?

ATTENDANT

I am astonished at the striking resemblance between the child and yourself; and, what is still more extraordinary, he seems to have taken to you kindly and submissively, though you are a stranger to him.

KING [*fondling the child*]

If he be not the son of the great sage, of what family does he come, may I ask?

ATTENDANT

Of the race of Puru.

KING [*aside*]

What! are we, then, descended from the same ancestry? This, no doubt, accounts for the resemblance she traces between the child and me. Certainly it has always been an established usage among the princes of Puru's race, —

>To dedicate the morning of their days
>To the world's weal, in palaces and halls,
>'Mid luxury and regal pomp abiding;
>Then, in the wane of life, to seek release
>From kingly cares, and make the hallowed shade
>Of sacred trees their last asylum, where
>As hermits they may practice self-abasement,
>And bind themselves by rigid vows of penance.

[*Aloud*] But how could mortals by their own power gain admission to this sacred region?

SAKOONTALA, OR THE LOST RING

Attendant

Your remark is just; but your wonder will cease when I tell you that his mother is the offspring of a celestial nymph, and gave him birth in the hallowed grove of Kasyapa.

King [aside]

Strange that my hopes should be again excited! [*Aloud.*] But what, let me ask, was the name of the prince whom she deigned to honor with her hand?

Attendant

How could I think of polluting my lips by the mention of a wretch who had the cruelty to desert his lawful wife?

King [aside]

Ha! the description suits me exactly. Would I could bring myself to inquire the name of the child's mother! [*Reflecting.*] But it is against propriety to make too minute inquiries about the wife of another man.

First Attendant [entering with the china peacock in her hand]

Sarva-damana, Sarva-damana, see, see, what a beautiful Sakoonta (bird).

Child [looking round]

My mother! Where? Let me go to her.

Both Attendants

He mistook the word Sakoonta for Sakoontala. The boy dotes upon his mother, and she is ever uppermost in his thoughts.

INDIA

Second Attendant

Nay, my dear child, I said, Look at the beauty of this Sakoonta.

King [*aside*]

What! is his mother's name Sakoontala? But the name is not uncommon among women. Alas! I fear the mere similarity of a name, like the deceitful vapor of the desert, has once more raised my hopes only to dash them to the ground.

Child

Dear nurse, what a beautiful peacock! [*Takes the toy.*]

First Attendant [*looking at the child: in great distress*]

Alas! alas! I do not see the amulet on his wrist.

King

Don't distress yourself. Here it is. It fell off while he was struggling with the young lion. [*Stoops to pick it up.*]

Both Attendants

Hold! hold! Touch it not, for your life. How marvelous! He has actually taken it up without the slightest hesitation. [*Both raise their hands to their breasts and look at each other in astonishment.*]

King

Why did you try to prevent my touching it?

First Attendant

Listen, great monarch. This amulet, known as "The Invincible," was given to the boy by the divine son of

SAKOONTALA, OR THE LOST RING

Marichi, soon after his birth, when the natal ceremony was performed. Its peculiar virtue is, that when it falls to the ground, no one excepting the father or mother of the child can touch it unhurt.

KING

And suppose another person touches it?

FIRST ATTENDANT

Then it instantly becomes a serpent, and bites him.

KING

Have you ever witnessed the transformation with your own eyes?

BOTH ATTENDANTS

Over and over again.

KING [*with rapture, aside*]

Joy! joy! Are then my dearest hopes to be fulfilled?
[*Embraces the child.*]

SECOND ATTENDANT

Come, my dear Suvrata, we must inform Sakoontala immediately of this wonderful event, though we have to interrupt her in the performance of her religious vows.
[*Exeunt.*]

CHILD [*to the king*]

Do not hold me. I want to go to my mother.

KING

We will go to her together, and give her joy, my son.

INDIA

CHILD

Dushyanta is my father, not you.

KING [*smiling*]

His contradiction convinces me only the more.

[*Enter* SAKOONTALA, *in widow's apparel, with her long hair twisted into a single braid*]

SAKOONTALA [*aside*]

I have just heard that Sarva-damana's amulet has retained its form, though a stranger raised it from the ground. I can hardly believe in my good fortune. Yet why should not Sanumati's prediction be verified?

KING [*gazing at Sakoontala*]

Alas! can this indeed be my Sakoontala?
Clad in the weeds of widowhood, her face
Emaciate with fasting, her long hair
Twined in a single braid, her whole demeanor
Expressive of her purity of soul:
With patient constancy she thus prolongs
The vow to which my cruelty condemned her.

SAKOONTALA [*gazing at the king, who is pale with remorse*]

Surely, this is not like my husband; yet who can it be that dares pollute by the pressure of his hand my child, whose amulet should protect him from a stranger's touch?

CHILD [*going to his mother*]

Mother, who is this man that has been kissing me and calling me his son?

SAKOONTALA, OR THE LOST RING

King

My best-beloved, I have indeed treated thee most cruelly, but am now once more thy fond and affectionate lover. Refuse not to acknowledge me as thy husband.

Sakoontala [*aside*]

Be of good cheer, my heart. The anger of Destiny is at last appeased. Heaven regards thee with compassion. But is he in very truth my husband?

King

Behold me, best and loveliest of women,
Delivered from the cloud of fatal darkness
That erst oppressed my memory. Again
Behold us brought together by the grace
Of the great lord of Heaven. So the moon
Shines forth from dim eclipse, to blend his rays
With the soft luster of his Rohini.

Sakoontala

May my husband be victorious —
   [*She stops short, her voice choked with tears.*]

King

O fair one, though the utterance of thy prayer
Be lost amid the torrent of thy tears,
Yet does the sight of thy fair countenance,
And of thy pallid lips, all unadorned
And colorless in sorrow for my absence,
Make me already more than conqueror.

Child

Mother, who is this man?

INDIA

SAKOONTALA

My child, ask the deity that presides over thy destiny.

KING [*falling at* SAKOONTALA'S *feet*]

Fairest of women, banish from thy mind
The memory of my cruelty; reproach
The fell delusion that o'erpowered my soul,
And blame not me, thy husband; 't is the curse
Of him in whom the power of darkness reigns,
That he mistakes the gifts of those he loves
For deadly evils. Even though a friend
Should wreathe a garland on a blind man's brow,
Will he not cast it from him as a serpent?

SAKOONTALA

Rise, my own husband, rise. Thou wast not to blame. My own evil deeds, committed in a former state of being, brought down this judgment upon me. How else could my husband, who was ever of a compassionate disposition, have acted so unfeelingly? [*The king rises.*] But tell me, my husband, how did the remembrance of thine unfortunate wife return to thy mind?

KING

As soon as my heart's anguish is removed, and its wounds are healed, I will tell thee all.

Oh! let me, fair one, chase away the drop
That still bedews the fringes of thine eye;
And let me thus efface the memory
Of every tear that stained thy velvet cheek,

SAKOONTALA, OR THE LOST RING

Unnoticed and unheeded by thy lord,
When in his madness he rejected thee.
[*Wipes away the tear.*]

SAKOONTALA [*seeing the signet ring on his finger*]

Ah! my dear husband, is that the Lost Ring?

KING

Yes; the moment I recovered it, my memory was restored.

SAKOONTALA

The ring was to blame in allowing itself to be lost at the very time when I was anxious to convince my noble husband of the reality of my marriage.

KING

Receive it back, as the beautiful twining plant receives again its blossom in token of its reunion with the spring.

SAKOONTALA

Nay; I can never more place confidence in it. Let my husband retain it.

[*Enter* MATALI]

MATALI

I congratulate Your Majesty. Happy are you in your reunion with your wife: happy are you in beholding the face of your own son.

KING

Yes, indeed. My heart's dearest wish has borne sweet fruit. But tell me, Matali, is this joyful event known to the great Indra?

INDIA

Matali [*smiling*]

What is unknown to the gods? But come with me, noble Prince, the divine Kasyapa graciously permits thee to be presented to him.

King

Sakoontala, take our child and lead the way. We will together go into the presence of the holy Sage.

Sakoontala

I shrink from entering the august presence of the great Saint, even with my husband at my side.

King

Nay; on such a joyous occasion it is highly proper. Come, come; I entreat thee. [*All advance.*]

[The Holy Sage Kasyapa explains that what has happened is not the fault of the King, but is due to the curse.
The Editor.]

Kasyapa

Know that when the nymph Menaka, the mother of Sakoontala, became aware of her daughter's anguish in consequence of the loss of the ring at the nymphs' pool, and of thy subsequent rejection of her, she brought her and confided her to the care of Aditi. And I no sooner saw her than I ascertained by my divine power of meditation, that thy repudiation of thy poor faithful wife had been caused entirely by the curse of Durvasas — not by thine own fault — and that the spell would terminate on the discovery of the ring.

SAKOONTALA, OR THE LOST RING

KING [*drawing a deep breath*]

Oh! what a weight is taken off my mind, now that my character is cleared of reproach.

SAKOONTALA

Joy! joy! My revered husband did not, then, reject me without good reason, though I have no recollection of the curse pronounced upon me. But, in all probability, I unconsciously brought it upon myself, when I was so distracted on being separated from my husband soon after our marriage. For I now remember that my two friends advised me not to fail to show the ring in case he should have forgotten me.

KASYAPA

At last, my daughter, thou art happy, and hast gained thy heart's desire. Indulge, then, no feeling of resentment against thy partner. See now, —

Though he repulsed thee, 't was the sage's curse
That clouded his remembrance; 't was the curse
That made thy tender husband harsh towards thee.
Soon as the spell was broken, and his soul
Delivered from its darkness, in a moment
Thou didst regain thine empire o'er his heart.
So on the tarnished surface of a mirror
No image is reflected, till the dust
That dimmed its wonted luster is removed.

KING

Holy father, see here the hope of my royal race.
[*Takes his child by the hand.*]

INDIA

Kasyapa

Know that he, too, will become the monarch of the whole earth. Observe, —

Soon, a resistless hero, shall he cross
The trackless ocean, borne above the waves
In an aerial car; and shall subdue
The earth's seven sea-girt isles. Now has he gained
As the brave tamer of the forest beasts,
The title Sarva-damana; but then
Mankind shall hail him as King Bharata,
And call him the supporter of the world.

King

We cannot but entertain the highest hopes of a child for whom your highness performed the natal rites.

Aditi

My reverend husband, should not the intelligence be conveyed to Kanwa, that his daughter's wishes are fulfilled, and her happiness complete? He is Sakoontala's foster-father. Menaka, who is one of my attendants, is her mother, and dearly does she love her daughter.

Sakoontala [*aside*]

The venerable matron has given utterance to the very wish that was in my mind.

Kasyapa

His penances have gained for him the faculty of omniscience, and the whole scene is already present to his mind's eye.

SAKOONTALA, OR THE LOST RING

KING

Then most assuredly he cannot be very angry with me.

KASYAPA

Nevertheless it becomes us to send him intelligence of this happy event, and hear his reply. What, ho there!

PUPIL

Holy father, what are your commands?

KASYAPA

My good Galava, delay not an instant, but hasten through the air and convey to the venerable Kanwa, from me, the happy news that the fatal spell has ceased, that Dushyanta's memory is restored, that his daughter Sakoontala has a son, and that she is once more tenderly acknowledged by her husband.

PUPIL

Your highness's commands shall be obeyed. [*Exit.*]

KASYAPA

And now, my dear son, take thy consort and thy child, re-ascend the car of Indra, and return to thy imperial capital.

KING

Most holy father, I obey.

KASYAPA

And accept this blessing —

INDIA

For countless ages may the god of gods,
Lord of the atmosphere, by copious showers
Secure abundant harvest to thy subjects;
And thou by frequent offerings preserve
The Thunderer's friendship! Thus, by interchange
Of kindly actions, may you both confer
Unnumbered benefits on earth and heaven!

King

Holy father, I will strive, as far as I am able, to attain this happiness.

Kasyapa

What other favor can I bestow on thee, my son?

King

What other can I desire? If, however, you permit me to form another wish, I would humbly beg that the saying of the sage Bharata be fulfilled, —

May kings reign only for their subjects' weal!
May the divine Saraswati, the source
Of speech, and goddess of dramatic art,
Be ever honored by the great and wise!
And may the purple self-existent god,
Whose vital energy pervades all space,
From future transmigrations save my soul!

[*Exeunt omnes.*]

V
THE MOGUL CONQUEST

HISTORICAL NOTE

IN 900 A.D. Buddhism was driven from India, but only to spread into other lands, and to win one half of the human race as converts. Meanwhile, Brahmanism had never lost its power. It had taken many points from Buddhism and also from the rites of the aborigines, and had developed into what was known as Hinduism, with its complicated system of castes. About the year 1000, Mohammedanism reached India, and now one fifth of the inhabitants profess that faith.

The Mohammedans entered a land not only as missionaries, but also as determined conquerors. India was no exception, and when that country was invaded by the Moguls, or Mongols, in 1526, under Bahar, it was found to be divided into many little principalities, each under the rule of either a Mohammedan or a Hindu prince. Bahar's son Akbar, afterwards called the Great, succeeded in uniting the empire partly by arms and partly by shrewd alliances. It was his grandson, Shah Jehan, who built the exquisite Taj Mahal. The empire became strong and magnificent. Under his son Aurungzebe its wealth and its area increased, but not its strength. The decline had begun. There were rebellions and invasions. The Mogul rulers had attained to their power partly by the aid of the Hindus, but they took no pains to conciliate their former helpers, who now became their enemies. The Hindu confederacies came into power, and the rule of the Moguls had passed.

PRINCE WITH ATTENDANTS IN A GARDEN

PRINCE WITH ATTENDANTS IN A GARDEN

(An Indian painting of the seventeenth century)

The Koran, following the literal interpretation of the second commandment, forbids Mohammedans to make the likeness of anything in heaven or on earth. But Akbar, greatest of the Mogul emperors, cared more for art than for the Koran, and attracted to his court a host of artists on whom he lavished money and honor without stint.

By referring to the records of his reign, we find that he ranked the master artists, of whom he employed a hundred, as officers in his army with corresponding pay and privileges, while the countless numbers of minor artists and apprentices were enrolled as members of the Imperial Bodyguard, or as common soldiers, and paid from eight to sixteen dollars a month. Besides this, a weekly inspection was held of their work, and talent was liberally rewarded. At Delhi, Agra, and other cities, Akbar formed magnificent libraries, covering the volumes with the richest bindings and illustrating them with splendid miniatures. The Imperial Library at Agra alone is said to have contained, in 1641, twenty-four thousand volumes, valued at the astounding sum of $3,600,000, an average of $150 a volume; and a single book, the Persian translation of the Mahābhārata, cost $200,000. These wonderful libraries were for the most part destroyed in the wars of the seventeenth and eighteenth centuries.

The picture shown here was painted as an illustration for a book. A prince is seated, in Oriental fashion, in his palace grounds, with his sword beside him, for the Moguls were fighters as well as patrons of the arts. A slave is offering him a cup of tea which she has drawn from one of the curiously shaped vessels standing on the tray in the foreground. A male attendant sits on the ground before him, and another stands behind with the brush, used to drive away disturbing insects, thrown over his shoulder. In the background are blossoming trees, and birds flying across a sky that is filled with conventionalized clouds. Especially noteworthy is the exquisite delicacy shown in the most minute details of the elaborate costumes and ornamentations.

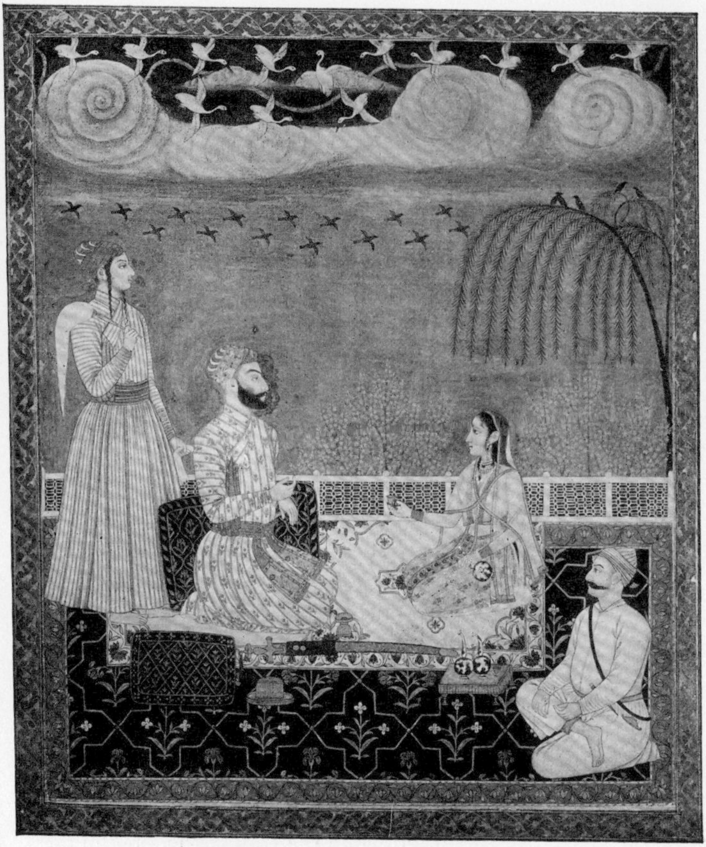

THE PEACOCK THRONE OF THE GREAT MOGUL, SHAH JEHAN

[Middle of seventeenth century]

BY JEAN BAPTISTE TAVERNIER, BARON OF AUBONNE

It should be stated that the Great Mogul has seven magnificent thrones, one wholly covered with diamonds, the others with rubies, emeralds, or pearls.

The principal throne, which is placed in the hall of the first court, is nearly of the form and size of our campbeds; that is to say, it is about six feet long and four wide. Upon the four feet, which are very massive, and from twenty to twenty-five inches high, are fixed the four bars which support the base of the throne, and upon these bars are ranged twelve columns, which sustain the canopy on three sides, there not being any on that which faces the court. Both the feet and the bars, which are more than eighteen inches long, are covered with gold inlaid and enriched with numerous diamonds, rubies, and emeralds. In the middle of each bar there is a large *balass* ruby, cut *en cabuchon*, with four emeralds round it, which form a square cross. Next in succession, from one side to the other along the length of the bars there are similar crosses, arranged so that in one the ruby is in the middle of four emeralds, and in another the emerald is in the middle and four *balass* rubies surround it. The emeralds are table-cut, and the intervals between the rubies and emeralds are covered with diamonds, the largest of which do not exceed ten to twelve carats in weight, all being showy stones, but very flat. There are also in some parts pearls set in gold, and upon one of the longer sides of the throne there are four steps to ascend it. Of the three cushions or pillows which are upon the throne, that which is placed behind the king's back is large and round like one of our bolsters, and the two others that are placed at his sides are flat. There is to be seen, moreover, a sword suspended from this throne, a mace, a round shield, a bow and quiver with arrows; and all these weapons, as also the cushions and steps, both of this throne and the other six, are covered over with stones which match those with which each of the thrones is respectively enriched.

I counted the large *balass* rubies on the great throne, and there are about one hundred and eight, all *cabuchons*, the least of which weighs one hundred carats; but there are some which weigh apparently two hundred and more. As for the emeralds, there are plenty of good color, but they have many flaws; the largest may weigh sixty carats and the least thirty carats. I counted about one hundred and sixteen; thus there are more emeralds than rubies.

The underside of the canopy is covered with diamonds and pearls, with a fringe of pearls all around, and above the canopy, which is a quadrangular-shaped dome, there is to be seen a peacock with elevated tail made of blue sapphires and other colored stones, the body being gold inlaid with precious stones, having a large ruby in front of the breast, from whence hangs a pear-shaped pearl of fifty carats or thereabouts, and of a somewhat yellow water. On both sides of the peacock there is a large bouquet of the same height as the bird,

THE PEACOCK THRONE OF SHAH JEHAN

and consisting of many kinds of flowers made of gold inlaid with precious stones. On the side of the throne which is opposite the court there is to be seen a jewel consisting of a diamond of from eighty to ninety carats' weight, with rubies and emeralds round it; and when the king is seated, he has this jewel in full view. But that which in my opinion is the most costly thing about this magnificent throne is, that the twelve columns supporting the canopy are surrounded with beautiful rows of pearls, which are round and of fine water, and weigh from six to ten carats each. At four feet distance from the throne there are fixed, on either side, two umbrellas, the sticks of which, for seven or eight feet in height, are covered with diamonds, rubies, and pearls. The umbrellas are of red velvet, and are embroidered and fringed all round with pearls.

This is what I have been able to observe regarding this famous throne, commenced by Tamerlane and completed by Shah Jehan; and those who keep the accounts of the king's jewels and of what this great work has cost, have assured me that it amounts to one hundred and seven lakhs of rupees.[1]

Behind this grand and magnificent throne there is placed a smaller one, which has the form of a bathing-tub. It is of an oval shape of about seven feet in length and five in breadth, and the outside is covered over with diamonds and pearls, but it has no canopy.

[1] About five million dollars.

THE TAJ MAHAL, THE MOST BEAUTIFUL TOMB IN THE WORLD

[Middle of seventeenth century]

BY BAYARD TAYLOR

[SHAH JEHAN was a famous builder of palaces and mosques. More beautiful than any of these, however, is the wondrously lovely Taj Mahal, which he built as the tomb of his favorite wife.

The Editor.]

I PURPOSELY postponed my visit to the Taj Mahal — the most renowned monument of Agra — until I had seen everything else in the city and its vicinity. The distant view of this matchless edifice satisfied me that its fame was well deserved. So pure, so gloriously perfect did it appear, that I almost feared to approach it, lest the charm should be broken. It is seen to best advantage from the tomb of Itmun e' Dowlah, the Prime Minister of Shah Jehan, which stands in a garden on the northern bank of the Jumna, directly opposite to the city. I spent an afternoon at this tomb and the Ram Bagh (Garden of Rama), two miles farther up the river. The former is a mausoleum of white marble, elegantly sculptured and inlaid, standing on a raised platform, from the corners of which rise marble minarets. Its design shows the same purity of taste, the same richness of fancy, which I had previously remarked in the Pearl Mosque, and afterward in the Taj.

The Ram Bagh is a garden which, I believe, formerly

THE TAJ MAHAL

belonged to the Mogul emperors, and is now kept in order as a place of recreation, by the Government. Too much praise cannot be awarded to the British rulers in India, for the care with which they have restored and protected all of these monuments of the past, expending large sums to prevent the mosques, palaces and tombs of the former rulers from falling into decay. On account of the humidity of the soil, and the abundance of insects and reptiles, the Ram Bagh is traversed by raised stone causeways, the principal of which inclose water tanks and fountains. It is a pleasant, shady retreat, with a stone balcony overhanging the rapid Jumna, and commanding a view of many ruined palaces on the opposite bank. There are suites of apartments, comfortably furnished, which are let to visitors at the rate of a rupee per day; but when the applications are frequent, no one is allowed to stay more than eight days, in order to give a chance to others. My friends brought their servants and a handsome tiffin, of which we all partook, in the largest chamber. We returned across the bridge of boats in the evening. The Hindoos had lighted lamps in front of the many little shrines facing the water, and in some of them stood persons waving a torch back and forth before the face of the god, crying out at the same time, "Ram, Ram, Ram!" "Ram, Seeta, Ram!" This ceremony, with the pouring of the Jumna water over the image, and decorating it with wreaths of flowers, appeared to be the only form of worship observed. There are more substantial offerings made, but if the god gets them, the Brahmins take care that he shall not keep them.

To return to the Taj — for the reader expects me to describe it, and I must comply, although reluctantly, for I am aware of the difficulty of giving an intelligible picture of a building, which has no counterpart in Europe, or even in the East. The mosques and palaces of Constantinople, the domed tent of Omar at Jerusalem, and the structures of the Saracens and Memlooks at Cairo, have nothing in common with it. The remains of Moorish art in Spain approach nearest to its spirit, but are only the scattered limbs, the torso, of which the Taj is the perfect type. It occupies that place in Saracenic art, which, during my visit to Constantinople, I mistakenly gave to the Solymanye Mosque, and which, in respect to Grecian art, is represented by the Parthenon. If there were nothing else in India, this alone would repay the journey.

The history and associations of the Taj are entirely poetic. It is a work inspired by Love, and consecrated to Beauty. Shah Jehan, the "Selim" of Moore's poem, erected it as a mausoleum over his queen, Noor Jehan, — "the Light of the World," — whom the same poet calls Noor Mahal, "the Light of the Harem," or more properly, "Palace." She is reputed to have been a woman of surpassing beauty, and of great wit and intelligence. Shah Jehan was inconsolable for her loss and has immortalized her memory in a poem, the tablets of which are marble, and the letters jewels: — for the Taj is poetry transmuted into form, and hence, when a poet sees it he hails it with the rapture of a realized dream. Few persons, of the thousands who sigh over the pages of "Lalla Rookh," are aware that the "Light of the Harem" was a real personage, and that her tomb is one of the wonders of the world. The native miniature painters in Delhi show you her portrait, painted on

THE TAJ MAHAL

ivory, — a small, rather delicate face, with large, dark piercing eyes, and black hair flowing from under a scarf adorned with peacock's feathers.

The Taj is built on the bank of the Jumna, rather more than a mile to the eastward of the Fort of Agra. It is approached by a handsome road, cut through the mounds left by the ruins of ancient palaces. Like the tomb of Akbar, it stands in a large garden, inclosed by a lofty wall of red sandstone, with arched galleries around the interior. The entrance is a superb gateway of sandstone, inlaid with ornaments and inscriptions from the Koran, in white marble. Outside of this grand portal, however, is a spacious quadrangle of solid masonry, with an elegant structure intended as a caravanseraï, on the opposite side. Whatever may be the visitor's impatience, he cannot help pausing to notice the fine proportions of these structures, and the rich and massive style of their architecture. The gate to the garden of the Taj is not so large as that of Akbar's tomb, but quite as beautiful in design. Passing under the open demi-vault, whose arch hangs high above you, an avenue of dark Italian cypresses appears before you. Down its center sparkles a long row of fountains, each casting up a single slender jet. On both sides, the palm, the banyan, and the feathery bamboo mingle their foliage; the song of birds meets your ear, and the odor of roses and lemon-flowers sweetens the air. Down such a vista, and over such a foreground, rises the Taj.

It is an octagonal building, or rather, a square with the corners truncated, and each side precisely similar. It stands upon a lofty platform, or pedestal, with a minaret at each corner, and this, again, is lifted on a vast terrace of solid masonry. An Oriental dome, swelling out boldly from the base into nearly two-thirds of a sphere, and tapering at the top into a crescent-tipped spire, crowns the edifice, rising from its center, with four similar, though much smaller domes, at the corners. On each side there is a grand entrance, formed by a single pointed arch, rising nearly to the cornice, and two smaller arches (one placed above the other) on either hand. The height of the building, from its base to the top of the dome, is two hundred and sixty-two feet, and of the minarets, about two hundred feet. But no words can convey an idea of the exquisite harmony of the different parts, and the grand and glorious effect of the whole structure, with its attendant minarets.

The material is of the purest white marble, little inferior to that of Carrara. It shines so dazzlingly in the sun, that you can scarcely look at it near at hand, except in the morning and evening. Every part — even the basement, the dome, and the upper galleries of the minarets — is inlaid with ornamental designs in marble of different colors, principally a pale brown, and a bluish violet variety. Great as are the dimensions of the Taj, it is as laboriously finished as one of those Chinese caskets of ivory and ebony, which are now so common in Europe. Bishop Heber truly said: "The Pathans designed like Titans, and finished like jewelers." Around all the arches of the portals and the windows — around the cornice and the domes — on the walls and in the passages, are inlaid chapters of the Koran, the letters being exquisitely formed of black marble. It is asserted that the whole of the Koran is thus inlaid, in the Taj, and I can readily believe it to be true. The

THE TAJ MAHAL

building is perfect in every part. Any dilapidations it may have suffered are so well restored that all traces of them have disappeared.

I ascended to the base of the building — a gleaming marble platform, almost on a level with the tops of the trees in the garden. Before entering the central hall, I descended to the vault where the beautiful Noor Jehan is buried. A sloping passage, the walls and floor of which have been so polished by the hands and feet of thousands, that you must walk carefully to avoid sliding down, conducts to a spacious vaulted chamber. There is no light but what enters the door, and this falls directly upon the tomb of the queen in the center. Shah Jehan, whose ashes are covered by a simpler cenotaph, raised somewhat above hers, sleeps by her side. The vault was filled with the odors of rose, jasmine, and sandalwood, the precious attars of which are sprinkled upon the tomb. Wreaths of beautiful flowers lay upon it, or withered around its base.

These were the true tombs, the monuments for display being placed in the grand hall above, which is a lofty rotunda, lighted both from above and below by screens of marble wrought in filigree. It is paved with blocks of white marble and jasper, and ornamented with a wainscoting of sculptured tablets, representing flowers. The tombs are sarcophagi of the purest marble, exquisitely inlaid with bloodstone, agate, cornelian, lapis-lazuli, and other precious stones, and surrounded with an octagonal screen six feet high, in the open tracery of which lilies, irises, and other flowers are interwrought with the most intricate ornamental designs. This is also of marble, covered with precious stones. From the resemblance of this screen and the workmanship of the tomb to Florentine mosaic, it is supposed by some to have been executed by an Italian artist; and I have even heard it stated that the Taj was designed by an Italian architect. One look at the Taj ought to assure any intelligent man that this is false — nay, impossible, from the very nature of the thing. The Taj is the purest Saracenic, in form, proportions, and ornamental designs. If that were not sufficient, we have still the name of the Moslem architect, sculptured upon the building.

I consider it extremely doubtful whether any Italian had anything to do with the work, though it is barely possible that one may have been employed upon the screen around the tombs. In the weekly account of the expenditures for the building of the Taj, there is a certain sum mentioned as paid to "the foreign stone-cutter," who may either have been Italian, Turkish, or Persian. As for the flowers, represented in bas-relief on the marble panels, it has been said that they are not to be found in India. Now these flowers, as near as they can be identified, are the tulip, the iris (both natives of Persia), and the lotus. But I noticed a curious feature in the sculpture, which makes it clear to me that the artist was a native. *The flowers lack perspective*, which would never have been the fault of an Italian artist of Shah Jehan's time — about the middle of the seventeenth century. Bishop Heber has declared that he recognized Italian art in the ornaments of the Taj, but he declared also that its minarets have no beauty, that the Fort of Agra is built of granite, and fell into many other glaring errors, both of taste and observation, which I have no time to point out.

THE TAJ MAHAL

The dome of the Taj contains an echo more sweet, pure, and prolonged than that in the Baptistry of Pisa, which is the finest in Europe. A single musical tone, uttered by the voice, floats and soars overhead, in a long, delicious undulation, fainting away so slowly that you hear it after it is silent, as you see, or seem to see, a lark you have been watching, after it is swallowed up in the blue of heaven. I pictured to myself the effect of an Arabic or Persian lament for the lovely Noor Jehan, sung over her tomb. The responses that would come from above, in the pauses of the song, must resemble the harmonies of angels in Paradise. The hall, notwithstanding the precious materials of which it is built, and the elaborate finish of its ornaments, has a grave and solemn effect, infusing a peaceful serenity of mind, such as we feel when contemplating a happy death. Stern, unimaginative persons have been known to burst suddenly into tears, on entering it; and whoever can behold the Taj without feeling a thrill that sends the moisture to his eye, has no sense of beauty in his soul.

The Taj truly is, as I have already said, a poem. It is not only a pure architectural type, but also a creation which satisfies the imagination, because its characteristic is Beauty. Did you ever build a Castle in the Air? Here is one, brought down to earth, and fixed for the wonder of ages; yet so light it seems, so airy, and, when seen from a distance, so like a fabric of mist and sunbeams, with its great dome soaring up, a silvery bubble, about to burst in the sun, that, even after you have touched it, and climbed to its summit, you almost doubt its reality. The four minarets which surround it are perfect — no other epithet will describe them. You cannot conceive of their proportions being changed in any way, without damage to the general effect. On one side of the Taj is a mosque with three domes, of red sandstone, covered with mosaic of white marble. Now, on the opposite side, there is a building precisely similar, but of no use whatever, except as a balance to the mosque, lest the perfect symmetry of the whole design should be spoiled. This building is called the *jowàb*, or "answer." Nothing can better illustrate the feeling for proportion which prevailed in those days — and proportion is Art.

In comparing these masterpieces of architecture with the Moorish remains in Spain, which resemble them most nearly, I have been struck with the singular fact, that while, at the central seats of the Moslem Empire, Art reached but a comparative degree of development, here, in India, and there, on the opposite and most distant frontiers, it attained a rapid and splendid culmination. The capitals of the Caliphs and the Sultans — Bagdad, Cairo, Damascus, and Constantinople — stand far below Agra and Delhi, Granada and Seville, in point of architecture, notwithstanding the latter cities have but few and scattered remains. It is not improbable that the Moorish architects, after the fall of Granada, gradually made their way to the eastward, and that their art was thus brought to India — or, at least, that they modified and improved the art then existing. The conquest of India by Baber (grandson of Tamerlane and grandfather of Akbar) is almost coeval with the expulsion of the Moors from Granada.

But the sun grows hot; it is nearly noon. We have spent three hours in and around the Taj, and we must leave it. Nothing that is beautiful can be given up without a pang, but if a man would travel, he must endure many such partings. I must add, however, before we go, that on the opposite bank of the Jumna there is an immense foundation-terrace, whereon, it is said, Shah Jehan intended to erect a tomb for himself, of equal magnificence, but the rebellion of his sons, and his own death, prevented it. What the gods permitted to Love, they forbade to Vanity. A sheikh, who takes care of the Taj, told me, that had the emperor carried out his design, the tombs were to have been joined by a bridge, with a silver railing on each side. He told me that the Taj, with its gateways, mosque, and other buildings attached, had cost seven crores of rupees — $35,000,000. This, however, is quite impossible, when we consider the cheapness of labor in those days, and I believe the real cost is estimated at £3,000,000 ($15,000,000), which does not seem exaggerated.

ON THE MARCH WITH AURUNGZEBE

[Reigned from 1658 to 1707]

BY FRANÇOIS BERNIER

[AURUNGZEBE was a son of the Shah Jehan who built the wonderful Taj Mahal. Aurungzebe overcame his brothers, and later put them to death. He imprisoned his father, and proclaimed himself emperor.

The Editor.]

THIS is indeed slow and solemn marching, what we here call *à la Mogole*. Lahor is little more than one hundred and twenty leagues or about fifteen days' journey from Delhi, and we have been nearly two months on the road. The king, it is true, together with the greater part of the army, diverge from the highway, in search of better ground for the sports of the field, and for the convenience of obtaining the water of the Gemna, which we had gone in search of to the right; and we leisurely skirted its bank, hunting and shooting amid grass so high as almost to conceal our horsemen, but abounding in every kind of game. We are now in a good town, enjoying repose; and I cannot better employ my time than in committing to paper the various particulars which have engaged my mind since I quitted Delhi. Soon I hope to conduct you to Kachemire, and to show you one of the most beautiful countries in the world.

Whenever the king travels in military pomp he has always two private camps; that is to say, two separate bodies of tents. One of these camps being constantly a day in advance of the other, the king is sure to find

ON THE MARCH WITH AURUNGZEBE

at the end of every journey a camp fully prepared for his reception. It is for this reason that these separate bodies of tents are called *peiche-kanes*, or houses which precede. The two *peiche-kanes* are nearly equal, and to transport one of them the aid of more than sixty elephants, two hundred camels, one hundred mules, and one hundred men-porters is required. The most bulky things are carried by the elephants, such as the large tents with their heavy poles, which on account of their great length and weight are made so as to be taken down into three pieces. The smaller tents are borne by the camels, and the luggage and kitchen utensils by the mules. To the porters are confided the lighter and more valuable articles, as the porcelain used at the king's table, the painted and gilt beds, and those rich *karguain* [cabinets] of which I shall speak hereafter.

One of the *peiche-kanes* has no sooner reached the place intended for the new encampment than the grand quartermaster selects some fine situation for the king's tents, paying, however, as much attention as possible to the exact symmetry of the whole camp. He then marks out a square, each side of which measures more than three hundred ordinary paces. A hundred pioneers presently clear and level this space, raising square platforms of earth on which they pitch the tents. The whole of this extensive square is then encompassed with *kanates*, or screens, seven or eight feet in height, secured by cords attached to pegs, and by poles fixed two by two in the ground, at every ten paces, one pole within and the other without, and each leaning upon the other. The *kanates* are made of strong cloth, lined with printed Indian calico, representing large vases of flowers. The royal entrance, which is spacious and magnificent, is in the center of one of the sides of the square, and the flowered calico of which it is composed, as well as that which lines the whole exterior face of this side of the square, is of much finer texture and richer than the rest.

The first and largest tent erected in the royal camp is named *am-kas*, being the place where the king and all the nobility keep the *mokam;* that is, where they assemble at nine o'clock in the morning for the purpose of deliberating on affairs of state and of administering justice. The kings of Hindustan seldom fail, even when in the field, to hold this assembly twice during the twenty-four hours, the same as when in the capital. The custom is regarded as a matter of law and duty, and the observance of it is rarely neglected.

The second tent, little inferior in size and somewhat farther within the inclosure, is called the *gosle-kane*, or the place for bathing. It is here that all the nobility meet every evening to pay their obeisance to the king, in the same manner as when the court is at Delhi. This evening assembly subjects the *Omrahs* to much inconvenience; but it is a grand and imposing spectacle in a dark night to behold, when standing at some distance, long rows of torches lighting these nobles, through extended lanes of tents, to the *gosle-kane*, and attending them back again to their own quarters. These flambeaux, although not made of wax, like ours in France, burn a long time. They merely consist of a piece of iron hafted in a stick, and surrounded at the extremity with linen rags steeped in oil, which are renewed, as occasion requires, by the *masalchis*, or link-boys, who carry the oil in long narrow-necked vessels of iron or brass.

ON THE MARCH WITH AURUNGZEBE

Still deeper in the square is the third tent, smaller than those I have spoken of, called *kaluet-kane*, the retired spot, or the place of the privy council. To this tent none but the principal ministers of state have access, and it is here that all the important concerns of the kingdom are transacted.

Advancing beyond the *kaluet-kane*, you come to the king's private tents, which are surrounded by small *kanates*, of the height of a man, some lined with *Maslipatam* chintz, painted over with flowers of a hundred different kinds, and others with figured satin, decorated with deep silken fringes.

Adjoining the royal tents are those of the *begums*, or princesses, and of the great ladies and principal female attendants of the seraglio. These tents are also inclosed on every side by rich *kanates;* and in the midst of them are the tents of the inferior female domestics and other women connected with the seraglio, placed generally in much the same order, according to the offices of the respective occupants.

The *am-kas*, and the five or six other principal tents, are elevated above the rest, as well for the sake of keeping off the heat as that they may be distinguished at a distance. The outside is covered with a strong and coarse red cloth, ornamented with large and variegated stripes; but the inside is lined with beautiful handpainted chintz, manufactured for the purpose at *Maslipatam*, the ornamentation of which is set off by rich figured satin of various colors, or embroideries of silk, silver, and gold, with deep and elegant fringes. Cotton mats, three or four inches in thickness, are spread over the whole floor, and these again are covered with a splendid carpet, on which are placed large square brocade cushions to lean upon. The tents are supported by painted and gilt pillars.

In each of the two tents wherein the king and nobility meet for deliberation is erected a stage, which is most sumptuously adorned, and the king gives audience under a spacious canopy of velvet or flowered silk. The other tents have similar canopies, and they also contain what are called *karguain*, or cabinets, the little doors of which are secured by silver padlocks. You may form some idea of them by picturing to yourself two small squares of our folding screens, the one placed upon the other, and both tied round with a silken cord in such a manner that the extremities of the sides of the upper square incline towards each other so as to form a kind of dome. There is this difference, however, between the *karguain* and our screens, that all their sides are composed of very thin and light deal boards painted and gilt on the outside, and embellished around with gold and silk fringe. The inside is lined with scarlet, flowered satin, or brocade.

I believe that I have omitted nothing of consequence contained within the great square.

In describing what is to be seen without, I shall first notice two handsome tents on either side of the grand entrance, or royal gate. Here is to be seen a small number of the choicest horses, saddled and superbly caparisoned, ready to be mounted upon any emergency, but intended rather for ceremony and parade.

On both sides of the same royal gate are ranged the fifty or sixty small field-pieces of which the stirrup-artillery is composed, and which fire a salute when the king enters his tent, by which the army is apprised of his arrival.

A free space, as extensive as may be convenient or practicable, is always kept in front of the royal entrance, and at its extremity there is a large tent called *nagar-kane*, i.e., drum room, because it contains the trumpets and the cymbals.

Close to this tent is another of a large size, called *tchauky-kane*, where the *Omrahs* in rotation mount guard for twenty-four hours, once every week. Most of them, however, order one of their own tents to be pitched in its immediate vicinity, where they find themselves more comfortable and are in greater privacy.

Within a short square of the three other sides of the great square are the tents of officers and others appropriated to particular purposes, which, unless there be local impediments, are always placed in the same relative situation. Every one of these tents has its particular appellation, but the names are difficult of pronunciation, and as it is not within my scope to teach you the language of the country, it may suffice to state that in one of them are deposited the arms of the king; in a second the rich harnesses; and in a third the vests of brocade, which are the presents generally made by the king. The fruits, the sweetmeats, the Ganges water, the saltpeter with which it is cooled, and the *betle*, are kept in four other tents. *Betle* is the leaf which, after it has undergone a certain preparation, is given as a mark of royal favor (like coffee in Turkey), and which when masticated sweetens the breath and reddens the lips. There are fifteen or sixteen other tents which serve for kitchens and their appurtenances; and in the midst of all these are the tents of a great number of officers and attendants. There are, lastly, six others, of considerable length, for led horses; and other tents for choice elephants and for the animals employed in hunting; for the birds of prey that invariably accompany the court, and are intended both for show and for field sports; for the dogs; the leopards for catching antelopes; the *nilghaux*, or gray oxen, which I believe to be a species of elk; the lions and rhinoceroses, brought merely for parade; the large Bengal buffaloes, which attack the lion; the tamed antelopes, frequently made to fight in the presence of the king.

The quarters of the monarch are understood to comprehend not only the great square, but the numerous tents situated without the square to which I have just drawn your attention. Their position is always in the center of the army, or as much so as the nature of the ground will admit. You will easily conceive that there is something very striking and magnificent in these royal quarters, and that this vast assemblage of red tents, placed in the center of a numerous army, produces a brilliant effect when seen from some neighboring eminence; especially if the country be open and offer no obstruction to the usual and regular distribution of the troops.

The first care of the grand quartermaster is, as before remarked, to choose a suitable situation for the royal tents. The *am-kas* is elevated above every other tent, because it is the landmark by which the order and disposition of the whole army is regulated. He then marks out the royal bazaars, from which all the troops are supplied. The principal bazaar is laid out in the form of a wide street, running through the whole extent of the army, now on the right, then on the left of the *am-kas*, and always as much as possible in the direction of the next day's encampment. The other royal bazaars, which are neither so long nor so spacious, generally cross this one, some on one side and some on another side of the king's quarters. All of them are distinguished by extremely long poles stuck in the ground at the distance of three hundred paces from each other, bearing red standards, and surmounted with the tails of the Great Tibet cows, which have the appearance of so many periwigs.

The quartermaster then proceeds to plan the quarters for the *Omrahs*, that there may always be the same observance of regularity, and that each nobleman may be placed at his usual distance from the royal square, whether on the right or on the left, so that no individual may be permitted to change the place allotted to him, or which he expressed a wish to occupy before the commencement of the expedition.

The description I have given of the great square is, in many particulars, applicable to the quarters of the *Omrahs* and Rajahs. In general they also have two *peiche-kanes*, with a square of *kanates* inclosing their principal tents and those of their wives. Outside this square are likewise pitched the tents of their officers and troopers, and there is a bazaar in the form of a street, consisting of small tents belonging to the followers of the army, who supply it with forage, rice, butter, and other necessary articles of life. The *Omrahs* need not, therefore, always have recourse to the royal bazaars, where indeed everything may be procured, almost the same as in the capital. A long pole is planted at both ends of each bazaar, and distinguished by a particular standard, floating in the air, as high as those of the royal bazaars, in order that the different quarters may be readily discerned from a distance.

The chief *Omrahs* and great Rajahs pride themselves on the loftiness of their tents, which must not, however, be too conspicuous, lest the king perceive it and command that the tents be thrown down, as he did on our late march. For the same reason, the outside must not be entirely red, there being none but the royal tents that can be of that color; and as a mark of proper respect every tent has also to front the *am-kas*, or quarters of the king.

The remainder of the ground, between the quarters of the monarch, those of the *Omrahs*, and the bazaars, is filled with the tents of *Mansebdars*, or inferior *Omrahs*, of tradespeople of every description, of civil officers and other persons, who for various reasons follow the army; and, last of all, the tents of those who serve in the light and heavy artillery. The tents are therefore very numerous, and cover a large extent of ground; though with respect both to their number and the space occupied by them very extravagant notions are formed. When the army halts in a fine and favorable country, which leaves it at liberty to adopt the well-understood rules and order of a circular encampment, I do not believe that this space measures more than two leagues, or perhaps two leagues and a half in circumference, including here and there several spots of unoccupied ground. It should be mentioned, however, that the heavy artillery, which requires a great deal of room, is commonly a day or two in advance of the army.

ON THE MARCH WITH AURUNGZEBE

What is said of the strange confusion that prevails in the camp, and of the alarm thereby occasioned to a newcomer, is also much exaggerated. A slight acquaintance with the method observed in the quartering of the troops will enable you to go, without much difficulty from place to place as your business may require; the king's quarters, the tents and standards peculiar to every *Omrah*, and the ensigns and "periwigs" of the royal bazaars, which are all seen from a great distance, serving, after a little experience, for unerring guides.

Sometimes, indeed, notwithstanding all these precautions, there will be uncertainty and disorder, particularly on the arrival of the army at the place of encampment in the morning, when every one is actively employed in finding and establishing his own quarters. The dust that arises often obscures the marks I have mentioned, and it becomes impossible to distinguish the king's quarter, the different bazaars, or the tents of the several *Omrahs*. Your progress is besides liable to be impeded by the tents then pitching, and by the cords extended by inferior *Omrahs*, who have no *peiche-kanes*, and by *Mansebdars* to mark their respective boundaries, and to prevent not only the public from passing through, but the fixing of any strange tent near their own, where their wives, if accompanying them, reside. A horde of their lusty varlets, with cudgels in their hands, will not suffer these cords to be removed or lowered; you then naturally retrace your steps, and find that while you have been employed in unavailing efforts to pass at one end, your retreat has been cut off at the other. There is now no means of extricating your laden camels but by menace and entreaty; outrageous passion, and calm remonstrance; seeming as if you would proceed to blows, yet carefully abstaining from touching any one; promoting a violent quarrel between the servants of both parties, and afterward reconciling them for fear of the consequences, and in this way taking advantage of a favorable moment to pass your camels. But the greatest annoyance is perhaps in the evening when business calls you to any distance. This is the time when the common people cook their victuals with a fire made of cow and camel dung and green wood. The smoke of so many fires of this kind, when there is little wind, is highly offensive, and involves the atmosphere in total darkness. It was my fate to be overtaken three or four times by this wide-spreading vapor. I inquired, but could not find my way. I turned and roamed about, ignorant whither I went. Once I was obliged to stop until the smoke dispersed, and the moon arose; and at another time I with difficulty reached the *aguacy-die*, at the foot of which I passed the night with my horse and servant. The *aguacy-die* resembles a lofty mast of a ship, but is very slender, and takes down in three pieces. It is fixed toward the king's quarters, near the tent called *nagarkane*, and during the night has a lighted lantern suspended from the top. This light is very useful, for it may be seen when every object is enveloped in impenetrable darkness. To this spot persons who lose their way resort, either to pass the night secure from all danger of robbers, or to resume their search after their own lodgings. The name *aguacy-die* may be translated Light of Heaven, the lantern when at a distance appearing like a star.

To prevent robberies every *Omrah* provides watchmen, who continually perambulate his particular quarters during the night, crying out, "Kaber-dar!" or, Have a care! and there are guards posted round the whole army at every five hundred paces, who kindle fires, and also cry out "Kaber-dar!" Besides these precautions, the *Cotoual*, or grand provost, sends soldiers in every direction, who especially pervade the bazaars, crying out and sounding a trumpet. Notwithstanding all these measures, robberies are often committed, and it is prudent to be always on the alert, not to rely too much on the vigilance of servants; and to repose at an early hour, so as to watch during the remainder of the night.

I will now proceed to describe the different modes of traveling adopted by the Great Mogul on these occasions. Most commonly, he is carried on men's shoulders in a *tact-ravan*, or field throne, wherein he sits. This *tact* is a species of magnificent tabernacle, with painted and gilt pillars, and glass windows, that are kept shut when the weather is bad. The four poles of the litter are covered either with scarlet or brocade, and decorated with deep fringes of silk and gold. At the end of each pole are stationed two strong and handsomely dressed men, who are relieved by eight other men constantly in attendance. Sometimes the king rides on horseback, especially when the weather is favorable for hunting; and at other times he is carried by an elephant in a *mikdember*, or in a *hauze*, which is by far the most striking and splendid style of traveling, as nothing can surpass the richness and magnificence of the harness and trappings. The *mikdember* is a small house, or square wooden tower, gilt and painted; and the *hauze*, an oval chair with a canopy on pillars, also superbly decorated with colors and gold.

In every march the king is accompanied by a great number of *Omrahs* and Rajahs, who follow him closely on horseback, placing themselves promiscuously in a body, without much method or regularity. On the morning of a journey, they assemble at break of day in the *am-kas*, with the exception of those who may be exempted by age or the nature of their office. They find these marches very fatiguing, especially on hunting-days, being exposed like a private soldier to the sun and dust, frequently until three o'clock in the afternoon.

These luxurious lords move along very differently when not in the train of the king: neither dust nor sun then annoys them, but they are stretched, as on a bed, in a *paleky*, closed and covered or not as may be found more agreeable; sleeping at ease until they reach their tent, where they are sure to find an excellent dinner, the kitchen and every necessary article having been sent forward the preceding night, immediately after supper. The *Omrahs* are always surrounded by a number of well-mounted cavaliers, called *gourze-berdars*, because they carry a kind of club, or silver mace. The king is also attended by many of them, who go before him, both on the right and on the left, together with a multitude of footmen. The *gourze-berdars* are picked, good-looking men, of fine figures, and are employed to convey orders and dispatches. With great sticks in their hands they drive everybody before them, and keep the way clear for the king.

The *Cours* follows the Rajahs, surrounded by a large number of players on cymbals and trumpets. The

Cours, as I before observed, consists of figures in silver, representing strange animals, hands, balances, fishes, and other mystical objects, borne at the end of large silver poles.

A numerous body of *Mansebdars* or inferior *Omrahs* comes next, well mounted, and equipped with sword, quiver and arrows. This body is much more numerous than that of *Omrahs*, which follows the king; because not only the *Mansebdars* who are on duty are obliged to assemble at break of day near the royal tent, for the purpose of accompanying the king, but there are many who join the train in the hope of attracting notice and preferment.

You are no doubt at a loss to conceive how so vast a number both of men and animals can be maintained in the field. The best solution of the difficulty will be found in the temperance of the Indians and simple nature of their diet. Of the five-score thousand troopers, not a tenth, no, not a twentieth part, eat animal food; they are satisfied with their *kichery*, a mess of rice and other vegetables, over which, when cooked, they pour melted butter. It should be considered too that camels endure fatigue, hunger, and thirst in a surprising degree, live upon little, and eat any kind of food. At the end of every march, they are left to browse in the fields, where everything serves for fodder. It is important likewise to observe that the same tradesmen who supply the bazaars in Delhi are compelled to furnish them in the camp; the shops of which they are composed being kept by the same persons whether in the capital or in the field.

These poor people are at great pains to procure forage:

they rove about from village to village, and what they succeed in purchasing, they endeavor to sell in the army at an advanced price. It is a common practice with them to clear, with a sort of trowel, whole fields of a peculiar kind of grass, which having beaten and washed, they dispose of in the camp at a price sometimes very high and sometimes inadequately low.

WOMEN OF THE PALACE AT PLAY

WOMEN OF THE PALACE AT PLAY

(An Indian painting of the seventeenth century)

To the Indian, as to all Asiatic artists, the most important part of a picture, and the first to be done, was the outline. This was filled in with squirrel-hair brushes, often, for the finest work, of but a single hair. The colors used were clear and extremely brilliant and were applied in layers, jewels and other ornaments being indicated in the best pictures by the insertion of diamond or pearl chips. The work was highly specialized, one man often drawing merely the outline, while another filled in the color, and sometimes a third and fourth finished the face and figures.

The Indo-Persian school of painters, of whose work the picture here shown is a good example, found their subjects almost entirely amid the pomp and magnificence with which the Mogul emperors were surrounded. Gorgeous scenes of the palace life and recreations of luxurious and pleasure-loving courts are mirrored in their work with an infinite elaboration and a richness of color that are unsurpassed in the history of art. They excelled also in portraiture, and have left a host of pictures of the Mogul kings and their courtiers that are marvels of fineness and accuracy.

This picture shows a favorite subject of Indian painters — the effect of fireworks against the blackness of night, a subject that has inspired European artists as well. A fête is in progress, and the women of the palace are amusing themselves with fireworks. The pavilions of the palace grounds are brilliantly lighted, the river beyond is dotted with illuminated boats, and the sky blazes with fire. It is a brilliant scene, drawn with a perfection of minute detail and a love of elaborate ornamentation possible only in the Orient.

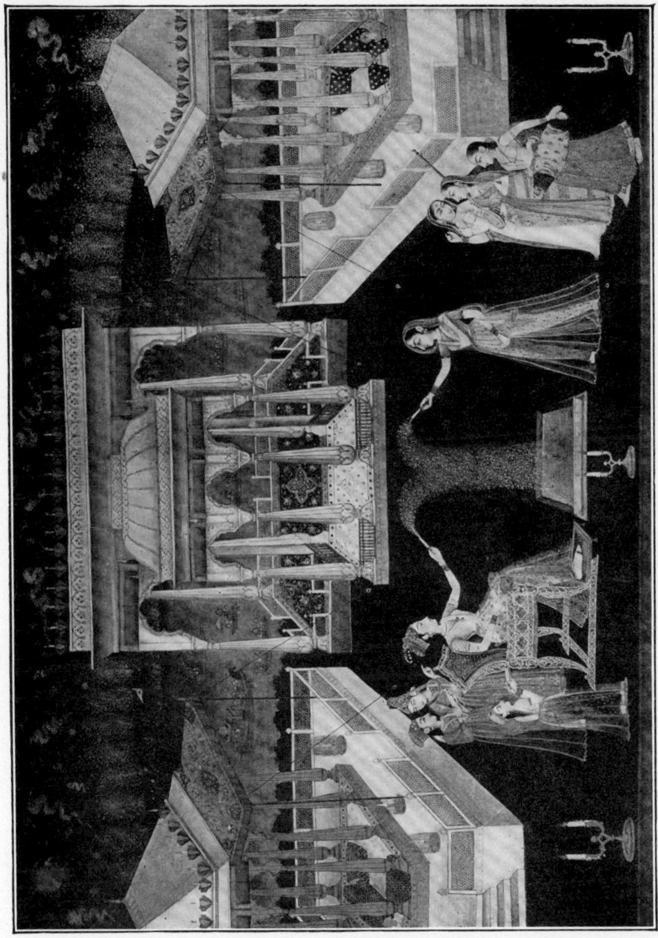

THE DECLINE OF THE MOGUL EMPIRE
[Eighteenth century]

BY THOMAS BABINGTON MACAULAY

THE empire which Baber and his Moguls reared in the sixteenth century was long one of the most extensive and splendid in the world. In no European kingdom was so large a population subject to a single prince, or so large a revenue poured into the treasury. The beauty and magnificence of the buildings erected by the sovereigns of Hindostan amazed even travelers who had seen St. Peter's. The innumerable retinues and gorgeous decorations which surrounded the throne of Delhi dazzled even eyes which were accustomed to the pomp of Versailles. Some of the great viceroys who held their posts by virtue of commissions from the Mogul ruled as many subjects as the King of France or the Emperor of Germany. Even the deputies of these deputies might well rank, as to extent of territory and amount of revenue, with the Grand Duke of Tuscany or the Elector of Saxony.

There can be little doubt that this great empire, powerful and prosperous as it appears on a superficial view, was yet, even in its best days, far worse governed than the worst governed parts of Europe now are. The administration was tainted with all the vices of Oriental despotism and with all the vices inseparable from the domination of race over race. The conflicting pretensions of the princes of the royal house produced a long series of crimes and public disasters. Ambitious lieutenants of the sovereign sometimes aspired to independence. Fierce tribes of Hindoos, impatient of a foreign yoke, frequently withheld tribute, repelled the armies of the Government from the mountain fastnesses, and poured down in arms on the cultivated plains. In spite of occasional convulsions which shook the whole frame of society, this great monarchy, on the whole, retained, during some generations, an outward appearance of unity, majesty, and energy. But throughout the long reign of Aurungzebe, the State, notwithstanding all that the vigor and policy of the prince could effect, was hastening to dissolution. After his death, which took place in the year 1707, the ruin was fearfully rapid. Violent shocks from without coöperated with an incurable decay which was fast proceeding within; and in a few years the empire had undergone utter decomposition. A succession of nominal sovereigns, sunk in indolence and debauchery, sauntered away life in secluded palaces, chewing *bhang*, fondling concubines, and listening to buffoons. A succession of ferocious invaders descended through the western passes, to prey on the defenseless wealth of Hindostan. A Persian conqueror crossed the Indus, marched through the gates of Delhi, and bore away in triumph those treasures of which the magnificence had astounded Roe and Bernier, — the Peacock Throne, on which the richest jewels of Golconda had been disposed by the most skillful hands of Europe, and the inestimable Mountain of Light, which, after many strange vicissitudes, lately shone in the bracelet of Runjeet Sing, and is now destined to adorn the hideous idol of Orissa. The Afghan soon fol-

THE DECLINE OF THE MOGUL EMPIRE

lowed to complete the work of devastation which the Persian had begun. The warlike tribes of Rajpootana threw off the Mussulman yoke. A band of mercenary soldiers occupied Rohilcund. The Seiks ruled on the Indus. The Jauts spread dismay along the Jumna. The highlands which border on the western seacoast of India poured forth a yet more formidable race, a race which was long the terror of every native power, and which, after many desperate and doubtful struggles, yielded only to the fortune and genius of England. It was under the reign of Aurungzebe that this wild clan of plunderers first descended from their mountains; and soon after his death, every corner of his wide empire learned to tremble at the mighty name of the Mahrattas. Many fertile vice royalties were entirely subdued by them. Their dominions stretched across the peninsula from sea to sea. Mahratta captains reigned at Poonah, at Gualior, in Guzerat, in Berar, and in Tanjore. Nor did they, though they had become great sovereigns, therefore cease to be freebooters. They still retained the predatory habits of their forefathers. Every region which was not subject to their rule was wasted by their incursions. Wherever their kettledrums were heard, the peasant threw his bag of rice on his shoulder, hid his small savings in his girdle, and fled with his wife and children to the mountains or the jungles, to the milder neighborhood of the hyena and the tiger. Many provinces redeemed their harvests by the payment of an annual ransom. Even the wretched phantom who still bore the imperial title stooped to pay this ignominious blackmail. The camp fires of one rapacious leader were seen from the walls of the palace of Delhi. Another, at the head of his innumerable cavalry, descended year after year on the ricefields of Bengal. Even the European factors trembled for their magazines. Less than a hundred years ago, it was thought necessary to fortify Calcutta against the horsemen of Berar; and the name of the Mahratta ditch still preserves the memory of the danger.

Wherever the viceroys of the Mogul retained authority they became sovereigns. They might still acknowledge in words the superiority of the house of Tamerlane; as a Count of Flanders or a Duke of Burgundy might have acknowledged the superiority of the most helpless driveler among the later Carlovingians. They might occasionally send to their titular sovereign a complimentary present, or solicit from him a title of honor. In truth, however, they were no longer lieutenants removable at pleasure, but independent hereditary princes. In this way originated those great Mussulman houses which formerly ruled Bengal and the Carnatic, and those which still, though in a state of vassalage, exercise some of the powers of royalty at Lucknow and Hyderabad.

In what was this confusion to end? Was the strife to continue during centuries? Was it to terminate in the rise of another great monarchy? Was the Mussulman or the Mahratta to be the Lord of India? Was another Baber to descend from the mountains, and to lead the hardy tribes of Cabul and Chorasan against a wealthier and less warlike race? None of these events seemed improbable. But scarcely any man, however sagacious, would have thought it possible that a trading company, separated from India by fifteen thousand miles of sea, and possessing in India only a few acres for purposes of commerce, would, in less than a hundred years, spread its empire from Cape Comorin to the eternal snow of the Himalayas; would compel Mahratta and Mahommedan to forget their mutual feuds in common subjection; would tame down even those wild races which had resisted the most powerful of the Moguls; and, having united under its laws a hundred millions of subjects, would carry its victorious arms far to the east of the Burrampooter, and far to the west of the Hydaspes, dictate terms of peace at the gates of Ava, and seat its vassal on the throne of Candahar.

VI
INDIA BECOMES A BRITISH PROVINCE

HISTORICAL NOTE

FROM the time of the invasion of Alexander the Great the world had never lost interest in India. In 1498, Vasco da Gama won the friendship of the Hindu Rajah of Calicut. The Portuguese at once made conquests in India, and in the sixteenth century had a monopoly of the trade and made strenuous efforts to convert the natives to Christianity. A century later, their monopoly of trade was disputed by the Dutch, who were then the strongest maritime power in the world. In 1600, the success of the Dutch in the Indian trade led to the formation of the famous English East India Company, followed by that of the French Company in 1664.

During the greater part of the time from 1746 to 1757 the French and English were at war in India. The result of the struggle was the overthrow of the French and the beginning of the British Empire in the East. In 1758, Robert Clive was made the first governor of Bengal. So far as territory is concerned, Clive and his conquests laid the foundations of the empire. Its administration was organized by Warren Hastings, who was in power from 1772 to 1785. Neither the period of his rule nor the years that immediately followed were times of peace. There were wars with the Marathas, the Afghans, and the Sikhs, with Mysore, Nepal, and Burma; but firmly and steadily the dominion of the English was increasing. One province after another came under the control of the East India Company, whose activities after the eighteenth century were almost wholly political. There was no haphazard progress, but a definite plan for making Great Britain the one power in the land. The native princes were made to understand that if they wished to remain princes, they must hold their domains not independently, but subject to the English. In 1857, the Sepoy Mutiny broke out. This made it clear that the Company was no longer able to administer the government of the land to the best advantage of either India or Britain. Its charter was taken away, and in 1858 India became a province of the Crown. In 1877, Queen Victoria assumed the title of Empress of India. This was proclaimed to the Indian princes at a durbar whose splendor surpassed the tales of Oriental magnificence.

HOW ROBERT CLIVE DEFENDED ARCOT

[1751]

BY THOMAS BABINGTON MACAULAY

[IN 1743, war broke out in Europe between France and England. The French now attacked Madras, which promptly surrendered. Among those who fled from the city was a young clerk of the East India Company named Robert Clive. This flight practically ended his clerkship, for he obtained an ensign's commission. His defense of Arcot was the most famous event of this war.

The Editor.]

CLIVE was now twenty-five years of age. After hesitating for some time between a military and a commercial life, he had at length been placed in a post which partook of both characters, that of commissary to the troops, with the rank of captain. The present emergency called forth all his powers. He represented to his superiors that, unless some vigorous effort were made, Trichinopoly would fall, the house of Anaverdy Khan would perish, and the French would become the real masters of the whole peninsula of India. It was absolutely necessary to strike some daring blow. If an attack were made on Arcot, the capital of the Carnatic, and the favorite residence of the Nabobs, it was not impossible that the siege of Trichinopoly would be raised. The heads of the English settlement, now thoroughly alarmed by the success of Dupleix, and apprehensive that, in the event of a new war between France and Great Britain, Madras would be instantly taken and destroyed, approved of Clive's plan, and intrusted the execution of it to himself. The young captain was put at the head of two hundred English soldiers, and three hundred sepoys, armed and disciplined after the European fashion. Of the eight officers who commanded this little force under him, only two had ever been in action, and four of the eight were factors of the Company, whom Clive's example had induced to offer their services. The weather was stormy; but Clive pushed on, through thunder, lightning, and rain, to the gates of Arcot. The garrison, in a panic, evacuated the fort, and the English entered it without a blow.

But Clive well knew that he should not be suffered to retain undisturbed possession of his conquest. He instantly began to collect provisions, to throw up works, and to make preparations for sustaining a siege. The garrison, which had fled at his approach, had now recovered from its dismay, and, having been swollen by large reinforcements from the neighborhood to a force of three thousand men, encamped close to the town. At dead of night, Clive marched out of the fort, attacked the camp by surprise, slew great numbers, dispersed the rest, and returned to his quarters without having lost a single man.

The intelligence of these events was soon carried to Chunda Sahib, who, with his French allies, was besieging Trichinopoly. He immediately detached four thousand men from his camp, and sent them to Arcot. They were speedily joined by the remains of the force which Clive had lately scattered. They were further strengthened by two thousand men from Vellore, and by a still more important reinforcement of a hundred and fifty French soldiers whom Dupleix dispatched from Pondi-

HOW ROBERT CLIVE DEFENDED ARCOT

cherry. The whole of this army, amounting to about ten thousand men, was under the command of Rajah Sahib, son of Chunda Sahib.

Rajah Sahib proceeded to invest the fort of Arcot, which seemed quite incapable of sustaining a siege. The walls were ruinous, the ditches dry, the ramparts too narrow to admit the guns, the battlements too low to protect the soldiers. The little garrison had been greatly reduced by casualties. It now consisted of a hundred and twenty Europeans and two hundred sepoys. Only four officers were left; the stock of provisions was scanty; and the commander, who had to conduct the defense under circumstances so discouraging, was a young man of five and twenty, who had been bred a bookkeeper.

During fifty days the siege went on. During fifty days the young captain maintained the defense, with a firmness, vigilance, and ability which would have done honor to the oldest marshal in Europe. The breach, however, increased day by day. The garrison began to feel the pressure of hunger. Under such circumstances, any troops so scantily provided with officers might have been expected to show signs of insubordination; and the danger was peculiarly great in a force composed of men differing widely from each other in extraction, color, language, manners, and religion. But the devotion of the little band to its chief surpassed anything that is related of the Tenth Legion of Cæsar or of the Old Guard of Napoleon. The sepoys came to Clive, not to complain of their scanty fare, but to propose that all the grain should be given to the Europeans, who required more nourishment than the natives of Asia. The thin gruel, they said, which was strained away from the rice, would suffice for themselves. History contains no more touching instance of military fidelity, or of the influence of a commanding mind.

An attempt made by the Government of Madras to relieve the place had failed. But there was hope from another quarter. A body of six thousand Mahrattas, half soldiers, half robbers, under the command of a chief named Morari Row, had been hired to assist Mahommed Ali; but thinking the French power irresistible, and the triumph of Chunda Sahib certain, they had hitherto remained inactive on the frontiers of the Carnatic. The fame of the defense of Arcot roused them from their torpor. Morari Row declared that he had never before believed that Englishmen could fight, but that he would willingly help them since he saw that they had spirit to help themselves. Rajah Sahib learned that the Mahrattas were in motion. It was necessary for him to be expeditious. He first tried negotiation. He offered large bribes to Clive, which were rejected with scorn. He vowed that, if his proposals were not accepted, he would instantly storm the fort, and put every man in it to the sword. Clive told him in reply, with characteristic haughtiness, that his father was an usurper, that his army was a rabble, and that he would do well to think twice before he sent such poltroons into a breach defended by English soldiers.

Rajah Sahib determined to storm the fort. The day was well suited to a bold military enterprise. It was the great Mahommedan festival which is sacred to the memory of Hosein the son of Ali. The history of Islam contains nothing more touching than the event which gave rise to that solemnity. The mournful legend relates how

HOW ROBERT CLIVE DEFENDED ARCOT

the chief of the Fatimites, when all his brave followers had perished round him, drank his latest draught of water, and uttered his latest prayer, how the assassins carried his head in triumph, how the tyrant smote the lifeless lips with his staff, and how a few old men recollected with tears that they had seen those lips pressed to the lips of the Prophet of God. After the lapse of near twelve centuries, the recurrence of this solemn season excites the fiercest and saddest emotions in the bosoms of the devout Moslem of India. They work themselves up to such agonies of rage and lamentation that some, it is said, have given up the ghost from the mere effect of mental excitement. They believe that whoever, during this festival, falls in arms against the infidels, atones by his death for all the sins of his life, and passes at once to the Garden of the Houris. It was at this time that Rajah Sahib determined to assault Arcot. Stimulating drugs were employed to aid the effect of religious zeal, and the besiegers, drunk with enthusiasm, drunk with *bhang*, rushed furiously to the attack.

Clive had received secret intelligence of the design, had made his arrangements, and, exhausted by fatigue, had thrown himself on his bed. He was awakened by the alarm, and was instantly at his post. The enemy advanced driving before them elephants whose foreheads were armed with iron plates. It was expected that the gates would yield to the shock of these living battering-rams. But the huge beasts no sooner felt the English musket balls than they turned round, and rushed furiously away, trampling on the multitude which had urged them forward. A raft was launched on the water which filled one part of the ditch. Clive, perceiving that his gunners at that post did not understand their business, took the management of a piece of artillery himself, and cleared the raft in a few minutes. Where the moat was dry, the assailants mounted with great boldness; but they were received with a fire so heavy and so well directed, that it soon quelled the courage even of fanaticism and of intoxication. The rear ranks of the English kept the front ranks supplied with a constant succession of loaded muskets, and every shot told on the living mass below. After three desperate onsets, the besiegers retired behind the ditch.

The struggle lasted about an hour. Four hundred of the assailants fell. The garrison lost only five or six men. The besieged passed an anxious night, looking for a renewal of the attack. But when day broke, the enemy were no more to be seen. They had retired, leaving to the English several guns and a large quantity of ammunition.

THE BLACK HOLE OF CALCUTTA
[1756]

BY THOMAS BABINGTON MACAULAY

The great province of Bengal, together with Orissa and Bahar, had long been governed by a viceroy, whom the English called Aliverdy Khan, and who, like the other viceroys of the Mogul, had become virtually independent. He died in 1756, and the sovereignty descended to his grandson, a youth under twenty years of age, who bore the name of Surajah Dowlah. Oriental despots are perhaps the worst class of human beings; and this unhappy boy was one of the worst specimens of his class. His understanding was naturally feeble, and his temper naturally unamiable. His education had been such as would have enervated even a vigorous intellect and perverted even a generous disposition. He was unreasonable, because nobody ever dared to reason with him, and selfish, because he had never been made to feel himself dependent on the good will of others. Early debauchery had unnerved his body and his mind. He indulged immoderately in the use of ardent spirits, which inflamed his weak brain almost to madness. His chosen companions were flatterers, sprung from the dregs of the people, and recommended by nothing but buffoonery and servility. It is said that he had arrived at that last stage of human depravity, when cruelty becomes pleasing for its own sake, when the sight of pain, as pain, where no advantage is to be gained, no offense punished, no danger averted, is an agreeable excitement. It had early been his amusement to torture beasts and birds; and, when he grew up, he enjoyed with still keener relish the misery of his fellow-creatures.

From a child Surajah Dowlah had hated the English. It was his whim to do so; and his whims were never opposed. He had also formed a very exaggerated notion of the wealth which might be obtained by plundering them; and his feeble and uncultivated mind was incapable of perceiving that the riches of Calcutta, had they been even greater than he imagined, would not compensate him for what he must lose, if the European trade, of which Bengal was a chief seat, should be driven by his violence to some other quarter. Pretexts for a quarrel were readily found. The English, in expectation of a war with France, had begun to fortify their settlement without special permission from the Nabob. A rich native, whom he longed to plunder, had taken refuge at Calcutta, and had not been delivered up. On such grounds as these Surajah Dowlah marched with a great army against Fort William.

The servants of the Company at Madras had been forced by Dupleix to become statesmen and soldiers. Those in Bengal were still mere traders, and were terrified and bewildered by the approaching danger. The governor, who had heard much of Surajah Dowlah's cruelty, was frightened out of his wits, jumped into a boat, and took refuge in the nearest ship. The military commandant thought that he could not do better than follow so good an example. The fort was taken after a feeble resistance; and great numbers of the English fell into the hands of the conquerors. The Nabob seated himself

THE BLACK HOLE OF CALCUTTA

with regal pomp in the principal hall of the factory, and ordered Mr. Holwell, the first in rank among the prisoners, to be brought before him. His Highness talked about the insolence of the English, and grumbled at the smallness of the treasure which he had found; but promised to spare their lives, and retired to rest.

Then was committed that great crime, memorable for its singular atrocity, memorable for the tremendous retribution by which it was followed. The English captives were left at the mercy of the guards, and the guards determined to secure them for the night in the prison of the garrison, a chamber known by the fearful name of the Black Hole. Even for a single European malefactor, that dungeon would, in such a climate, have been too close and narrow. The space was only twenty feet square. The air holes were small and obstructed. It was the summer solstice, the season when the fierce heat of Bengal can scarcely be rendered tolerable to natives of England by lofty halls and by the constant waving of fans. The number of the prisoners was one hundred and forty-six. When they were ordered to enter the cell, they imagined that the soldiers were joking; and, being in high spirits on account of the promise of the Nabob to spare their lives, they laughed and jested at the absurdity of the notion. They soon discovered their mistake. They expostulated; they entreated; but in vain. The guards threatened to cut down all who hesitated. The captives were driven into the cell at the point of the sword, and the door was instantly shut and locked upon them.

Nothing in history or fiction, not even the story which Ugolino told in the sea of everlasting ice, after he had wiped his bloody lips on the scalp of his murderer, approaches the horrors which were recounted by the few survivors of that night. They cried for mercy. They strove to burst the door. Holwell, who, even in that extremity, retained some presence of mind, offered large bribes to the jailers. But the answer was that nothing could be done without the Nabob's orders, that the Nabob was asleep, and that he would be angry if anybody woke him. Then the prisoners went mad with despair. They trampled each other down, fought for the places at the windows, fought for the pittance of water with which the cruel mercy of the murderers mocked their agonies, raved, prayed, blasphemed, implored the guards to fire among them. The jailers in the mean time held lights to the bars, and shouted with laughter at the frantic struggles of their victims. At length the tumult died away in low gaspings and moanings. The day broke. The Nabob had slept off his debauch, and permitted the door to be opened. But it was some time before the soldiers could make a lane for the survivors, by piling up on each side the heaps of corpses on which the burning climate had already begun to do its loathsome work. When at length a passage was made, twenty-three ghastly figures, such as their own mothers would not have known, staggered one by one out of the charnel house. A pit was instantly dug. The dead bodies, a hundred and twenty-three in number, were flung into it promiscuously, and covered up.

But these things which, after the lapse of more than eighty years, cannot be told or read without horror, awakened neither remorse nor pity in the bosom of the savage Nabob. He inflicted no punishment on the murderers. He showed no tenderness to the survivors.

THE BLACK HOLE OF CALCUTTA

Some of them, indeed, from whom nothing was to be got, were suffered to depart; but those from whom it was thought that anything could be extorted were treated with execrable cruelty. Holwell, unable to walk, was carried before the tyrant, who reproached him, threatened him, and sent him up the country in irons, together with some other gentlemen who were suspected of knowing more than they chose to tell about the treasures of the Company. These persons, still bowed down by the sufferings of that great agony, were lodged in miserable sheds, and fed only with grain and water, till at length the intercessions of the female relations of the Nabob procured their release. One Englishwoman had survived that night. She was placed in the harem of the Prince at Moorshedabad.

THE IMPEACHMENT OF WARREN HASTINGS
[1785]

BY THOMAS BABINGTON MACAULAY

[WARREN HASTINGS became governor of India in 1772. Upon his return to England in 1785, he was impeached for oppressing the natives, and was tried by the House of Lords. The following extract pictures the beginning of his trial. It dragged along for seven years. He was finally pronounced innocent.

The Editor.]

THE place was worthy of such a trial. It was the great hall of William Rufus, the hall which had resounded with acclamations at the inauguration of thirty kings, the hall which had witnessed the just sentence of Bacon and the just absolution of Somers, the hall where the eloquence of Strafford had for a moment awed and melted a victorious party inflamed with just resentment, the hall where Charles had confronted the High Court of Justice with the placid courage which has half redeemed his fame. Neither military nor civil pomp was wanting. The avenues were lined with grenadiers. The streets were kept clear by cavalry. The peers, robed in gold and ermine, were marshaled by the heralds under Garter King-at-arms. The judges in their vestments of state attended to give advice on points of law. Near a hundred and seventy lords, three fourths of the Upper House as the Upper House then was, walked in solemn order from their usual place of assembling to the tribunal.

THE IMPEACHMENT OF WARREN HASTINGS

The junior baron present led the way, George Eliott, Lord Heathfield, recently ennobled for his memorable defense of Gibraltar against the fleets and armies of France and Spain. The long procession was closed by the Duke of Norfolk, Earl Marshal of the realm, by the great dignitaries, and by the brothers and sons of the King. Last of all came the Prince of Wales, conspicuous by his fine person and noble bearing. The gray old walls were hung with scarlet. The long galleries were crowded by an audience such as has rarely excited the fears or the emulation of an orator. There were gathered together, from all parts of a great, free, enlightened, and prosperous empire, grace and female loveliness, wit and learning, the representatives of every science and of every art. There were seated round the Queen the fair-haired young daughters of the House of Brunswick. There the Ambassadors of great Kings and Commonwealths gazed with admiration on a spectacle which no other country in the world could present. There Siddons, in the prime of her majestic beauty, looked with emotion on a scene surpassing all the imitations of the stage. There the historian of the Roman Empire thought of the days when Cicero pleaded the cause of Sicily against Verres, and when, before a senate which still retained some show of freedom, Tacitus thundered against the oppressor of Africa. There were seen, side by side, the greatest painter and the greatest scholar of the age. The spectacle had allured Reynolds from that easel which has preserved to us the thoughtful foreheads of so many writers and statesmen, and the sweet smiles of so many noble matrons. It had induced Parr to suspend his labors in that dark and profound mine from which he had extracted a vast treasure of erudition, a treasure too often buried in the earth, too often paraded with injudicious and inelegant ostentation, but still precious, massive, and splendid. There appeared the voluptuous charms of her to whom the heir of the throne had in secret plighted his faith. There too was she, the beautiful mother of a beautiful race, the St. Cecilia whose delicate features, lighted up by love and music, art has rescued from the common decay. There were the members of that brilliant society which quoted, criticized, and exchanged repartees, under the rich peacock hangings of Mrs. Montague. And there the ladies whose lips, more persuasive than those of Fox himself, had carried the Westminster election against palace and treasury, shone round Georgiana, Duchess of Devonshire.

The Sergeants made proclamation. Hastings advanced to the bar, and bent his knee. The culprit was indeed not unworthy of that great presence. He had ruled an extensive and populous country, had made laws and treaties, had sent forth armies, had set up and pulled down princes. And in his high place he had so borne himself that all had feared him, that most had loved him, and that hatred itself could deny him no title to glory, except virtue. He looked like a great man, and not like a bad man. A person small and emaciated, yet deriving dignity from a carriage which, while it indicated deference to the Court, indicated also habitual self-possession and self-respect, a high and intellectual forehead, a brow pensive but not gloomy, a mouth of inflexible decision, a face pale and worn, but serene, on which was written, as legibly as under the picture in the council chamber at Calcutta, *Mens æqua in arduis;* such was the aspect with which the great proconsul presented himself to his judges.

His counsel accompanied him, men all of whom were afterwards raised by their talents and learning to the highest posts in their profession, the bold and strong-minded Law, afterwards Chief Justice of the King's Bench; the more humane and eloquent Dallas, afterwards Chief Justice of the Common Pleas; and Plomer, who, near twenty years later, successfully conducted in the same high court the defense of Lord Melville, and subsequently became Vice-Chancellor and Master of the Rolls.

But neither the culprit nor his advocates attracted so much notice as the accusers. In the midst of the blaze of red drapery, a space had been fitted up with green benches and tables for the Commons. The managers, with Burke at their head, appeared in full dress. The collectors of gossip did not fail to remark that even Fox, generally so regardless of his appearance, had paid to the illustrious tribunal the compliment of wearing a bag and sword. Pitt had refused to be one of the conductors of the impeachment; and his commanding, copious, and sonorous eloquence was wanting to that great muster of various talents. Age and blindness had unfitted Lord North for the duties of a public prosecutor; and his friends were left without the help of his excellent sense, his tact, and his urbanity. But, in spite of the absence of these two distinguished members of the Lower House, the box in which the managers stood contained an array of speakers such as perhaps had not appeared together since the great age of Athenian eloquence. There were Fox and Sheridan, the English Demosthenes and the

INDIA

English Hyperides. There was Burke, ignorant, indeed, or negligent of the art of adapting his reasonings and his style to the capacity and taste of his hearers, but in amplitude of comprehension and richness of imagination superior to every orator, ancient or modern. There, with eyes reverentially fixed on Burke, appeared the finest gentleman of the age, his form developed by every manly exercise, his face beaming with intelligence and spirit, the ingenious, the chivalrous, the high-souled Windham. Nor, though surrounded by such men, did the youngest manager pass unnoticed. At an age when most of those who distinguish themselves in life are still contending for prizes and fellowships at college, he had won for himself a conspicuous place in Parliament. No advantage of fortune or connection was wanting that could set off to the height his splendid talents and his unblemished honor. At twenty-three he had been thought worthy to be ranked with the veteran statesmen who appeared as the delegates of the British Commons, at the bar of the British nobility. All who stood at that bar, save him alone, are gone, culprit, advocates, accusers. To the generation which is now in the vigor of life, he is the sole representative of a great age which has passed away. But those who, within the last ten years, have listened with delight, till the morning sun shone on the tapestries of the House of Lords, to the lofty and animated eloquence of Charles Earl Grey are able to form some estimate of the powers of a race of men among whom he was not the foremost.

The charges and the answers of Hastings were first read. The ceremony occupied two whole days, and was rendered less tedious than it would otherwise have been

THE IMPEACHMENT OF WARREN HASTINGS

by the silver voice and just emphasis of Cowper, the clerk of the court, a near relation of the amiable poet. On the third day Burke rose. Four sittings were occupied by his opening speech, which was intended to be a general introduction to all the charges. With an exuberance of thought and a splendor of diction which more than satisfied the highly raised expectation of the audience, he described the character and institutions of the natives of India, recounted the circumstances in which the Asiatic empire of Britain had originated, and set forth the constitution of the Company and of the English Presidencies. Having thus attempted to communicate to his hearers an idea of Eastern society, as vivid as that which existed in his own mind, he proceeded to arraign the administration of Hastings as systematically conducted in defiance of morality and public law. The energy and pathos of the great orator extorted expressions of unwonted admiration from the stern and hostile Chancellor, and, for a moment, seemed to pierce even the resolute heart of the defendant. The ladies in the galleries, unaccustomed to such displays of eloquence, excited by the solemnity of the occasion, and perhaps not unwilling to display their taste and sensibility, were in a state of uncontrollable emotion. Handkerchiefs were pulled out; smelling-bottles were handed round; hysterical sobs and screams were heard; and Mrs. Sheridan was carried out in a fit. At length the orator concluded. Raising his voice till the old arches of Irish oak resounded, "Therefore," said he, "hath it with all confidence been ordered by the Commons of Great Britain, that I impeach Warren Hastings of high crimes and misdemeanors. I impeach him in the name of the Commons' House of Parliament, whose trust he has betrayed. I impeach him in the name of the English nation, whose ancient honor he has sullied. I impeach him in the name of the people of India, whose rights he has trodden under foot, and whose country he has turned into a desert. Lastly, in the name of human nature itself, in the name of both sexes, in the name of every age, in the name of every rank, I impeach the common enemy and oppressor of all."

INDIAN CUSTOMS AND MANNERS IN 1840

BY HON. MOUNTSTUART ELPHINSTONE

The food of the common people, both in the country and in towns, is unleavened bread with boiled vegetables, clarified butter or oil, and spices. Smoking tobacco is almost the only luxury. Some few smoke intoxicating drugs; and the lowest castes only, and even they rarely, get drunk with spirits. Drunkenness is confined to damp countries, such as Bengal, the Concans, and some parts of the south of India. It increases in our territories where spirits are taxed; but is so little of a natural propensity that the absolute prohibition of spirits, which exists in most native states, is sufficient to keep it down. Opium, which is used to great excess in the west of Hindostan, is peculiar to the Rajputs and does not affect the lower classes. All but the poorest people chew betel (a pungent aromatic leaf), with the hard nut of the areca, mixed with a sort of lime made from shells, and with various spices, according to the person's means. Some kinds of fruit are cheap and common.

The upper classes, at least the Bramin part of them, have very little more variety; it consists in the greater number of kinds of vegetables and spices, and in the cookery. Assafœtida is a favorite ingredient, as giving to some of their richer dishes something of the flavor of flesh. The caution used against eating out of dishes or on carpets defiled by other castes gives rise to some curious customs. At a great Bramin dinner, where twenty or thirty different dishes and condiments are placed before each individual, all are served in vessels made of leaves sewed together. These are placed on the bare floor, which, as a substitute for a tablecloth, is decorated for a certain distance in front of the guests with patterns of flowers, etc., very prettily laid out in lively-colored sorts of sand, spread through frames in which the patterns are cut, and swept away after dinner. The inferior castes of Hindus eat meat, and care less for their vessels; metal, especially, can always be purified by scouring. In all classes, however, the difference of caste leads to a want of sociability. A soldier, or any one away from his family, cooks his solitary meal for himself, and finishes it without a companion, or any of the pleasures of the table, but those derived from taking the necessary supply of food. All eat with their fingers, and scrupulously wash before and after meals.

Though they have chess, a game played with tables and dice as backgammon is, and cards (which are circular, in many suits, and painted with Hindu gods, etc., instead of kings, queens, and knaves), yet the great indoor amusement is to listen to singing interspersed with slow movements which can scarcely be called dancing. The attitudes are not ungraceful, and the songs are pleasing; but it is, after all, a languid and monotonous entertainment; and it is astonishing to see the delight that all ranks take in it; the lower orders, in particular, often standing for whole nights to enjoy this unvaried amusement.

These exhibitions are now often illuminated, when in rooms, by English chandeliers; but the true Hindu way of lighting them up is by torches held by men, who feed the flame with oil from a sort of bottle constructed for the purpose. For ordinary household purposes they use lamps of earthenware or metal.

In the houses of the rich, the doorways are hung with quilted silk curtains; and the doors, the arches, and other woodwork in the rooms are highly carved. The floor is entirely covered with a thin mattress of cotton, over which is spread a clean white cloth to sit on; but there is no other furniture of any description. Equals sit in opposite rows down the room. A prince or great chief has a seat at the head of the room between the rows, very slightly raised by an additional mattress, and covered with a small carpet of embroidered silk. This, with a high round embroidered bolster behind, forms what is called a *masnad* or *gadi*, and serves as a throne for sovereigns under the rank of king.

Great attention is paid to ceremony. A person of distinction is met a mile or two before he enters the city; and a visitor is received (according to his rank) at the outer gate of the house, at the door of the room, or by merely rising from the seat. Friends embrace if they have not met for some time. Bramins are saluted by joining the palms, and raising them twice or thrice to the forehead: with others, the salute with one hand is used, so well known by the Mahometan name of *salaam*. Bramins have a peculiar phrase of salutation for each other. Other Hindus on meeting repeat twice the name of the god Rama. Visitors are seated with strict attention to their rank, which on public occasions it often takes much previous negotiation to settle. Hindus of rank are remarkable for their politeness to inferiors, generally addressing them by some civil or familiar term, and scarcely ever being provoked to abusive or harsh language. The lower classes are courteous in their general manners among themselves, but by no means so scrupulous in their language when irritated. All visits end by the master of the house presenting betel leaf with areca nut, etc., to the guest: it is accompanied by attar of roses or some other perfume put on the handkerchief, and rosewater sprinkled over the person; and this is the signal for taking leave. At first meetings and at entertainments, trays of shawls and other materials for dresses are presented to the guests, together with pearl necklaces, bracelets, and ornaments for the turban of jewels: a sword, a horse, and an elephant are added when both parties are men of high rank. Such presents are also given to meritorious servants, to soldiers who have distinguished themselves, and to poets or learned men: they are showered on favorite singers and dancers.

At formal meetings nobody speaks but the principal persons, but in other companies there is a great deal of unrestrained conversation. The manner of the Hindus is polite, and their language obsequious. They abound in compliments and expressions of humility, even to their equals, and when they have no object to gain. They seldom show much desire of knowledge or disposition to extend their thoughts beyond their ordinary habits. Within that sphere, however, their conversation is shrewd and intelligent, often mixed with lively and satirical observations.

The rich rise at the same hour as the common people, or perhaps not quite so early; perform their devotions in their own chapels; dispatch private and other business with their immediate officers and dependents; bathe, dine, and sleep. At two or three they dress, and appear in their public apartments, where they receive visits and transact business till very late at night. Some also listen to music till late: but these occupations are confined to the rich, and in general a Hindu town is quiet soon after dark.

Entertainments, besides occasions of rare occurrence, as marriages, etc., are given on particular festivals, and sometimes to show attention to particular friends. Among themselves they commence with a dinner; but the essential part of the entertainment is dancing and singing, sometimes diversified with jugglers and buffoons; during which time perfumes are burned, and the guests are dressed with garlands of sweet-smelling flowers; presents, as above described, are no less essential.

Among the most striking of the religious exhibitions is that of the capture of Lanka, in honor of Rama, which is necessarily performed out of doors. Lanka is represented by a spacious castle with towers and battlements, which are assailed by an army dressed like Rama and his followers, with Hanuman and his monkey allies. The combat ends in the destruction of Lanka, amidst a blaze of fireworks which would excite admiration in any part of the world, and in a triumphal procession sometimes conducted in a style of grandeur which might become a more important occasion.

This festival is celebrated in another manner, and with still greater splendor, among the Mahrattas. It is the day on which they always commence their military operations; and the particular event which they commemorate is Rama's devotions and his plucking a branch from a certain tree before he set out on his expedition. A tree of this sort is planted in an open plain near the camp or city; and all the infantry and guns, and as many of the cavalry as do not accompany the prince, are drawn up on each side of the spot, or form a wide street leading up to it. The rest of the plain is filled with innumerable spectators. The procession, though less regular than those of Mahometan princes, is one of the finest displays of the sort in India. The chief advances on his elephant, preceded by flags and gold and silver sticks or maces, and by a phalanx of men on foot bearing pikes of fifteen or sixteen feet long. On each side are his nobles and military leaders on horseback, with sumptuous dresses and caparisons, and each with some attendants selected for their martial appearance; behind are long trains of elephants with their sweeping housings, some with flags of immense size, and glittering with gold and embroidery; some bearing *howdahs*, open or roofed, often of silver, plain or gilt, and of forms peculiarly Oriental: around and behind is a cloud of horsemen, their trappings glancing in the sun, and their scarfs of cloth of gold fluttering in the wind, all overtopped by sloping spears and waving banners; those on the flanks dashing out, and returning after displaying some evolutions of horsemanship: the whole moving, mixing, and continually shifting its form as it advances, and presenting one of the most animated and gorgeous spectacles that is ever seen, even in that land of barbarous magnificence. As the chief approaches, the guns are fired, the infantry discharge their pieces, and the procession moves on with accelerated speed, exhibiting a lively picture of an attack by a great body of cavalry on an army drawn up to receive them.

When the prince has performed his devotions and plucked his bough, his example is followed by those around him: a fresh salvo of all the guns is fired, and at the signal, the other troops break off, and each man snatches some leaves from one of the fields of tall grain which is grown for the purpose near the spot: each sticks his prize in his turban, and all exchange compliments and congratulations. A grand durbar, at which all the court and military officers attend, closes the day.

There is less grandeur, but scarcely less interest, in the fairs and festivals of the common people. These have a strong resemblance to fairs in England, and exhibit the same whirling machines and the same amusements and occupations. But no assemblage in England can give a notion of the lively effect produced by the prodigious concourse of people in white dresses and bright-colored scarfs and turbans, so unlike the black head-dresses and dusky habits of the North. Their taste for gaudy shows and processions and the mixture of arms and flags give also a different character to the Indian fairs. The Hindus enter into the amusements of these meetings with the utmost relish, and show every sign of peaceful festivity and enjoyment. They may, on all these occasions, have some religious ceremony to go through, but it does not take up a moment, and seldom occupies a thought. At the pilgrimages, indeed, the long anticipation of the worship to be performed, the example of other pilgrims invoking the god aloud, and the sanctity of the place, concur to produce stronger feelings of devotion. There are also more ceremonies to be gone through, and sometimes these are joined in by the whole assembly; when the thousands of eyes directed to one point, and of voices shouting one name, is often impressive even to the least interested spectator. But even at pilgrimages, the feeling of amusement is much stronger than that of religious zeal; and many such places are also among the most celebrated marts for the transfer of merchandise and for all the purposes of a fair.

The regular dress of all Hindus is probably that which has been mentioned as used in Bengal, and which is worn by all strict Bramins. It consists of two long pieces of white cotton cloth, one of which is wrapped round the middle and tucked up between the legs, while part hangs down a good deal below the knees; the other is worn over the shoulders, and occasionally stretched over the head, which has no other covering. The head and beard are shaved, but a long tuft of hair is left on the crown. Mustachios are also worn, except perhaps by strict Bramins. Except in Bengal, all Hindus who do not affect strictness now wear the lower piece of cloth smaller and tighter, and over it a white cotton or chintz or silk tunic, a colored muslin sash round the middle, and a scarf of the same material over the shoulders, with a turban; some wear loose drawers like the Mahometans.

The full dress is a long white gown of almost transparent muslin, close over the body, but in innumerable loose folds below the waist. This, with the sash and turban, bracelets, necklaces, and other jewels and ornaments, make the dress complete. As this dress is partly borrowed from the Mahometans, and cannot be very ancient, it is singular that it should be accurately represented in some of the figures of kings on the tombs at Thebes in Egypt, where the features, attitudes, and everything else are, by a remarkable coincidence (for it can be nothing more) exactly what is seen in a Hindu rajah of the present day.

The dress of the women is nearly the same as that first described for the men; but both the pieces of cloth are much larger and longer, and they are of various bright colors as well as white. Both sexes wear many ornaments. Men even of the lower orders wear earrings, bracelets, and necklaces. They are sometimes worn as a convenient way of keeping all the money the owner has; but the necklaces are sometimes made of a particular berry that hardens into a rough but handsome dark brown bead, and sometimes of particular kinds of wood turned; and these are mixed alternately with beads of gold or coral. The neck and legs are bare; but on going out, embroidered slippers with a long point curling up are put on, and are laid aside again on entering a room or a palanquin. Children are loaded with gold ornaments, which gives frequent temptation to child-murder.

It is well known that Indian widows sometimes sacrifice themselves on the funeral pile of their husbands, and that such victims are called *sattis* (suttees). The practice is ascribed by our missionaries to the degraded condition to which a woman who outlives her husband is condemned. If the motive were one of so general an influence, the practice would scarcely be so rare. It is more probable that the hopes of immediately entering on the enjoyment of heaven and of entitling the husband to the same felicity, as well as the glory attending such a voluntary sacrifice, are sufficient to excite the few enthusiastic spirits who go through this awful trial.

The mode of cremation is various: in Bengal, the

living and dead bodies are stretched on a pile where strong ropes and bamboos are thrown across them so as to prevent any attempt to rise. In Orissa, the woman throws herself into the pyre, which is below the level of the ground. In the Deckan, the woman sits down on the pyre, with her husband's head in her lap, and remains there till suffocated, or crushed by the fall of a heavy roof of logs of wood, which is fixed by cords to posts at the corners of the pile.

The sight of a widow burning is a most painful one; but it is hard to say whether the spectator is most affected by pity or admiration. The more than human serenity of the victim, and the respect which she receives from those around her, are heightened by her gentle demeanor and her care to omit nothing in distributing her last presents, and paying the usual marks of courtesy to the bystanders; while the cruel death that awaits her is doubly felt from her own apparent insensibility to its terrors. The reflections which succeed are of a different character, and one is humiliated to think that so feeble a being can be elevated by superstition to a self-devotion not surpassed by the noblest examples of patriots or martyrs.

I have heard that in Guzerat women about to burn are often stupefied with opium. In most other parts this is certainly not the case. Women go through all the ceremonies with astonishing composure and presence of mind, and have been seen seated, unconfined, among the flames, apparently praying, and raising their joined hands to their heads with as little agitation as at their ordinary devotions.

On the other hand, frightful instances have occurred

INDIAN CUSTOMS AND MANNERS IN 1840

of women bursting from amidst the flames, and being thrust back by the assistants. One of these diabolical attempts was made in Bengal, when an English gentleman happened to be among the spectators, and succeeded in preventing the accomplishment of the tragedy; but next day he was surprised to encounter the bitterest reproaches from the woman for having been the occasion of her disgrace and the obstacle to her being then in heaven enjoying the company of her husband and the blessings of those she had left behind.

The practice is by no means universal in India. It never occurs to the south of the river Kishna; and under the Bombay presidency, including the former sovereignty of the Bramin Peshwas, it amounts to thirty-two in a year. In the rest of the Deckan it is probably more rare. In Hindostan and Bengal it is so common that some hundreds are officially reported as burned annually within the British dominions alone.

[The Emperor Akban tried to put an end to the burning of widows, but did not succeed. As the Hindus insisted that the rite was a part of their religion, the English did not for many years venture to oppose it by the making of any law. At length, Lord William Bentinck, Governor-General, proposed in 1829 a regulation in Council declaring all who abetted the *satti* (suttee) to be guilty of "culpable homicide." There was opposition on the part of Europeans as well as natives, but the regulation was carried.

The Editor.]

THE RELIEF OF LUCKNOW

BY ROBERT TRAILL SPENCE LOWELL

Oh, that last day in Lucknow fort!
    We knew that it was the last;
That the enemy's lines crept surely on,
    And the end was coming fast.

To yield to that foe meant worse than death;
    And the men and we all worked on;
It was one day more of smoke and roar,
    And then it would all be done.

There was one of us, a corporal's wife,
    A fair, young, gentle thing,
Wasted with fever in the siege,
    And her mind was wandering.

She lay on the ground, in her Scottish plaid,
    And I took her head on my knee;
"When my father comes hame frae the pleugh,"
    she said,
    "Oh, then please waken me."

She slept like a child on her father's floor,
    In the flecking of woodbine shade,
When the house-dog sprawls by the open door,
    And the mother's wheel is stayed.

JESSIE'S DREAM

JESSIE'S DREAM

BY FREDERICK GOODALL
(*English Artist*, 1822–1904)

THE natives of India were restless and unhappy under British rule, and in 1857 this discontent burst out into the Sepoy Rebellion. The sepoys, or native soldiers serving under British officers, were supplied with cartridges greased with the fat of the pig. To touch this was to lose caste. The blunder was remedied at once, but it was too late. The outburst began at Meerut; but its worst manifestations were at Cawnpur, Lucknow, and Delhi. At Cawnpur, the Europeans were besieged for nineteen days. On the promise of safety, they surrendered, but only to be cut down in a terrible massacre. At Lucknow, the feeble garrison held out for months, and were rescued in their last extremity by an army of relief under Sir Colin Campbell.

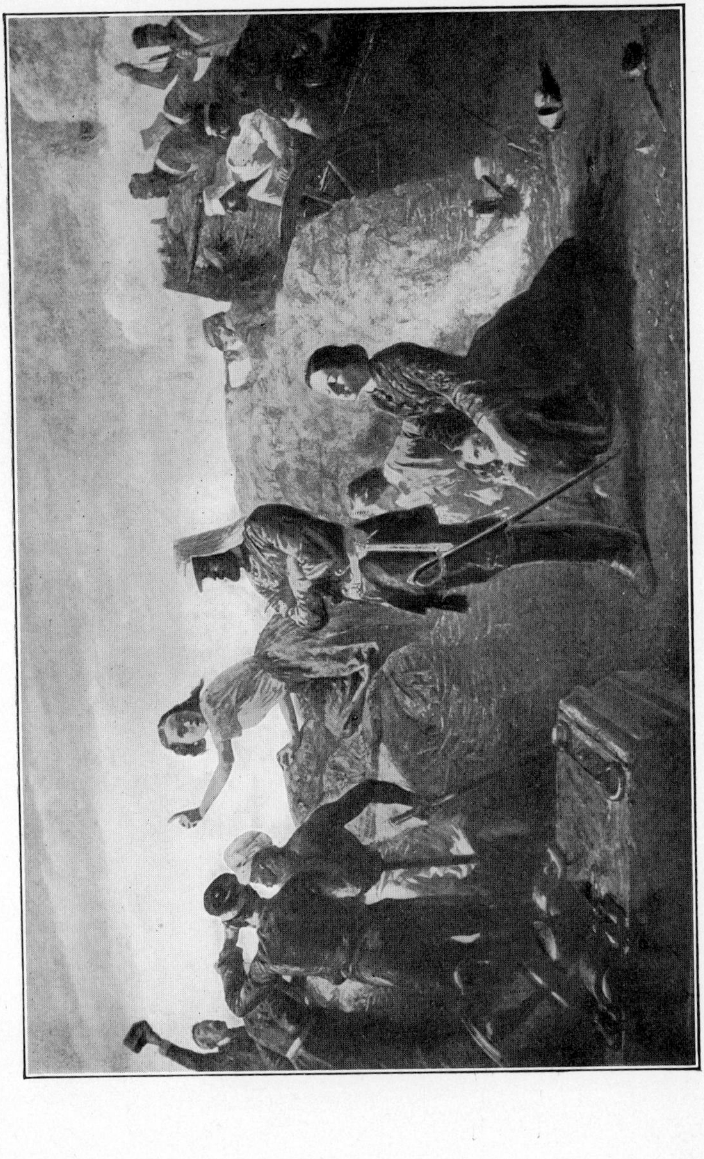

THE RELIEF OF LUCKNOW

It was smoke and roar and powder-stench,
    And hopeless waiting for death;
And the soldier's wife, like a full-tired child,
    Seemed scarce to draw her breath.

I sank to sleep, and I had my dream
    Of an English village-lane,
And wall and garden; — but one wild scream
    Brought me back to the roar again.

There Jessie Brown stood listening
    Till a sudden gladness broke
All over her face; and she caught my hand
    And drew me near as she spoke: —

"The Hielanders! Oh, dinna ye hear
    The slogan far awa'?
The McGregor's. Oh! I ken it weel;
    It's the grandest o' them a'!

"God bless the bonny Hielanders!
    We're saved! we're saved!" she cried;
And fell on her knees; and thanks to God
    Flowed forth like a full flood-tide.

Along the battery line her cry
    Had fallen among the men,
And they started back; — they were there to die;
    But was life so near them, then?

INDIA

They listened for life; the rattling fire
    Far off, and that far-off roar,
Were all, and the colonel shook his head,
    And they turned to their guns once more.

But Jessie said, "The slogan's done;
    But winna ye hear it noo?
'The Campbells are comin''? It's no a dream;
    Our succors hae broken through!"

We heard the roar and the rattle afar,
    But the pipes we could not hear;
So the men plied their work of hopeless war,
    And knew that the end was near.

It was not long ere it made its way, —
    A thrilling, ceaseless sound:
It was no noise from the strife afar,
    Or the sappers under ground.

It *was* the pipes of the Highlanders!
    And now they played "Auld Lang Syne."
It came to our men like the voice of God,
    And they shouted along the line.

And they wept, and shook one another's hands,
    And the women sobbed in a crowd;
And every one knelt down where he stood,
    And we all thanked God aloud.

That happy time, when we welcomed them,
    Our men put Jessie first;

THE RELIEF OF LUCKNOW

And the general gave her his hand, and cheers
   Like a storm from the soldiers burst.

And the pipers' ribbons and tartan streamed,
   Marching round and round our line;
And our joyful cheers were broken with tears,
   As the pipes played "Auld Lang Syne."

WHEN QUEEN VICTORIA BECAME EMPRESS OF INDIA

[1877]

BY FIELD-MARSHAL LORD ROBERTS

[THE PRINCE OF WALES, afterwards King Edward VII, paid a visit to India as a mark of honor to the native princes who had aided the English in their efforts to govern the land. This visit was followed by Queen Victoria's assumption of the title of Empress of India.

The Editor.]

IN the autumn of 1876 preparations were commenced for the "Imperial Assemblage," which it was announced by the Viceroy would be held at Delhi on the first day of January, 1877, for the purpose of proclaiming to the Queen's subjects throughout India the assumption by Her Majesty of the title of "Empress of India." To this assemblage Lord Lytton further announced that he proposed "to invite the governors, lieutenant-governors, and heads of administration from all parts of the Queen's Indian dominions, as well as the princes, chiefs, and nobles in whose persons the antiquity of the past is associated with the prosperity of the present, and who so worthily contribute to the splendor and stability of this great empire."

Delhi was selected as the place where the meeting between the Queen's representative and the great nobles of India could most appropriately be held, and a committee was appointed to make the necessary arrangements. As a member of the committee I was deputed to proceed to Delhi, settle about the sites for the camps, and carry out all details in communication with the local authorities. The Viceroy impressed upon me that the assemblage was intended to emphasize the Proclamation Lord Canning issued eighteen years before, by which the Queen assumed the direct sovereignty of her Eastern possessions, and that he wished no trouble or expense to be spared in making the ceremony altogether worthy of such a great historical event.

I returned to Simla in October, when my wife and I accompanied the commander-in-chief on a very delightful march over the Jalauri Pass through the Kulu Valley to Chamba and Dalhousie. Our party consisted of the chief, his doctor (Bradshaw), Persian interpreter (Moore), General and Mrs. Lumsden, and ourselves. The first slight shower of snow had just fallen on the Jalauri Pass, and as we crossed over we disturbed a number of beautiful snow-pheasants and minals busily engaged in scratching it away to get at their food. The scenery on this march is very fine and varied; for the most part the timber and foliage are superb, and the valleys are very fertile and pretty, lying close under the snow-capped mountains.

Having inspected the "Hill stations," we proceeded to Peshawar, where the Viceroy had arranged to hold a conference with the lieutenant-governor of the Punjab and the commissioner of Peshawar about frontier affairs.

Early in December I was back again at Delhi, where I found the arrangements for the several camps progressing most satisfactorily, and canvas cities rising up in every direction. I had previously chosen the site of the old cantonment for the camps of the Viceroy, the commander-in-chief, and the principal officials, while for the assemblage itself I had selected ground about three miles off.

The chiefs and princes were all settled in their several camps ready to meet the Viceroy, who, on his arrival, in a few graceful words welcomed them to Delhi, and thanked them for responding to his invitation. He then mounted with Lady Lytton, on a state elephant, and a procession was formed, which, I fancy, was about the most gorgeous and picturesque which has ever been seen, even in the East. The magnificence of the native princes' retinues can hardly be described; their elephant-housings were of cloth of gold, or scarlet-and-blue cloths embroidered in gold and silver. The *howdahs* were veritable thrones of the precious metals, shaded by the most brilliant canopies, and the war-elephants belonging to some of the Central India and Rajputana chiefs formed a very curious and interesting feature. Their tusks were tipped with steel; they wore shields on their foreheads, and breastplates of flashing steel; chain-mail armor hung down over their trunks and covered their backs and sides; and they were mounted by warriors clad in chain-mail, and armed to the teeth. Delhi must have witnessed many splendid pageants, when the Rajput, the Moghul, and the Mahratta dynasties, each in its turn, was at the height of its glory; but never before had princes and chiefs of every race and creed come from all parts of Hindustan, vying with each other as to the magificence of their *entourage*, and met together with the same object, that of acknowledging and doing homage to one supreme ruler.

The next few days were spent by Lord Lytton in

receiving the sixty-three ruling princes of India according to the strictest etiquette. Each prince, with his suite, was met at the entrance to the camp, and conducted up the street to the durbar tent by mounted officers, the salute to which he was entitled being fired while the procession moved on. He was then presented by the Foreign Secretary to the Viceroy, who placed him on a chair on his right, immediately below a full-length portrait of Her Majesty. A satin banner, richly embroidered with the chief's armorial bearings surmounted by the imperial crown, was next brought in by Highland soldiers and planted in front of the throne, when the Viceroy, leading the particular chief towards it, thus addressed him: "I present Your Highness with this banner as a personal gift from Her Majesty the Queen, in commemoration of her assumption of the title of Empress of India. Her Majesty trusts that it may never be unfurled without reminding you not only of the close union between the throne of England and your loyal and princely house, but also of the earnest desire of the paramount power to see your dynasty strong, prosperous, and permanent."

His Excellency then placed round the chief's neck a crimson ribbon, to which was attached a very handsome gold medal with the Queen's head engraved on it, adding: "I further decorate you, by command of Her Majesty. May this medal be long worn by yourself, and long kept as an heirloom in your family in remembrance of the auspicious date it bears."

The first of January, 1877, saw the Queen proclaimed Empress of India. The ceremony was most imposing, and in every way successful. Three tented pavilions

INDIA

had been constructed on an open plain. The throne-pavilion in the center was a very graceful erection, brilliant in hangings and banners of red, blue, and white satin magnificently embroidered in gold with appropriate emblems. It was hexagonal in shape, and rather more than two hundred feet in circumference. In front of this was the pavilion for the ruling chiefs and high European officials, in the form of a semicircle eight hundred feet long. The canopy was of Star of India blue-and-white satin embroidered in gold, each pillar being surmounted by an imperial crown. Behind the throne was the stand for the spectators, also in the form of a semicircle divided in the middle, and likewise canopied in brilliant colors. Between these two blocks was the entrance to the area.

Each chief and high official sat beneath his own banner, which was planted immediately behind his chair, and they were all mixed up as much as possible to avoid questions of precedence, the result being the most wonderful mass of color, produced from the intermingling of British uniforms and plumes with gorgeous Eastern costumes, set off by a blaze of diamonds and other precious stones.

All the British troops brought to Delhi for the occasion were paraded to the north, and the troops and retainers belonging to the native chiefs to the south, of the pavilion. Guards of honor were drawn up on either side of the throne, and at each opening by which the ruling chiefs were to enter the pavilion.

The guests being all seated, a flourish of trumpets by the heralds exactly at noon announced the arrival of the Viceroy. The military bands played a march, and Lord Lytton, accompanied by Lady Lytton, their daughters, and his staff, proceeded to the pavilion. His Excellency took his seat upon the throne, arrayed in his robes as Grand Master of the Star of India, the National Anthem was played, the guards of honor presented arms, while the whole of the vast assemblage rose as one man. The chief herald was then commanded to read the proclamation. A flourish of trumpets was again sounded, and Her Majesty was proclaimed Empress of India.

When the chief herald had ceased reading, the royal standard was hoisted, and a salute of one hundred and one salvos of artillery was fired, with a *feu-de-joie* from the long line of troops. This was too much for the elephants. As the *feu-de-joie* approached nearer and nearer to them, they became more and more alarmed, and at last scampered off, dispersing the crowd in every direction. When it ceased, they were quieted and brought back by their mahouts, only to start off again when the firing recommenced; but, as it was a perfectly bare plain, without anything for the great creatures to come in contact with, there was no harm done beyond a severe shaking to their riders. As the sound of the last salvo died away, the Viceroy addressed the assemblage. When he had ceased speaking, the assembly again rose en masse and joined the troops in giving several ringing cheers.

His Highness the Maharaja Sindhia then spoke as follows: "Shah in Shah Padishah. May God bless you. The princes of India bless you, and pray that your sovereignty and power may remain steadfast forever."

Sir Salar Jung rose in behalf of the boy Nizam and said: "I am desired by His Highness the Nizam to re-

INDIA

quest Your Excellency to convey to Her Majesty, on the part of himself and the chiefs of India, the expression of their hearty congratulations on the assumption of the title of Empress of India, and to assure the Queen that they pray for her, and for the enduring prosperity of her Empire, both in India and England."

The Maharajas of Udaipur and Jaipur, in the name of the United Chiefs of Rajputana, begged that a telegram might be sent to the Queen, conveying their dutiful and loyal congratulations; and the Maharaja of Kashmir expressed his gratification at the tenor of the Viceroy's speech, and declared that he should henceforth consider himself secure under the shadow of Her Majesty's protecting care.

It is difficult to overrate the political importance of this great gathering. It was looked upon by most of the ruling chiefs as the result of the Prince of Wales's visit, and rejoiced in as an evidence of Her Majesty's increased interest in, and appreciation of, the vast Empire of India with its many different races and peoples.

VII
THE INDIA OF TO-DAY

HISTORICAL NOTE

THE Executive Government of India is vested in the Viceroy, who is appointed by the sovereign of Great Britain, assisted by a council of five members, each of whom has charge of a department of the executive. The Viceroy, however, can overrule a majority vote of the council. There is a national congress, but the native Indian has little idea of a national life or even of India as a whole. Nine tenths of the civil employees are natives, as are also two thirds of the army; but the high-salaried positions are in the hands of the English, one of the things that causes much discontent. The English Government recognizes no favored sect in religious faith, but pays grants to Hindu temples and Mohammedan mosques alike; and finds room for both Protestants and Roman Catholics as chaplains. In December, 1911, King George and Queen Mary visited their Indian Empire. The capital was changed to Delhi, and in that city a magnificent durbar was held to celebrate the coronation of the sovereigns.

WHAT IS CASTE?

BY SIR WILLIAM WILSON HUNTER

[DURING the eighth and ninth centuries, Brahmanism became more powerful than Buddhism. It developed into the form of faith known as Hinduism. As a social league, Hinduism is based upon the laws of caste.

The Editor.]

INDIAN caste rests upon three distinct systems of division; namely, upon race, occupation, and geographical position. It is very difficult even to guess at the number of the Indian castes. But there are not fewer than three thousand of them which have separate names, and which regard themselves as separate classes. The different castes cannot intermarry with each other, and most of them cannot eat together. The ordinary rule is that no Hindu of good caste can touch food cooked by a man of inferior caste. By rights, too, each caste should keep to its own occupation. Indeed, there has been a tendency to erect every separate kind of employment or handicraft in each separate province into a distinct caste. But, as a matter of practice, the castes often change their occupation, and the lower ones sometimes raise themselves in the social scale. Thus the Vaisya caste were in ancient times the tillers of the soil. They have in most provinces given up this toilsome occupation, and the Vaisyas are now the great merchants and bankers of India. Their fair skins, intelligent faces, and polite bearing must have altered since the days when

INDIA

their forefathers ploughed, sowed, and reaped under the hot sun. Such changes of employment still occur on a smaller scale throughout India.

The system of caste exercises a great influence upon the industries of the people. Each caste is, in the first place, a trade-guild. It ensures the proper training of the youth of its own special craft; it makes rules for the conduct of the caste-trade; it promotes good feeling by feasts or social gatherings. The famous manufactures of mediæval India, its muslins, silks, cloth of gold, inlaid weapons, and exquisite work in precious stones — were brought to perfection under the care of the castes or trade-guilds. Such guilds may still be found in full work in many parts of India. Thus, in the Northwestern Districts of Bombay, all heads of artisan families are ranged under their proper trade-guild. The trade-guild or caste prevents undue competition among the members, and upholds the interest of its own body in any dispute arising with other craftsmen.

In 1873, for example, a number of bricklayers in Ahmadabad could not find work. Men of this class sometimes added to their daily wages by rising very early in the morning, and working overtime. But when several families complained that they could not get employment, the bricklayers' guild met, and decided that as there was not enough work for all, no member should be allowed to work in extra hours. In the same city, the clothdealers in 1872 tried to cut down the wages of the sizers or men who dress the cotton cloth. The sizers' guild refused to work at lower rates and remained six weeks on strike. At length they arranged their dispute, and both the trade-guilds signed a stamped agreement fixing the rates for the future. Each of the higher castes or trade-guilds in Ahmadabad receives a fee from young men on entering their business. The revenue derived from these fees, and from fines upon members who break caste rules, is spent in feasts to the brethren of the guild, and in helping the poorer craftsmen or their orphans. A favorite plan of raising money in Surat is for the members of the trade to keep a certain day as a holiday, and to shut up all their shops except one. The right to keep open this one shop is put up to auction, and the amount bid is expended on a feast. The trade-guild or caste allows none of its members to starve. It thus acts as a mutual assurance society and takes the place of a poor law in India. The severest social penalty which can be inflicted upon a Hindu is to be put out of his caste.

THE AMUSEMENTS OF AN EASTERN KING

[Nineteenth century]

BY A MEMBER OF THE HOUSEHOLD OF NUSSIR-U-DEEN, LATE KING OF OUDE

The favor and intimacy which the European members of the household enjoyed were by no means pleasing to the higher native nobility of Oude—nay, were altogether displeasing. This was natural enough; for the nawab and the commander of the forces and the "general" at the head of the police, Rajah Buktar Singh by name, were all secondary beings when the barber was by.

"It is not right or proper for these gentlemen," urged the nawab, "to enter into the presence with their shoes and boots on. We never do. Your Majesty is somewhat over-condescending in allowing it. Believe me, Your Majesty's august father, of happy memory, Ghazi-u-deen, the great and magnificent, would never have suffered it."

The king was taken aback for a moment at this bold speech from one usually so humble and so pliant; but Rushon-u-Dowlah had screwed his courage to the speaking point, and was not to be answered with a look.

"Am I a greater man than the King of England, nawab?" asked His Majesty.

"Your Majesty is the greatest king in India — greater than the Emperor of Delhi. May the asylum of

THE AMUSEMENTS OF AN EASTERN KING

the world live a thousand years!" Such was the wily courtier's evasive answer.

"Rushon-u-Dowlah," said the king, "am I a greater man than the King of England?"

"It's not for Your Majesty's servant to say that any one is greater than his lord."

"Listen to me, nawab; and you, general, listen to me. The King of England is my master; and these gentlemen would go into his presence with their shoes on. Shall they not come into mine, then? Do they come before me with their hats on? Answer me, Your Excellency."

"They do not, Your Majesty."

"No; that is *their* way of showing respect. *They* take off their hats and *you* take off your shoes. But, come, now, let us have a bargain. Wallah, but I will get them to take off their shoes and leave them without, as you do, if you will take off your turban and leave it without as they do."

The nawab never said a word more on the subject. He was silenced. The loss of the turban is the greatest of indignities among Mussulmans. "May my father's head be uncovered, if I do!" is no uncommon asseveration with them when urged to perform what they will not, or when anxious to show that the commission of an action is far from their thoughts.

The above conversation, which surprised us all so much that the king got his secretary to make a note of it, — for everything done at court is chronicled, — will show that the king was no fool, when he allowed his judgment and his reason to guide him. It was only when governed by foolish whim or drunken caprice that he was childish and absurd. . . .

INDIA

We were in a large walled-in garden at Chaungunge, one of the park palaces. The garden might have been some three or four acres in extent, and was surrounded with a high wall. Some one had been describing the game of leap-frog to His Majesty or else he had seen some pictures of it, and it had taken his fancy mightily. The natives were left without the garden, the heavy gates were swung to, and His Majesty commanded that we should forthwith begin. The captain of the body-guard "made a back" for the tutor, the librarian stood for the portrait-painter. Away we went, like schoolboys, beginning with very "low backs," for none of us were very expert in the game, but gradually "making backs" higher and higher. Tutor, barber, captain, librarian, portrait-painter — off we were like overgrown schoolboys, now up, now down. It was hot work, I assure you.

The king, however, did not long stand a quiet spectator of the scene; he would try, too. His Majesty was very thin, and not over-strong. I happened to be nearest him at the time; and he ran toward me, calling out. I "made a back" for him, and he went over easily enough. He was very light and a good horseman, so that he succeeded in the vault. He then stood for me. I would have given a good deal to have been excused; but he would not have it so, and to have refused would have been to have offended him mortally.

I ran, vaulted, down went the back, down I went with it; and His Majesty the King and the author of these reminiscences went rolling together among the flower-beds. He got up annoyed.

"Boppery bopp, but you are as heavy as an elephant!" he exclaimed.

THE AMUSEMENTS OF AN EASTERN KING

I was afraid he would have been in a passion, but he was not. The barber adroitly made a back for him forthwith, and over he went blithely. The tutor, a thin, spare man, was the lightest of our party, and the king made a back for him and succeeded in getting him safely over. It was then all right. Away they went, vaulting and standing, round and round, until His Majesty was tired out and wanted iced claret to cool him. The game was frequently renewed afterward. . . .

It was about Christmas-time. Christmas is called in India the great day of the sahibs; and we were conversing about it in this very garden at Chaungunge where the leap-frog had been first tried.

Christmas sports led to a description of what winter was; winter led to snow; snow to snowballing. We described to His Majesty the art and pastime of snowballing as well as we could. To a man who had never seen snow it was not easy to describe it vividly.

The garden abounded with a large yellow flower, peculiar to India, the smaller varieties of which are used to ornament houses in Calcutta at Christmas-time. It is not quite so large as a dahlia, but somewhat similar in appearance. When snowballing had been described to the king as well as we could describe it, he pulled three or four of these yellow flowers and threw them at the librarian, who happened to be the most distant of the party. Like good courtiers, all followed the royal example, and soon every one was pelting right and left. These yellow flowers were our snowballs, and we all entered into the game with hearty good will. The king bore his share in the combat right royally, discharging three missiles for one that was aimed at him. He laughed and enjoyed the sport amazingly. Before we had concluded, we were all a mass of yellow leaves; they stuck about our hair and clothes and on the king's hat in a tenacious way. What the gardeners must have thought of the matter when they came to set the garden to rights again, we did not stop to conjecture. It was enough that the king was amused. He had found out a new pleasure, and enjoyed it as long as those yellow flowers continued in bloom.

AN IDOL CAR WITH STONE WHEELS

AN IDOL CAR WITH STONE WHEELS

The lumbering car with the four wheels of stone is one of those used in religious processions to carry the idol. The starting of such a car is thus described by "Pierre Loti": —

"The horns give the signal, and hundreds of arms, with tensely knotted muscles, fix themselves on the cables. All the young men, even the most noble Brahmins, join in united effort, partly from pleasure and partly from a sense of duty. Now they make ready. With a grace that is almost feminine, and which contrasts strongly with their proud masculine eyes and thin broad shoulders, they unknot their heavy coils of hair; then raising their arms, which many bracelets encircle, retie them into a tighter knot.

"The second signal, a fury of tom-toms, and a more imperious blast of the horn, is answered by an outcry of human tongues, whilst the cables stretch under the effort of straining muscles. However, the enormous machine does not move, for it has become embedded in the ground since last year's procession. . . .

"'Run! fetch the levers and the tackle, we must have them.' Whole trunks of trees are brought on the shoulders of the porters, the leveled end is placed under the wheel which will not move, ten men sit astride on the end that projects into the air and spring up and down, whilst others pull ahead at the ropes and pulleys.

"The huge structure trembles. There is a great cry of joy, and the car starts off.

"The wheels of Vishnu's car commence to revolve, tearing up the earth with four deep furrows. The car moves, accompanied by the groans of straining axles, a creaking of bending wood, and the din of human voices and sacred trumpets. There is an immense overflow of childish joy; white teeth glimmer in mouths which are opened widely with shouts of triumph, and the air is filled with waving arms."

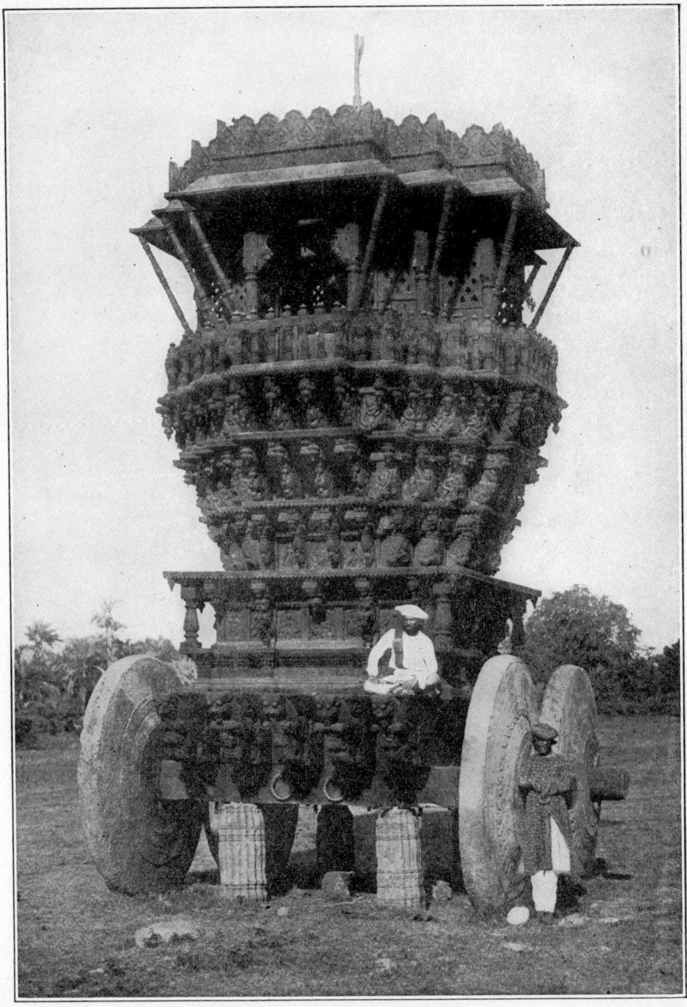

HOW THE MOHAMMEDANS KEEP THE FESTIVAL OF THE MOHURRIM

[Nineteenth century]

BY A MEMBER OF THE HOUSEHOLD OF NUSSIR-U-DEEN, LATE KING OF OUDE

THE month of Mohurrim — one of the Arabic months — is the anniversary of the death of two early leaders of "the faithful," near relatives of Mohammed himself, Hassan and Hosein, and is observed by more than one half the Mohammedan population of India, including the court of Lucknow, as a period of deep humiliation and sorrowful remembrance; — by more than one half of the Mohammedan population, because, as every one knows, "the faithful" are divided into two great sects, the Shiahs and the Sunnis. The Turks are Sunnis, the Persians Shiahs — generally speaking, indeed, the western Mussulmans, from the Euphrates to the Atlantic, are Sunnis; the eastern, from the Euphrates to Java, are Shiahs.

The Mohurrim, as the festival is called, scarcely ever passes over in India without contests between the two great parties — between those who regard the deaths of Hassan and Hosein as barbarous murders on the one side, that is the Shiahs, and those who, on the other, look upon them as having been usurpers, and lawfully put to death by the true head of "the faithful" — the reigning calif. These latter are the Sunnis.

On the first day of the Mohurrim, the vast Mohammedan population appears to be suddenly snatched away from all interest and employment in the affairs of earth. The streets are deserted, every one is shut up in his house, mourning with his family. On the second, again, the streets are crowded; but with people in mourning attire, parading along the thoroughfares in funeral procession to the tombs set up here and there as tributes of respect to the memory of Hassan and Hosein. These tombs are representations of the mausoleum at Kerbela, or Neshed, on the banks of the Euphrates, in which the two chiefs were buried; and are either contained in an *emanbarra* belonging to a chief or in the house of some wealthy Mussulman. The tomb model, or *tazia*, belonging to the King of Oude, was made for His Majesty's father in England; it was composed of green glass with gold mouldings, and was regarded as peculiarly holy.

The *emanbarra* is usually erected for the purpose of celebrating the Mohurrim, and is not unfrequently intended, as was the king's, for the final resting-place of the heads of the family to which it belongs. The representation of the tomb of Hassan and Hosein is placed, at the period of Mohurrim, against the wall facing Mecca, under a canopy, which consisted in the royal *emanbarra* of green velvet embroidered with gold. A pulpit is placed opposite, usually of the same material as the model, in which the reader of the service — the officiating priest, as we should call him — stands with his face to Mecca and his back to the tomb. This pulpit consists simply of a small raised platform, without railing or parapet of any kind, on which the reader sits or stands, as he may find most convenient.

During the entire period of the Mohurrim, large wax

THE FESTIVAL OF THE MOHURRIM

lights, red and green, are kept burning round the tomb, and mourning assemblies are held in the *emanbarra* twice a day; those in the evening being by far the most attractive and the most generally attended. It was a fine thing to see the king, in his splendid mourning suit and with a crown on his head decorated with feathers from the bird of paradise, taking his place in front of the reader — his long train of native attendants coming in two by two afterward, with downcast faces and sorrowing mien, while the wax candles and the brilliant chandeliers threw an intense light upon the scene. It was interesting to observe the profound quiet which reigned, until broken by the reader of the service; the audience always awaiting the commencement of the reading or the recitation in the same humble and sorrowing attitude in which they entered.

The lights are flaring upon the broad turbans; the glittering interior of the *emanbarra*, with chandeliers and wax tapers, its gilding and its banners, its fringes and its embroideries, is a blaze of light. The preacher is reciting an account of the death of the two chiefs, his keen black eyes glowing with animation as he proceeds — his audience, at first so solemn and so quietly sad, being gradually wound up to passionate bursts of grief. The orator groans aloud as he recapitulates the disastrous story; his audience is deeply moved. Tears trickle from the eyes of more than one bearded face, sobs and groans issue from the others. At length, as if with a sudden unpremeditated burst, but really at the proper part of the service, the audience utters forth the names "Hassan!" "Hosein!" in succession, beating the breast the while in cadence. At first somewhat gently and in a

INDIA

low tone are the names uttered, but afterward louder and more loud, until the whole *emanbarra* rings again with the excited, prolonged, piercing wail. For fully ten minutes does this burst of grief continue — the beating of the breast, the loud uttering of the names, the beating ever louder and more resounding, the utterance gradually increasing in shrillness and piercing energy; until, in a moment, all is hushed again, and silence, as of deep affliction, falls like a pall upon the assembly.

But man requires refreshment after his labor, whether that labor consists in being whirled across a frozen country with a biting east wind in one's teeth, at the rate of thirty miles an hour, or shouting "Hassan" and "Hosein" for ten minutes in uninterrupted succession and beating the breast with the thermometer at ninety. Sherbet is now handed round. The king and the members of his family indulge in that perfection of smoking, — the hookah, — while the others take a savory stimulant from their belts and proceed to chew it, until the reading of the service recommences, and the time rolls round again for renewed thumping, renewed shouting of "Hassan" and "Hosein," and a renewed respite. At the conclusion a funeral dirge is chanted, called the *moorseah;* and being in the vernacular, this portion of the service is much prized by all, because comprehended by all. The *moorseah* ended, the whole assembly rises, and recapitulates simultaneously the names of all the true leaders of "the faithful," ending with curses upon the usurping califs.

Nor is it only in their visits to the *emanbarra* and joining in the service that the Shiah families express their sympathy with and sorrow for the sufferings of the

THE FESTIVAL OF THE MOHURRIM

lost chiefs. Every kind of luxury is put aside during this month of Mohurrim. The commonest and hardest *charpoys*, or a simple mat upon the floor, are substituted for the luxurious cushions and well-wadded mattresses on which they usually recline. Their fare is of the coarsest. Hot curries and savory pilaws are eschewed, and common barley bread, rice, and boiled peas are substituted. The usual ornaments are laid aside — a great deprivation of the ladies' pleasures and comforts, for the contemplation of her jewelry is one of the most pleasing and constant employments of the Indian belle.

In Lucknow they believe that they have the metal crest of the banner of Hosein (conveyed thither long ago by a poor pilgrim from the West), and the relic is regarded as peculiarly sacred. The building in which it is contained is called the Durgah; and thither the banners used in the Mohurrim are brought by thronging multitudes with great display upon the fifth day. The Durgah is fully five miles from the king's palace — a magnificent building, a beautiful specimen of that style of architecture which Bishop Heber aptly calls the Oriental Gothic. In the center of this building the sacred crest is fixed aloft on a pole, the whole elevated upon a platform hung round with flags and emblematic devices.

On the morning of the fifth day of Mohurrim, crowds of all ranks and classes of the people might be seen issuing from Lucknow to visit the Durgah, each little party bearing its own banners. On such occasions the Orientals love to display their wealth. The procession from the royal *emanbarra* was of course the most magnificent. Six or eight elephants with silver trappings first appeared, the men upon them bearing the banners to

INDIA

be blessed. A guard of soldiers accompanied the elephants. Then came a sort of chief mourner, bearing a black pole supporting two swords hung from a reversed bow. Then came the king himself and the male members of his family with his favorite *moluvies*. To these succeeded a charger called Dhull-dhull, the name of the horse Hosein rode when he lost his life. A white Arab of elegant proportions was usually employed for this purpose, whose reddened legs and sides (from which arrows, apparently buried in his body, projected) indicated the sufferings of both horse and rider. A turban in the Arabian style and a bow and quiver of arrows are fixed upon the saddle of Dhull-dhull; and a beautifully embroidered saddlecloth contrasts finely with the spotless white coat of the animal — the trappings all of solid gold. Attendants, gorgeously dressed, accompany the horse with *chowries* (for beating away flies) made of the yak's tail. Following Dhull-dhull might be seen troops of the king's servants, regiments of horse and foot, and a crowd of idlers.

The banners are borne through the Durgah, presented to the sacred crest, and touched, and then taken out again at the opposite door to make room for others. All day long does this ceremony continue. Fresh crowds constantly arrive from Lucknow, some waiting till the afternoon in expectation of an easier journey, some delayed by accident. Fifty thousand banners so hallowed in the course of the day I have heard of as being no extraordinary number.

From a burial to a wedding is often but a step in human life, and nowhere is that step shorter than in the East. The Mohurrim, a season of mourning and of grief

— or woe, depression, and penance — contains also the representation of a wedding! This wedding is commemorated on the seventh day of the fast and is called *Mayndieh*. It is held in remembrance of the marriage of the favorite daughter of Hosein to her cousin Cossim on the very day that Hosein lost his life at Kerbela. The *Mayndieh* is a great wedding procession, which sets out at night; that of the inferior being directed toward the *emanbarra* of the superior — that of the nawab, or native prime minister, usually directing its course, for instance, to the *emanbarra* of the king.

The *emanbarra* on this day was fitted up of course with extraordinary splendor, worthy to receive the expensive and gorgeous *Mayndieh;* and when the preparations were complete, the public were admitted to gaze upon the glittering though somewhat bizarre scene. They crowded the vast hall in thousands; some admiring the strangely varied collection of chandeliers, one of which alone, as I well remember, contained more than a hundred wax lights; others gazing upon the colored lamps — amber, blue, and green; others examining the glittering tomb of the *emauns* with its decorations, a huge lion on one side, and the royal arms, two fish *embowed and respecting each other* (as the heralds have it) upon the other. The streaming flags astonished the more lively; and the silver representations of the gates of Mecca, of the tent of Hosein, and of the tomb of Kerbela, all placed upon silver tables, gave ample food for thought and calculations to the more sordid; while the variety of arms and armor hung round the walls attracted the attention of the warriors. The whole of the decorations were rather showy and glittering than tasteful, exciting not so much admiration of the beauty of the scene as wonder at the display.

But the roll of musketry without has already announced that the wedding procession is advancing — a wedding and a burial both performed in one day, and strangely commemorated together; for Cossim was buried the day he was married. The roll of musketry has sounded, and the king's messengers come in, in great numbers, to clear the hall. They know their duty and what is expected of them; while the people, on their part, still linger around the objects of their contemplations. Hustling and friendly pushing will not do — the gazers have not yet feasted their eyes, and *will* not be hustled out. How London policemen would clear the place of the fierce-looking, well-bearded Mussulmans I do not know; but the king's messengers and peons adopt a very summary method of procedure. They have three times announced with a loud voice that the place must be cleared; and still hundreds are gathered round the tombs and round the silver models, and many gaping admirers still contemplate the dazzling lights. There is no time to be lost, and messengers and peons proceed forthwith to enforce the departure of the more tardy. Their bamboos are flourished and well-thonged whips are produced. Blows resound upon the backs of the lagging gazers — good sturdy blows often, by no means a joke — and the recipients growl and move on. Not a loiterer, however, returns the salute — the messengers and peons have right on their side; this whipping and flagellation is the *dustoor*, the custom, and therefore must be right. Occasionally a more than ordinarily severe stroke elicits a sudden facing round of the well-

THE FESTIVAL OF THE MOHURRUM

bearded *floggee;* while the flogger still flourishes his cane or his whip, and looks the indignant sufferer full in the face. *Donkeys* and *dogs*, and even *pigs* (the most opprobrious of epithets to the ear of a Mussulman), they will call each other in irritated and rapid colloquy; but still the loiterer moves on toward the door, however loudly or fiercely he may retort in words, rubbing the outraged part the while manfully, and wagging his beard violently in indignant remonstrance; without any answering blow, however, — no angry retaliation comes from the hand or dagger. Custom has decided the matter, and custom and right are synonymous east of the Indus.

And now all is ready for the wedding procession, which has been gradually drawing near. The *emanbarra* is silent again. The doors by which the people went out are closed, and the vast quadrangle in front, brilliantly lit up, is thrown open. The elephants and horses are left without; but the crowd of soldiers and bearers of presents and attendant musicians almost fill up the spacious square — the beautiful tessellated pavement is completely hidden.

First, through the lines of soldiers filing to right and left, are borne in the wedding presents. Richly decorated attendants advance, carrying silver trays laden with sweetmeats and dried fruits, miniature beds of flowers, and garlands of sweet jasmine; while fireworks are let off as they enter the doors. A covered conveyance, — that of the bride, — the exterior of silver, such as is used by the highest of the female nobility, follows the wedding presents, accompanied by richly decorated attendants bearing torches. Then come the bands of music and other torchbearers; and with glad sounds the whole procession enters, and makes the round of the vast hall. The presents are deposited near the model of the tomb, in readiness to be taken to the place of burial a few days after. But scarcely has the richly decorated wedding procession passed into the *emanbarra* when another company, with downcast countenances and in mourning garb, draws nigh. The wedding and the death occurred on the same day, and so the funeral pomp follows hard upon the *Mayndich*.

The model of the tomb of Cossim, duly supported on a bier, is brought in by the attendants, and a sad mourning procession accompanies it. Sometimes even a horse, duly trained for the purpose, accompanies the party. It is regarded as the horse of Cossim, and bears his embroidered turban, his scimitar, his bow and arrows; while over it is held a royal umbrella, the emblem of sovereignty, and a gorgeously worked *aftadah*, or sun-symbol. The horse, if he be admitted to the interior, is one, of course, upon which dependence can be placed; and makes the round of the spacious hall with a solemnity and steadiness of gait befitting the occasion.

So much for what goes on within, where the usual service succeeds to the processions. But there is a part of the ceremony proceeding without the courtyard infinitely more to the taste of the populace than the gloom and distress which characterize the principal actors in the funeral scene. Without the courtyard — for that is a place which may not be desecrated by the great unwashed — crowds have collected, of all ages and of both sexes; there is crushing and amusement, laughter and groaning and objurgation, as in all crowds. They are awaiting the distribution of coin, which always accom-

THE FESTIVAL OF THE MOHURRIM

panies a wedding, and which is never omitted upon the occasion of the *Mayndieh* commemorating the marriage of Cossim and the daughter of Hosein. Small silver coins are scattered right and left by officers appointed for the purpose, with a lavish expenditure that would astonish the European. It is a part of the religion of the Mussulman to be liberal at such a time, and he cares not for the cost.

It is on record at Lucknow that one of these Mohurrims cost a reigning nawab upward of three hundred thousand pounds; the costly nature of the processions and trappings — the munificence to the poor — the lavish display of expensive dresses and appointments, never used again, need not astonish us therefore. The wealth of the Mohammedan population of any part of India may be safely estimated by the displays they make at Mohurrim. Were all this valuable mourning and embroidery, this display of silvering and gilding, to be retained from year to year to be used at each successive Mohurrim, the expense would be very different. Such, however, is not the case; what has once been used is not permitted to be used again. All is distributed among the poor and needy on the conclusion of the fast; so that the populace do not want incitement to make the commemoration of the Mohurrim as enthusiastic as possible.

But we have not yet ended with the season of gloom and despondency. All these services at the *emanbarras* — all this consecration of banners and parading of wedding and funeral processions, is but preliminary to a final display of a still more imposing character. The chiefs lie dead — their deaths alone have been hitherto commemorated — that is, the deaths of Hassan and Hosein.

INDIA

The funeral and the burial have yet to come; for this funeral vast preparations have been made, while for the burial, an imitation of the burial-ground at Kerbela has been duly set apart by each family of large possessions ages before.

These burial-grounds are all at a considerable distance from the walls of the town; and at the earliest dawn of day the populace issues forth in thousands, to witness or to take part in the various ceremonies which accompany the burial of the tomb-models, together with the food and other articles always put into a Mohammedan grave.

As the funeral of Hosein was a military spectacle, so, on this occasion, is every endeavor made to give as military a character as possible to the display. Banners are exhibited, bands play, matchlocks and guns and pistols are fired off, shields are clashed together, and no sound is wanting which serves to bring before the mind's eye the mimicry of military pageants. The poor man, with his little company, falls into the rear of the rich man's larger assembly, that he may get on the faster thereby; for the crowds are dense, and the smaller bands have no little difficulty in making a way for themselves. Besides, some of those heretical Sunnis may be lying in wait, to attack or to interrupt; for they, miserable unbelievers! regard the whole display as worse than foolish, as almost impious, in fact.

Each procession is marshaled much in the same order; first, the consecrated banners, carried aloft upon long poles, the bearers of the poles usually seated in an elephant *howdah*. The large displays will have two or three, or even six elephants so employed. A band of music, discoursing such dirges as their instruments will accomplish and custom prescribes, follows the elephants; — where all are playing, procession jostling procession, company pressing against company, each with its band, it may be easily imagined that the sounds produced are not of the most harmonious. The sword-bearer — with the two glittering blades hung aloft upon a black pole, and suspending beneath a reversed bow, near its summit — comes after the band. He is supported by men on each side, who also bear aloft black poles, to which are attached streamers of long black unspun silk.

Then comes the horse — Dhull-dhull — as on the former occasion of the consecration of the banners, attended by numerous servants. Two grooms hold the bridle, one upon either side; an officer marches at his head with the sun-symbol; another holds over him a royal umbrella; others accompany him with gilt and silvered staves, while running messengers follow with small triangular green banners. The chain armor, gold-embroidered turban, sword, and belt, are all fixed upon the saddle of Dhull-dhull; while often the owner of the animal and head of the procession walks after the horse as a sort of chief mourner. A walk of some miles amid such steaming crowds is by no means a pleasant journey.

The bearers of incense, in gold and silver censers, succeed. The censers are suspended by means of chains made of the same material, and are thus waved to and fro, as the march proceeds — much as they are waved at the foot of the altar in Roman Catholic cathedrals on the Continent. The *lahbaun*, a sweet-smelling resin which is burnt in the censers, is probably the very frankincense so frequently mentioned in the Bible. The reader of the funeral service follows, usually attended by the proprietor of the tomb-model and his friends. Always barefooted, and often without any covering upon their heads, do these mourners follow in sad procession. It is no unusual thing to see their heads disfigured with chaff and dust — the more striking symbols of profound grief.

The tomb-model, or *tazia*, is borne next; above which a canopy of green cloth or velvet, embroidered with gold or silver in the more showy processions, is spread, elevated upon poles and carried by several men stationed at the side. The model of Cossim's tomb; the covered conveyance of his bride; the trays of wedding presents, with all the other accompaniments of the marriage procession, follow in order; and lastly, camels and elephants, bearing representations of the tent equipage and warlike train of Hosein, as he marched from Medina to Kerbela.

These are all the parts of the procession proper; but, in addition to these, Oriental charity always demands a train of elephants, the *howdahs* on which are filled with confidential servants distributing bread and money among the poor. The bread so distributed is believed by the Mussulman ladies to possess certain peculiar virtues of its own, very superior to those of the ordinary staff of life. They will commission their servants to bring them a morsel of such, even though they may themselves distribute or cause to be distributed, large quantities! Its being given on the great day of the Mohurrim constitutes it holy, sacred, and peculiar.

All along the march, as the various processions wind

THE FESTIVAL OF THE MOHURRIM

by different roads over the country, guns, pistols, rifles, and matchlocks are discharged, while the mourning cry, "Hassan!" "Hosein!" is heard at intervals swelling out from the mighty throng.

The ordinary ceremony of burial is gone through on the procession reaching the appointed place — the model of the burial-ground at Kerbela. The tomb-model, with its various accompaniments of wedding trays and wedding presents, — fruits, flowers, and incense, — all are committed to the earth, a grave having been previously prepared for the purpose. It is at this part of the ceremony that the long pent-up animosity between the Shiahs and the Sunnis usually finds vent, and the mimic burial is often made the occasion of loss of life and bloody feuds between the contending factions.

SUNDAY IN THE BRITISH ARMY IN INDIA
[Nineteenth century]
BY REV. ARTHUR MALE

SUNDAY morning in camp! Ah, you say, very different from Sunday morning at home in England. Yes, of course, it is necessarily very different. No church-going bell sounding over hill and dale, and summoning the simple villagers to some ivy-covered church on the hillside, or clanging through the quiet streets of the big town, where the orderly groups of people, all in their Sunday best, are wending their way to some old time-honored temple. Certainly these accompaniments of the English Sabbath day are all wanting. But if you suppose for a moment that amid the bustling realities of active war, the stern and multifarious duties which belong to a campaign, the Sabbath is forgotten, and the worship which belongs to the day ignored, you are very much mistaken. "Tommy Atkins" is no heathen. And one of the privileges which belong to his profession is that he is allowed to worship God according to the dictates of his own conscience. No man need be a worse man morally for going into the army. Many a man has become a better man. Indeed, speaking from large experience and personal observation, I have always regarded the army as a great school of training and discipline; where the man who, in civil life, lacking the restraints and helps which belong to army discipline, would, through sheer weakness of character, rapidly

SUNDAY IN THE BRITISH ARMY IN INDIA

degenerate into a worthless fellow, receives the very aid that he needs, to give him some moral backbone, and is thus made into a very decent man, and when he leaves the service becomes a respectable citizen. Whereas, if a man be radically bad — bad through and through — he soon finds his measure taken in the army. It is a bad refuge for him, and ten to one he is soon drummed out with ignominy, as unworthy to wear the Queen's uniform. The time for regarding the ranks of the British army as filled with the scum and offscouring of society has gone by; and the scorn with which some people affect to regard our soldiers can only arise from ignorance or groundless prejudice. From close contact with the British soldier, and a personal experience extending over many years, I can honestly say that some of the grandest qualities which go to make a noble character in man, I have seen over and over again exemplified in him. Who so unshaken in discipline, so patient in suffering, so ready for any sacrifice or service in the cause of Queen and country! Many of the lads die in the alien land and are laid in some far-distant grave, where no mother can come and weep at her boy's quiet resting-place. Have they not nobly earned the kindly interest and sympathy of the people at home, for whom they thus toil and march and fight in every part of the world? In the name of all that is just, putting aside the question of kindliness and charity, let us hear no more of scorn for our soldiers. It is an injustice and a folly.

In the army there are now four recognized religious denominations, — the Church of England, the Presbyterian, the Wesleyan, and the Roman Catholic. When a man enlists he is questioned as to his "religion," as it is called; and he is compelled to make choice of one of these four parties, which choice is then recorded, with other items, against his name and number. He can, of course, afterwards "change his religion," as the men term it, by explaining his reasons to the officer commanding his regiment. The Sunday parade service, at which attendance is compulsory, unless a man be on guard or otherwise fulfilling some duty, is never by any chance omitted, if it be at all possible to hold it. Usually it takes place in the morning, often soon after dawn, though sometimes I have known it "in orders" for the afternoon.

On the previous day arrangements, as to time and locality, are made at the office of the Adjutant-General, and all such particulars inserted in the General Orders for the day, and are, therefore, known throughout the force, however large or widely scattered. Sometimes, indeed, it happens that owing to the wide disposition of a large force, portions of which may be miles apart, several parade services are held at various points, the chaplain going from one to another in succession until he has reached all the men of his "persuasion."

Thus, on Sunday morning, the Church of England party would be seen marching away to some central spot in the camp, headed, most probably, by one of the regimental bands. There, by the side of the simple lectern, consisting of the big drum, perhaps, the chaplain would await their coming, and around him, in hollow square formation, the men would presently be drawn up facing inwards on three sides, himself and any of the staff who attended the service forming the fourth. And there, under the broad canopy of heaven, the true sacrifice of worship has risen from many a sincere, hon-

SUNDAY IN THE BRITISH ARMY IN INDIA

est heart, hidden under the scarlet tunic or the blue jacket. A parade service was no opportunity for a long sermon. Straight truth, put into plain words, "able to be understanded of the common people," and kept within the limits of fifteen minutes or thereabouts, was what well suited the soldier. He does not object to hard hitting, but you must be quick about it, and it will not be the less effective. Happy the chaplain who is able to let his men have the chance of a good sing. They dearly love it. I had specially printed and prepared a large number of very thin, pamphlet-like hymn-books, containing a score or so of well-known hymns, and sufficiently portable to be carried around and distributed at each service in a few moments. I never heard anything grander, I think, than the vast volume of musical song that used to rise and swell from hearts sincere at our Sunday morning parade service. And surely the ministry of song may be credited with some strange subtle power to touch the deep-down chords in men's hearts, and help them up to better things, when stern denunciation of sin and the most pleading voice of a man may fail.

Thus also the Presbyterian party would be marching towards another quarter of the camp, the pipers of some Scotch regiment swinging along at the head and discoursing their weird music, so dear to the heart of the Scotsman.

And yonder the Wesleyan party, too, would be gathering in its appointed place, including most likely all the Nonconformists of the force.

And then in some secluded spot the Roman Catholic chaplain would arrange his simple altar, and around him would be gathered the devout worshipers who held his creed. Parade service usually lasted about three-quarters of an hour. No wisdom was shown by the chaplain who prolonged it beyond that limit.

Most of the chaplains held a voluntary service in the evening, which the men might attend or not as they chose. A good number of men used to come; and generally a very hearty and earnest service was the result.

While we lay here at Jellalabad it was my custom, in accordance with the wish of some of the men, to hold a short religious meeting — somewhat after the fashion of a Bible reading — almost every evening. This was held, not in the open air, for it was then very cold at night, but in a large tent attached to one of the regimental hospitals. I was very much amused at the zeal of one of the apothecaries, who, good-hearted fellow that he was, used to boil up a great *degchee* of tea, to serve as a kind of loving-cup for the men ere they dispersed. This little meeting rapidly became very popular in the camp. Let us not for a moment hint that bribery and corruption in the form of the tea *degchee* was the influence which stimulated the men and brought them together. But so it was that at the appointed hour a goodly number might be seen in undress quietly wending their way towards the apothecary's tent, every man of them armed with his tin canteen for drinking purposes. At first the men sat about on the ground, or on boxes, taking up a good deal of room. But as our numbers multiplied it was needful to economize space, and the following ingenious method of seating was adopted: Tent-pegs were driven into the ground at intervals, two pegs being crossed so as to form a forked rest; and on these were placed long ten-foot

SUNDAY IN THE BRITISH ARMY IN INDIA

dooley poles — the poles on which the *dooleys*, or stretchers for carrying the sick were slung. These were fixed row after row, and although the result was not quite like a well-cushioned armchair, the accommodation was marvelously enlarged, till the tent interior was a living mass of men. How our numbers increased, and the ambition of our men, too, resulting in a kind of church building of their own, I shall have occasion to narrate later on.

But there were other methods of spending the evening pleasantly, for all sorts of contrivances were set to work to make the weary hours pass. One of the other chaplains used to read every night to the men whatever of interest he could lay hold of, they gathering around him smoking their pipes and listening with a good deal of appreciation.

But the great evening's entertainment was the "sing-song," as the men dubbed it. A big space, amphitheatrical in shape, was roughly dug out, and so arranged that many hundreds of men could find some sort of sitting accommodation; while in the center was a flat space, called by courtesy the platform. Somebody was master of ceremonies, though little ceremony was observed beyond that of calling out the name of the singer or reciter, as he appeared. First uprose a stalwart young officer, Hamilton, of the Guides Cavalry, who gave a song in good style. A gallant fellow he! But a few weeks more, and he was to lead his men in charge against the fierce Kujianis at Futtehabad — his chief slain by his side — and he sweeping through the masses of the foe to save the life of a native officer and win his Victoria Cross. And then a few more months were to pass, and with

INDIA

Cavagnari, Kelly, and Jenkins, he was to meet a soldier's death, after many a deed of "derring do," in the gateway of the embassy at Kabul. All this, however, was in the future, and was now mercifully hidden from knowledge. Then young Gunner Burke, of the Artillery, sang a comical ditty telling of a tempestuous voyage in a barge from Deptford to London Bridge, which provoked broad grins, especially from the Cockneys. After him a Post-Office official, who had to accompany the force, and who hailed unmistakably from the Emerald Isle, sang of the little "Cruiskeen Lawn" and of "Shan Van Vocht," and other equally Republican songs. He was succeeded by Sergeant Moon, of the Tenth Hussars, who gave a very clever topical song of his own composing, dealing with the circumstances in which we now found ourselves, and with poor Shere Ali, and the Oxus River boundary, and Russian sympathy, and so on. A very good song it was, and well put together, testifying both to Moon's literary and musical skill. And the men responded to every point, political or otherwise, with huge guffaws and cheers. But now, last of all, modest young corporal of the same gallant regiment stood up to add his part to the evening's entertainment. He was but a boy, smooth-faced, and not too robust-looking, and, indeed, I remembered to have talked with him in hospital not so long before. But as his sweet, clear, baritone voice, gentle-toned at first, rang out over the plain, I noticed a hush gradually falling upon the assembly. The loud laughter is stilled, and the men are sitting smoking and silently gazing at the singer, who can just be discerned by the flickering light of the single lantern. And why the hush? Ah! the great quietness has fallen upon the spirits of

SUNDAY IN THE BRITISH ARMY IN INDIA

those rollicking men, because the words of the song have wafted their thoughts away from the wild Afghan land to the old home in England. It was only a simple old English ditty called, I think, "The Vacant Chair." [1] But as the words of the chorus came around —

> "We shall meet, but we shall miss him,
> There will be one vacant chair," —

there were only a few who could join quietly in it, and those with a certain tremor in their voice. They knew well enough that there would be a vacant chair in many a cottage home in England ere this campaign closed: the place where the soldier son used to sit, but which would know him no more.

And then with a verse of the National Anthem joined in with loyal enthusiasm, the "sing-song" used to close.

[1] This song was written in Worcester, Massachusetts, in the time of the Civil War.

The Editor.

CAMP LIFE IN INDIA

BY SIR MONIER MONIER-WILLIAMS

My only room was, of course, a tent. It had four doors and no windows, and a fifth door leading into a kind of lean-to, or small annex, fitted up with a large bath. Happily no one need trouble himself with a portable bath in India, because this indispensable convenience is found everywhere The tent had a lining of blue and yellow chintz, and for a carpet a stout blue and white cotton cloth laid on flax straw. All the doors had two coverings, or rather flaps, one of the same material as the tent, the other a kind of wire screen, called a *chick*, to let in air, and keep out as far as possible inquisitive intruders — not men and women, but huge bees, wasps, grasshoppers, squirrels, snakes, and all manner of winged and creeping things innumerable. For furniture there were two or three chairs, a dressing-table, and a good iron bedstead with hard mattresses, woolen pillows, and mosquito curtains, well tucked in all round. Let the reader, then, imagine me comfortably ensconced, after my month's voyages and travels, within my four canvas walls, and looking forward with pleasant anticipations to an undisturbed sleep in a veritable bed — my first since leaving England.

I go through every needful purificatory rite in my strange lavatory, and emerge refreshed from my tent door to peep at the scene outside and take my bearings. I find that we are in a large field or common, on one side of the Mehmoodabad station. The camp consists of about a dozen tents, all under large spreading trees, with which the whole park-like country round is beautifully wooded. Most of the trees are new to me — the mango, the banian, the pipal, the tamarind, the nim, and the Japanese acacia with its lovely yellow flowers. No tent is ever pitched under a tamarind. It is supposed, I believe, to exhale too much carbonic acid during the nighttime. The mango and nim are the tent-pitcher's favorite trees. Under one mango there is a large pavilion-like erection for the collector and his wife. Then there is another double tent, which serves as a dining-room and drawing-room, of ample dimensions, fitted up with carpets, tables, bookcases, easy-chairs, sewing-machine, and harmonium: two or three others for visitors like myself; another for the baby and its *ayahs;* another for the Portuguese butler; and of course a capacious tent, with annexes, which together serve for the collector's *kutchery*, magisterial court, and other offices.

On one side under the dense foliage of a banian is a circular canvas erection without any roof. This is the kitchen, where excellent dinners are cooked by means of two bricks and a hole in the ground. A little removed from the tents is the stable, an open space quite unprotected, except by foliage, where four Arab horses and two ponies are tethered by their heels, each attended by its man. Near them stand carriages, carts, and a curious vehicle called a *tonga*, usually drawn by two ponies. It has two seats back to back, suspended on two wheels, and is covered by an awning. Not far off an all but nude Bhisti, dark as a Negro, is seen plying his occupation. He supplies the camp with water, by means of two water-skins slung over the back of a bullock. Ranging about the field in promiscuous places are other bullocks, buffaloes, goats, sheep, geese, ducks, and fowls. The bullocks are for the carts, the buffaloes and goats for producing milk and butter. The other creatures come in usefully as raw material, out of which the excellent dinners before alluded to are supplied. A sheep in these country places only costs, I am told, about four rupees, or eight shillings. It is, however, a melancholy reflection that infliction of death is essential to the maintenance of an Englishman's life. For life is everywhere exuberant around me, and every living thing seems to enjoy itself, as if it were certain of being unmolested. Natives never willingly destroy life. They cannot enter into an Englishman's desire for venting his high spirits on a fine day by killing game of some kind. "Live and let live" is their rule of conduct towards the inferior creation.

I walk about admiring every living creature, especially the birds — the hoopoo with its lovely crest hopping about near me, the doves very like those at home, the bright parrots, the jays, the woodpeckers. Then little gray and brown streaked squirrels are playing all around me. They jump about with wonderful agility, peer in at the tent doors, and try to secure little bits of cotton for their nests. The sounds are not always melodious. I hear a screeching note above my head. It comes from a kind of gray and red toucan seated trustfully on a branch, and quite undisturbed by my presence. Then another discordant cry, and a rush — a number of natives are driving away a troop of big, gray, mischievous monkeys, some with little baby-monkeys clinging to them. They soon repel the invaders, but

CAMP LIFE IN INDIA

only by shouting in rather harsh vernacular, "The monkey-people, the monkey-people!" To shoot a monkey would be nothing short of sacrilege. I venture to follow the retreating intruders, but am arrested by hedges of prickly pear. Then I fall into ecstasies over the creepers, many of them of gigantic size, which twine themselves everywhere, covering hedges, bushes, and trees with their brilliant red, orange, and white flowers.

I must not omit to mention that dotted about the field are mounted and unmounted sepoys, with here and there a belted government servant (called a *patti-wala*, or *patta-wala*, because distinguished by a belt) — all within call — all ready to answer instantaneously to the sahib's summons, and eager to execute his behests. As to the big collector sahib himself, in the eyes of the people of his district he is every inch a king. He speaks like one, acts like one, and really has the power of one. He says to one man, "Come," and he cometh, and to another "Go," and he goeth. His title of collector gives a very inadequate idea of his real duties and authority; unless it be taken to mean that in him all the administrative functions of the district are collected and comprehended. He not only collects the revenue, but has high judicial powers, and the whole welfare of a small territory is committed to him. He superintends police, civil engineering, road-making, rural economy, municipal government, sanitation, education, every conceivable matter.

But if every collector is a small king, every Englishman in India is regarded as a petty prince. Obsequious natives watch his movements, and hang upon his words. I try to stroll about, but as I circle leisurely round the compound, attendant satellites hover about my path. I am evidently expected to develop wants of some kind or other in the course of my ramble. I ransack my store of correct Hindustani just imported from Europe for the most polite way of requesting to be left alone; but I feel as helpless as a child, and as shy as a new boy at school. Disconcerted and humiliated, I long for a little temporary obscurity, and hastily hide my head within the walls of my tent. But my tenacious followers are not to be shaken off so easily. I am conscious of being vigilantly watched through my barrier of canvas. By way of experiment I utter the magical formula, "Qui hai?" and a dusky form seems to rise out of the ground as if by magic. There he stands in an attitude of abject reverence and attention, waiting for me to issue my commands either in the best Gujarat or purest Hindustani. But I do not rise to the occasion. I am not sure whether to be exhilarated by the opportunity of bringing my knowledge of Indian languages into play, or depressed by an uncomfortable consciousness of blank inability to deliver myself of any well-turned and highly idiomatic sentence expressive of a simple desire to know the dinner-hour. Just at this juncture I hear a commanding voice call out in the distance "Khana lao." This is the collector's brief and business-like order for dinner. I repair with relief to the drawing-room and dining-room. The collector and his wife, beaming with hospitality, make me sit down at a well-appointed dinner-table. I have a French menu placed before me. I eat a dinner cooked with Parisian skill, I drink wine fit for an emperor, and am waited on by a stately butler and half a dozen stately waiters in imposing costumes, who move about with noiseless tread behind my chair, and anticipate every eccentricity of my appetite. I am evidently on enchanted ground, and can only think of Aladdin in the "Arabian Nights."

Dinner over, we sit out in the open air. The moon is shining with a luster unknown in Northern latitudes. We recline on lounging-chairs round a blazing wood fire, not sorry to wrap ourselves up in our warm plaids. I retire early to my tent and compose myself for the luxurious slumber I had anticipated. But I am too excited to sleep immediately. With difficulty I gain the borderland between consciousness and unconsciousness. What is that sound, half snort, half snuffle, close to my head? I start, and sit up. Can it be the Brahmani bull I saw just before dinner roaming about at large in full enjoyment of a kind of sacred independence? Cautiously and guardedly I open my mosquito curtains, intending to seize the nearest weapon of defense. *Clink, clink! Clank, clank!* Thank goodness, that must be the guard parading close to my tent; and sure enough there are sounds of a rush, and a chase, and a genuine bull's bellow, which gradually diminish and fade away in the distance.

Again I compose myself, but as night advances begin to be aware that a number of other strange sounds are intensifying, outside and inside my tent — croaks squeaks, grunts, chirps, hums, buzzes, whizzes, whistles, rustles, flutters, scuffles, scampers, and nibbles. Harmless sounds proceeding from harmless creatures! I reason with myself. A toad is attracted by the water in my bathroom, a rat has scented out my traveling-biscuits, mosquitoes and moths are trying to work their way through my curtains, a vampire bat is hanging from

INDIA

the roof of my tent, crickets and grasshoppers are making themselves at home on my floor. "Quite usual, of course," I say to myself, "in these hot climates, and quite to be expected!" Ah, but that hissing sound! Do not cobras hiss? The hissing subsides, and is succeeded by a melancholy moan. Is that the hooting of an owl? No! the moan has changed to a prolonged yell, increasing in an alarming manner. Yell is taken up by yell, howl by howl. Awful sounds come from all directions. Surely a number of peasants are being murdered in the adjoining fields. I am bound to get up and rush to the rescue. No, no, I remember. I saw a few jackals slinking about the camp in the evening.

Once more I try to compose myself, disgusted with my silly sensitiveness. Shriek, shriek, and a thundering roar! The midnight luggage-train is passing with a screaming whistle fifty yards from my head. At last I drop off exhausted into a troubled slumber. I dream of bulls, snakes, tigers, and railway collisions. A sound of many voices mingles with my perturbed visions. Crowds of natives are collecting for the six o'clock train two hours before sunrise. They talk, chatter, jabber, shout, and laugh to beguile the tedium of waiting. At five minutes to six the station bell rings violently, and my servant appears with my *chota haziri*, or little breakfast. I start up, dress quickly, remembering that I am expected to drink a cup of hot tea, and go out like a veteran Anglo-Indian, to "eat the air," before the sun is well up.

I conform to the spirit of the trite precept, *Si Romæ fueris, Romano vivito more;* but the collector and his wife are out before me, and are seen mounting their horses and starting off to scour the country in every direction for an hour or so. I find the morning breeze bites keenly, and am glad to walk briskly up and down the camp. I amuse myself by watching the gradual gathering of natives around the *kutchery* — two or three policemen with a prisoner; a cheerful-looking man in a red turban and white garments carrying a paper or petition of some kind; several emaciated, half-naked villagers bowed down to the dust with the weight of their poverty and grievances; a decrepit old man attended by a decrepit old woman; underlings who come to deliver reports or receive instructions; other persons who come to be advised, encouraged, scolded, or praised, and others who appear to have nothing to do, and to do it very successfully. Every one has an air of quiet resignation, and nearly all squat on the ground, awaiting the collector sahib's return with imperturbable patience. All these cases are disposed of by the collector in person after our eight o'clock breakfast.

At eleven the post comes in; that is, a running messenger, nearly naked, brings in a pile of letters on his head from the neighboring town. The collector is immersed in a sea of papers until our next meal. Meanwhile a visitor from a neighboring station makes his appearance riding on a camel, and is received in the drawing-room by the collector's wife. Then a deputation of Brahmans is seen approaching. They have come to greet me on my arrival; some of them are Pandits. A mat is spread for them in a vacant tent. They enter without shoes, make respectful salaams, and squat round me in a semicircle. I thoughtlessly shake hands with the chief Pandit, a dignified, venerable old gentleman, forgetful that the touch of a *Mleccha* (English barbarian) will entail upon him laborious purificatory ceremonies on his return to his own house. We then exchange compliments in Sanskrit, and I ask them many questions, and propound difficulties for discussion. Their fluency in talking Sanskrit surprises me, and certainly surpasses mine. We English scholars treat Sanskrit as a dead language, but here in India I am expected to speak it as if it were my mother-tongue. Once or twice I find myself floundering disastrously, but the polite Pandits help me out of my difficulties. Two hours pass away like lightning, the only drawback to general harmony being that all the Pandits try to speak at once. I find that no one thinks of terminating the visit. Native visitors never venture to depart till the sahib says plainly, "You may go." I begin to think of the most polite Sanskrit formula for breaking up my conclave, when I am saved from all awkwardness by a call to tiffin.

In the afternoon the sun acquires canicular power, the thermometer rises to eighty-two, and the temperature is about as trying as that of the hottest day of an English summer. Under the combined influence of tiffin, heat, exhilaration, humiliation, and general excitement, I am compelled to doze away an hour or two, till it is time to walk with the collector to a neighboring *baoli*, or old underground well, now unused and falling into ruins, but well worth a visit. It is more like a small subterranean tank than a well, and the descent to it is by a long flight of stone steps, surrounded by cool stone chambers built of solid masonry, and supported by handsome pillars. In Eastern countries, benevolent men who have become rich and wish to benefit their fellow-creatures before they die, construct wells and tanks, much as we build hospitals in Europe. I return with the collector to his camp as the sun sets.

So much for my first day's experiences.

THE TOWERS OF SILENCE

BY SIR MONIER MONIER-WILLIAMS

THE Parsis are descendants of the ancient Persians who were expelled from Persia by the Muhammadan conquerors, and who first settled at Surat between eleven and twelve hundred years ago. According to the last census they do not number more than seventy thousand souls, of whom about fifty thousand are found in the city of Bombay, the remaining twenty thousand in different parts of India, but chiefly in Gujarat and the Bombay Presidency. Though a mere drop in the ocean of 241,000,000 inhabitants, they form a most important and influential body of men, emulating Europeans in energy and enterprise, rivaling them in opulence, and imitating them in many of their habits. Their vernacular language is Gujarati, but nearly every adult speaks English with fluency, and English is now taught in all their schools. Their Benevolent Institution for the education of at least one thousand boys and girls is in a noble building, and is a model of good management. Their religion, as delivered in its original purity by their prophet Zoroaster, and as propounded in the Zand-Avasta, is monotheistic, or, perhaps, rather pantheistic, in spite of its philosophical dualism, and in spite of the apparent worship of fire and the elements, regarded as visible representations of the Deity. Its morality is summed up in three precepts of two words each — "Good thoughts," "Good words," "Good deeds"; of

THE TOWERS OF SILENCE

which the Parsi is constantly reminded by the triple coil of his white cotton girdle. In its origin the Parsi system is closely allied to that of the Hindu Aryans — as represented in the Veda — and has much in common with the more recent Brahmanism. Neither religion can make proselytes.

A man must be born either a Brahman or a Parsi; no power can convert him into either one or the other. One notable peculiarity, however, distinguishes Parsiism. Nothing similar to its funeral rites prevails among other nations; though the practice of exposing bodies on the tops of rocks is said to prevail among the Buddhists of Bhotan.

And truly among the interesting contrasts which everywhere meet the eye of an observant European traveler, when he first arrives at Bombay, may especially be noted the different methods adopted by the adherents of different creeds for the disposal of their dead.

There in Bombay one may see, within a short distance of each other, the Christian cemetery, the Muhammadan graveyard, the Hindu burning-ground, and the Parsi Dakhmas, or Towers of Silence. These latter are erected in a garden, on the highest point of Malabar Hill — a beautiful rising ground on the north side of Back Bay, noted for the bungalows and compounds of the European and wealthier inhabitants of Bombay scattered in every direction over its surface.

The garden is approached by a well-constructed private road, all access to which, except to Parsis, is barred by strong iron gates. I obtained leave to visit the Towers on two different occasions, and thanks to the omnipotent Sir Jamsetjee, no obstacles impeded my advance. Each time I made my appearance before the massive gates they flew open before me as if by magic. I drove rapidly through a park-like inclosure, and found the courteous Secretary of the Parsi Panchayat, Mr. Nasarwanjee Byramjee, awaiting my arrival at the entrance to the garden. On the occasion of my first visit he took me at once to the highest point in the consecrated ground, and we stood together on the terrace of the largest of the three Sagris, or Houses of Prayer, which overlook the five Towers of Silence. These Sagris are indispensable adjuncts to all Parsi burial-towers in large towns such as Bombay, Surat, and Poona, but are not found attached to them in less important localities. They are not only places of prayer, they are sanctuaries for the sacred fire, which, when once kindled and consecrated by solemn ceremonial, is fed day and night with incense and fragrant sandal by a priest appointed for the purpose, and never extinguished. It is noteworthy that the wall of the Bombay Sagri has an aperture or apertures, so arranged that the light streaming from the sacred fire, or from a consecrated oil-lamp, kept burning throughout the night, may pass through similar apertures in the parapets of the towers, and fall on the bodies lying in the interior. The view we enjoyed when standing near the principal Sagri can scarcely be surpassed by any in the world. Beneath us lay the city of Bombay partially hidden by cocoanut groves, with its beautiful bay and harbor glittering in the brilliant December light. Beyond stretched the magnificent range of the Ghauts, while immediately around us extended a garden, such as can only be seen in tropical countries. No

THE TOWERS OF SILENCE

English nobleman's garden could be better kept, and no pen could do justice to the glories of its flowering shrubs, cypresses, and palms. It seemed the very ideal, not only of a place of sacred silence, but of peaceful rest.

But what are those five circular structures which appear at intervals rising mysteriously out of the foliage? They are masses of solid masonry, massive enough to last for centuries, built of the hardest black granite, and covered with white chunam, the purity and smoothness of which are disfigured by patches of black fungus-like incrustations. Towers they scarcely deserve to be called; for the height of each is quite out of proportion to its diameter. The largest of the five may be described as an upright cylindrical stone structure, in shape and solidity not unlike a gigantic millstone, about fourteen feet high and ninety feet in diameter, resting on the ground in the midst of the garden. It is built of solid granite, except in the center, where a well, ten feet deep and about fifteen across, leads down to an excavation under the masonry, containing four drains at right angles to each other, terminated by holes filled with sand, or in some cases, with charcoal. Round the upper and outer edge of this circular structure, and completely hiding its upper surface from view, is a high stone parapet. This is constructed so as to seem to form one piece with the solid stone-work, and being, like it, covered with chunam, gives the whole erection, when viewed from the outside, the appearance of a low tower. Clearly, one great object aimed at by the Parsis in the construction of these strange depositories of their dead is solidity. We saw two or three enormous massive stones lying on the ground, which had been rejected by the

INDIA

builders simply because they contained almost invisible veins of quartz, through which it was possible that impure particles might find their way, and be carried, in the course of centuries, by percolating moisture, into the soil. Earth, water, and fire are, according to Zoroaster, sacred symbols of the wisdom, goodness, and omnipotence of the Deity, and ought never, under any circumstances, to be defiled. Especially ought every effort to be made to protect Mother Earth from the pollution which would result if putrefying corpses were allowed to accumulate in the ground. Hence the disciples of Zoroaster spare neither trouble nor expense in erecting solid and impenetrable stone platforms fourteen feet thick for the reception of their dead. The cost of erection is greatly increased by the circumstance that the Towers ought always to be placed on high hills, or in the highest situations available. I was informed by the Secretary that the largest of the five Towers was constructed at an outlay of three lakhs (300,000) of rupees.[1]

The oldest and smallest of the five was built two hundred years ago, when the Parsis first settled in Bombay, and is now only used by the Modi family, whose forefathers built it; and here the bones of many kindred generations are commingled. The next oldest was erected in 1756, and the other three during the succeeding century. A sixth Tower stands quite apart from the others. It is square in shape, and only used for persons who have suffered death for heinous crimes. The bones of convicted criminals are never allowed to mingle with those of the rest of the community.

But the strangest feature in these strange, unsightly

[1] About $97,500.

THE TOWERS OF SILENCE

structures, so incongruously intermixed with graceful cypresses and palms, exquisite shrubs, and gorgeous flowers, remains to be described. Though wholly destitute of ornament, and even of the simplest moulding, the parapet of each Tower possesses an extraordinary coping, which instantly attracts and fascinates the gaze. It is a coping formed, not of dead stone, but of living vultures. These birds, on the occasion of my visit, had settled themselves side by side in perfect order, and in a complete circle around the parapets of the Towers, with their heads pointed inwards, and so lazily did they sit there and so motionless was their whole mien that, except for their color, they might have been carved out of the stone-work.

And now as to the interior of the Towers, the upper surface of the massive granite column is divided into compartments by narrow grooved ridges of stone, radiating like the spokes of a wheel from the central well. These stone ridges form the sides of seventy-two shallow open receptacles or coffins, arranged in three concentric rings, the last of the three encircling the central well. The ridges are grooves — that is, they have narrow channels running down their whole length, which channels are connected by side ducts with the open coffins, so as to convey all moisture to the central well, and into the lower drains. The number three is emblematical of Zoroaster's three moral precepts, "Good thoughts, good words, and good deeds," and the seventy-two open stone receptacles represent the seventy-two chapters of his Yasna, a portion of the Zand-Avasta.

Each concentric circle of open stone coffins has a pathway surrounding it, the object of which is to make each receptacle accessible to the corpse-bearers. Hence there are three concentric circular pathways, the outermost of which is immediately below the parapet, and these three pathways are crossed by another conducting from the solitary door which admits the corpse-bearers from the exterior, and which must face the east, to catch the rays of the rising sun. In the outermost circle of stone coffins, which stands for "good deeds," are placed the bodies of males; in the middle, symbolizing "good words," those of females; in the inner and smallest circle, nearest the well, representing "good thoughts," those of children. Each Tower is consecrated with solemn religious ceremonies, and after its consecration no one, except the corpse-bearers, — not even a high-priest, — is allowed to enter, or to approach within thirty feet of the immediate precincts.

The first funeral I witnessed was that of a child. While I was engaged in conversation with the Secretary outside the Fire-Temple, a sudden stir among the vultures made us raise our heads. At least a hundred birds, collected round one of the Towers, began to show symptoms of excitement, while others swooped down from neighboring trees. The cause of this sudden abandonment of their previous apathy soon revealed itself. A funeral procession was seen to be approaching. However distant the house of a deceased person, and whether he be young or old, rich or poor, high or low in rank, his body is always carried to the Towers by the official corpse-bearers, the mourners walking behind. The corpse-bearers are properly divided into two classes, named Nasa-salars and Khandhias. The former alone are privileged to enter the Towers, but they are assisted

THE TOWERS OF SILENCE

in carrying the bier by the Khandhias, and they carry the dead bodies of little children without the aid of the Khandhias. As these Nasa-salars are supposed to contract impurity in the discharge of their duty, they are obliged to submit to certain social disadvantages. For instance, they are generally expected to eat apart from the rest of the community at social gatherings. They enjoy, however, a compensating advantage in being highly paid for the work they have to do.

Before they removed the body of the child from the house where its relatives were assembled, funeral prayers were recited, and the corpse was exposed to the gaze of the sacred dog.

[The dog, because of its faithfulness, is greatly loved by the Parsis, and they feed it as a sacred duty and pleasure. In olden times dead bodies were given to dogs to consume; but in these days a piece of bread is fed to the one that follows the corpse. Moreover, for three days after burial the soul of the dead man is supposed to be in great danger of being attacked by evil spirits, and from these the dog is believed to deliver him.]

Then the body, swathed in a white sheet, was placed on a curved metal trough, open at both ends, and the corpse-bearers, dressed in pure white garments, proceeded with it towards the Towers. They were followed by the mourners at a distance of at least thirty feet, in pairs, also dressed in white, and each couple joined by holding a white handkerchief between them. When the two corpse-bearers reached the path leading by a steep incline to the door of the Tower, the mourners, about eight in number, turned back and entered one of the prayer-houses. "There," said the Secretary, "they repeat certain Gathas, and pray that the spirit of the deceased may be safely transported on the fourth day after death to its final resting-place."

The Tower selected for the child's burial was one in which other members of the same family had before been laid. The two bearers speedily unlocked the door, reverently conveyed the body of the child into the interior, and, unseen by any one, laid it uncovered in one of the open stone receptacles nearest the central well. In two minutes they reappeared with the empty bier and white cloth. But scarcely had they closed the door when a dozen vultures swooped down upon the body, and were rapidly followed by flights of others. In five minutes more we saw the satiated birds fly back and lazily settle down again upon the parapet. They had left nothing behind but a skeleton. Meanwhile the bearers were seen to enter a building shaped like a huge barrel. There, as the Secretary informed me, they changed their clothes and washed themselves. Shortly afterwards we saw them come out and deposit their cast-off funeral garments on a stone receptacle near at hand. Not a thread leaves the garden, lest it should carry defilement into the city. Fresh garments were supplied at each funeral. In a fortnight, or at most four weeks, the same bearers return, and with gloved hands and implements resembling tongs, place the dry skeleton in the central well. There the bones find their last resting-place, and there the dust of whole generations of Parsis commingling is left undisturbed for centuries.

The revolting sight of the gorged vultures made me turn my back on the Towers with ill-concealed abhorrence. I asked the Secretary how it was possible to

THE TOWERS OF SILENCE

become reconciled to such a usage. His reply was nearly in the following words: "Our Prophet Zoroaster, who lived six thousand years ago, taught us to regard the elements as symbols of the Deity. Earth, fire, water, he said, ought never, under any circumstances, to be defiled by contact with putrefying flesh. Naked, he said, we came into the world, and naked we ought to leave it. But the decaying particles of our bodies should be dissipated as rapidly as possible, and in such a way that neither Mother Earth nor the beings she supports should be contaminated in the slightest degree. In fact, our Prophet was the greatest of health officers, and following his sanitary laws, we built our Towers on the tops of the hills, above all human habitations. We spare no expense in constructing them of the hardest materials, and we expose our putrescent bodies in open stone receptacles, resting on fourteen feet of solid granite, not necessarily to be consumed by vultures, but to be dissipated in the speediest manner, and without the smallest possibility of polluting the earth, or contaminating a single living being dwelling thereon. God, indeed, sends the vultures, and, as a matter of fact, these birds do their appointed work much more expeditiously than millions of insects would do, if we committed our bodies to the ground. In a sanitary point of view nothing can be more perfect than our plan. Even the rain-water which washes our skeletons is conducted by channels into purifying charcoal. Here in these five Towers rest the bones of all the Parsis that have lived in Bombay for the last two hundred years. We form a united body in life, and we are united in death. Even our leader, Sir Jamsetjee, likes to feel that when he dies he will be reduced to perfect equality with the poorest and humblest of the Parsi community."

When the Secretary had finished his defense of the Towers of Silence, I could not help thinking that however much such a system may shock our European feelings and ideas, yet our own method of interment, if regarded from a Parsi point of view, may possibly be equally revolting to Parsi sensibilities.

THE LAST VOYAGE

THE LAST VOYAGE

BY EDWIN L. WEEKS

(*American painter*, 1849-1903)

THIS crossing of the Ganges is a race with death. According to the belief of pious Hindus, the soul of even the man who has lived a worthy life may at death enter into the form of a donkey or other beast of burden, should he be so unfortunate as to die on the right bank of the stream. If he dies on the left, however, he enters directly into paradise. This is why the comrade of the old fakir lying in the boat is fanning him sedulously and trying to keep the breath of life in him until he can be laid in the shadow of some temple in Benares on the opposite shore, and so attain at once to eternal peace.

The boat is pointed toward the wide flight of steps leading up to the temple. Wooden platforms are built out over the stream for the convenience of washing and bathing. There, too, sit the devout, and, sheltered by their big straw umbrellas, they meditate hour after hour. In the center of the background is the burning-ghat. Here the bodies of the better classes are burned in the open air.

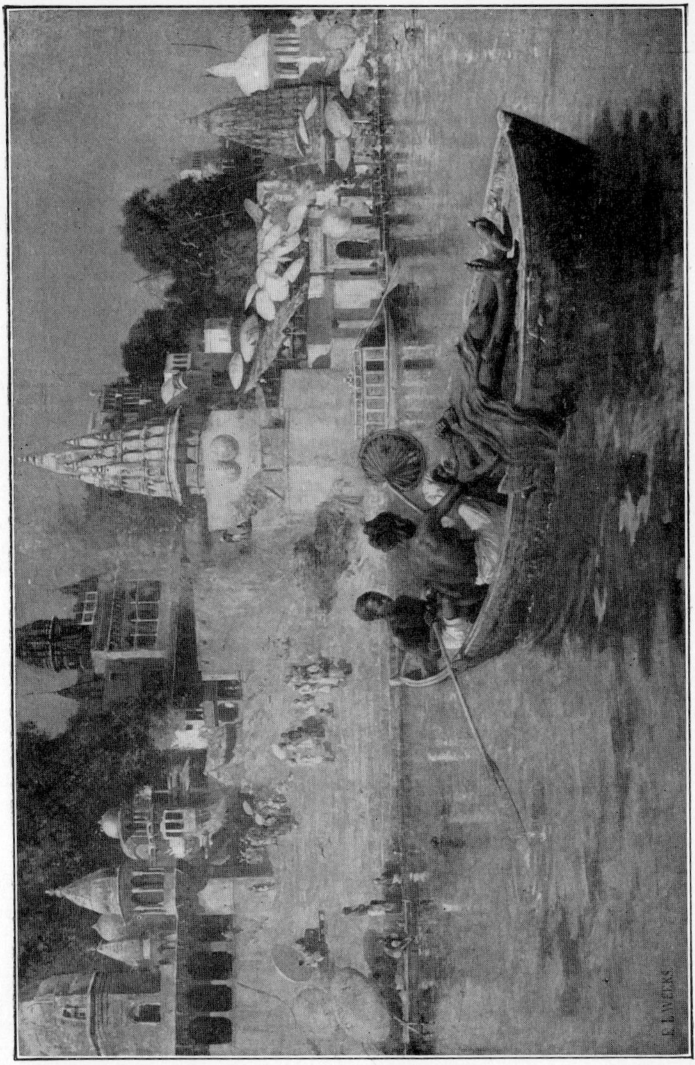
E. L. WEEKS

FABLES BY RAMAKRISHNA, A BRAHMAN SAINT OF TO-DAY

WHO KILLED THE SACRED COW?

A BRAHMAN was laying down a garden and looked after it day and night. One day a cow straying into the garden browsed away a mango sapling which was one of the most carefully watched trees of the Brahman. The Brahman, seeing the cow destroy his favorite plant, gave it such a sound beating that it died of the injuries received. The news soon spread like wildfire that the Brahman had killed the sacred animal.

Now the Brahman when taxed with the sin denied it, saying, "No, I have not killed the cow; it is my hand that has done it, and as Indra is the presiding Deity of the hand, if any one has incurred the guilt of killing the cow, it is Indra and not I."

Indra in his heaven heard all this, assumed the shape of an old Brahman, came to the owner of the garden and said, "Sir, whose garden is this?"

Brahman. — Mine.

Indra. — It is a beautiful garden. You have got a skillful gardener, for see how neatly and artistically he has planted the trees!

Brahman. — Well, sir, that is also my work. The trees are planted under my personal supervision and direction.

Indra. — Indeed! O, you are very clever. But who has laid out this road? It is very ably planned and neatly executed.

INDIA

Brahman. — All this has been done by me.

Then Indra with joined hands said, "When all these things are yours, and you take credit for all the works done in the garden, it is hard lines for poor Indra to be held responsible for the killing of the cow."

BEWARE OF THE ELEPHANT

The master said, "Everything that exists is God." The pupil understood it literally, but not in the true spirit. While he was passing through a street, he met with an elephant. The driver shouted aloud from his high place, "Move away, move away!" The pupil argued in his mind, "Why should I move away? I am God, so is the elephant also God. What fear has God of himself?" Thinking thus he did not move. At last the elephant took him up by his trunk and dashed him aside. He was severely hurt, and going back to his master he related the whole adventure. The master said, "All right, you are God. The elephant is God too, but God in the shape of the elephant-driver was warning you also from above. Why did you not pay heed to his warnings?"

LIKE FINDS LIKE

A sage was lying in a deep trance by a roadside. A thief passing by saw him and thought within himself, "This fellow, lying here, is a thief. He has been breaking into some house by night and now sleeps exhausted. The police will very soon be here to catch him, so let me escape in time." Thus thinking, he ran away. Soon after, a drunkard came upon the sage and said, "Hallo! thou hast fallen into the ditch by taking a drop too much. I am steadier than thou, and am not going to tumble." Last of all came a sage, and understanding that a great sage was in a trance, he sat down and touched him and began to rub gently his holy feet.

THE CUP OF OIL

Once upon a time conceit entered the heart of the divine sage Narada and he thought there was no greater devotee than himself. Reading his heart the Lord Sri Vishnu said, "Narada, go to such and such a place, there is a great Bhakta of mine there, and cultivate his acquaintance." Narada went there and found an agriculturist who rose early in the morning, pronounced the name of Hari only once, and taking his plough went out to till the ground all day long. At night he went to bed after pronouncing the name of Hari once more. Narada said within himself, "How can this rustic be called a lover of God? I see him busily engaged in worldly duties, and he has no signs of a pious man in him." Narada then went back to the Lord and said all he thought of his new acquaintance. The Lord said, "Narada, take this cup full of oil, go round the city and come back with it, but beware lest a drop of it fall to the ground." Narada did as he was told, and on his return he was asked, "Well, Narada, how often did you remember me in your walk?" "Not once, my Lord," replied Narada, "and how could I when I had to watch this cup brimming over with oil?" The Lord then said, "This one cup of oil did so divert your attention that even you did forget me altogether, but look to that rustic who, carrying the heavy load of a family, still remembers me twice every day."

THE CORONATION DURBAR OF 1911

BY JOHN FINNEMORE

THE first peep of dawn on the Great Day of the Durbar, the day when the King and Queen of England were to be proclaimed Emperor and Empress of India, saw vast crowds of people swarming out of Delhi to seek places in the huge amphitheater, whence they might view the wondrous scene. As the light grew, so the crowds thickened. They came from all directions, and many had come great distances, for people were there from every corner of India.

Another great throng streamed from the vast Durbar Camp, and all met on the wide plain where the King-Emperor's Durbar was to be held. Here two amphitheaters with sloping banks had been built, one small and one large. The small one was an open half circle twelve hundred feet long from point to point, and facing north.

The larger one was also a semicircle, half a mile long from point to point, facing south, looking into the small amphitheater, and partly surrounding it. This huge sweep was a vast mound of earth, covered in part with seats, and also affording standing-room for great crowds of spectators. The smaller amphitheater was roofed, and here were gathered the princes and chiefs who had come to do homage to their emperor, the officials who rule India, the guests, and the great people. The larger was unroofed, and as it swiftly filled, the sun shone on bril-

THE CORONATION DURBAR OF 1911

liant pools and masses of color, relieved by broad bands of white and cream, where a throng of Moslems had gathered in their spotless robes. At one point a great number of children had been seated, and each division wore its own color, so that the vast group looked like a lovely mosaic, picked out in many shades.

But it was upon the splendor of the smaller amphitheater that all eyes were turned, and especially upon its center, where a large, canopied platform projected. Upon this platform stood two splendid throne-chairs facing the people who sat in the small amphitheater. This was the place where the King-Emperor would receive the homage of his feudatory princes. This dais was shaded by a canopy supported by sixteen golden pillars. The roof of the canopy was of rich crimson velvet, the inner lining of beautiful and costly silks.

Yet this was not the spot where the Emperor and Empress would face their people, and be shown to all as the rulers of India. A much loftier dais had been erected midway between the two horns of the small amphitheater. This, the great throne dais, was a series of platforms, narrowing like a pyramid, until the small, topmost platform was reached, and here were placed two magnificent thrones, glittering in crimson and gold. The dais was crowned by a golden dome, and this shining splendor marked the central point of the great day and the wonderful scene. The inner part of the small amphitheater was kept clear; it was an open stretch of smooth green lawns, with wide, clean gravel paths running through them. But the open space between the throne dais and the great amphitheater was filled with masses of troops drawn from every branch of the Durbar army, and beyond the serried array of soldiery rose the huge outer ring, with its marvelous living tapestry, as if some vast and many-colored shawl had been draped along the slope of the great mound.

As the morning grew older, the seats in the small amphitheater swiftly filled, till all had taken their places, and the most splendid assembly which the world can show had been completely mustered. The radiance and beauty of this gathering of princes was marvelous. It was a sea of rich and delicate coloring, as the light played on gorgeous robes of golden and silver brocade, shot with every hue of the rainbow, and decked with magnificent jewels, with diamonds, pearls, rubies, emeralds, for which the farthest corners of ancient treasure-houses had been ransacked, for which, in other days, princes had made war upon each other and armies had met in mortal combat.

"Most of the princes wore an outer robe of honor, made of pure cloth of gold, or of cloth of gold shot with silver. Beneath this pliant metal was often a sheen of rose or green or orange, which was scarcely visible in the full sunlight, but lent an exquisite richness to the owner's lightest movement beneath the shade of the roof. Above or beneath this outer robe were the jewels of the princely house, generally ropes of filbert-shaped pearls in festoons of ten, twelve, or fifteen at a time. Besides these, necklets of diamonds, emeralds, and rubies sparkled upon head-dress and sword-hilt, upon brooch and button and shoulder-knot."

In comparison with the splendor of the native princes, the dresses of the European ladies present were quite outshone. "They seemed swallowed up beside this

THE CORONATION DURBAR OF 1911

softly moving radiance of silken and golden magnificence." The native ladies were, of course, not to be seen. At the back of the amphitheater were several inclosures guarded by close lattices; from these the wives of princes and other great native ladies watched the Durbar. At no other Durbar have so many native ladies been present, and the Delhi Durbar is noted for the elaborate arrangements which have been made to enable *zenana* ladies to see the stately pageant.

At eleven o'clock the massed bands, sixteen hundred strong, which had been performing selections of music, ceased playing. A thrill ran through every spectator; conversation ceased; all were on the alert; the Durbar was about to begin. The wild scream of bagpipes was heard in the distance, and kilted troops swung into the arena; it was a guard of honor from the Black Watch to be posted at the throne dais. The Highlanders were followed by a second guard of honor furnished by native troops — tall, soldierly Sikhs, who were posted opposite the first guard. A third guard of honor was composed of sailors and marines.

Now the troops in the arena burst into a tempest of cheers. A band of old men, some in uniform, some in civilian dress, were marching slowly into the arena. They were veterans, both British and Indian, and more than a hundred of them had fought in the Great Mutiny. Scarce had the old warriors gained their places than the troops sprang to attention: the Viceroy was coming. Into the arena swept the carriage of the man, Lord Hardinge, who rules India for the King. As the carriage drew up at the canopied dais, the whole vast assembly rose and stood in their honor, as the Governor-General

INDIA

and Lady Hardinge were conducted to their places. Now there was a short wait, and every eye was strained towards the point where the central figures of this most wonderful pageant would appear.

Suddenly the guns began to roar. It was the Royal Salute they were firing, and the King and Queen were near at hand. One hundred and one times the thunder of the saluting cannon rang out, and at every discharge six pieces were fired together. Then came in sight the bobbing white helmets of Hussars, still at the trot, and next a battery of Artillery pounded along, every scrap of steel polished till it shone out like a mirror, then more Hussars, big, splendid Sikh Lancers clad in scarlet, three tall Lifeguardsmen in glittering cuirasses, and next the Imperial carriage, which moved slowly after it entered the arena.

The Emperor and Empress now made their progress through ranks of saluting troops, and past great bodies of cheering spectators, until they gained the canopied dais. Their reception was tremendous. From the moment they came into sight until they had gained the dais the whole vast assembly was on its feet, greeting them with a thunderous roar of welcome. At the dais, they were received by the Governor-General and the great officials, and were conducted up the crimson-carpeted steps to the splendid throne-chairs. Pages of honor in most gorgeous dresses bore Their Majesties' trains, and draped them over the steps of the dais when the Emperor and Empress were seated. These boys were of the noblest blood of India, two of them rulers in their own right, the Maharajahs of Bharatpur and Jodhpur, the others being heirs of princely houses.

THE CORONATION DURBAR OF 1911

Permission was now asked of the King-Emperor that the Durbar might begin. It was given, and was signified by the shrill sweet music of a fanfare of trumpets and a tattoo on the drums — a tattoo which began with a soft mutter that swelled to a thunderous roll, and died away. Amid a profound silence the King-Emperor was seen to rise, and all remained standing while he delivered a short speech, in which he expressed his pleasure at being able to visit India, and to announce in person that he had come to the throne, and to receive for himself the loyal homage of the Indian princes. He promised to maintain Indian rights and privileges, and prayed for the welfare of the country.

When the Imperial speech was ended, the ceremony of offering homage began at once. At the head of those who approached the throne were the Governor-General and his Council, the men who govern India. Next came the ruling chiefs, led by the Nizam of Hyderabad, the Gaekwar of Baroda, the Maharajahs of Mysore and Cashmere. Then came the proud procession of the Rajput chiefs, "the gentlemen of Asia," led by the ruler of Jaipur, wearing the chief treasure of his house, the most costly necklace in India. The little ruler of Jodhpur slipped from his post among the pages beside the throne, and came in his place among the chiefs to do homage. He was resplendent in dazzling cloth of gold, and wore, hanging over his right eye, a richly jeweled miniature of his grandfather.

Another tiny chief was the boy-ruler of Bahawalpur, clad in deep crimson heavily embroidered with gold, and with waving plumes thick with flashing diamonds. So they passed in gorgeous brocades or shimmering cloth

INDIA

of gold, the chiefs of Central India, of Baluchistan, of Sikkim, far in the northern highlands. Amidst this glittering procession of princes one figure caught every eye, that of the only woman who rules in India, the Begum of Bhopal, whose presence at the Coronation in London the June before was well remembered. She was wrapped from head to foot in a robe of gold lacework, and wore a rich crown of gold filigree. As she passed, the Empress leaned a little forward to greet her.

After the ruling chiefs had gone by, the representatives of the various provinces did homage, and with each province came the native rulers, who are under the control of the province. The provinces were led by Madras, the oldest of them all, "Clive's Province," and among the native chiefs was the ruler of Travancore. The ropes upon ropes of most magnificent pearls which he wore caused quite a sensation, but then he rules over the great pearl-fisheries of the South, and for generations the divers have been seeking these treasures of the sea for his family.

Next came the Bombay Province, and among its princes was the Jam of Nawanagar, once Prince Ranjitsinghi, the "Ranji" beloved on English cricket-fields. And still they came, province after province, each with its band of feudatory chiefs, until the last of the long procession had filed by. It took forty minutes for these rulers to pass their over-lord.

Now came the moment for the great event of the day — the showing of the Emperor and Empress to their Indian subjects, the proclaiming of their Imperial rank. Up to this time, you must remember, they had been

THE CORONATION DURBAR OF 1911

seated on the smaller dais, the canopied dais which faced the small amphitheater where the princes were gathered. Here the ceremony of homage, which had just concluded, was performed. But behind Their Majesties was standing the great throne dais between the horns of the little amphitheater and facing the open arena and the great amphitheater. The mass of people on the latter had seen but little of the ceremony of homage. But now the Emperor and Empress were about to mount on high, to take their seat on the lofty throned dais, to be seen of all men.

Leaving the smaller dais, the King-Emperor led the Queen-Empress by the hand along a raised way which led to the great throned dais. A brilliant procession was formed. The trains of the magnificent robes of State worn by the King and Queen were borne by the splendidly dressed pages, and a glittering array of attendants escorted them to the high-raised thrones below the golden dome. To shield them from the strong sunshine, scarlet and gold umbrellas of State were held above their heads, and many rich emblems of authority were borne in their train.

When the throned dais was reached, the ascent was made slowly, and as it was made, the ascending group thinned, until the great figures of the day stepped on high, alone. There were four platforms to this dais, each platform being like a broad step of a pyramid. On the first platform the guard of honor was posted. On the second platform the attendants were left. On the third platform the great officers came to a stand; and now stepping up, the King-Emperor and Queen-Empress gained the fourth and topmost dais and stood there, alone, facing the vast mass of people, their faces to the North, whence they had come.

It was the climax of the day, the crowning monument of all the pomp and circumstance of the great ceremony. Alone, in most gorgeous robes, crowned with light, surrounded by a chosen and splendid retinue, Their Majesties stood out, the center of a sea of faces, the focus of the blessings and devotion of a myriad of human beings, all swayed and bent by one common impulse, as the wind sways the corn. Overhead, the rich crimson and gold of the spreading canopy, fitly framed the scene within the pavilion, and a special richly embroidered shamiana was suspended above Their Imperial Majesties' heads. The phrase of a very, very ancient Indian writer came into the mind as one watched. One could understand his quaint words that "the glory of the Emperor spread roundabout, like the sound of a great gong rung in the canopy of the skies."

Now came a veritable scene of romance, the Proclamation itself. From the massed bands in the arena a loud burst of music rang out, with bugles pealing and drums rolling their muttered thunder. From the plain beyond came faint, sweet, silver-clear notes in reply; then there rode into the arena the tall, stately figure of a herald, the Royal Standard blazoned on his tabard glittering in the sun, and attended by a native herald and twenty-four trumpeters. There were twelve British and twelve Indian trumpeters; all rode white horses, and blew loud fanfares on their silver trumpets as they rode round the arena and drew up before the throne.

Here the first herald read, in English, the Proclama-

THE CORONATION DURBAR OF 1911

tion of the Coronation of King George, and his magnificent voice rolled far across the wide arena. Then the second herald, a great Punjaub magnate, repeated the Proclamation in the native tongue. Out rang the silver trumpets once more, and the first notes of "God Save the King" swelled from the massed bands. The cannon thundered in salute, the troops in the arena presented arms, all rose and stood: the King-Emperor had been proclaimed in the Great Durbar. On roared the salute of one hundred and one guns, and in the intervals the troops beyond the amphitheater fired a *feu-de-joie*, a rattle of musketry passing down the long lines posted from the Durbar ground to the Imperial tents below the ridge.

When the thunder of the guns had died away, and the clouds of smoke had drifted over, the Viceroy advanced and announced the will and pleasure of the Emperor. The chief points were that, in token of this great day, a large sum of money should be devoted to education in India, that the Victoria Cross should be open to Indian as well as British troops, and that certain prisoners and debtors should be set free from prison. After this announcement had been made the chief herald swiftly wheeled his horse round, rose in his stirrups, waved his helmet above his head, and called for three cheers for the King-Emperor. The response was tremendous. The vast multitude gave vent to their excitement and delight in a roar of applause which rang to the very skies. Surely never yet did any monarch of the world listen to so whole-hearted a greeting in which so many people and races took part, and all owning his sway! Then the second herald called for cheers for the

Queen-Empress, and again there broke forth a wildly enthusiastic outburst of deafening acclaim. When the cheering died down within the arena, it was heard traveling away in the distance as the troops and crowds beyond the amphitheater took it up, and the volume of sound rolled down to the great camp below the ridge.

There was still one thrilling moment to come in this stirring day. When the King and Queen had left their lofty thrones and returned to the canopied dais, the King rose and made an announcement which took every one by surprise. As a rule, all that the chief figures have to say and do on such occasions is well known beforehand, and no one dreams of anything unexpected. But of the last announcement the secret had been kept in most wonderful fashion, and when the King said that the capital of India was to be transferred from Calcutta to Delhi, he was heard in open-mouthed wonder. He spoke also of changes to be made in the shaping of provinces, but these were almost lost in thinking of the great and striking decision which restored its former glory to the Mistress of India.

This thrilling announcement, made by the King-Emperor himself, formed a fitting close to a thrilling occasion. It was received as its importance demanded. "People looked at each other in swift surprise. Then in a flash the whole vast audience was aflame with enthusiasm, and deafening and prolonged cheers arose."

The Durbar was now closed, and the rulers left the arena at a walking pace, amid the cheers of the populace who hailed their Emperor and Empress with delight. Presently the magnificent procession disappeared through a western opening in the arena, and the Durbar was over. It had been a glorious and undimmed success, in which the chief actors had played their parts with a quiet, simple dignity, which won the respect and regard of all beholders.

SIAM

HISTORICAL NOTE

THE kingdom of Siam has fabulous history in generous supply, but little that is authentic before the middle of the fourteenth century. There is a tradition that the Siamese kings were descended from Buddha, and Buddhism is the religion of the country; but when or how it was introduced, no one can say. After 1350, there were two centuries of peace, then two centuries of warfare. Finally, Burma seized the land; then China. In 1782, the country fell into the hands of a Chinese general, Yaut Fa, from whom succeeding kings are descended. By the encroachments of France on the east and England on the northwest and southwest, the Siamese territories have been somewhat narrowed; and the country is now recognized as divided into two "spheres of influence," one under the control of France, the other under that of England.

THE RECEPTION OF A WHITE ELEPHANT

BY MRS. A. H. LEONOWENS

Almost all white animals are held in reverence by the Siamese, because they were once superior human beings, and the white elephant, in particular, is supposed to be animated by the spirit of some king or hero. Having once been a great man, he is thought to be familiar with the dangers that surround the great, and to know what is best and safest for those whose condition in all respects was once his own. He is hence supposed to avert national calamity, and bring prosperity and peace to a people.

From the earliest times the kings of Siam and Burmah have anxiously sought for the white elephant, and having had the rare fortune to procure one, have loaded it with gifts and dignities, as though it were a conscious favorite of the throne. When the governor of a province of Siam is notified of the appearance of a white elephant within his bailiwick, he immediately commands that prayers and offerings shall be made in all the temples, while he sends out a formidable expedition of hunters and slaves to take the precious beast, and bring it in in triumph. As soon as he is informed of its capture, a special messenger is dispatched to inform the king of its sex, probable age, size, complexion, deportment, looks, and ways; and in the presence of His Majesty this bearer of glorious tidings undergoes the painfully pleasant operation of having his mouth, ears, and nostrils stuffed with gold. Especially is the lucky wight — perhaps some half-wild woodsman — who was first to spy the illustrious monster munificently rewarded. Orders are promptly issued to the woons and wongses of the several districts through which he must pass to prepare to receive him royally, and a wide path is cut for him through the forests he must traverse on his way to the capital. Wherever he rests he is sumptuously entertained, and everywhere he is escorted and served by a host of attendants, who sing, dance, play upon instruments, until he reaches the banks of the Meinam, where a great floating palace of wood, surmounted by a gorgeous roof and hung with crimson curtains, awaits him. The roof is literally thatched with flowers, ingeniously arranged so as to form symbols and mottoes, which the superior beast is supposed to decipher with ease. The floor of this splendid float is laid with gilt matting, curiously woven, in the center of which his four-footed lordship is installed in state, surrounded by an obsequious and enraptured crowd of mere bipeds, who bathe him, perfume him, fan him, feed him, sing and play to him, flatter him. His food consists of the finest herbs, the tenderest grass, the sweetest sugar-cane, the mellowest plantains, the brownest cakes of wheat, served on huge trays of gold and silver; and his drink is perfumed with the fragrant flower of the *dok mallee*, the large native jessamine.

Thus, in more than princely state, he is floated down the river to a point within seventy miles of the capital, where the king and his court, all the chief personages of the kingdom, and a multitude of priests, both Buddhist and Brahmin, accompanied by troops of players and

THE RECEPTION OF A WHITE ELEPHANT

musicians, come out to meet him, and conduct him with all the honors to his stable palace. A great number of cords and ropes of all qualities and lengths are attached to the raft, those in the center being of fine silk (figuratively, "spun from a spider's web"). These are for the king and his noble retinue, who with their own hands make them fast to their gilded barges; the rest are secured to the great fleet of lesser boats. And so, with shouts of joy, beating of drums, blare of trumpets, boom of cannon, a hallelujah of music, and various splendid revelry, the great Chang Phoouk is conducted in triumph to the capital.

Here, in a pavilion, temporary but very beautiful, he is welcomed with imposing ceremonies by the custodians of the palace and the principal personages of the royal household. The king, his courtiers, and the chief priests being gathered round him, thanksgiving is offered up; and then the lordly beast is knighted, after the ancient manner of the Buddhists, by pouring upon his forehead consecrated water from a chank-shell.

The titles reserved for the Chang Phoouk vary according to the purity of the complexion (for these favored creatures are rarely true albinos, — salmon or flesh-color being the nearest approach to white in almost all the historic "white elephants" of the courts of Burmah and Siam) and the sex; for though one naturally has recourse to the masculine pronoun in writing of a transmigrated prince or warrior, it often happens that prince or warrior has, in the medlied mask of metempsychosis, assumed a female form. Such, in fact, was the case with the stately occupant of the stable palace at the court of Maha Mongkut; and she was distinguished by the high-sounding appellation of Maa Phya Seri Wongsah Ditsarah Krasaat,—"August and Glorious Mother, Descendant of Kings and Heroes."

For seven or nine days, according to certain traditions, the Chang Phoouk is fêted at the temporary pavilion, and entertained with a variety of dramatic performances; and these days are observed as a general holiday throughout the land. At the expiration of this period he is conducted with great pomp to his sumptuous quarters within the precincts of the first king's palace, where he is received by his own court of officers, attendants, and slaves, who install him in his fine lodgings, and at once proceed to robe and decorate him. First, the court jeweler rings his tremendous tusks with massive gold, crowns him with a diadem of beaten gold of perfect purity and adorns his burly neck with heavy golden chains. Next his attendants robe him in a superb velvet cloak of purple, fringed with scarlet and gold; and then his court prostrate themselves around him and offer him royal homage.

When his lordship would refresh his portly person in the bath, an officer of high rank shelters his noble head with a great umbrella of crimson and gold, while others wave golden fans before him. On these occasions he is invariably preceded by musicians, who announce his approach with cheerful minstrelsy and songs.

If he falls ill, the king's own leech prescribes for him, and the chief priests repair daily to his palace to pray for his safe deliverance and sprinkle him with consecrated waters and anoint him with consecrated oils. Should he die, all Siam is bereaved, and the nation, as one man, goes into mourning for him. But his body is not burned;

THE RECEPTION OF A WHITE ELEPHANT

only his brains and heart are thought worthy of that last and highest honor. The carcass, shrouded in fine white linen and laid on a bier, is carried down the river with much wailing and many mournful dirges, to be thrown into the Gulf of Siam.

In 1862, a magnificent white — or, rather, salmon-colored — elephant was "bagged," and preparations on a gorgeous scale were made to receive him. A temporary pavilion of extraordinary splendor sprang up as if by magic before the eastern gate of the palace; and the whole nation was wild with joy; when suddenly came awful tidings, — he had died!

No man dared tell the king. But the Kralahome — that man of prompt expedients and unfailing presence of mind — commanded that the preparation should cease instantly, and that the building should vanish with the builders. In the evening His Majesty came forth as usual to exult in the glorious work. What was his astonishment to find no vestige of the splendid structure that had been so nearly completed the night before. He turned, bewildered, to his courtiers, to demand an explanation, when suddenly the terrible truth flashed into his mind. With a cry of pain he sank down upon a stone, and gave vent to an hysterical passion of tears; but was presently consoled by one of his children, who, carefully prompted in his part, knelt before him and said: "Weep not, O my father! The stranger lord may have left us but for a time." The stranger lord, fatally pampered, had succumbed to astonishment and indigestion.

A few days after the mournful event the king read to me a curious description of the defunct monster, and showed me parts of his skin preserved, and his tusks, which in size and whiteness surpassed the finest I had ever seen. "His [that is, the elephant's] eyes were light blue, surrounded by salmon-color; his hair fine, soft, and white; his complexion pinkish white; his tusks like long pearls; his ears like silver shields; his trunk like a comet's tail; his legs like the feet of the skies; his tread like the sound of thunder; his looks full of meditation; his expression full of tenderness; his voice the voice of a mighty warrior; and his bearing that of an illustrious monarch."

That was a terrible affliction, to the people not less than to the king.

On all occasions of state, — court receptions, for example, — the white elephant, gorgeously arrayed, is stationed on the right of the inner gate of the palace, and forms an indispensable as well as a conspicuous figure of the picture.

When the Siamese ambassadors returned from England, the chief of the embassy — a man remarkable for his learning and the purity of his character, who was also first cousin to the Supreme King — published a quaint pamphlet, describing England and her people, their manners and customs and dwellings, with a very particular report of the presentation of the embassy at court. Speaking of the personal appearance of Queen Victoria, he says: "One cannot but be struck with the aspect of the august Queen of England, or fail to observe that she must be of pure descent from a race of goodly and warlike kings and rulers of the earth, in that her eyes, complexion, and above all her bearing, are those of a beautiful and majestic white elephant."

THE WHITE ELEPHANT

BY HEINRICH HEINE

Great Mashawasant, the Siam King,
Has half of India under his wing,
Twelve kings, with the Great Mogul, obey
His rule, and acknowledge his sovereign sway.

Each year, with banner, trumpet, and drum,
To Siam the trains with the tribute come;
Many thousand camels, with backs piled high
With the costliest treasures of earth, draw nigh.

When the camels he sees with their heavy piles,
The soul of the king in secret smiles;
But in public in truth he always deplores
That his storehouses serve not to hold all his stores.

Yet these storehouses all are so lofty and spacious,
So full of magnificence, so capacious,
The reality's splendor surpasses in glory
The Arabian Nights' most wondrous story.

The "Castle of Indra" call they the hall,
In which are displayed the deities all,
The golden images, chiseled with care,
And all incrusted with jewels so rare.

Full thirty thousand their numbers are:
Their ugliness passes description far;

SIAM

A compound of men and animals dread,
With many a hand and many a head.

In the "Hall of Purple" one wonderingly sees
Some thirteen hundred coral trees,
As big as palms, a singular sight,
With spiral branches, a forest bright.

The floor of the purest crystal is made,
And all the trees are in it displayed,
While pheasants of glittering plumage gay
Strut up and down in a dignified way.

The ape on which the monarch doth dote
A ribbon of silk wears round his throat,
Whence hangs the key that opens the hall
Which people the "Chamber of Silence" call.

All kinds of jewels of value high
All over the ground here scattered lie
Like common peas, with diamonds rare,
That in size with the egg of a fowl compare.

On sacks that stuffed with pearls appear
The monarch is wont to stretch himself here;
The ape lies down by the monarch proud,
And both of them slumber and snore aloud.

But the king's most precious, costly treasure,
His happiness, his soul's first pleasure,
The joy and the pride of the Mahawasant,
Is truly his snow-white elephant.

THE WHITE ELEPHANT

As a home for a guest so highly respected
A splendid palace the king has erected;
Gay lotos-headed columns uphold
Its roof, all covered with plates of gold.

Three hundred heralds stand at the gate,
As the elephant's guard of honor to wait;
And kneeling down with low-bent back
There serve him a hundred eunuchs black.

For his proboscis the daintiest meat
On golden dishes they bring him to eat;
From silver buckets he drinks his wine,
Well seasoned with spices and sweet and fine.

With perfumes they rub him, and otto of roses,
On his head a chaplet of flowers reposes,
The richest shawls that are made in the East
As carpets serve for the dignified beast.

AFGHANISTAN

HISTORICAL NOTE

AFGHANISTAN was conquered by Alexander the Great, and from his time until the middle of the eighteenth century, indeed, almost to the present day, it has been constantly changing masters. The conqueror of the eighteenth century, Nadir Shah, was assassinated, and succeeded by one of his officers. Since that time the country has been independent, but her annals have been a story of anarchy, revolt, and warfare. In 1838, England restored an exiled shah. The result was a bitter war between the Afghans and the British, followed a few years later by a second struggle, in which the British were successful. An Afghan revolt was put down by General Roberts's march to Kandahar, which won for him his title of Lord Roberts of Kandahar. Since then the land had been practically under British control.

"THE HILL OF BONES"

[1878]

BY REV. ARTHUR MALE

[IN 1838 war broke out between Afghanistan and England. Four years later, the British army was destroyed while retreating through Kurd-Kabul Pass. The visit to the "Hill of Bones," described in the text, took place in 1878, during a second war.

The Editor.]

WHILE we lay at Gundamuk it was but natural that our thoughts often went back to the sad episodes of the former Afghan campaign of 1841 and 1842. Not very far from our camp — perhaps four or five miles — the people of the country still pointed out the remains of "Burnes Sahib's" camp, a few mud walls standing to mark the spot where our forces, when going up to Kabul, were *cantoned* for a while. Among them were Sir Alexander Burnes, Macnaughten, Elphinstone, and others. Then, after a period of garrison in Kabul, there came the sudden and fierce rising of November 2, 1841, when Macnaughten was treacherously slain while holding a parley with Akbar Khan in view of the British garrison who were on the walls of the city. After this came the episode of retreat. The force, diminished in number and weakened by sickness, were promised safe conduct through the passes if they would give up the city they had defended so long and retire to India. They did so, or essayed to do so. And then the arch-traitor, Akbar

AFGHANISTAN

Khan, who knew no honor, lined the cliffs en route with his overwhelming numbers. They hung upon the flanks of the retreating army, harrying them, and cutting off the stragglers day after day. Some sixteen thousand souls, of whom perhaps forty-five hundred were fighting men, the rest servants and camp-followers, left Kabul. On they struggled with desperate valor, almost at the outset having to abandon their baggage. It was winter-time, and the snow lay thickly on the road. Thus while the multitudes dropped under the fire which ever poured upon them from the high rocks which lined the Pass, many, very many, perished from the cold, lying down at night in their bed of snow, and rising not again at morning dawn. At last, when bullet, sword, and cold had ended the struggles of almost all the native soldiers and camp-followers, the miserable remnant of the force, consisting mainly of men of the Forty-fourth, a few Artillery men, and a score or so of officers, and numbering, all told, barely a hundred fighting men, with two or three hundred camp-followers, reached the vicinity of Gundamuk, or at least a spot some eight miles from our present camp. The day before they had crossed the stream called the Surkh Ab, or "Red Water," fighting hand-to-hand with their foe for the passage. And now what more could they do? Strength was gone, and hope was almost dead. Six officers were chosen and sent to ride as hard as their miserable ponies would carry them to Jellalabad, some thirty-five miles off, where Sale and Havelock were gallantly holding out, to seek help. It was a forlorn hope, for the journey was fraught with fearful peril. How could six worn-out men ever anticipate a safe ride through a wild country swarming with fierce tribesmen.

THE HILL OF BONES

But they started. Meanwhile the handful of fighting men who remained gathered on the summit of a round-topped hill. And there, a desperate band, they resolved to fight, and, if no help came, to die, selling their lives as dearly as possible. And they did it. Standing shoulder to shoulder in old heroic British fashion, surrounded by a perfect sea of Ghilzai tribesmen, and the fierce warriors of Akbar, they held their foe at bay till all their ammunition was gone. Then the waves of the sea closed in and swept on and over them, for every man had fallen in his tracks.

And what about the forlorn hope? For a while fortune seemed to favor them. Half the distance had been accomplished without molestation. But at the village of Futtehabad (nigh unto the spot of our fight with the Kujianis a few weeks since) they turned aside — fatal mistake — and sought milk and refreshment from some of the villages. It was given. But while partaking of it, all unsuspicious of treachery, the false villagers attacked them; and though they defended themselves with desperate courage, five were slain. One only, Dr. Brydon, an army surgeon, escaped. Fighting his way through the traitors, he gained the open path, and though pursued for many a mile, with his broken sword he managed to beat off his assailants and then distance them.

About midday on January 13, 1842, a sentry pacing the walls of Jellalabad called aloud that he saw a mounted man slowly wending his way across the barren plain towards the city. Many glasses were leveled, and they could just discern a European supporting himself on a miserable country pony, faint with travel, and perhaps wounded too. Who could he be? they asked one

AFGHANISTAN

another, as a thrill passed over them; for the very sight of the solitary stranger seemed to bring them forebodings of disaster. Slowly they led him through the city gate, faint, bleeding, covered with wounds, grasping still the fragment of sword which had been shattered in the conflict for life. It was Brydon, the sole survivor of the force which had left Kabul to return to India, and, with the exception of the hostages who were in captivity, the only living remnant of Elphinstone's army. Riding over the very same pathway as poor Brydon, when I was going back to India, how vividly did I recall Miss Thompson's marvelous picture, where with such strange fidelity she depicts the weary, wounded man clinging to his worn-out, gasping pony. It is the same path today, as you look out from the Kabul gate of Peshawar, with the selfsame solitary tree standing at the corner where it bends away to the left.

With the various remembrances of this old dark page in our history all around us, it was not strange that some of us desired to see a little more closely the very spots where some of these events had taken place.

One morning accordingly two of us rode out beyond our lines, and towards the Jugdullok Pass, accompanied by an old Kujiani who knew the country around, and every spot of interest. The old fellow professed to remember well the time of the last campaign from 1839 to 1842. The names of our leaders then were familiar to him, Pollock and Sale, Elphinstone, Burnes, and Macnaughten. For six miles he led us across the stony plain, and by tortuous hill-paths, until we came out upon a broad stretch of country which led away, we could see, to the entrance of one of the passes. And here on the

THE HILL OF BONES

flat ground, the hills away in the distance, and no cover or protection near, we found the remains of the old mud walls, and even the remnants of huts, which had once formed part of the cantonments of Burnes. He was our envoy to the Court of Kabul, and a most distinguished Oriental scholar and traveler. But for some time before proceeding to the capital he had been permanently "cantoned" in this spot. With sad interest we moved along the broken walls, and tried to imagine the scene of thirty-nine years ago, when in this spot the little European force were located and lived, surrounded by tribes who were at any rate hostile in heart, aliens in a strange land.

But there was more than this to see, and so we turned to our old guide, one of whose accomplishments, very important to us, was that he could understand a little Hindustani.

"Larai ki jagah kahan hai, buddha?" "Where is the place of fight, old man?" said we. And the old man said not a word, but pointing with his finger forward, silently led us on. Away to our right, perhaps two miles off, we could see a conical hill rising out of the plain, round-topped and solitary. The hill ranges were around it, but distant. It stood alone, a monument itself! We did not say much as we neared it. Both my companion and myself were thinking of the old tragedy and its consummation on that hilltop. We thought of the devoted band who had struggled down the passes from Kabul, fighting every inch of the way; men, women, camp-followers, and soldiers dropping in their tracks under murderous fire or savage attack; or perchance lying down at night, weary of life, to rise no more. We thought of them, — a diminished band, indeed, — sixteen thousand souls reduced to about five hundred; forty-five hundred soldiers to a bare hundred — reaching the river four miles ahead and finding the ford and bridge barred by an overwhelming host of savage foes. But they cut their way through, and came on — thus far. And here they paused awhile, and then climbed the hill yonder to die. We could see it all again after a lapse of thirty-seven years. The little band toiling with painful effort up the hillside, and forming up on the top shoulder to shoulder — at bay. The fierce tribesmen gathering round, closing in more and more, the band of heroes lessening moment by moment; and then the great wave of the human sea around surging over them and burying them away out of sight unshaken in discipline, undaunted in spirit, faithful unto death!

We reached the bottom of the hill. My companion, who had brought his photographic apparatus with him, and was anxious to get a view first from the base, waited to do it, the Kujiani with him. I slowly ascended; my horse, which belonged to a hill breed, climbing like a cat among the big rocks that covered the side. Soon I reached the summit, and prepared to look upon the very spot where our gallant fellows had made their death stand. There it must be, I thought, towards the center. And I made my way towards it. The summit of the hill was of fairly large extent; but as I came nearer the middle, I saw that there the surface seemed strangely white. What could it be? I hurried forward; and to my horror there I saw gathered together in a great heap the skeleton bones of that heroic band. There, where the men had fallen, their remains had been lying for thirty-seven long years, bleached by the sun, and swept by

THE HILL OF BONES

every tempest which had broken on that hilltop. It was a ghastly sight. But it was not the ghastliness so much as the sadness of it that struck me most of all. Alien feet had trodden around that hill summit; the wild shepherds who tended their mountain sheep and goats, Kujiani and Ghilzai tribesmen, all had looked upon that open sepulcher; but never before had foot of brother Englishman been there, nor had friendly eyes lighted on the unburied remains. Here were truly the "relics of a lost army." I shouted to my companion, who was still at the bottom of the hill manipulating his camera, and waiting for a peep of brighter light to get a good view.

The day had been gloomy, in consonance, I seemed to feel, with the sad sight on which I had been gazing. I understood now why our Kujiani friend had been quite content to stay below, while I went up alone. He knew what I should find; but he had told us nothing to prepare us for the sight. In response to my shout, Burke, leaving his camera, came hastily up, and looked with horror and amazement on what again revealed itself, as we together came to the center of the hill. They were truly the remains of our poor fellows. Probably when Pollock's avenging force, after relieving the "Illustrious Garrison" at Jellalabad, had marched on up the passes towards Kabul, they had found the bodies here and had buried them out of sight by covering them with a great stone cairn. This, no doubt, had been subsequently rudely cast down by the Afghans belonging to the tribes around, and the bodies left shamefully exposed; the Mussulman creed allowing them to desecrate the place of sepulcher, but not the dead bodies themselves. This was the general opinion. And, indeed, in connection with our own campaign we had cases where graves in which we had laid some of our men to rest were rudely broken open, — outrage enough, indeed, — but the remains within not otherwise disturbed.

Burke brought up his camera, and from the top of a neighboring height took a picture of the "Hill of Bones," as it afterward came to be called. It was a gloomy, weird picture enough! All around were the mountain spurs reaching down to the barren plain, the furthermost peaks still capped with snow. Yonder away the dark entrance to the Jugdullok Pass. And here in the middle the one solitary round-topped hill — monument and grave at once. Two human forms could be discerned, myself and the old Kujiani, who had now been induced to come up too; we two looking down sadly on the gathered bones of the brave men, as they lay resting on God's earth, and looking up into the face of God's heaven.

When we returned to camp we unfolded the tale of what we had found, and arrangements were made soon after for the reverent burial of the bones. A detachment was sent out, and over the great grave they raised a tall obelisk, which no doubt still marks the spot.

PERSIA

I
THE MIGHTY EMPIRE

HISTORICAL NOTE

MANY centuries ago the Aryans made their way to the countries known later as Media and Persia. At first the Medes were by far the stronger. They struggled fiercely with the Assyrians of Mesopotamia, and finally succeeded, with the aid of the Babylonians, in overcoming them and burning their capital, Nineveh. The Persians had been under the sway of the Medes, but they revolted against their rulers, and Cyrus, the Persian king, became sovereign of the united nations. His kingdom stretched from the Indus River to the Mediterranean Sea, and from the Caspian Sea to the Persian Gulf. Vast as it was, it did not content his son Cambyses, and before long Phœnicia, Egypt, and all northern Africa were added to his dominions. His successor Darius also longed for wider territories. He overcame northwestern India, and twice he attempted to invade Greece. On his first invasion, his ships were shattered in a storm; on the second, he was utterly routed at Marathon. His son Xerxes also attempted to conquer Greece, and at first he met with success. He overcame the Spartans at Thermopylæ and tore down Athens. This was the end of his good fortune. His fleet was destroyed, and he returned to Persia. His general, Mardonius, remained, but he was routed in a furious battle at Platæa.

SOHRAB'S LAST CONTEST

BY MATTHEW ARNOLD

[OF all the heroes of the Persian legends, the greatest was Rustum. His exploits were numerous enough to have needed the work of at least a score of champions for more than a score of years. While he was away from his own country, his wife bore him a son, Sohrab; but lest Rustum should send for the boy to train him to become a warrior, she bade a messenger say to her husband that their child was a girl.

This was how it came to pass, some years later, that Rustum and Sohrab, being on opposite sides, met in single combat, wherein Sohrab received his death wound. He declares: —

"The mighty Rustum shall avenge my death,
My father, whom I seek through all the world!
He shall avenge my death, and punish thee."

The Editor.]

AND he saw that youth,
Of age and looks to be his own dear son,
Piteous and lovely, lying on the sand,
Like some rich hyacinth which by the scythe
Of an unskillful gardener has been cut,
Mowing the garden grass-plots near its bed,
And lies, a fragrant tower of purple bloom,
On the mown, dying grass: so Sohrab lay,
Lovely in death, upon the common sand.
And Rustum gaz'd on him with grief, and said: —
"O Sohrab, thou indeed art such a son
Whom Rustum, wert thou his, might well have lov'd.

PERSIA

Yet here thou errest, Sohrab, or else men
Have told thee false: thou art not Rustum's son,
For Rustum had no son; one child he had,
But one: a girl who with her mother now
Plies some light female task, nor dreams of us;
Of us she dreams not, nor of wounds, nor war."

  But Sohrab answer'd him in wrath; for now
The anguish of the deep-fix'd spear grew fierce,
And he desir'd to draw forth the steel,
And let the blood flow free, and so to die;
But first he would convince his stubborn foe.
And, rising sternly on one arm, he said: —
"Man, who art thou who dost deny my words?
Truth sits upon the lips of dying men;
And falsehood, while I liv'd, was far from mine.
I tell thee, prick'd upon this arm I bear
That seal which Rustum to my mother gave,
That she might prick it on the babe she bore."

  He spoke; and all the blood left Rustum's cheeks,
And his knees totter'd, and he smote his hand
Against his breast, his heavy-mailed hand,
That the hard iron corslet clank'd aloud;
And to his heart he press'd the other hand,
And in a hollow voice he spake, and said: —
"Sohrab, that were a proof which could not lie!
If thou show this, then art thou Rustum's son."

  Then, with weak hasty fingers, Sohrab loos'd
His belt, and near the shoulder bar'd his arm,
And show'd a sign in faint vermilion points
Prick'd: as a cunning workman, in Pekin,
Pricks with vermilion some clear porcelain vase,
An emperor's gift; at early morn he paints,

SOHRAB'S LAST CONTEST

And all day long; and, when night comes, the lamp
Lights up his studious forehead and thin hands:
So delicately prick'd the sign appear'd
On Sohrab's arm, the sign of Rustum's seal.
It was that griffin, which of old rear'd Zal,
Rustum's great father, whom they left to die,
A helpless babe, among the mountain-rocks;
Him that kind creature found, and rear'd, and lov'd:
Then Rustum took it for his glorious sign.
And Sohrab bar'd that image on his arm,
And himself scann'd it long with mournful eyes,
And then he touch'd it with his hand, and said: —

"How say'st thou? Is that sign the proper sign
Of Rustum's son, or of some other man's?"

He spoke; but Rustum gaz'd, and gaz'd, and stood
Speechless; and then he utter'd one sharp cry:
O boy — thy father! and his voice chok'd there.
And then a dark cloud pass'd before his eyes,
And his head swam, and he sank down to earth.
But Sohrab crawl'd to where he lay, and cast
His arms about his neck, and kiss'd his lips,
And with fond faltering fingers strok'd his cheeks,
Trying to call him back to life; and life
Came back to Rustum: and he op'd his eyes,
And they stood wide with horror; and he seiz'd
In both his hands the dust which lay around,
And threw it on his head, and smirch'd his hair,
His hair, and face, and beard, and glittering arms;
And strong convulsive groanings shook his breast,
And his sobs chok'd him; and he clutch'd his sword,
To draw it, and forever let life out.
But Sohrab saw his thought, and held his hands,

PERSIA

And with a soothing voice he spake, and said: —
 "Father, forbear! for I but meet to-day
The doom which at my birth was written down
In Heaven; and thou art Heaven's unconscious hand.
Surely my heart cried out that it was thou,
When first I saw thee; and thy heart spoke too,
I know it: but fate trod those promptings down
Under its iron heel; fate, fate engag'd
The strife, and hurl'd me on my father's spear.
But let us speak no more of this: I find
My father; let me feel that I have found!
Come, sit beside me on this sand, and take
My head betwixt thy hands, and kiss my cheeks,
And wash them with thy tears, and say: *My son!*
Quick! quick! for number'd are my sands of life,
And swift; for like the lightning to this field
I came, and like the wind I go away:
Sudden, and swift, and like a passing wind.
But it was writ in Heaven that this should be."

 So said he, and his voice releas'd the heart
Of Rustum, and his tears broke forth: he cast
His arms round his son's neck, and wept aloud,
And kiss'd him. And awe fell on both the hosts,
When they saw Rustum's grief; and Ruksh, the horse,
With his head bowing to the ground, and mane
Sweeping the dust, came near, and in mute woe
First to the one, then to the other, mov'd
His head, as if inquiring what their grief
Might mean; and from his dark compassionate eyes,
The big warm tears roll'd down, and cak'd the sand.
But Rustum chid him with stern voice, and said: —

 "Ruksh, now thou grievest; but, O Ruksh, thy feet

SOHRAB'S LAST CONTEST

Should first have rotted on their nimble joints,
Or e'er they brought thy master to this field!"
　　But Sohrab look'd upon the horse and said: —
"Is this, then, Ruksh? How often, in past days,
My mother told me of thee, thou brave steed,
My terrible father's terrible horse! and said
That I should one day find thy lord and thee.
Come, let me lay my hand upon thy mane!
O Ruksh, thou art more fortunate than I:
For thou hast gone where I shall never go,
And snuff'd the breezes of my father's home.
And thou hast trod the sands of Seistan,
And seen the River of Helmund, and the Lake
Of Zirrah; and the aged Zal himself
Has often strok'd thy neck, and given thee food,
Corn in a golden platter, soak'd with wine,
And said: *O Ruksh, bear Rustum well!* — but I
Have never known my grandsire's furrow'd face,
Nor seen his lofty house in Seistan,
Nor slak'd my thirst at the clear Helmund stream
But lodg'd among my father's foes, and seen
Afrasiab's cities only: Samarcand,
Bokhara, and lone Khiva in the waste,
And the black Toorkmun tents; and only drunk
The desert rivers: Moorghab and Tejend,
Kohik, and where the Kalmuks feed their sheep,
The northern Sir; and this great Oxus stream,
The yellow Oxus, by whose brink I die."
　　Then, with a heavy groan, Rustum bewail'd: —
"Oh, that its waves were flowing over me!
Oh, that I saw its grains of yellow silt
Roll tumbling in the current o'er my head!"

PERSIA

But, with a grave mild voice, Sohrab replied: —
"Desire not that, my father! thou must live:
For some are born to do great deeds, and live,
As some are born to be obscur'd, and die.
Do thou the deeds I die too young to do,
And reap a second glory in thine age:
Thou art my father, and thy gain is mine.
But come: thou seest this great host of men
Which follow me; I pray thee, slay not these!
Let me entreat for them: what have they done?
They follow'd me, my hope, my fame, my star.
Let them all cross the Oxus back in peace.
But me thou must bear hence, not send with them,
But carry me with thee to Seistan,
And place me on a bed, and mourn for me;
Thou, and the snow-hair'd Zal, and all thy friends.
And thou must lay me in that lovely earth,
And heap a stately mound above my bones,
And plant a far-seen pillar over all,
That so the passing horseman on the waste
May see my tomb a great way off, and cry:
*Sohrab, the mighty Rustum's son, lies there,
Whom his great father did in ignorance kill!*
And I be not forgotten in my grave."

And, with a mournful voice, Rustum replied: —
"Fear not! as thou hast said, Sohrab, my son,
So shall it be: for I will burn my tents,
And quit the host, and bear thee hence with me,
And carry thee away to Seistan,
And place thee on a bed, and mourn for thee,
With the snow-headed Zal, and all my friends.
And I will lay thee in that lovely earth,

SOHRAB'S LAST CONTEST

And heap a stately mound above thy bones,
And plant a far-seen pillar over all,
And men shall not forget thee in thy grave.
And I will spare thy host; yea, let them go:
Let them all cross the Oxus back in peace.
What should I do with slaying any more?
For would that all that I have ever slain
Might be once more alive: my bitterest foes,
And they who were call'd champions in their time,
And through whose death I won that fame I have!
And I were nothing but a common man,
A poor, mean soldier, and without renown,
So thou mightest live too, my son, my son!
Or rather would that I, even I myself,
Might now be lying on this bloody sand,
Near death, and by an ignorant stroke of thine,
Not thou of mine! and I might die, not thou,
And I, not thou, be borne to Seistan;
And Zal might weep above my grave, not thine,
And say: *O son, I weep thee not too sore,*
For willingly, I know, thou met'st thine end!
But now in blood and battles was my youth,
And full of blood and battles is my age;
And I shall never end this life of blood."
    Then, at the point of death, Sohrab replied: —
"A life of blood indeed, thou dreadful man!
But thou shalt yet have peace; only not now,
Not yet: but thou shalt have it on that day,
When thou shalt sail in a high-masted ship,
Thou and the other peers of Kai Khosroo,
Returning home over the salt blue sea,
From laying thy dear master in his grave."

PERSIA

And Rustum gaz'd in Sohrab's face, and said: —
"Soon be that day, my son, and deep that sea!
Till then, if fate so wills, let me endure."

He spoke; and Sohrab smil'd on him, and took
The spear, and drew it from his side, and eas'd
His wound's imperious anguish; but the blood
Came welling from the open gash, and life
Flow'd with the stream; all down his cold white side
The crimson torrent ran, dim now and soil'd,
Like the soil'd tissue of white violets
Left, freshly gather'd, on their native bank,
By children whom their nurses call with haste
Indoors from the sun's eye; his head droop'd low,
His limbs grew slack; motionless, white, he lay,
White, with eyes clos'd; only when heavy gasps,
Deep heavy gasps, quivering through all his frame,
Convuls'd him back to life, he open'd them,
And fix'd them feebly on his father's face;
Till now all strength was ebb'd: and from his limbs
Unwillingly the spirit fled away,
Regretting the warm mansion which it left,
And youth, and bloom, and this delightful world.

So, on the bloody sand, Sohrab lay dead:
And the great Rustum drew his horseman's cloak
Down o'er his face, and sate by his dead son.
As those black granite pillars, once high-rear'd
By Jemshid in Persepolis, to bear
His house, now 'mid their broken flights of steps
Lie prone, enormous, down the mountain side:
So, in the sand, lay Rustum by his son.

And night came down over the solemn waste,
And the two gazing hosts, and that sole pair,

SOHRAB'S LAST CONTEST

And darken'd all; and a cold fog, with night,
Crept from the Oxus. Soon a hum arose,
As of a great assembly loos'd, and fires
Began to twinkle through the fog; for now
Both armies mov'd to camp, and took their meal;
The Persians took it on the open sands
Southward, the Tartars by the river marge:
And Rustum and his son were left alone.

WHEN CYRUS THE GREAT WAS A BOY

[Early part of sixth century B.C.]

BY XENOPHON

At that time Astyages sent for his daughter and her son; for he was desirous to see him, having heard that he was a handsome and excellent child. Accordingly Mandane went to her father, and took her son Cyrus with her.

As soon as she arrived, and Cyrus knew Astyages to be his mother's father, he instantly, as being a boy naturally affectionate, embraced him, just as if he had been previously brought up with him, and had long loved him; and, observing him adorned with paint about his eyes and color applied to his face, and with artificial hair, things that are customary amongst the Medes (for purple coats, cloaks, collars about the neck, and bracelets on the wrists are all Median decorations; but amongst the Persians at home, even at this day, their habits are much coarser, and their diet more simple), observing the dress of his grandfather, and fixing his eyes on him, he said, "O mother, how handsome my grandfather is!"

His mother then asking him which he thought the more handsome, his father or his grandfather, Cyrus answered, "Of the Persians, mother, my father is much the most handsome; but of all the Medes that I have seen, either upon the road or at the gates of the palace, my grandfather is far the most handsome."

Astyages, then, embracing Cyrus in return, put on him a fine robe, did him honor, and decorated him with

WHEN CYRUS THE GREAT WAS A BOY

collars and bracelets; and, whenever he went abroad, took him with him on a horse with a bridle of gold, just as he himself used to go about. Cyrus, being a boy fond of what was fine and honorable, was pleased with the robe, and extremely delighted at learning to ride; for, amongst the Persians, from its being difficult to breed horses, and difficult even to ride in a country so mountainous, it is a rare thing to see a horse.

Astyages, when he was supping with his daughter and Cyrus, wishing the boy to sup as agreeably as possible, that he might the less regret what he had left at home, had several dishes set before him, with sauces and meats of all kinds; when, as they relate, Cyrus said: —

"How much trouble, grandfather, you have at your meals, if you must stretch out your hands to all these dishes, and taste of all these kinds of meat!"

"What, then," said Astyages, "do you not think this entertainment much finer than what you have in Persia?"

To this question Cyrus is said to have replied: —

"No, grandfather; for with us the way to be satisfied is much plainer and straighter than with you; since among us plain bread and meat conduct us to that object; you indeed pursue the same object with us, but, after rambling in many windings up and down, you at last scarcely reach the point at which we have arrived long before you."

"But, child," said Astyages, "it is not with pain that we ramble through these windings; if you taste," said he, "you will find that these things are pleasant."

"But, grandfather," said Cyrus, "I observe you yourself show an aversion to these dishes."

PERSIA

"From what do you guess," inquired Astyages, "that you express such an opinion?"

"Because I remark," said he, "that when you touch your bread, you do not wipe your hand upon anything, but when you touch any one of these dishes, you immediately wipe your hand upon your napkin, as if you were quite uneasy that it had touched them."

On receiving this answer Astyages said: "If you think so, then, at least eat heartily of plain meat, that you may return home a stout youth"; and as he said this, he directed various kinds of flesh, both of tame and wild animals, to be presented to him.

Cyrus, when he saw this variety of meats, is reported to have said: —

"And do you give me all these meats, grandfather, to do with them what I please?"

"Yes, indeed," said Astyages; "I make you a present of them."

Then Cyrus, taking of the several meats, is said to have distributed them to the servants about his grandfather, saying to each, "I give this to you, because you take pleasure in teaching me to ride; this to you, because you gave me a javelin, for I have it still; this to you, because you serve my grandfather well; this to you, because you honor my mother"; and to have proceeded thus, till he had distributed all the meat that he had received.

Astyages then said, "And do you give nothing to this Sacian, my cup-bearer, whom I value above all?"

This Sacian was a handsome person, and had the honor to introduce to Astyages any that wanted to see

WHEN CYRUS THE GREAT WAS A BOY

him, and to exclude such as he did not think it seasonable to admit.

Cyrus on this is said to have answered rather flippantly, as a boy not yet grown bashful: —

"For what reason is it, grandfather, that you value this Sacian so much?"

Astyages replied jestingly. "Do you not see," said he, "how properly and gracefully he pours out my wine?" For these cup-bearers to kings perform their business very cleverly; they pour in the wine without spilling, and give the cup, holding it on three fingers, and presenting it in such a manner as to put it most conveniently into the hand of the person who is to drink.

"Bid the Sacian give me the cup, grandfather," said Cyrus, "that I also, by gracefully pouring in wine for you to drink, may gain your favor if I can."

Astyages bade the Sacian give him the cup; and Cyrus, taking it, rinsed the cup so well, as he had observed the Sacian to do, settled his countenance so gravely, and brought and presented the cup to his grandfather so prettily as to afford much laughter to his mother and Astyages.

Cyrus then, laughing out, leaped up to his grandfather, and, kissing him, cried out, "O Sacian, you are undone; I will turn you out of your office; for I will pour out wine better than you in other respects, and I will not drink the wine myself." For these cup-bearers to kings, when they give the cup, dip a little out with a smaller cup, which they pour into their left hand and swallow; so that, in case they mix poison in the cup, it may be of no profit to them.

Upon this, Astyages said, joking: —

PERSIA

"And why, Cyrus, when you imitated the Sacian in everything else, did not you swallow some of the wine?"

"Because, to say the truth," said he, "I was afraid there might have been poison mixed in the cup; for, when you entertained your friends upon your birthday, I plainly perceived that he had poured in poison for you all."

"And how, child," said he, "did you know this?"

"Because," said he, "I saw you all disordered both in mind and body; for, in the first place, what you do not allow us boys to do, that you did yourselves; for you all cried out together, and yet could not understand each other; next you fell to singing very ridiculously; and, without attending to the singer, you swore that he sang admirably; then, though each told stories of his own strength, when you rose up and fell to dancing, you were not only unable to dance properly, but were unable even to stand upright; at length, you all entirely forgot yourselves, you, that you were the king, and they, that you were their ruler; and then, for the first time, I discovered that it was equal liberty of speech that you were practicing; for you never ceased to speak."

Astyages then said, —

"Is your father, child, never intoxicated when he drinks?"

"No, indeed," said he.

"What does he, then?"

"Why, he quenches his thirst, and suffers no further harm; for I believe, grandfather," says he, "it is not a Sacian that pours out wine for him."

His mother then said: —

WHEN CYRUS THE GREAT WAS A BOY

"But why, child, do you thus make war upon the Sacian?"

Cyrus is said to have replied: —

"Why, indeed, because I hate him; for, very often, when I am desirous to run to my grandfather, this disagreeable fellow hinders me. But pray, grandfather," said he, "allow me to have the government of him for three days."

"How would you govern him?" said Astyages.

Cyrus replied: —

"Why, standing as he does, just at the entrance, when he had a mind to go in to dinner, I would tell him that it is not yet possible for him to get his dinner, because 'he was busy with certain people': then, when he came to supper, I would tell him that 'he was bathing': and, if he was very eager to eat, I would tell him that 'he was with the women': and so on, till I had tormented him as he torments me when he keeps me from you."

Such amusement did he afford them at meals; at other times of the day, if he perceived his grandfather or his mother's brother in want of anything, it was difficult for any one to be beforehand with him in doing it; for Cyrus was extremely delighted to gratify them in anything that lay in his power.

But when Mandane was preparing to return home to her husband, Astyages requested her to leave Cyrus with him. She made answer, that she was willing to gratify her father in everything; but that she should think it unkind to leave the child against his will.

Upon this, Astyages said to Cyrus: —

"Child, if you will stay with me, in the first place, the Sacian shall not have the command of your access to me; but, whenever you wish to come in, it shall be in your own power to do so; and the oftener you come," said he, " the more I shall think myself obliged to you. You shall also have the use of all my horses, and of as many more as you please; and, when you go away, you shall take as many of them as you please with you. At meals, too, you shall take whatever way you please to what appears to you to be sufficient. As for the animals that are now in the park, I give them to you; and will collect others of all kinds, which you shall hunt when you have learned to ride, and shall strike them down with your bow and javelin, as grown men do. Boys I will find you for playfellows; and whatever else you may desire, if you tell me of it, you shall not fail to have it."

When Astyages had said this, Cyrus's mother asked him whether he would stay or go. He did not at all hesitate, but at once said that he would stay. And being asked by his mother for what reason, it is said that he answered: —

"Because, mother, at home I am, and am accounted, superior to my equals in age both in throwing the javelin and in shooting with the bow; but here, I well know that, in horsemanship, I am inferior to the boys of my age; and be assured, mother, this grieves me very much. But if you leave me here, and I learn to be a horseman, I conceive that when I am in Persia, I shall easily master them there, who are so good at all exercises on foot; and when I come amongst the Medes, I shall endeavor by becoming the best of good horsemen for my grandfather's sake, to be a support to him."

His mother is reported to have said, "But how, child,

WHEN CYRUS THE GREAT WAS A BOY

will you be instructed here in the knowledge of justice, when your masters are there?"

"Oh, mother," said Cyrus, "I understand that accurately already."

"How do you know that?" said Mandane.

"Because my teacher," said he, "appointed me to give judgment to others, as being very exact in the knowledge of justice myself. But yet," added he, "for not having decided rightly, in one case, I received some stripes. The case was this: A bigger boy, who had a little coat, taking the coat off a little boy, that had a larger one, put on him his own coat, and put on himself the little boy's coat. I, therefore, giving judgment between them, decided that it was best that each should keep the coat that best fitted him. Upon this, the master beat me, telling me that, when I should be constituted judge of what fitted best, I might determine in this manner; but that when I was to judge whose the coat was, I must consider what just possession is; whether he that took a thing from another by force should have it, or he who made it or purchased it should possess it; and then he told me that what was according to law was just, and that what was contrary to law was an act of violence; and impressed upon me accordingly, that a judge ought to give his opinion in conformity with the law. So, mother," said he, "I understand what is just in all cases very exactly; or, if I am at all deficient, my grandfather here will teach it me."

"But, child," said she, "the same things are not accounted just with your grandfather here, and yonder in Persia; for among the Medes, your grandfather has made himself master of all; but amongst the Persians, it is accounted just that each should have equal rights with his neighbors. Your father is the first to execute what is appointed by the whole state, and submits to what is appointed; his own inclination is not his standard of action, but,the law. Take care then, that you are not beaten to death at home, if you come thither having learned from your grandfather not what belongs to a king, but what belongs to a tyrant; an ingredient in which is, to think that you yourself ought to have more than others."

"Oh, mother," said Cyrus, "your father is much better able to teach one to have less than to have more. Do you not see," said he, "that he has taught all the Medes to have less than himself? Be well assured, therefore, that your father will not dismiss me, nor any one, from about him, instructed to encroach upon others."

HOW CYRUS THE GREAT WON THE LAND OF GOLD

[546 B.C.]

BY JACOB ABBOTT

[IN the country of Lydia, the mountains were rich in gold, and the rivers flowed over sands of gold. It was the country in which King Midas of the "golden touch" is fabled to have lived. In the sixth century before Christ, a struggle took place between King Crœsus of Lydia and King Cyrus, who had become ruler of the Medes and the Persians.
The Editor.]

As soon as Cyrus had become established on his throne as King of the Medes and Persians, his influence and power began to extend westward toward the confines of the empire of Crœsus, King of Lydia. Crœsus was aroused from the dejection and stupor into which the death of his son had plunged him by this threatening danger. He began to consider very earnestly what he could do to avert it.

The river Halys, a great river of Asia Minor, which flows northward into the Black Sea, was the eastern boundary of the Lydian empire. Crœsus began to entertain the design of raising an army and crossing the Halys to invade the empire of Cyrus, thinking that that would perhaps be safer policy than to wait for Cyrus to cross the Halys, and bring the war upon him. Still, the enterprise of invading Persia was a vast undertaking, and the responsibility great of being the aggressor in the contest.

PERSIA

After carefully considering the subject in all its aspects, Crœsus found himself still perplexed and undecided.

The Greeks had a method of looking into futurity, and of ascertaining, as they imagined, by supernatural means, the course of future events, which was peculiar to that people; at least no other nation seems ever to have practiced it in the precise form which prevailed among them. It was by means of the oracles. There were four or five localities in the Grecian countries which possessed, as the people thought, the property of inspiring persons who visited them, or of giving to some natural object certain supernatural powers by which future events could be foretold. The three most important of these oracles were situated respectively at Delphi, at Dodona, and at the Oasis of Jupiter Ammon.

Delphi was a small town built in a sort of valley, shaped like an amphitheater, on the southern side of Mount Parnassus. Mount Parnassus is north of the Peloponnesus, not very far from the shores of the Gulf of Corinth. Delphi was in a picturesque and romantic situation, with the mountain behind it, and steep, precipitous rocks descending to the level country before. These precipices answered instead of walls to defend the temple and the town. In very early times a cavern or fissure in the rocks was discovered at Delphi, from which there issued a stream of gaseous vapor, which produced strange effects on those who inhaled it. It was supposed to inspire them. People resorted to the place to obtain the benefit of these inspirations, and of the knowledge which they imagined they could obtain by means of them. Finally, a temple was built, and a priestess resided constantly in it, to inhale the vapor and give the

HOW CYRUS WON THE LAND OF GOLD

responses. When she gave her answers to those who came to consult the oracle, she sat upon a sort of three-legged stool, which was called the sacred tripod. These stools were greatly celebrated as a very important part of the sacred apparatus of the place. This oracle became at last so renowned, that the greatest potentates, and even kings, came from great distances to consult it, and they made very rich and costly presents at the shrine when they came. These presents, it was supposed, tended to induce the god who presided over the oracle to give to those who made them favorable and auspicious replies. The deity that dictated the predictions of this oracle was Apollo.

There was another circumstance, besides the existence of the cave, which signalized the locality where this oracle was situated. The people believed that this spot was the exact center of the earth, which of course they considered as one vast plain. There was an ancient story that Jupiter, in order to determine the central point of creation, liberated two eagles at the same time, in opposite quarters of the heavens, that they might fly toward one another, and so mark the middle point by the place of their meeting. They met at Delphi.

Another of the most celebrated oracles was at Dodona. Dodona was northwest of Delphi, in the Epirus, which was a country in the western part of what is now Turkey in Europe, and on the shores of the Adriatic Sea. The origin of the oracle at Dodona was, as the priestesses there told Herodotus, as follows: In very ancient times, two black doves were set at liberty in Thebes, which was a very venerable and sacred city of Egypt. One flew toward the north and the other toward the west. The former crossed the Mediterranean, and then continued its flight over the Peloponnesus, and over all the southern provinces of Greece, until it reached Dodona. There it alighted on a beech-tree, and said, in a human voice, that that spot was divinely appointed for the seat of a sacred oracle. The other dove flew to the Oasis of Jupiter Ammon.

There were three priestesses at Dodona in the days of Herodotus. Their names were Promenea, Timarete, and Nicandre. The answers of the oracle were, for a time, obtained by the priestesses from some appearances which they observed in the sacred beech on which the dove alighted, when the tree was agitated by the wind. In later times, however, the responses were obtained in a still more singular manner. There was a brazen statue of a man, holding a whip in his hand. The whip had three lashes, which were formed of brazen chains. At the end of each chain was an *astragalus*, as it was called, which was a row of little knots or knobs, such as were commonly appended to the lashes of whips used in those days for scourging criminals.

These heavy lashes hung suspended in the hand of the statue over a great brazen caldron, in such a manner that the wind would impel them, from time to time, against its sides, causing the caldron to ring and resound like a gong. There was, however, something in this resonance supernatural and divine; for, though it was not loud, it was very long continued, when once the margin of the caldron was touched, however gently, by the lashes. In fact, it was commonly said that if touched in the morning, it would be night before the reverberations would have died entirely away. Such a belief could be very

HOW CYRUS WON THE LAND OF GOLD

easily sustained among the common people; for a large, open-mouthed vessel like the Dodona caldron, with thin sides formed of sonorous metal, might be kept in a state of continual vibration by the wind alone.

They who wished to consult this oracle came with rich presents both for the priestesses and for the shrine, and when they had made the offerings, and performed the preliminary ceremonies required, they propounded their questions to the priestesses, who obtained the replies by interpreting, according to certain rules which they had formed, the sounds emitted by the mysterious gong.

The second black dove which took its flight from Thebes alighted, as we have already said, in the Oasis of Jupiter Ammon. This oasis was a small fertile spot in the midst of the deserts of Africa, west of Egypt, about a hundred miles from the Nile, and somewhat nearer than that to the Mediterranean Sea. It was first discovered in the following manner: A certain king was marching across the deserts, and his army, having exhausted their supplies of water, were on the point of perishing with thirst, when a ram mysteriously appeared, and took a position before them as their guide. They followed him, and at length came suddenly upon a green and fertile valley, many miles in length. The ram conducted them into this valley, and then suddenly vanished, and a copious fountain of water sprung up in the place where he had stood. The king, in gratitude for this divine interposition, consecrated the spot and built a temple upon it, which was called the temple of Jupiter Ammon. The dove alighted here, and ever afterward the oracles delivered by the priests of this temple were considered as divinely inspired.

PERSIA

These three were the most important oracles. There were, however, many others of subordinate consequence, each of which had its own peculiar ceremonies, all senseless and absurd. At one there was a sort of oven-shaped cave in the rocks, the spot being inclosed by an artificial wall. The cave was about six feet wide and eight feet deep. The descent into it was by a ladder. Previously to consulting this oracle certain ceremonies were necessary, which it required several days to perform. The applicant was to offer sacrifices to many different deities and to purify himself in various ways. He was then conducted to a stream in the neighborhood of the oracle, where he was to be anointed and washed. Then he drank a certain magical water, called the water of forgetfulness, which made him forget all previous sorrows and cares. Afterward he drank of another enchanted cup, which contained the water of remembrance; this was to make him remember all that should be communicated to him in the cave. He then descended the ladder, and received within the cave the responses of the oracle.

At another of these oracles, which was situated in Attica, the magic virtue was supposed to reside in a certain marble statue, carved in honor of an ancient and celebrated prophet, and placed in a temple. Whoever wished to consult this oracle must abstain from wine for three days, and from food of every kind for twenty-four hours preceding the application. He was then to offer a ram as a sacrifice; and afterward, taking the skin of the ram from the carcass, he was to spread it out before the statue and lie down upon it to sleep. The answers of the oracle came to him in his dreams.

But to return to Crœsus. He wished to ascertain, by

consulting some of these oracles, what the result of his proposed invasion of the dominions of Cyrus would be, in case he should undertake it; and in order to determine which of the various oracles were most worthy of reliance, he conceived the plan of putting them all to a preliminary test. He effected this object in the following manner: —

He dispatched a number of messengers from Sardis, his capital, sending one to each of the various oracles. He directed these messengers to make their several journeys with all convenient dispatch; but, in order to provide for any cases of accidental detention or delay, he allowed them all one hundred days to reach their several places of destination. On the hundredth day from the time of their leaving Sardis, they were all to make applications to the oracles, and inquire what Crœsus, King of Lydia, was doing at that time. Of course he did not tell them what he should be doing; and as the oracles themselves could not possibly know how he was employed by any human powers, their answers would seem to test the validity of their claims to powers divine.

Crœsus kept the reckoning of the days himself with great care, and at the hour appointed on the hundredth day, he employed himself in boiling the flesh of a turtle and of a lamb together in a brazen vessel. The vessel was covered with a lid, which was also of brass. He then awaited the return of the messengers. They came in due time, one after another, bringing the replies which they had severally obtained. The replies were all unsatisfactory, except that of the oracle at Delphi. This answer was in verse, as, in fact, the responses of that oracle always were. The priestess who sat upon the tripod was accustomed to give the replies in an incoherent and half-intelligible manner, as impostors are very apt to do in uttering prophecies, and then the attendant priests and secretaries wrote them out in verse.

The verse which the messenger brought back from the Delphic tripod was in Greek; but some idea of its style, and the import of it, is conveyed by the following imitation: —

> "I number the sands, I measure the sea,
> What's hidden to others is known to me.
> The lamb and the turtle are simmering slow
> With brass above them and brass below."

Of course, Crœsus decided that the Delphic oracle was the one that he must rely upon for guidance in respect to his projected campaign. And he now began to prepare to consult it in a manner corresponding with the vast importance of the subject, and with his own boundless wealth. He provided the most extraordinary and sumptuous presents. Some of these treasures were to be deposited in the temple, as sacred gifts, for permanent preservation there. Others were to be offered as a burnt sacrifice in honor of the god. Among the latter, besides an incredible number of living victims, he caused to be prepared a great number of couches, magnificently decorated with silver and gold, and goblets and other vessels of gold, and dresses of various kinds richly embroidered, and numerous other articles, all intended to be used in the ceremonies preliminary to his application to the oracle. When the time arrived, a vast concourse of people assembled to witness the spectacle. The animals were sacrificed, and the people feasted on the flesh; and when these ceremonies were concluded, the couches, the goblets, the utensils of every kind, the dresses, everything, in short, which had been used on the occasion, were heaped up into one great sacrificial pile, and set on fire. Everything that was combustible was consumed, while the gold was melted, and ran into plates of great size, which were afterward taken out from the ashes. Thus it was the workmanship only of these articles which was destroyed and lost by the fire. The gold, in which the chief value consisted, was saved. It was gold from the Pactolus.

Besides these articles, there were others made, far more magnificent and costly, for the temple itself. There was a silver cistern or tank, large enough to hold three thousand gallons of wine. This tank was to be used by the inhabitants of Delphi in their great festivals. There was also a smaller cistern, or immense goblet, as it might, perhaps, more properly be called, which was made of gold. There were also many other smaller presents, such as basins, vases, and statues, all of silver and gold, and of the most costly workmanship. The gold, too, which had been taken from the fire, was cast again, a part of it being formed into the image of a lion, and the rest into large plates of metal for the lion to stand upon. The image was then set up upon the plates, within the precincts of the temple.

There was one piece of statuary which Crœsus presented to the oracle at Delphi, which was, in some respects, more extraordinary than any of the rest. It was called the bread-maker. It was an image representing a woman, a servant in the household of Crœsus, whose business it was to bake the bread. The reason that induced Crœsus to honor this bread-maker with a statue of gold was, that on one occasion during his childhood she had saved his life. The mother of Crœsus died when he was young, and his father married a second time. The second wife wished to have some one of *her* children, instead of Crœsus, succeed to her husband's throne. In order, therefore, to remove Crœsus out of the way, she prepared some poison and gave it to the bread-maker, instructing her to put it into the bread which Crœsus was to eat. The bread-maker received the poison and promised to obey. But, instead of doing so, she revealed the intended murder to Crœsus, and gave the poison to the queen's own children. In gratitude for this fidelity to him, Crœsus, when he came to the throne, caused this statue to be made, and now he placed it at Delphi, where he supposed it would forever remain. The memory of his faithful servant was indeed immortalized by the measure, though the statue itself, as well as all these other treasures, in process of time disappeared. In fact, statues of brass or of marble generally make far more durable monuments than statues of gold; and no structure or object of art is likely to be very permanent among mankind unless the workmanship is worth more than the material.

Crœsus did not proceed himself to Delphi with these presents, but sent them by the hands of trusty messengers, who were instructed to perform the ceremonies required, to offer the gifts, and then to make inquiries of the oracle in the following terms: —

"Crœsus, the sovereign of Lydia and of various other kingdoms, in return for the wisdom which has marked your former declarations, has sent you these gifts. He now furthermore desires to know whether it is safe for

HOW CYRUS WON THE LAND OF GOLD

him to proceed against the Persians, and if so, whether it is best for him to seek the assistance of any allies."

The answer was as follows: —

"If Crœsus crosses the Halys, and prosecutes a war with Persia, a mighty empire will be overthrown. It will be best for him to form an alliance with the most powerful States of Greece."

Crœsus was extremely pleased with this response. He immediately resolved on undertaking the expedition against Cyrus; and to express his gratitude for so favorable an answer to his questions, he sent to Delphi to inquire what was the number of inhabitants in the city, and, when the answer was reported to him, he sent a present of a sum of money to every one. The Delphians, in their turn, conferred special privileges and honors upon the Lydians and upon Crœsus in respect to their oracle, giving them the precedence in all future consultations, and conferring upon them other marks of distinction and honor.

At the time when Crœsus sent his present to the inhabitants of Delphi, he took the opportunity to address another inquiry to the oracle, which was, whether his power would ever decline. The oracle replied in a couplet of Greek verse, similar in its style to the one recorded on the previous occasion.

It was as follows: —

"Whene'er a mule shall mount upon the Median throne,
Then, and not till then, shall great Crœsus fear to lose his own."

This answer pleased the king quite as much as the former one had done. The allusion to the contingency of a mule's reigning in Media he very naturally regarded as only a rhetorical and mystical mode of expressing an utter impossibility. Crœsus considered himself and the continuance of his power as perfectly secure. He was fully confirmed in his determination to organize his expedition without any delay, and to proceed immediately to the proper measures for obtaining the Grecian alliance and aid which the oracle had recommended.

There were, in fact, three inducements which combined their influence on the mind of Crœsus, in leading him to cross the Halys, and invade the dominions of the Medes and Persians: first, he was ambitious to extend his own empire; secondly, he feared that if he did not attack Cyrus, Cyrus would himself cross the Halys and attack him; and, thirdly, he felt under some obligation to consider himself the ally of Astyages, and thus bound to espouse his cause, and to aid him in putting down, if possible, the usurpation of Cyrus, and in recovering his throne. He felt under this obligation because Astyages was his brother-in-law; for the latter had married, many years before, a daughter of Alyattes, who was the father of Crœsus. This, as Crœsus thought, gave him a just title to interfere between the dethroned king and the rebel who had dethroned him. Under the influence of all these reasons combined, and encouraged by the responses of the oracle, he determined on attempting the invasion.

The first measure which he adopted was to form an alliance with the most powerful of the States of Greece, as he had been directed to do by the oracle. After much inquiry and consideration, he concluded that the Lacedæmonian State was the most powerful. Their chief city was Sparta, in the Peloponnesus. They were a warlike, stern, and indomitable race of men, capable of bearing

HOW CYRUS WON THE LAND OF GOLD

every possible hardship, and of enduring every degree of fatigue and toil, and they desired nothing but military glory for their reward. This was a species of wages which it was very easy to pay; much more easy to furnish than coin, even for Crœsus, notwithstanding the abundant supplies of gold which he was accustomed to obtain from the sands of the Pactolus.

Crœsus sent ambassadors to Sparta to inform the people of the plans which he contemplated, and to ask their aid. He had been instructed, he said, by the oracle at Delphi, to seek the alliance of the most powerful of the States of Greece, and he accordingly made application to them. They were gratified with the compliment implied in selecting them, and acceded readily to his proposal. Besides, they were already on very friendly terms with Crœsus; for, some years before, they had sent to him to procure some gold for a statue which they had occasion to erect, offering to give an equivalent for the value of it in such productions as their country afforded. Crœsus supplied them with the gold that they needed, but generously refused to receive any return.

In the mean time, Crœsus went on, energetically, at Sardis, making the preparations for his campaign. One of his counselors, whose name was Sardaris, ventured, one day, strongly to dissuade him from undertaking the expedition. "You have nothing to gain by it," said he, "if you succeed, and everything to lose if you fail. Consider what sort of people these Persians are whom you are going to combat. They live in the most rude and simple manner, without luxuries, without pleasures, without wealth. If you conquer their country, you will find nothing in it worth bringing away. On the other hand, if they conquer you, they will come like a vast band of plunderers into Lydia, where there is everything to tempt and reward them. I counsel you to leave them alone, and to remain on this side the Halys, thankful if Cyrus will be contented to remain on the other."

But Crœsus was not in a mood of mind to be persuaded by such reasoning.

When all things were ready, the army commenced its march and moved eastward, through one province of Asia Minor after another, until they reached the Halys. This river is a considerable stream, which rises in the interior of the country, and flows northward into the Euxine Sea. The army encamped on the banks of it, and some plan was to be formed for crossing the stream. In accomplishing this object, Crœsus was aided by a very celebrated engineer who accompanied his army, named Thales. Thales was a native of Miletus, and is generally called in history, Thales the Milesian. He was a very able mathematician and calculator, and many accounts remain of the discoveries and performances by which he acquired his renown.

For example, in the course of his travels, he at one time visited Egypt, and while there, he contrived a very simple way of measuring the height of the pyramids. He set up a pole on the plain in an upright position, and then measured the pole and also its shadow. He also measured the length of the shadow of the pyramid. He then calculated the height of the pyramid by this proportion: as the length of shadow of the pole is to that of the pole itself, so is the length of the shadow of the pyramid to its height.

Thales was an astronomer as well as a philosopher and

HOW CYRUS WON THE LAND OF GOLD

engineer. He learned more exactly the true length of the year than it had been known before; and he also made some calculations of eclipses, at least so far as to predict the year in which they would happen. One eclipse which he predicted happened to occur on the day of a great battle between two contending armies. It was cloudy, so that the combatants could not see the sun. This circumstance, however, which concealed the eclipse itself, only made the darkness which was caused by it the more intense. The armies were much terrified at this sudden cessation of the light of day, and supposed it to be a warning from heaven that they should desist from the combat.

Thales the Milesian was the author of several of the geometrical theorems and demonstrations now included in the Elements of Euclid. The celebrated fifth proposition of the first book, so famous among all the modern nations of Europe as the great stumbling block in the way of beginners in the study of geometry, was his. The discovery of the truth expressed in this proposition, and of the complicated demonstration which establishes it, was certainly a much greater mathematical performance than the measuring of the altitude of the pyramids by their shadow.

But to return to Crœsus. Thales undertook the work of transporting the army across the river. He examined the banks, and found, at length, a spot where the land was low and level for some distance from the stream. He caused the army to be brought up to the river at this point, and to be encamped there, as near to the bank as possible, and in as compact a form. He then employed a vast number of laborers to cut a new channel for the waters, behind the army, leading out from the river above, and rejoining it again at a little distance below. When this channel was finished, he turned the river into its new course, and then the army passed without difficulty over the former bed of the stream.

The Halys being thus passed, Crœsus moved on in the direction of Media. But he soon found that he had not far to go to find his enemy. Cyrus had heard of his plans through deserters and spies, and he had for some time been advancing to meet him. One after the other of the nations through whose dominions he had passed, he had subjected to his sway, or at least, brought under his influence by treaties and alliances, and had received from them all reinforcements to swell the numbers of his army. One nation only remained — the Babylonians. They were on the side of Crœsus. They were jealous of the growing power of the Medes and Persians, and had made a league with Crœsus, promising to aid him in the war. The other nations of the East were in alliance with Cyrus, and he was slowly moving on, at the head of an immense combined force, toward the Halys, at the very time when Crœsus was crossing the stream.

The scouts, therefore, that preceded the army of Crœsus on its march, soon began to fall back into the camp, with intelligence that there was a large armed force coming on to meet them, the advancing columns filling all the roads, and threatening to overwhelm them. The scouts from the army of Cyrus carried back similar intelligence to him. The two armies accordingly halted and began to prepare for battle. The place of their meeting was called Pteria. It was in the province of Cappadocia, and toward the eastern part of Asia Minor.

A great battle was fought at Pteria. It was continued

HOW CYRUS WON THE LAND OF GOLD

all day, and remained undecided when the sun went down. The combatants separated when it became dark, and each withdrew from the field. Each king found, it seems, that his antagonist was more formidable than he had imagined, and on the morning after the battle they both seemed inclined to remain in their respective encampments, without evincing any disposition to renew the contest.

Crœsus, in fact, seems to have considered that he was fortunate in having so far repulsed the formidable invasion which Cyrus had been intending for him. He considered Cyrus's army as repulsed, since they had withdrawn from the field, and showed no disposition to return to it. He had no doubt that Cyrus would now go back to Media again, having found how well prepared Crœsus had been to receive him. For himself, he concluded that he ought to be satisfied with the advantage which he had already gained, as the result of one campaign, and return again to Sardis to recruit his army, the force of which had been considerably impaired by the battle, and so postpone the grand invasion till the next season. He accordingly set out on his return. He dispatched messengers, at the same time, to Babylon, to Sparta, to Egypt, and to other countries with which he was in alliance, informing these various nations of the great battle of Pteria and its results, and asking them to send him, early in the following spring, all the reinforcements that they could command, to join him in the grand campaign which he was going to make the next season.

He continued his march homeward without any interruption, sending off, from time to time, as he was moving through his own dominions, such portions of his troops as desired to return to their homes, enjoining upon them to come back to him in the spring. By this temporary disbanding of a portion of his army, he saved the expense of maintaining them through the winter.

Very soon after Crœsus arrived at Sardis, the whole country in the neighborhood of the capital was thrown into a state of universal alarm by the news that Cyrus was close at hand. It seems that Cyrus had remained in the vicinity of Pteria long enough to allow Crœsus to return, and to give him time to dismiss his troops and establish himself securely in the city. He then suddenly resumed his march, and came on toward Sardis with the utmost possible dispatch. Crœsus, in fact, had no announcement of his approach, until he heard of his arrival.

All was now confusion and alarm, both within and without the city. Crœsus hastily collected all the forces that he could command. He sent immediately to the neighboring cities, summoning all the troops in them to hasten to the capital. He enrolled all the inhabitants of the city that were capable of bearing arms. By these means he collected, in a very short time, quite a formidable force, which he drew up, in battle array, on a great plain not far from the city, and there waited, with much anxiety and solicitude, for Cyrus to come on.

The Lydian army was superior to that of Cyrus in cavalry, and as the place where the battle was to be fought was a plain, which was the kind of ground most favorable for the operations of that species of force, Cyrus felt some solicitude in respect to the impression which might be made by it on his army. Nothing is more terrible than the onset of a squadron of horse when

HOW CYRUS WON THE LAND OF GOLD

charging an enemy upon the field of battle. They come in vast bodies, sometimes consisting of many thousands, with the speed of the wind, the men flourishing their sabers and rending the air with the most unearthly cries, those in advance being driven irresistibly on by the weight and impetus of the masses behind. The dreadful torrent bears down and overwhelms everything that attempts to resist its way. They trample one another and their enemies together promiscuously in the dust; the foremost of the column press on with the utmost fury, afraid quite as much of the headlong torrent of friends coming on behind them, as of the line of fixed and motionless enemies who stand ready to receive them before. These enemies, stationed to withstand the charge, arrange themselves in triple or quadruple rows, with the shafts of their spears planted against the ground, and the points directed forward and upward to receive the advancing horsemen. These spears transfix and kill the foremost horses; but those that come on behind, leaping and plunging over their fallen companions, soon break through the lines and put their enemies to flight, in a scene of indescribable havoc and confusion.

Crœsus had large bodies of horse, while Cyrus had no efficient troops to oppose them. He had a great number of camels in the rear of his army, which had been employed as beasts of burden to transport the baggage and stores of the army on their march. Cyrus concluded to make the experiment of opposing these camels to the cavalry. It is frequently said by the ancient historians that the horse has a natural antipathy to the camel, and cannot bear either the smell or the sight of one, though this is not found to be the case at the present day. However the fact might have been in this respect, Cyrus determined to arrange the camels in his front as he advanced into battle. He accordingly ordered the baggage to be removed, and, releasing their ordinary drivers from the charge of them, he assigned each one to the care of a soldier, who was to mount him, armed with a spear. Even if the supposed antipathy of the horse for the camel did not take effect, Cyrus thought that their large and heavy bodies, defended by the spears of their riders, would afford the most effectual means of resistance against the shock of the Lydian squadrons that he was now able to command.

The battle commenced, and the squadrons of horse came on. But, as soon as they came near the camels, it happened that, either from the influence of the antipathy above referred to, or from alarm at the novelty of the spectacle of such huge and misshapen beasts, or else because of the substantial resistance which the camels and the spears of their riders made to the shock of their charge, the horses were soon thrown into confusion and put to flight. In fact, a general panic seized them, and they became totally unmanageable. Some threw their riders; others, seized with a sort of frenzy, became entirely independent of control. They turned, and trampled the foot soldiers of their own army under foot, and threw the whole body into disorder. The consequence was, that the army of Crœsus was wholly defeated; they fled in confusion, and crowded in vast throngs through the gates into the city, and fortified themselves there.

Cyrus advanced to the city, invested it closely on all sides, and commenced a siege. But the appearances

HOW CYRUS WON THE LAND OF GOLD

were not very encouraging. The walls were lofty, thick, and strong, and the numbers within the city were amply sufficient to guard them. Nor was the prospect much more promising of being soon able to reduce the city by famine. The wealth of Crœsus had enabled him to lay up almost inexhaustible stores of food and clothing, as well as treasures of silver and gold. He hoped, therefore, to be able to hold out against the besiegers until help should come from some of his allies. He had sent messengers to them, asking them to come to his rescue without any delay, before he was shut up in the city.

The city of Sardis was built in a position naturally strong, and one part of the wall passed over rocky precipices which were considered entirely impassable. There was a sort of glen or rocky gorge in this quarter, outside of the walls, down which dead bodies were thrown on one occasion subsequently, at a time when the city was besieged, and beasts and birds of prey fed upon them there undisturbed, so lonely was the place and so desolate. In fact, the walls that crowned these precipices were considered absolutely inaccessible, and were very slightly built and very feebly guarded. There was an ancient legend that, a long time before, when a certain Males was King of Lydia, one of his wives had a son in the form of a lion, whom they called Leon, and an oracle declared that if this Leon were carried around the walls of the city, it would be rendered impregnable, and should never be taken. They carried Leon, therefore, around, so far as the regular walls extended. When they came to this precipice of rocks, they returned, considering that this part of the city was impregnable without any such ceremony. A spur or eminence from the mountain of

PERSIA

Tmolus, which was behind the city, projected into it at this point, and there was a strong citadel built upon its summit.

Cyrus continued the siege fourteen days, and then he determined that he must, in some way or other, find the means of carrying it by assault, and to do this he must find some place to scale the walls. He accordingly sent a party of horsemen around to explore every part, offering them a large reward if they would find any place where an entrance could be effected. The horsemen made the circuit, and reported that their search had been in vain. At length a certain soldier, named Hyræades, after studying for some time the precipices on the side which had been deemed inaccessible, saw a sentinel, who was stationed on the walls above, leave his post and come climbing down the rocks for some distance to get his helmet, which had accidentally dropped down. Hyræades watched him both as he descended and as he returned. He reflected on this discovery, communicated it to others, and the practicability of scaling the rock and the walls at that point was discussed. In the end, the attempt was made and was successful. Hyræades went up first, followed by a few daring spirits who were ambitious of the glory of the exploit. They were not at first observed from above. The way being thus shown, great numbers followed on, and so large a force succeeded in thus gaining an entrance that the city was taken.

In the dreadful confusion and din of the storming of the city, Crœsus himself had a very narrow escape from death. He was saved by the miraculous speaking of his deaf-and-dumb son — at least, such is the story. Cyrus had given positive orders to his soldiers, both before the

HOW CYRUS WON THE LAND OF GOLD

great battle on the plain and during the siege, that, though they might slay whomever else they pleased, they must not harm Crœsus, but must take him alive. During the time of the storming of the town, when the streets were filled with infuriated soldiers, those on the one side wild with the excitement of triumph, and those on the other maddened with rage and despair, a party, rushing along, overtook Crœsus and his helpless son, whom the unhappy father, it seems, was making a desperate effort to save. The Persian soldiers were about to transfix Crœsus with their spears, when the son, who had never spoken before, called out, "It is Crœsus; do not kill him." The soldiers were arrested by the words, and saved the monarch's life. They made him prisoner, and bore him away to Cyrus.

Crœsus had sent, a long time before, to inquire of the Delphic oracle by what means the power of speech could be restored to his son. The answer was, that that was a boon which he had better not ask; for the day on which he should hear his son speak for the first time would be the darkest and most unhappy day of his life.

Cyrus had not ordered his soldiers to spare the life of Crœsus in battle from any sentiment of humanity toward him, but because he wished to have his case reserved for his own decision. When Crœsus was brought to him a captive, he ordered him to be put in chains, and carefully guarded. As soon as some degree of order was restored in the city, a large funeral pile was erected, by his directions, in a public square, and Crœsus was brought to the spot. Fourteen Lydian young men, the sons, probably, of the most prominent men in the state, were with him. The pile was large enough for them all,

and they were placed upon it. They were all laid upon
the wood. Crœsus raised himself and looked around,
surveying with extreme consternation and horror the
preparations which were making for lighting the pile.
His heart sank within him as he thought of the dreadful fate that was before him. The spectators stood by
in solemn silence, awaiting the end. Crœsus broke this
awful pause by crying out, in a tone of anguish and
despair, —

"O Solon! Solon! Solon!"

The officers who had charge of the execution asked
him what he meant. Cyrus, too, who was himself personally superintending the scene, asked for an explanation. Crœsus was, for a time, too much agitated and distracted to reply. There were difficulties in respect to
language, too, which embarrassed the conversation, as
the two kings could speak to each other only through an
interpreter. At length Crœsus gave an account of his
interview with Solon, and of the sentiment which the
philosopher had expressed, that no one could decide
whether a man was truly prosperous and happy till it
was determined how his life was to end. Cyrus was
greatly interested in this narrative; but, in the mean
time, the interpreting of the conversation had been slow,
a considerable period had elapsed, and the officers had
lighted the fire. The pile had been made extremely
combustible, and the fire was rapidly making its way
through the whole mass. Cyrus eagerly ordered it to be
extinguished. The efforts which the soldiers made for
this purpose seemed, at first, likely to be fruitless; but
they were aided very soon by a sudden shower of rain,
which, coming down from the mountains, began, just at

this time, to fall; and thus the flames were extinguished, and Crœsus and the captives saved.

Cyrus immediately, with a fickleness very common among great monarchs in the treatment of both enemies and favorites, began to consider Crœsus as his friend. He ordered him to be unbound, brought him near his person, and treated him with great consideration and honor.

Crœsus remained after this for a long time with Cyrus, and accompanied him in his subsequent campaigns. He was very much incensed at the oracle at Delphi for having deceived him by its false responses and predictions, and thus led him into the terrible snare into which he had fallen. He procured the fetters with which he had been chained when placed upon the pile, and sent them to Delphi, with orders that they should be thrown down upon the threshold of the temple — the visible symbol of his captivity and ruin — as a reproach to the oracle for having deluded him and caused his destruction. In doing this, the messengers were to ask the oracle whether imposition like that which had been practiced on Crœsus was the kind of gratitude it evinced to one who had enriched it by such a profusion of offerings and gifts.

To this the priests of the oracle said in reply that the destruction of the Lydian dynasty had long been decreed by the Fates, in retribution for the guilt of Gyges, the founder of the line. He had murdered his master, and usurped the throne, without any title to it whatever. The judgments of Heaven had been denounced upon Gyges for this crime, to fall on himself or on some of his descendants. The Pythian Apollo at Delphi had done all in his power to postpone the falling of the blow until after the death of Crœsus, on account of the munificent benefactions which he had made to the oracle; but he had been unable to effect it: the decrees of Fate were inexorable. All that the oracle could do was to postpone — as it had done, it said, for three years — the execution of the sentence, and to give Crœsus warning of the evil that was impending. This had been done by announcing to him that his crossing the Halys would cause the destruction of a mighty empire, meaning that of Lydia; and also by informing him that when he should find a mule upon the throne of Media he must expect to lose his own. Cyrus, who was descended, on the father's side, from the Persian stock, and on the mother's from that of Media, was the hybrid sovereign represented by the mule.

When this answer was reported to Crœsus, it is said that he was satisfied with the explanations, and admitted that the oracle was right, and that he himself had been unreasonable and wrong.

THE SEVEN SLEEPERS OF EPHESUS, IN THE LAND OF LYDIA

[249–251 A.D.]

BY JOHANN WOLFGANG VON GOETHE

Six young men of Cæsar's household
Fled before their master's anger;
As a god he claimed their worship,
Though a sorry god was he.
For an insect, ever buzzing,
Still annoyed him at the banquet,
Still disturbed his rest and pleasure.
All the chasing of his servants
Could not drive away the torment.
Ever round the head of Cæsar
Did the angry creature hover,
Threatening with its poisoned sting:
Still it flew, and swiftly circling
Made confusion at the table,
Messenger of Baalzebub,
The infernal god of flies.

"Ha!" — so spake the youths together, —
"He a god that fears an insect!
Can a god be thus molested?
Does a god, like wretched mortals,
Feast and revel at the banquet?
Nay! to Him, the one, the only,
Who the sun and moon created,

PERSIA

Who hath made the stars in glory,
Shall we henceforth bend the knee!"

So they spake and left the palace,
Left it in their trim apparel;
By a shepherd led, they hastened
To a cave was in the mountain,
And they all went gliding in.

And the shepherd's dog came after,
Though they strove to drive him from them;
Thrust himself toward his master,
Licked their hands in dumb entreaty,
That he might remain their fellow;
And lay down with them to sleep.

But the wrath of Cæsar kindled,
When he knew that they had left him;
All his former love departed,
All his thought was vengeance only.
Out in quest he sent his people,
Traced them to the mountain-hollow.
Not to fire nor sword he doomed them;
But he bade great stones be lifted
To the entrance of the cavern;
Saw it fastened up with mortar;
And so left them in their tomb.

But the youths lay calmly sleeping;
And the angel, their protector,
Spake before the throne of glory:
" I have watched beside the sleepers,

THE SEVEN SLEEPERS OF EPHESUS

Made them turn in slumber ever,
That the damps of yonder cavern
Should not cramp their youthful limbs;
And the rocks around I've opened,
That the sun at rising, setting,
May give freshness to their cheeks.
So they lie in rest and quiet,
In the bliss of happy dreams."
So they lay; and still, beside them,
Lay the dog in peaceful slumber,
Never whimpering in his sleep.

Years came on, and years departed;
Till at last the young men wakened;
And the wall, so strongly fastened,
Now had fallen into ruin,
Crumbled by the touch of ages.
Then Iamblicus, the youngest,
And the goodliest of them all,
Seeing that the shepherd trembled,
Said, "I pray you now, my brothers,
Let me go to seek provision;
I have gold; my life I'll venture;
Tarry till I bring you bread."
Ephesus, that noble city,
Then, for many a year, had yielded
To the faith of the Redeemer,
Jesus. (Glory to his name!)

And he ran unto the city;
At the gate were many warders.
Armèd men on tower and turret,

PERSIA

But he passed them all unchallenged;
To the nearest baker's went he,
And in haste demanded bread.

"Ha! young rogue," exclaimed the baker,
"Surely thou hast found a treasure;
That old piece of gold betrays thee!
Give me, or I shall denounce thee,
Half the treasure thou hast found."

And Iamblicus denied it;
But the baker would not listen,
Brawling till the watch came forward.
To the king they both were taken;
And the monarch, like the baker,
But a higher right asserting,
Claimed to share the treasure too.

But at last the wondrous story,
Which the young man told the monarch,
Proved itself by many tokens.
Lord was he of that same palace,
Whither he was brought for judgment;
For he showed to them a pillar,
In the which a stone when loosened
Led unto a treasure chamber,
Heaped with gold and costly jewels.
Straightway came in haste his kindred,
All his clan came thronging round him,
Eager to advance their claim;
Each was nearer than the other.
And Iamblicus, the blooming,

THE SEVEN SLEEPERS OF EPHESUS

Young in face and form and feature,
Stood an ancestor among them.
All bewildered heard he legends
Of his son and of his grandsons,
Fathers of the men before him.
So amazed he stood and listened,
Patriarch in his early manhood;
While the crowd around him gathered,
Stalwart men, and mighty captains,
Him, the youngest, to acknowledge
As the founder of their race!
And one token with another
Made assurance doubly certain;
None could doubt the wondrous story
Of himself and of his comrades.
Shortly, to the cave returning,
King and people all go with him,
And they saw him enter in.
But no more to king or people
Did the Chosen reappear.
For the seven, who long had tarried, —
Nay, but they were eight in number,
For the faithful dog was with them, —
Thenceforth from the world were sundered.
The most blessed angel Gabriel,
By the will of God Almighty,
Walling up the cave forever,
Led them unto Paradise.

KING DARIUS AND THE FLYING SCYTHIANS
[513 B.C.]

BY HERODOTUS; RETOLD BY ALFRED J. CHURCH

KING DARIUS, being lord of all Asia, wherein were great multitudes of men and much wealth, purposed to make war against the Scythians, desiring also to punish them for their wrongdoing in time past. Now their wrongdoing had been this. They had invaded Asia in the days of the Medes, and had ruled it for twenty and eight years, and when the years were ended had gone back to their own land. About which going back there is this to be told. When they were come to the border of the land, they found an army drawn out in battle array against them; and this army was of their own slaves. But when they had fought with the slaves many times and could not prevail, one of them said to his fellows: "Men of Scythia, we do ill, fighting against these slaves. Come, let us cast aside our spears and take each one of us his whip. For so long as they see us with arms in our hands they count themselves to be our equals, but when they shall see the whips they will remember that we are their masters." This the Scythians did, and it was so with the slaves, that when they saw the whips they fled.

King Darius therefore prepared to make war against the Scythians, requiring soldiers from some nations, and from some ships, and commanding others that they should make a bridge over the Thracian Bosphorus. But in the mean time Artabanus, that was brother to the

KING DARIUS AND THE FLYING SCYTHIANS

king, would have persuaded him not to go against the Scythians, as being men that had no possessions; but he could not prevail. And when the king was now about to depart from Susa, which is the chief city of Persia, there came to him one Œobazus, entreating of him that he would suffer one of his sons to tarry at home, for he had three sons and all were in the army. Then the king said that because Œobazus was his friend and asked but a small thing, all his sons should tarry at home. Whereat the man was greatly rejoiced; but the king sent his executioners and slew them all. In this fashion did they tarry at home.

When the king was come to the Bosphorus he set up two pillars of white marble, whereon he inscribed the names of all the nations as many as were in his army; and indeed of all that he ruled none were absent. The writing on the one pillar was Persian and on the other Greek. Now the number of the men was seven hundred thousand, besides those that were in the ships, and of ships there were six hundred. After this he crossed by the bridge, which Mæandrius of Samos had made over the Bosphorus, commanding the Ionians that they should sail along the shore to the river Danube and should make a bridge across the river, and so tarry till he should come. Then he went on his way through the land of Thrace till he came to the river Tearus. Of this river they say that the water thereof healeth diseases both of men and beasts beyond all others. It has thirty and eight springs flowing from one and the same rock, of which some are cold and some are hot. Here the king pitched his camp, and beside the river he set up a pillar by it, whereon was written, "To the Tearus, which is the best

PERSIA

and fairest of all rivers, came Darius, son of Hystaspes, King of the Persians, being the best and fairest of all men."

At this time the Getæ, that are called Immortal, submitted themselves to him. This they did without fighting, though they are counted the most valiant and righteous of all the Thracians. The cause wherefore they are called Immortal is this. They believe that they die not, but that such as seem to die go to their god Zalmoxis. And every fifth year they send a messenger to Zalmoxis with a message concerning the things which they need. They cast lots who shall be this messenger; and their manner of sending him is this. Some of them stand in order holding up three spears; and others take the messenger whom they would send to Zalmoxis by the hands and the feet, and throw him from above on to the spears. If the man die they hold that Zalmoxis is gracious to them; but if he die not, they blame the messenger, saying that he is a wicked man; and then they look for another. But the message they give him while he is yet alive. These Thracians shoot arrows into the sky when there is thunder and lightning, and threaten the gods, holding that there is in truth no god but this Zalmoxis. As for this Zalmoxis, some say that he was a slave in Samos, and that his master was Pythagoras, and that when he had gathered much wealth he went back to his country; and that he affirmed that neither he nor they that were his disciples should die, but should come to a country full of all manner of all good things; and that while he taught these things he made for himself a dwelling under the earth; and that when this dwelling was finished he vanished out of the sight of the Thracians and dwelt therein for three years; and that afterward

KING DARIUS AND THE FLYING SCYTHIANS

he showed himself again to the Thracians, so that they believed all that he had taught them.

After this the king came to the Danube; which when he had crossed, he said to the Ionians that they should loose the bridge and follow him. But when the Ionians were now about to loose it, a certain Coës, who was captain of the men of Mitylene, spake thus to the king, having first heard that the king would willingly hear his opinion: "This land into which thou goest, O King, hath in it neither fields nor cities; for which reason I would have thee leave this bridge, and leave also them that made it to guard it. For if we prosper in this journey and find the Scythians, then shall we have a way of return, and if we find them not, we shall also have a way. For that we shall turn our backs before the Scythians in battle, I fear not; but only, that not being able to find them, we may wander a long time, and so suffer many things. And I say not this that I may myself be left behind, only I set forth the opinion that I hold to be best for thee, O King: but as for myself I will go with thee, and will not be left behind." These words pleased Darius very much; and he said to Coës, "Man of Lesbos, if I return in peace, come to my house, that I may recompense thee for thy good counsel." After this he took a thong, and tied in it sixty knots, and calling the kings of the Ionians, said to them, " My former purpose concerning the bridge is changed. Take, therefore, this thong, and do thus with it. Loose one knot every day, from the day when I shall depart hence to fight with the Scythians. And if I come not back when all these knots shall have been loosed, then sail back to your own land; but for sixty days, according to the number of the knots, keep this bridge with all the care that ye may." And when he had said this, he went on his way searching for the Scythians.

Now the Scythians, knowing that they could not stand against the Persians in battle, sent messengers to the nations roundabout that they should help them, for that the Persians had it in their mind to conquer the whole country. And when the kings of these nations had met in council together, eight kings in all, the assembly soon divided, for three were willing to help the Scythians, but five were not willing, saying that the Scythians had invaded the land of Asia and were now suffering punishment for their misdeeds. When this was told to the Scythians they considered what they might best do; and it seemed best that they should not join battle with the Persians, but should flee before them, filling the springs and the wells, and destroying the pasture. For this end they divided themselves into two armies; whereof one, being one third part of the whole, having with them also the Sauromatæ, should go toward the river Tanais, if the Persians should pursue them, but if the Persians turned back, should pursue in their turn; and the remainder, having with them the Geloni and the Budini, should go toward the country of the five nations that would not help them, that the Persians might lay waste the country of these nations. But their wagons, wherein their wives and their children are wont to live, and their flocks and herds, save such only as they needed for food, they sent away, bidding them go northward.

After this, the swiftest of their horsemen went forth to meet the Persians, and found them encamped at a place that is three days' journey from the Danube. And

KING DARIUS AND THE FLYING SCYTHIANS

when the Persians saw the Scythian horsemen they followed on their track, and pursued them a very long way till they came to the desert. Here Darius halted and made his camp by the river Oarus, and began to build eight great forts. But as the Scythians could nowhere be seen he left the forts unfinished, and marched toward the west. And as he marched he came upon the greater army of the Scythians, and these also gave way before him, having always a day's journey between them and the Persians; and they led them to the towns of those nations that were not willing to help them. All these countries the Persians wasted, save only the country of the Agathyrsi; for these came down armed to their borders, and were ready to fight with the Scythians.

And when this had been done many days, Darius, being now weary, sent a horseman to Idanthyrsus, King of the Scythians, saying, "Why flyest thou ever in this fashion? If thou thinkest thyself able to meet me in battle, stay from thy wanderings and fight with me; but if thou confessest thyself to be not worthy, cease from this running, and send gifts as to thy master, even earth and water, and let us talk together." To this Idanthyrsus, King of the Scythians, made answer: "I never feared any man that I should flee before him; and I fear not thee, nor indeed do I now any other thing than that which I am wont to do in peace. But if thou wilt know why we do not fight with thee, hearken: we have neither city nor field for which we should fear, lest they should be taken or plundered, and so join battle with thee. Yet, if thou art minded by all means to fight with us, we have the tombs of our fathers. Find ye these, and seek to destroy them, and ye shall know right soon whether we will fight for the tombs of our fathers or no. But till thou do this we will not fight with thee till we be so minded. And as to what thou sayest of a master, know that our masters are Zeus only, whose son I am, and Vesta, that is Queen of the Scythians. As to these gifts of earth and water, I will not send them; but I will send such as is meet for thee to receive."

This answer the herald brought back to Darius; but when the kings of the Scythians heard this talk of masters and slaves they were very wroth, and they sent the smaller part of their army to treat with the Ionians at the bridge; but with the larger part they determined not to give way any more before the Persians, but to attack them while they were gathering food. This the Scythians did; and the horsemen of the Persians always fled before their horsemen; but when the foot-soldiers came to the help of the horsemen, then the Scythians gave place. Also they made many attacks on the Persians by night. One thing, indeed, there was that hindered them. There is neither ass nor mule in the whole land of Scythia; and it often fell out that when the horsemen of the Scythians were pursuing the Persians, the asses in their camp would bray; and when the horses heard it they would be astonished and stand still, pricking up their ears, for they had not heard such sound before nor seen the shape of an ass.

Now the Persians were troubled at what befell them; and when the Scythians saw this, they sought to keep them in their country that they might come utterly to want. For this end they left some of their flocks with the shepherds behind them when they themselves departed to some other place. And the Persians coming

KING DARIUS AND THE FLYING SCYTHIANS

upon the flocks and laying hold of them, were much encouraged, and so were the more willing to tarry in the country. But when this had been done many times, at last King Darius was in sore straits and knew not what he should do. Then the King of the Scythians knowing this sent a herald with gifts to Darius, and the gifts were these: a bird, and a mouse, and a frog, and five arrows. And the Persians inquired of the herald that brought the gifts what they might signify; but the man made answer that of this he knew nothing, but that it had been commanded him to give the gifts to the king and then depart straightway, but that the Persians might themselves discover, if only they were wise, what the gifts signified. And King Darius judged that the purpose of the Scythians was this, to give themselves up to him (which is commonly done by the giving of earth and water), for he considered that the mouse liveth in the earth, and eateth the fruits thereof even as doth a man, and that the frog liveth in the water, and that the bird is most like to the horse, and that as to the arrows these signified their arms which they gave up to him. This, indeed, was the opinion of King Darius; but the judgment of Gobryas about the matter was widely different. (This Gobryas was one of the seven who slew the Magian.) He indeed interpreted the gift after this fashion: Unless ye become as birds and fly up into the air, or as mice and burrow in the earth, or as frogs and leap into the water, ye shall not go back, but shall be smitten with these arrows that ye die. Thus Gobryas judged about the gifts.

But in the mean while one of the armies of the Scythians, that which had gone eastward to the Tanais, having returned by the way by which they went, came to the Danube and had speech with the Ionians that guarded the bridge, saying, "Men of Ionia, we come to you offering freedom if only ye will hearken unto us. We hear that Darius when he departed bade you guard the bridge for sixty days only, and that if he came not back within these sixty days, ye should loose the bridge and so depart to your own country. Now if ye do after these words ye shall have no blame either from him or from us. Tarry therefore for the appointed days and afterward depart." And when the Ionians said that they would do so the Scythians went their way.

Then this army of the Scythians departed; and the other army set themselves in battle array against Darius, having both horse and foot, and purposing to fight against him. And it so fell out when the two armies were drawn up the one over against the other, that a hare ran through the midst of the army of the Scythians, and when the Scythians saw it they left care of the battle and pursued after the hare. And Darius, seeing that the Scythians were in much confusion and shouted aloud, inquired what this might mean that the enemy were so disturbed. And when he knew that they were busy pursuing the hare he turned to them to whom he was wont to speak at other times also, and said to them, "Surely these men have a great scorn for us; and surely also Gobryas interpreted the gifts and their signification aright. Seeing then that these things are so, we need good counsel that we may return in safety." And Gobryas said, "O King, I knew before that these men were hard to deal with; and now I know it the more certainly when I see how they scoff at us. My judgment

KING DARIUS AND THE FLYING SCYTHIANS

therefore is this: so soon as it shall be night, let us light the fires in the camp, as we are wont to do at other times, and let us tie up the asses in their place, and let us so depart, leaving behind us such as be least able to endure hardships. And let us do this before that the Scythians go to the Danube and loose the bridge, or that the Ionians themselves consider that they may do us this hurt." This was the counsel of Gobryas; and so soon as it was night Darius followed it. He left such of the soldiers as were sick, and such as were of least account, if they should perish, and he caused them to tie up the asses in their places in the camp, and so departed. And the cause why he left the asses and the sick men behind was this: the asses he left that they might make a noise, and the men because they could not make haste in marching. But to these he said that his purpose was to attack the Scythians with the better part of his army, and that they in the mean while should guard the camp. This Darius said to them that were left, and having caused the camp-fires to be lighted he so departed, and made with all the speed that he could for the Danube. And the asses, missing the noise of the multitude about them, made themselves the more noise, which when the Scythians heard they made no doubt but that the Persians were yet in their camp.

But when the day was come they that had been left behind of the Persians, judging that they had been betrayed by King Darius, surrendered themselves to the Scythians, and told what had been done. And the Scythians, so soon as they heard it, pursued after the Persians with both their armies, and with the nations also that had come to their help; and they pursued,

PERSIA

going straight to the Danube. But the Persians and the Scythians fell not in with each other for this cause, namely, that the army of the Persians was for the most part of foot-soldiers, and they knew not the way, for indeed in the land of Scythia there are not roads duly made; but the Scythians were horsemen, and they knew the shortest ways. For this cause they fell not in with each other; but the Scythians came to the bridge of the Danube by a long time the first. And when they found that the Persians were not yet come to the bridge, they spake to the Ionians that were in the ships, saying, "Men of Ionia, the days that were numbered to you are now passed, and ye do wrong still tarrying here by the bridge. And if ye have done this heretofore in fear, fear ye no longer; but leave the bridge with all speed, and go on your way rejoicing, and be free, thanking the Gods and the Scythians for these benefits. And as for the man that was your master, we will so order things with him that he shall not make war against any man hereafter forever." When they heard this the Ionians took counsel together. Then Miltiades the Athenian, who was King of the Chersonese that is near the Hellespont, advised that they should do according to the saying of the Scythians, and so set the Ionians free. But the advice of Histiæus of Miletus was contrary to this, for he said, "Each one of us is king in his own city by reason of the power of Darius; and if this power be overthrown, then shall we be overthrown also, and neither he nor any man will be king in Miletus, or indeed in any of the cities, seeing that they would all of them wish to be governed by the people rather than be governed by a king."

KING DARIUS AND THE FLYING SCYTHIANS

When the other kings heard this they turned straightway to the opinion of Histiæus, though before they had followed the opinion of Miltiades. And as they judged it most expedient for themselves, so they did forthwith. For they loosed that part of the bridge which was toward the Scythians, and they loosed it for the length of a bow-shot. And this they did in order that, though they did nothing, they might yet seem to be doing something, and that the Scythians might not take the bridge by force, and so cross the Danube. And while they were loosing the bridge on the side of the Scythians they affirmed that they were about to do as the Scythians had counseled them. For Histiæus came forward in the name of all, and spake, saying, "Ye men of Scythia, ye have come to us with counsel that is right welcome, and are zealous on our behalf to good purpose. And as ye have advised us well, so will we serve you faithfully. For we will loose this bridge, even as ye now see us do, and we will work with all our might that we may have the freedom which we desire. Do ye, therefore, while we are loosing the bridge, go and seek for these oppressors, and when ye have found them, avenge yourselves and us also upon them in such manner as they deserve."

When the Scythians heard these words they believed a second time that the Ionians spake the truth, and so departed, seeking the Persians. Yet did they miss them altogether, and for this cause, for which indeed they were themselves to blame, namely, that they had destroyed the pastures and filled up the wells. For if they had not done this thing they could easily have found the Persians. But now the counsel that seemed to have been most excellently devised turned out ill for them.

PERSIA

For the Scythians indeed went through their country seeking the Persians where there was food for their horses and wells of water, for they thought that of a surety the enemy would return by this way. But the Persians did not so, but kept to their own trail which they had made marching from the Danube; and so at last, after many things suffered, they came to the river and the bridge. But as they came in the night-time, and the one end of the bridge had been loosed, they were for a while in great fear lest the Ionians should have left them. Now there was with Darius a certain Egyptian, whose voice was louder than the voice of all other men; and Darius commanded this man that he should go down to the edge of the river, and call to Histiæus of Miletus. This he did, and Histiæus heard him call the first time, and straightway brought the ships and joined the bridge, so that the army of the Persians passed over and escaped.

But when the Scythians came again to the river, having missed the Persians a second time, they had great wrath against the Ionians. And from that day they are wont to say of the Ionians that, if they be called freemen, then be they the most cowardly and vile of all the nations upon earth; and if they be counted slaves, then there are no slaves more mean and worthless.

HOW XERXES SET OUT TO CONQUER GREECE

[480 B.C.]

BY HERODOTUS

[DARIUS, King of Persia, tried in vain to conquer Greece. When his son Xerxes came to the throne in 486 B.C., he, too, made the same attempt. An account of his disastrous failure is given in volume IV, "The Great Persian Invasion."
The Editor.]

XERXES thus levied his army, searching out every region of the continent. For from the reduction of Egypt, he was employed four whole years in assembling his forces, and providing things necessary for the expedition. In the course of the fifth year he began his march with a vast multitude of men; for of the expeditions with which we are acquainted, this was by far the greatest, so that that of Darius against the Scythians appears nothing in comparison with this; nor the Scythian, when the Scythians pursuing the Cimmerians, and invading the Medic territory, subdued almost the whole of the upper part of Asia, on account of which Darius afterward attempted to inflict vengeance on them; nor, according to what is related, that of the Atridæ against Ilium; nor that of the Mysians and Teucrians, which took place before the Trojan War, who, having passed over into Europe by the Bosphorus, subdued all the Thracians, and went down to the Ionian Sea, and marched southward as far as the river Peneus.

PERSIA

All these expeditions, and any others, if there have been any besides them, are not to be compared with this one. For what nation did not Xerxes lead out of Asia against Greece? What stream, being drunk, did not fail him, except that of great rivers? Some supplied ships; others were ordered to furnish men for the infantry, from others cavalry were required, from others transports for horses, together with men to serve in the army; others had to furnish long ships for the bridges, and others provisions and vessels.

And first of all, as those who had first attempted to double Mount Athos had met with disasters, preparations were being made for nearly three years about Athos; for triremes were stationed at Eleus in the Chersonese, and proceeding from thence, men of every nation from the army dug under the lash; and they went in succession; and the people who dwelt round Athos dug also. Bubares, son of Megabazus, and Artachæus, son of Artæus, both Persians, presided over the work. Athos is a vast and celebrated mountain, stretching into the sea, and inhabited by men. Where the mountain terminates toward the continent, it is in the form of a peninsula, and is an isthmus of about twelve stades: this is a plain with hills of no great height from the sea of the Acanthians to the sea which is opposite Torone. On this isthmus, in which Mount Athos terminates, stands Sana, a Grecian city; but those within Sana, and situate on Athos itself, which the Persian then was proceeding to make insular instead of continental, are the following, Dion, Olophyxus, Acrothoon, Thyssus, and Cleonæ. These are the cities which occupy Mount Athos.

They made the excavation as follows: the barbarians

XERXES SETS OUT TO CONQUER GREECE

divided the ground among the several nations, having drawn a straight line near the city of Sana; and when the trench was deep, some standing at the bottom continued to dig, and others handed the soil that was dug out to men who stood above on ladders; they again in turn handed it to others, until they reached those that were at the top; these last carried it off and threw it away. To all the rest, except the Phœnicians, the brink of the excavation falling in gave double labor, for as they made the upper opening and the lower of equal dimensions, this must necessarily happen. But the Phœnicians show their skill in other works, and especially did so in this; for having received the portion that fell to their share, they dug it, making the upper opening of the trench twice as large as it was necessary for the trench itself to be; and as the work proceeded, they contracted it gradually, so that when they came to the bottom, the work was equal in width to the rest: near adjoining is a meadow, where they had a market and bazaar, and great abundance of meal was brought to them from Asia.

According to my deliberate opinion, Xerxes ordered this excavation to be made from motives of ostentation, wishing to display his power, and to leave a memorial of himself; for though it was possible, without any great labor, to have drawn the ships over the isthmus, he commanded them to dig a channel for the sea of such a width that two triremes might pass through rowed abreast. And the same persons, to whom the excavation was committed, were ordered also to throw a bridge over the river Strymon.

These things, then, he thus contrived: he also caused

cables of papyrus and of white flax to be prepared for the bridges, having ordered the Phœnicians and Egyptians also to lay up provisions for the army, that neither the men nor the beasts of burden might suffer from famine on their march toward Greece; and having informed himself of the situations of the places, he ordered them to lay up the provisions where it was most convenient, conveying them to various quarters in merchant-ships and transports from all parts of Asia. Of these provisions the largest quantity they conveyed to a place called Leuce-Acte, in Thrace; some were ordered to Tyrodiza of the Perinthians, others to Doriscus, others to Eion on the Strymon, and others to Macedonia.

While these men were employed in their appointed task, the whole land forces, having been assembled, marched with Xerxes to Sardis, having set out from Critalla in Cappadocia, for it was ordered that all the troops throughout the continent, that were to march with Xerxes himself, should be assembled at that place. Now which of the generals, bringing the best-appointed troops, received the gifts promised by the king, I am unable to mention; for I am not at all aware that they came to any decision on this point. They then, when having crossed the river Halys they entered Phrygia, marching through that country, arrived at Celænæ, where rise the springs of the Mæander, and of another river not less than the Mæander, which is called the Catarractes, which, springing up in the very forum of the Celænians, discharges itself into the Mæander; in this city, also, the skin of Silenus Marsyas is suspended, which, as the Phrygians report, was stripped off and suspended by Apollo.

XERXES SETS OUT TO CONQUER GREECE

In this city Pythius, son of Atys, a Lydian, being in waiting, entertained the whole army of the king and Xerxes himself with most sumptuous feasts, and he offered money, wishing to contribute toward the expense of the war. When Pythius offered money, Xerxes asked the Persians near him who this Pythius was, and what riches he possessed, that he made such an offer. They answered, "O King, this is the person who presented your father Darius with the golden plane tree and the vine; and he is now the richest man we know of in the world, next to yourself."

Xerxes, surprised with these last words, next asked Pythius what might be the amount of his wealth. He said, "O King, I will not conceal it from you, nor will I pretend to be ignorant of my own substance, but as I know it perfectly I will tell you the exact truth. As soon as I heard you were coming down to the Grecian sea, wishing to present you with money for the war I made inquiry, and found by computation that I had two thousand talents of silver, and of gold four millions of Daric staters, all but seven thousand.[1] These I freely give you; for myself, I have sufficient subsistence from my slaves and lands."

Thus he spoke; but Xerxes, delighted with his offer, replied: "My Lydian friend, since I left the Persian country I have met with no man to the present moment who was willing to entertain my army, or who, having come into my presence, has voluntarily offered to contribute money toward the war. But you have entertained my army magnificently and have offered

---

[1] The silver talent of the Greeks was equal to about $1000, the Daric stater to about $5.40.

me vast sums; therefore, in return for this, I confer on you the following rewards: I make you my friend, and will make up the sum of four millions of staters from my own treasures, by adding the seven thousand; so that the four millions may not be short of seven thousand, but the full sum may be completed by me. Do you retain what you have acquired, and be careful always to continue such as you are; for if you do this you shall never repent, either now or hereafter."

Having said this, and performed his promises, he continued his march; and passing by a city of the Phrygians called Anaua, and a lake from which salt is obtained, he arrived at Colossæ, a considerable city of Phrygia, in which the river Lycus, falling into a chasm of the earth, disappears; then reappearing after a distance of about five stades, it also discharges itself into the Mæander. From Colossæ the army, advancing toward the boundaries of the Phrygians and Lydians, arrived at the city of Cydrara, where a pillar, planted in the ground, and erected by Crœsus, indicates the boundaries by an inscription.

When from Phrygia he entered Lydia, the way dividing into two, that on the left leading to Caria, the other on the right to Sardis, by which latter a traveler is compelled to cross the river Mæander, and to pass by the city of Callatebus, in which confectioners make honey with tamarisk and wheat; Xerxes, going by this way, met with a plane tree, which, on account of its beauty, he presented with golden ornaments, and, having committed it to the care of one of the immortals, on the next day he arrived at Sardis, the capital of the Lydians.

On his arrival at Sardis, he first of all sent heralds to

XERXES SETS OUT TO CONQUER GREECE

Greece to demand earth and water, and to require them to provide entertainment for the king; except that he did not send either to Athens or Lacedæmon, but he did to every other place. And he sent the second time for earth and water for the following reason; such as had not given them before when Darius sent, he thought would then certainly do so through fear; wishing, therefore, to know this for certain, he sent. And after this he prepared to march to Abydos.

In the mean while, those who were appointed had joined the Hellespont from Asia to Europe. There is in the Chersonese on the Hellespont, between the city of Sestos and Madytus, a craggy shore extending into the sea, directly opposite Abydos: there, not long after these events, under Xanthippus, son of Ariphron, a general of the Athenians, having taken Artayctes, a Persian, governor of Sestos, they impaled him alive against a plank; for he, having brought women into the temple of Protesilaus at Elæus, committed atrocious crimes.

To this shore, then, beginning at Abydos, they, on whom this task was imposed, constructed bridges, the Phœnicians one with white flax, and the Egyptians the other with papyrus. The distance from Abydos to the opposite shore is seven stades. When the strait was thus united, a violent storm arising, broke in pieces and scattered the whole work.

When Xerxes heard of this, being exceedingly indignant, he commanded that the Hellespont should be stricken with three hundred lashes with a scourge, and that a pair of fetters should be let down into the sea. I have moreover heard that with them he likewise sent branding instruments to brand the Hellespont. He certainly charged those who flogged the waters to utter these barbarous and impious words: "Thou bitter water! thy master inflicts this punishment upon thee, because thou hast injured him, although thou hadst not suffered any harm from him; and King Xerxes will cross over thee, whether thou wilt or not; it is with justice that no man sacrifices to thee, because thou art both a deceitful and briny river!" He accordingly commanded them to chastise the sea in this manner, and to cut off the heads of those who had to superintend the joining of the Hellespont.

They on whom this thankless office was imposed carried it into execution; and other engineers constructed bridges; and they constructed them in the following manner. They connected together pentecounters and triremes, under that toward the Euxine Sea, three hundred and sixty; and under the other, three hundred and fourteen, obliquely in respect of the Pontus, but in the direction of the current in respect of the Hellespont, that it might keep up the tension of the cables. Having connected them together, they let down very long anchors, some on the one bridge toward the Pontus, on account of the winds that blew from it within; others on the other bridge toward the west and the Ægean, on account of the south and southeast winds. They left an opening as a passage through between the pentecounters, and that in three places, that any one who wished might be able to sail into the Pontus in light vessels, and from the Pontus outward. Having done this, they stretched the cables from the shore, twisting them with wooden capstans, not as before using the two kinds separately, but assign-

XERXES SETS OUT TO CONQUER GREECE

ing to each two of white flax and four of papyrus. The thickness and quality were the same, but those of flax were stronger in proportion, every cubit weighing a full talent. When the passage was bridged over, having sawn up trunks of trees, and having made them equal to the width of the bridge, they laid them regularly upon the extended cables; and having laid them in regular order, they then fastened them together. And having done this, they put brushwood on the top; and having laid the brushwood in regular order, they put earth over the whole; and having pressed down the earth, they drew a fence on each side, that the beasts of burden and horses might not be frightened by looking down upon the sea.

When the works at the bridges were completed, and those at Mount Athos, as well as the mounds at the mouths of the canal, which had been made on account of the tide, in order that the mouths of the trench might not be choked up, and news was brought that the canal was entirely completed; thereupon the army, having wintered at Sardis, and being fully prepared, set out at the beginning of the spring from thence toward Abydos. But as it was on the point of setting out, the sun, quitting his seat in the heavens, disappeared, though there were no clouds, and the air was perfectly serene, and night ensued in the place of day. When Xerxes saw and perceived this, it occasioned him much uneasiness; he therefore inquired of the magi what the prodigy might portend. They answered that "the deity foreshows to the Greeks the extinction of their cities"; adding, "that the sun is the portender of the future to the Greeks, and the moon to the Persians." Xerxes, having heard this, was much delighted, and set out upon his march.

As he was leading his army away, Pythius the Lydian, terrified by the prodigy in the heavens, and emboldened by the gifts, went to Xerxes the king, and spoke thus: "Sire, would you indulge me by granting a boon I should wish to obtain, which is easy for you to grant, and of great importance to me." Xerxes, expecting that he would wish for anything rather than what he did ask, said that he would grant his request, and bade him declare what he wanted; whereupon he, when he heard this, spoke confidently as follows: "Sire, I have five sons; and it happens that they are all attending you in the expedition against Greece. But do you, O King, pity me, who am thus advanced in years, and release one of my sons from the service, that he may take care of me and my property. Take the other four with you, and, having accomplished your designs, may you return home."

Xerxes was highly incensed, and answered as follows: "Base man! hast thou dared, when I am marching in person against Greece, and taking with me my children, and brothers, and kinsmen, and friends, to make mention of thy son? thou, who art my slave, and who wert bound in duty to follow me with all thy family, even with thy wife. Now learn this well, that the spirit of man dwells in his ears; which, when it hears pleasing things, fills the whole body with delight, but when it hears the contrary, swells with indignation. When, therefore, you did well, and gave promise of the like, you cannot boast of having surpassed the king in generosity; but now that you have adopted a more shameless conduct, you shall not receive your deserts, but less than

XERXES SETS OUT TO CONQUER GREECE

your deserts; for your hospitality preserves four of your children, but you shall be punished with the loss of the one whom you cherish most." When he had given this answer, he immediately commanded those whose office it was to execute such orders, to find out the eldest of the sons of Pythius, and to cut his body in two; and having so done, to deposit the halves, one on the right of the road, the other on the left; and that the army should pass between them.

When they had done this, the army afterward passed between. The baggage-bearers and beasts of burden first led the way; after them came a host of all nations promiscuously, not distinguished: after more than one half of the army had passed, an interval was left, that they might not mix with the king's troops. Before him a thousand horsemen led the van, chosen from among all the Persians; and next to them a thousand spearmen, those also chosen from among all, carrying their lances turned downward to the earth. After these came ten sacred horses called Nisæan, gorgeously caparisoned. These horses are called Nisæan on the following account: there is a large plain in the Medic territory which is called the Nisæan; now this plain produces these large horses. Behind these ten horses was placed the sacred chariot of Jupiter, drawn by eight white horses; behind the horses followed a charioteer on foot, holding the reins; because no mortal ever ascends this seat. Behind this came Xerxes himself, on a chariot drawn by Nisæan horses; and a charioteer walked at his side, whose name was Patiramphes, son of Otanes, a Persian.

In this manner, then, Xerxes marched out of Sardis, and whenever he thought right, he used to pass from the chariot to a covered carriage. Behind him marched a thousand spearmen, the bravest and most noble of the Persians, carrying their spears in the usual manner; and after them another body of a thousand horse, chosen from among the Persians: after the cavalry came ten thousand men chosen from the rest of the Persians; these were infantry; and of these, one thousand had golden pomegranates on their spears instead of ferules, and they inclosed the others all round; but the nine thousand, being within them, had silver pomegranates. Those also that carried their spears turned to the earth had golden pomegranates, and those that followed nearest to Xerxes had golden apples. Behind the ten thousand foot were placed ten thousand Persian cavalry; and after the cavalry was left an interval of two stades; and then the rest of the throng followed promiscuously.

The army directed its march from Lydia to the river Caicus and the Mysian territory; and proceeding from the Caicus, leaving Mount Canæ on the left, passed through Atarneus to the city Carina. From thence it marched through the plain of Thebes, and passing by the city of Adramyttium and the Pelasgian Antrandus, and keeping Mount Ida on the left, it entered the territory of Ilium. But before this, as the army halted during the night under Mount Ida, thunder and lightning fell upon them, and destroyed a considerable number of the troops on the spot.

When the army arrived at the Scamander, which was the first river since they had set out on their march from Sardis, whose stream failed and did not afford sufficient drink for the army and beasts of burden; when, accordingly, Xerxes arrived at this river, he went up to

XERXES SETS OUT TO CONQUER GREECE

the Pergamus [1] of Priam, being desirous of seeing it; and having seen it, and inquired into every particular, he sacrificed a thousand oxen to the Ilian Minerva, and the magi poured out libations to the honor of the heroes. After they had done this, a panic fell on the camp during the night, and at the dawn of day they marched from thence, on the left skirting the city of Rhœtium, and Ophrynium, and Dardanus, which borders on Abydos, and on the right the Gergithæ Teucrians.

When they were at Abydos, Xerxes wished to behold the whole army; and there had been previously erected on a hill at this place, for his express use, a lofty throne of white marble; the people of Abydos had made it, in obedience to a previous order of the king. When he was seated there, looking down toward the shore, he beheld both the land army and the fleet; and when he beheld them, he desired to see a contest take place between the ships; and when it had taken place, and the Sidonian Phœnicians were victorious, he showed himself exceedingly gratified both with the contest and the army.

And when he saw the whole Hellespont covered by the ships, and all the shores and the plains of Abydos full of men, Xerxes thereupon pronounced himself happy, but afterward shed tears.

Artabanus, his paternal uncle, having observed him, the same who had before freely declared his opinion, and advised Xerxes not to invade Greece; this man, having perceived Xerxes shedding tears, addressed him thus: "O King, how very different from each other are what you are now doing and what you did a little while ago! for having pronounced yourself happy, now you weep."

[1] That is, "the citadel."

PERSIA

He answered, "Commiseration seized me when I considered how brief all human life is, since of these, numerous as they are, not one shall survive to the hundredth year." But Artabanus replied, saying, "We suffer during life other things more pitiable than this; for in this so brief life, there is not one, either of these or of others, born so happy, that it will not occur to him, not only once but oftentimes, to wish rather to die than to live; for calamities befalling him, and diseases disturbing him, make life, though really short, appear to be long; so that death, life being burdensome, becomes the most desirable refuge for man; and the deity, having given us to taste of sweet existence, is found to be jealous of his gift."

Xerxes answered, saying, "Artabanus, of human life, which is such as you have described it, let us say no more, nor let us call evils to mind, now that we have good things before us."

Xerxes again summoned the most distinguished of the Persians, and when they were assembled he addressed them as follows: "O Persians, I have called you together to desire this of you, that you would acquit yourselves like brave men, and not disgrace the former exploits of the Persians, which are great and memorable; but let each and all of us together show our zeal, for this which we are endeavoring to accomplish is a good common to all. On this account, then, I call on you to apply yourselves earnestly to the war; for, as I am informed, we are marching against brave men; and if we conquer them, no other army in the world will dare to oppose us. Now, then, let us cross over, having first offered up prayers to the gods who protect the Persian territory."

XERXES SETS OUT TO CONQUER GREECE

That day they made preparations for the passage over; and on the following they waited for the sun, as they wished to see it rising, in the mean time burning all sorts of perfumes on the bridges, and strewing the road with myrtle branches. When the sun rose, Xerxes, pouring a libation into the sea out of a golden cup, offered up a prayer to the sun that no such accident might befall him as would prevent him from subduing Europe until he had reached its utmost limits. After having prayed, he threw the cup into the Hellespont, and a golden bowl, and a Persian sword, which they call acinace; but I cannot determine with certainty whether he dropped these things into the sea as an offering to the sun, or whether he repented of having scourged the Hellespont, and presented these gifts to the sea as a compensation.

When these ceremonies were finished, the infantry and all the cavalry crossed over by that bridge which was toward the Pontus, and the beasts of burden and attendants by that toward the Ægean. First of all, the ten thousand Persians led the van, all wearing crowns, and after them the promiscuous host of all nations. These crossed on that day. On the following, first the horsemen, and those who carried their lances downward: these also wore crowns; next came the sacred horses and the sacred chariot; afterward Xerxes himself, and the spearmen, and the thousand horsemen; after them the rest of the army closed the march, and at the same time the ships got under weigh to the opposite shore. I have also heard that Xerxes crossed over last of all.

Xerxes, when he had crossed over into Europe, saw the army crossing over under the lash: his army crossed over in seven days and seven nights without halting at all. On this occasion, it is related that when Xerxes had crossed over the Hellespont, a certain Hellespontine said, "O Jupiter, why, assuming the form of a Persian, and taking the name of Xerxes, do you wish to subvert Greece, bringing all mankind with you, since without them it was in your power to do this?"

II
DAYS OF DECLINE

HISTORICAL NOTE

THE failure of Xerxes to conquer Greece marked the end of Persian greatness. The kingdom, apparently strong and flourishing, was really weak and in its decline. In the year 334 B.C., Alexander the Great with a small army of Macedonians and Greeks invaded Persia and conquered Darius III, the last of the Persian kings. After the death of Alexander and the breaking-up of his kingdom, the Parthians came into power. Their contests with the Romans brought about confusion and weakness, and one Artaxerxes, who claimed to be a descendant of the family of Cyrus, succeeded in making himself sovereign and the founder of a dynasty which continued for more than four hundred years. The most famous ruler of this line was Khosru, who reigned 531–79 A.D. His justice and wisdom and valor in arms were the themes of many a native poet. This glory was short-lived. First, the Romans, then the Mohammedan Arabs invaded the land. Then came the Seljooks, the Tartars, the leader Tamerlane with a new horde of Mongols, and the Afghans; and there were periods of revolution and anarchy marked by revolting tales of perfidy and cruelty. For more than a thousand years the history of Persia has been a long, uninteresting story of constantly changing divisions of the kingdom, of new dynasties, of murders, invasions, and wars.

THE LAST KING OF PERSIA[1]

[334 B.C.]

BY PLUTARCH (ABRIDGED)

[IN 401 B.C., the brother of the Persian king hired some Greek soldiers to help him seize the kingdom. He and the Greek generals were slain. The men made their way back to Greece and reported that the Persian kingdom was not nearly so strong as had been supposed. These two events encouraged Alexander the Great, King of Macedonia, to lead in 334 B.C. an army into Asia against Persia.

The Editor.]

THERE was at this time in Darius's army a Macedonian refugee, named Amyntas, one who was pretty well acquainted with Alexander's character. This man, when he saw Darius intended to fall upon the enemy in the passes and defiles, advised him earnestly to keep where he was, in the open and extensive plains, it being the advantage of a numerous army to have field-room enough when it engages with a lesser force. Darius, instead of taking his counsel, told him he was afraid the enemy would endeavor to run away, and so Alexander would escape out of his hands. "That fear," replied Amyntas, "is needless, for assure yourself that far from avoiding you, he will make all the speed he can to meet you, and is now most likely on his march towards you." But Amyntas's counsel was to no purpose, for Darius immediately decamping, marched into Cilicia, at the same time that Alexander advanced into Syria to meet

[1] From *Plutarch's Lives*. Corrected and translated by A. H. Clough. Copyright (U.S.A.), 1876, by Little, Brown, and Company.

him; and missing one another in the night, they both turned back again. Alexander, greatly pleased with the event, made all the haste he could to fight in the defiles, and Darius to recover his former ground, and draw his army out of so disadvantageous a place. For now he began to perceive his error in engaging himself too far in a country in which the sea, the mountains, and the river Pinarus running through the midst of it, would necessitate him to divide his forces, render his horse almost unserviceable, and only cover and support the weakness of the enemy. Fortune was not kinder to Alexander in the choice of the ground, than he was careful to improve it to his advantage. For being much inferior in numbers, so far from allowing himself to be outflanked, he stretched his right wing much further out than the left wing of his enemies, and fighting there himself in the very foremost ranks, put the barbarians to flight. In this battle he was wounded in the thigh, Chares says by Darius, with whom he fought hand to hand. But in the account which he gave Antipater of the battle, though indeed he owns he was wounded in the thigh with a sword, though not dangerously, yet he takes no notice who it was that wounded him.

Nothing was wanting to complete this victory, in which he overthrew above an hundred and ten thousand of his enemies, but the taking the person of Darius, who escaped very narrowly by flight. However, having taken his chariot and his bow, he returned from pursuing him, and found his own men busy in pillaging the barbarians' camp, which (though to disburden themselves, they had left most of their baggage at Damascus) was exceedingly rich. But Darius's tent, which was full of splendid furniture, and quantities of gold and silver, they reserved for Alexander himself, who after he had put off his arms, went to bathe himself, saying, "Let us now cleanse ourselves from the toils of war in the bath of Darius." "Not so," replied one of his followers, "but in Alexander's rather; for the property of the conquered is, and should be called the conqueror's." Here, when he beheld the bathing vessels, the water-pots, the pans, and the ointment boxes, all of gold, curiously wrought, and smelt the fragrant odors with which the whole place was exquisitely perfumed, and from thence passed into a pavilion of great size and height, where the couches and tables and preparations for an entertainment were perfectly magnificent, he turned to those about him and said, "This, it seems, is royalty."

But as he was going to supper, word was brought him that Darius's mother and wife and two unmarried daughters, being taken among the rest of the prisoners, upon the sight of his chariot and bow were all in mourning and sorrow, imagining him to be dead. After a little pause, more livelily affected with their affliction than with his own success, he sent Leonnatus to them, to let them know Darius was not dead, and that they need not fear any harm from Alexander, who made war upon him only for dominion; they should themselves be provided with everything they had been used to receive from Darius. This kind message could not but be very welcome to the captive ladies, especially being made good by actions no less humane and generous. For he gave them leave to bury whom they pleased of the Persians, and to make use for this purpose of what garments and furniture they thought fit out of the booty. He diminished nothing of their equipage, or of the attentions and respect formerly paid them, and allowed larger pensions for their maintenance than they had before.

Darius wrote him a letter, and sent friends to intercede with him, requesting him to accept as a ransom of his captives the sum of a thousand talents, and offering him in exchange for his amity and alliance, all the countries on this side the river Euphrates, together with one of his daughters in marriage. These propositions he communicated to his friends; and when Parmenio told him, that for his part, if he were Alexander, he should readily embrace them, "So would I," said Alexander, "if I were Parmenio." Accordingly, his answer to Darius was, that if he would come and yield himself up into his power, he would treat him with all possible kindness; if not, he was resolved immediately to go himself and seek him. But the death of Darius's wife made him soon after regret one part of this answer, and he showed evident marks of grief at being thus deprived of a further opportunity of exercising his clemency and good nature, which he manifested, however, as far as he could, by giving her a most sumptuous funeral.

Among the attendants who waited in the queen's chamber, and were taken prisoners with the women, there was one Tireus, who getting out of the camp, fled away on horseback to Darius, to inform him of his wife's death. He, when he heard it, beating his head, and bursting into tears and lamentations, said, "Alas! how great is the calamity of the Persians! Was it not enough that their king's consort and sister was a prisoner in her lifetime, but she must, now she is dead also, be but meanly and obscurely buried?" "O King," replied the

THE FAMILY OF DARIUS AT THE FEET OF ALEXANDER THE GREAT

THE FAMILY OF DARIUS AT THE FEET OF ALEXANDER THE GREAT

BY PAUL VERONESE
(*Italy*, 1530(?)–1588)

In the course of the wars of Alexander the Great with Darius of Persia, he captured the mother, wife, and two daughters of his antagonist. He sent at once to assure them that Darius was not dead, and that they themselves would be treated with the utmost respect — a promise which was kept to the letter. Some time later, the wife of Darius died, and her conqueror buried her with ceremonies of the utmost magnificence. According to Plutarch, Alexander had never even looked upon her face, so that Veronese's painting is rather what might have been than what was.

To attempt to make dress and other accessories those of the event portrayed, was a thing which probably never entered the mind of a sixteenth-century painter; and therefore the costumes in this picture are by no means those of Alexander's day, but exhibit the fashions and the gorgeousness of the Italian Renaissance.

Paul Veronese, the painter of this picture, was a "decorative painter of the highest rank." His delight was to portray men and women at luxurious banquets and in the gorgeous costumes of pageantry. He was a fine draughtsman and a "narrative painter," that is, his pictures may be depended upon to tell stories and to portray upon the faces of the different characters their feelings and emotions.

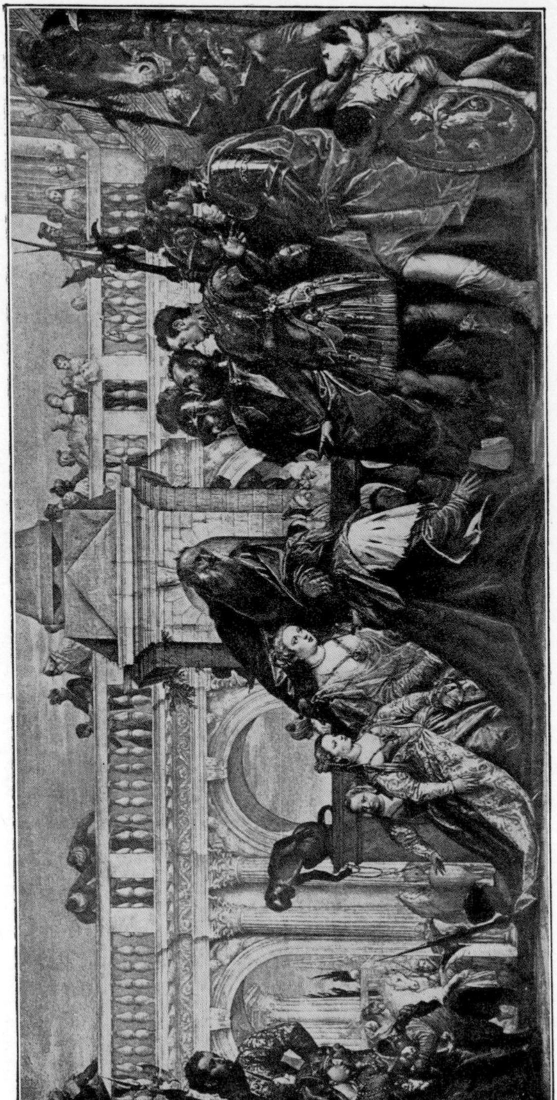

attendant, "as to her funeral rites, or any respect or honor that should have been shown in them, you have not the least reason to accuse the ill fortune of your country; for to my knowledge neither your queen Statira when alive, nor your mother, nor children, wanted anything of their former happy condition, unless it were the light of your countenance, which I doubt not but the lord Oromasdes will yet restore to its former glory. And after her decease, I assure you, she had not only all due funeral ornaments, but was honored also with the tears of your very enemies; for Alexander is as gentle after victory, as he is terrible in the field."

Darius, breaking away from him into the other division of the tent, where his friends and courtiers were, lifted up his hands to heaven, and uttered this prayer: "Ye gods," said he, "of my family, and of my kingdom, if it be possible, I beseech you to restore the declining affairs of Persia, that I may leave them in as flourishing a condition as I found them, and have it in my power to make a grateful return to Alexander for the kindness which in my adversity he has shown to those who are dearest to me. But if, indeed, the fatal time be come, which is to give a period to the Persian monarchy, if our ruin be a debt that must be paid to the divine jealousy and the vicissitude of things, then I beseech you grant that no other man but Alexander may sit upon the throne of Cyrus." Such is the narrative given by the greater number of the historians.

But to return to Alexander. After he had reduced all Asia on this side the Euphrates, he advanced towards Darius, who was coming down against him with a million of men. In his march, a very ridiculous passage happened. The servants who followed the camp, for sport's sake divided themselves into two parties, and named the commander of one of them Alexander, and of the other Darius. At first they only pelted one another with clods of earth, but presently took to their fists and at last, heated with the contention, they fought in good earnest with stones and clubs, so that they had much ado to part them; till Alexander, upon hearing of it, ordered the two captains to decide the quarrel by single combat, and armed him who bore his name himself, while Philotas did the same to him who represented Darius. The whole army were spectators of this encounter, willing from the event of it to derive an omen of their own future success. After they had fought stoutly a pretty long while, at last he who was called Alexander had the better, and for a reward of his prowess had twelve villages given him, with leave to wear the Persian dress. So we are told by Eratosthenes.

But the great battle of all that was fought with Darius, was not, as most writers tell us, at Arbela, but at Gaugamela, which, in their language, signifies the camel's house, forasmuch as one of their ancient kings having escaped the pursuit of his enemies on a swift camel, in gratitude to his beast, settled him at this place, with an allowance of certain villages and rents for his maintenance. It came to pass that in the month Boëdromion, about the beginning of the feast of Mysteries at Athens, there was an eclipse of the moon, the eleventh night after which, the two armies being now in view of one another, Darius kept his men in arms, and by torchlight took a general review of them. But Alexander, while his soldiers slept, spent the night before his tent

THE LAST KING OF PERSIA

with his diviner Aristander, performing certain mysterious ceremonies, and sacrificing to the god Fear. In the mean while the oldest of his commanders, and chiefly Parmenio, when they beheld all the plain between Niphates and the Gordyæan Mountains shining with the lights and fires which were made by the barbarians and heard the uncertain and confused sound of voices out of their camp, like the distant roaring of a vast ocean, were so amazed at the thoughts of such a multitude, that after some conference among themselves, they concluded it an enterprise too difficult and hazardous for them to engage so numerous an enemy in the day, and therefore meeting the king as he came from sacrificing, besought him to attack Darius by night, that the darkness might conceal the danger of the ensuing battle. To this he gave them the celebrated answer, "I will not steal a victory," which though some at the time thought a boyish and inconsiderate speech, as if he played with danger, others, however, regarded as an evidence that he confided in his present condition, and acted on a true judgment of the future, not wishing to leave Darius, in case he were worsted, the pretext of trying his fortune again, which he might suppose himself to have, if he could impute his overthrow to the disadvantage of the night, as he did before to the mountains, the narrow passages, and the sea. For while he had such numerous forces and large dominions still remaining, it was not any want of men or arms that could induce him to give up the war, but only the loss of all courage and hope upon the conviction of an undeniable and manifest defeat.

After they were gone from him with this answer, he laid himself down in his tent and slept the rest of the night more soundly than was usual with him, to the astonishment of the commanders, who came to him early in the morning, and were fain themselves to give order that the soldiers should breakfast. But at last, time not giving them leave to wait any longer, Parmenio went to his bedside, and called him twice or thrice by his name, till he waked him, and then asked him how it was possible, when he was to fight the most important battle of all, he could sleep as soundly as if he were already victorious. "And are we not so, indeed," replied Alexander, smiling, "since we are at last relieved from the trouble of wandering in pursuit of Darius through a wide and wasted country, hoping in vain that he would fight us?" And not only before the battle, but in the height of the danger, he showed himself great, and manifested the self-possession of a just foresight and confidence. For the battle for some time fluctuated and was dubious. The left wing, where Parmenio commanded, was so impetuously charged by the Bactrian horse that it was disordered and forced to give ground, at the same time that Mazæus had sent a detachment round about to fall upon those who guarded the baggage, which so disturbed Parmenio, that he sent messengers to acquaint Alexander that the camp and baggage would be all lost unless he immediately relieved the rear by a considerable reinforcement drawn out of the front. This message being brought him just as he was giving the signal to those about him for the onset, he bade them tell Parmenio that he must have surely lost the use of his reason, and had forgotten, in his alarm, that soldiers, if victorious, become masters of their enemies' baggage; and if defeated, instead of taking care of their wealth or their slaves, have nothing more to do but to fight gallantly and die with honor. When he had said this, he put on his helmet, having the rest of his arms on before he came out of his tent, which were a coat of the Sicilian make, girt close about him, and over that a breastpiece of thickly quilted linen, which was taken among other booty at the battle of Issus. The helmet, which was made by Theophilus, though of iron, was so well wrought and polished, that it was as bright as the most refined silver. To this was fitted a gorget of the same metal, set with precious stones. His sword, which was the weapon he most used in fight, was given him by the king of the Citieans, and was of an admirable temper and lightness. The belt which he also wore in all engagements, was of much richer workmanship than the rest of his armor. It was a work of the ancient Helicon, and had been presented to him by the Rhodians, as a mark of their respect to him. So long as he was engaged in drawing up his men, or riding about to give orders or directions, or to view them, he spared Bucephalus, who was now growing old, and made use of another horse; but when he was actually to fight, he sent for him again, and as soon as he was mounted, commenced the attack.

He made the longest address that day to the Thessalians and other Greeks, who answered him with loud shouts, desiring him to lead them on against the barbarians; upon which he shifted his javelin into his left hand, and with his right lifted up towards heaven, besought the gods, as Callisthenes tells us, that if he was of a truth the son of Jupiter, they would be pleased to assist and strengthen the Grecians. At the same time the augur Aristander, who had a white mantle about him, and a crown of gold on his head, rode by and showed them an eagle that soared just over Alexander, and directed his flight towards the enemy; which so animated the beholders, that after mutual encouragements and exhortations, the horse charged at full speed, and were followed in a mass by the whole phalanx of the foot. But before they could well come to blows with the first ranks, the barbarians shrunk back, and were hotly pursued by Alexander, who drove those that fled before him into the middle of the battle, where Darius himself was in person, whom he saw from a distance over the foremost ranks, conspicuous in the midst of his life-guard, a tall and fine-looking man, drawn in a lofty chariot, defended by an abundance of the best horse, who stood close in order about it, ready to receive the enemy. But Alexander's approach was so terrible, forcing those who gave back upon those who yet maintained their ground, that he beat down and dispersed them almost all. Only a few of the bravest and valiantest opposed the pursuit, who were slain in their king's presence, falling in heaps upon one another, and in the very pangs of death striving to catch hold of the horses. Darius now seeing all was lost, that those who were placed in front to defend him were broken and beat back upon him, that he could not turn or disengage his chariot without great difficulty, the wheels being clogged and entangled among the dead bodies, which lay in such heaps as not only stopped, but almost covered the horses, and made them rear and grow so unruly that the frighted charioteer could govern them no longer, in this extremity was glad to quit his chariot and his arms, and mounting, it is said, upon a mare that had been taken from her foal, betook himself

THE LAST KING OF PERSIA

to flight. But he had not escaped so either, if Parmenio had not sent fresh messengers to Alexander, to desire him to return and assist him against a considerable body of the enemy which yet stood together, and would not give ground. For, indeed, Parmenio is on all hands accused of having been sluggish and unserviceable in this battle, whether age had impaired his courage, or that, as Callisthenes says, he secretly disliked and envied Alexander's growing greatness. Alexander, though he was not a little vexed to be so recalled and hindered from pursuing his victory, yet concealed the true reason from his men, and causing a retreat to be sounded, as if it were too late to continue the execution any longer, marched back towards the place of danger, and by the way met with the news of the enemy's total overthrow and flight.

This battle being thus over, seemed to put a period to the Persian empire; and Alexander, who was now proclaimed king of Asia, returned thanks to the gods in magnificent sacrifices, and rewarded his friends and followers with great sums of money, and places, and governments of provinces.

He now set forth to seek Darius, expecting he should be put to the hazard of another battle, but heard he was taken and secured by Bessus, upon which news he sent home the Thessalians, and gave them a largess of two thousand talents over and above the pay that was due to them. This long and painful pursuit of Darius, for in eleven days he marched thirty-three hundred furlongs, harassed his soldiers so that most of them were ready to give it up, chiefly for want of water. While they were in this distress, it happened that some Macedonians who

PERSIA

had fetched water in skins upon their mules from a river they had found out, came about noon to the place where Alexander was, and seeing him almost choked with thirst, presently filled an helmet and offered it him. He asked them to whom they were carrying the water; they told him to their children, adding, that if his life were but saved, it was no matter for them, they should be able well enough to repair that loss, though they all perished. Then he took the helmet into his hands, and looking round about, when he saw all those who were near him stretching their heads out and looking earnestly after the drink, he returned it again with thanks without tasting a drop of it: "For," said he, "if I alone should drink, the rest will be out of heart." The soldiers no sooner took notice of his temperance and magnanimity upon this occasion, than they one and all cried out to him to lead them forward boldly, and began whipping on their horses. For whilst they had such a king, they said they defied both weariness and thirst, looked upon themselves to be little less than immortal. But though they were all equally cheerful and willing, yet not above threescore horse were able, it is said, to keep up, and to fall in with Alexander upon the enemy's camp, where they rode over abundance of gold and silver that lay scattered about, and passing by a great many chariots full of women that wandered here and there for want of drivers, they endeavored to overtake the first of those that fled, in hopes to meet with Darius among them. And at last, after much trouble, they found him lying in a chariot, wounded all over with darts, just at the point of death. However, he desired they would give him some drink; and when he had drunk a little cold water, he told Polystratus, who gave it him, that it had become the last extremity of his ill fortune to receive benefits and not be able to return them. "But Alexander," said he, "whose kindness to my mother, my wife, and my children I hope the gods will recompense, will doubtless thank you for your humanity to me. Tell him, therefore, in token of my acknowledgment, I give him this right hand," with which words he took hold of Polystratus's hand and died. When Alexander came up to them, he showed manifest tokens of sorrow, and, taking off his own cloak, threw it upon the body to cover it. And some time afterwards, when Bessus was taken, he ordered him to be torn in pieces in this manner. They fastened him to a couple of trees which were bound down so as to meet, and then being let loose, with a great force returned to their places, each of them carrying that part of the body along with it that was tied to it. Darius's body was laid in state, and sent to his mother with pomp suitable to his quality. His brother Exathres, Alexander received into the number of his intimate friends.

DARA

BY JAMES RUSSELL LOWELL

WHEN Persia's scepter trembled in a hand
Wilted with harem-heats, and all the land
Was hovered over by those vulture ills
That snuff decaying empire from afar,
Then, with a nature balanced as a star,
Dara arose, a shepherd of the hills.

He who had governed fleecy subjects well
Made his own village by the selfsame spell
Secure and quiet as a guarded fold;
Then, gathering strength by slow and wise degrees
Under his sway, to neighbor villages
Order returned, and faith and justice old.

Now when it fortuned that a king more wise
Endued the realm with brain and hands and eyes,
He sought on every side men brave and just;
And having heard our mountain shepherd's praise,
How he refilled the mould of elder days,
To Dara gave a satrapy in trust.

So Dara shepherded a province wide,
Nor in his viceroy's scepter took more pride
Than in his crook before; but envy finds
More food in cities than on mountains bare;
And the frank sun of natures clear and rare
Breeds poisonous fogs in low and marsh minds.

DARA

Soon it was hissed into the royal ear,
That, though wise Dara's province, year by year,
Like a great sponge, sucked wealth and plenty up,
Yet, when he squeezed it at the king's behest,
Some yellow drops, more rich than all the rest,
Went to the filling of his private cup.

For proof, they said, that, wheresoe'er he went,
A chest, beneath whose weight the camel bent,
Went with him; and no mortal eye had seen
What was therein, save only Dara's own;
But, when 't was opened, all his tent was known
To glow and lighten with heaped jewels' sheen.

The king set forth for Dara's province straight,
There, as was fit, outside the city's gate,
The viceroy met him with a stately train,
And there, with archers circled, close at hand,
A camel with the chest was seen to stand:
The king's brow reddened, for the guilt was plain.

"Open me here," he cried, "this treasure-chest!"
'T was done; and only a worn shepherd's vest
Was found therein. Some blushed and hung the head;
Not Dara; open as the sky's blue roof
He stood, and, "O my lord, behold the proof
That I was faithful to my trust," he said.

"To govern men, lo all the spell I had!
My soul in these rude garments ever clad
Still to the unstained past kept true and leal,

379

PERSIA

    Still on these plains could breathe her mountain air,
    And fortune's heaviest gifts serenely bear,
  Which bend men from their truth and make them reel.

"For ruling wisely I should have small skill,
    Were I not lord of simple Dara still;
    That scepter kept, I could not lose my way."
    Strange dew in royal eyes grew round and bright,
    And strained the throbbing lids; before 't was night
  Two added provinces blest Dara's sway.

THE BUILDING OF THE BRIDGE OF TUS

[Firdusi lived about 935-1020 A.D.]

BY ELIZABETH A. REED

[WHILE Shah Mahmud was ruler of Persia, the idea occurred to him that it would be an excellent thing to have the history of his country put into verse. He tested the ability of various "literary folk" among his subjects, and at length decided that the poet Firdusi should be favored with the commission. Firdusi's poem is known as the "Shah Namah, or book of Kings."

The Editor.]

THIS celebrated poet [Firdusi], whose true name was Abul Kasin, was a native of Tus, a city of Khorasas, and many happy hours of his boyhood were spent on the banks of the beautiful river that swept along its course near his home. But the rebellious waters occasionally flooded their banks, leaving ruin in their path, and the dream of the young poet's life was the hope that some day he might command the means to build a suitable bridge over this turbulent stream, and also to confine its rising waters within banks of solid masonry. When, therefore, he received the royal commission to write the long Persian poem, he felt that this great public improvement was within his reach, and he gladly undertook the task. After several samples of his poem had been presented to the shah, the prime minister was ordered to pay the poet a thousand drachms of gold for every thousand couplets which he produced until the work was completed.

A magnificent residence was erected for Firdusi near the palace of the king, and the best painters of the age were employed to cover the walls with the portraits of kings and heroes, with paintings of battles and sieges, with the most imposing military scenes, and everything that could excite the martial valor and fire the imagination of the writer.

The only member of the court with whom the poet was not upon friendly terms was the conceited prime minister, who expected, and generally received almost as much adulation from the court poets as the king himself. Firdusi refused to render him this servile homage, and not only so, but finally ignored him to such an extent that he would not go to his house to receive the payment of gold coin which became due upon the completion of each thousand couplets. The only reason he gave for this was that he preferred to receive the whole amount at once, and thereby be enabled to carry out his favorite project and build a bridge in his native city.

All of these little exhibitions of animosity on the part of the poet combined to make him offensive to the vizier, and gave opportunities to other envious courtiers to cultivate the favor of the prime minister by flatteries of himself, and curses upon the head of Firdusi.

At the end of thirty years of hard work the "Shah Namah" was completed, consisting of sixty thousand couplets. The vizier then revenged himself upon the poet by misrepresenting the condition of the treasury to the king, and urging upon him the absurdity of paying such an enormous price for a poem, he finally induced him to send to the poet sixty thousand drachms of silver instead of the gold which he had promised.

Firdusi was coming out of his bath when the bags of silver arrived from the treasury, and learning the value

THE BUILDING OF THE BRIDGE OF TUS

of their contents, he contemptuously gave them away, giving recklessly and without judgment, until the sum was exhausted.

This insult to the shah was duly reported and exaggerated by the prime minister, and while the monarch was furious with rage, the poet, at the suggestion of the vizier, was condemned to be trampled to death by elephants. His apartment, however, being close to the royal residence, he took advantage of that fact and threw himself at the king's feet, suing for pardon, and this was granted him upon the condition of his immediate departure from the city. Sick at heart, and burning with indignation, he sought the apartment of the king's favorite attendant, Ayaz, who had always been a faithful friend to the bard. To him Firdusi related his story, and from him received the fullest sympathy. Here he wrote a bitter poetic invective against the shah, and having sealed it up, requested Ayaz to deliver it to him after the poet's departure, and also to choose the time for doing so when some defeat had rendered the shah more low-spirited than usual. [This was in part.]

> "In Mahmud shall we hope to find
> One virtue to redeem his mind?
> A mind no generous transports fill,
> To truth, to faith, to justice chill.
>
> "Son of a slave. His diadem
> In vain may glow with many a gem.
> Exalted high in power and place,
> Outbursts the meanness of his race.
>
> "Oh, Mahmud, though thou fear'st me not,
> Heaven's vengeance will not be forgot.
> Shrink, tyrant, from my words of fire.
> And tremble at a poet's ire."

PERSIA

The indignant and unfortunate bard escaped from Ghizni by night, on foot and alone, for his friends dared not incur the enmity of the king by rendering him any assistance. Ayaz alone had the generous courage to brave the shah's displeasure by aiding the refugee. He sent a trusty slave after him, who soon overtook him, and giving him a horse and a sum of money and other little comforts for his journey, besought him in the name of Ayaz to hasten out of the territory of Shah Mahmud if he valued his life.

In the mean time reports of the vizier's animosity and of the sultan's cowardice were spread all over the country, exciting universal detestation of the king and his minister. The accounts of the poet's misfortunes and the king's injustice reached Muhteshim, the Prince of Kohistan, about the time the fugitive approached the seat of government. This prince was the dear friend of Shah Mahmud, and bound to him by ties of gratitude for countless favors; but he hesitated not to show his respect for genius, and he sent a deputation of learned and distinguished men to meet Firdusi and invite him to the royal presence. In the midst of this flattering and honorable reception Muhteshim learned that the offended poet intended to publish a satirical work, holding up to the detestation of the world the treachery of Mahmud, and he endeavored to dissuade him from this act of revenge, which he considered unworthy of the greatest literary genius of the age. The poet afterwards sent him a hundred indignant couplets, that the prince might destroy them himself. Firdusi stated in a letter sent with the lines that, although he dreaded not the anger of Mahmud, still, out of grateful friendship for the

THE BUILDING OF THE BRIDGE OF TUS

generous Muhteshim, he gave up the cutting rebuke. The closing paragraph states that —

"On thy account, most amiable prince, do I now consent to transfer my just revenge from this vain world to a higher court."

Muhteshim presented Firdusi with a goodly sum of money and forwarded him on his journey, fearful lest the sultan's rage or the vizier's malice might overtake and ruin him.

This proved to be a wise precaution, for the king had discovered a sarcastic epigram which Firdusi had written on the wall of the great mosque the night of his departure, and on the next day Ayaz delivered to the furious monarch the insulting letter which the poet had left with him for that purpose, and a large reward was offered for the apprehension of the fugitive. At length, however, the sultan received a long letter from his friend Muhteshim, who related his meeting with Firdusi, now, in his old age, a penniless wanderer, after having devoted the best years of his life in the constant exercise of his great talents for the execution of his king's wishes, and gently reproached the shah for allowing himself to be imposed upon by the evil advice of malicious courtiers; he also informed him of the forgiving spirit the poet had manifested in destroying his own brilliant satire which was composed at the monarch's expense, and closed the letter by quoting the couplet which Firdusi had used in the letter to himself.

The complaints from his subjects also began to come to the royal ears, and all of this, together with the reproaches of his own conscience, produced in his mind a strange combination of grief and rage, of indignation and regret. He disgraced the malicious vizier, and fined him sixty thousand drachms of gold, the same amount which he had prevented him from paying to Firdusi, and deeply regretted his own injustice to the gifted bard; but still he could not forgive the cutting satire of the letter which had taunted him with his low birth as being one of the causes of his cowardice and meanness.

Firdusi was protected by the Arabian Government, and after some years returned and lived with his family at Tus; but he was old, grieved, and broken down, and at last he died in his quiet home, at the age of eighty-three. In the mean time Shah Mahmud, hearing of his return to Tus, and anxious to render justice, though tardily, to the man he had wronged, sent an envoy with sixty thousand drachms of gold, together with quantities of silks, brocades, velvets, and other costly presents, to Firdusi as a peace offering. But as the royal train of loaded camels entered one gate of the city, a mournful procession went out of another, and followed the dead poet to the place of his burial.

The shah's ambassadors offered the presents intended for Firdusi to his only daughter, but she possessed her father's spirit, and haughtily dismissed the courtiers, rejecting their gifts with proud disdain.

The shah, wishing to make some offering to the memory of the departed poet, ordered the sum which had been intended for him to be expended in erecting a caravansery and bridge in Tus, in accordance with Firdusi's lifelong ambition. These monuments of the poet's fame and of the king's tardy justice existed for many years, until destroyed by an invading army.

LITTLE STORIES FROM SADI, A PERSIAN AUTHOR OF THE TWELFTH CENTURY

I

NEVER had I complained of the vicissitudes of fortune or saddened my face at the revolution of the heavens except once on a time when my foot was naked, and I had not wherewithal to purchase a shoe. Entering the great mosque of Nufah, I saw there a man who had no feet. Then I converted my lament into gratitude and praise for the goodness of God, and bore my want of shoes with patience.

II

Feridun ordered his Chinese embroiderers to embroider around his pavilion: "Thou who art of an understanding heart, be good to the wicked, for the good are great and happy of themselves."

III

I have heard that for a whole week no wayfarers had come to claim the hospitality of the Friend of God [Abraham]. From a cheerful habit he would not eat his morning meal unless some necessitous traveler arrived on his journey. He went out and looked out on every side, and surveyed every point of the valley. He saw only, like a reed in the desert, one solitary man, whose hair was white with the snows of age. He addressed him with a courteous welcome, and gave him an invitation after the custom of the liberal: "O dear to me as the apple of mine eye, do me the kindness to eat of my bread and of my salt." Gladly he assented, leaped up, and quickened his step, for he knew the character of the inviter — on whom be peace!

They who ministered to the hospitality of the Friend of God seated the poor old man in the seat of honor. He commanded, and they prepared the table, and his companions placed themselves around it. But when the company began, "In the name of God," no voice from the old man reached the ear. Then he said: "O thou that hast seen many days, I perceive that thou art not pious and earnest as an old man should be. Is it not proper when thou eatest thy daily bread, to name the name of the Lord who gave it?"

He replied: "I have not followed thy way, for I was never taught it by the priest of the Fire-Worshipers."

Then the Prophet of good omen knew that the old man was an Infidel, doomed to perdition. And when he found him to be an alien, he assailed him with contumelies as a wicked wretch too unholy to consort with the holy.

· Then came an angel from the Creator, who reproved him sternly, saying, "I have bestowed upon him life and daily food for a hundred years, and is he become to thee an abomination in a single day? If he hath offered up his adoration before Fire, art thou therefore to withdraw from him the hand of benevolence?"

IV

I have heard that an old man on a pilgrimage to the Holy Place at each step made two head-bowings in prayer. So warmly was he pursuing his path towards

God that he paused not to pluck out a thorn from his foot. At last, through the temptations of his treacherous heart, his acts appeared so praiseworthy in his own sight that, through the machinations of the Evil One, he was well-nigh falling into the pit, persuading himself that he could not by any possibility walk on any road preferable to this; and had the mercy of God not intervened, his vainglory would have hurried him on to destruction.

But his good genius in an inaudible voice whispered to him: "O happy and fortune-favored man! Think not that, because thou hast discharged a service of prayer, thou hast brought into this court a graceful free-will offering. To give peace to a single heart by a kindly act is worth more than a thousand head-bowings in prayer!"

V

I have heard that King Toghrul came in his rounds on a Hindu sentinel. The snow was falling thick, and it rained in torrents, and he shivered with the cold like the star Canopus. The heart of the king was moved with compassion, and he said: "Thou shalt put on my fur mantle. Wait a moment at the end of the terrace, and I will send it out by the hand of a slave."

Meanwhile a piercing wind was blowing, and the king walked into his royal hall. There the sight of a lovely lady so enchanted him that the poor sentinel entirely slipped his memory. As though the wintry cold was not suffering enough, to his evil fortune were added the pangs of disappointment!

III
STORIES OF MODERN PERSIA

HISTORICAL NOTE

DURING the nineteenth century there were three wars between Persia and Russia over the ownership of Georgia. These resulted in Persia's being obliged to pay Russia a large indemnity, to cede to her wide tracts of land, and to grant her the right of navigation in the Caspian Sea. In 1848 Nasr 'd-Din began his long reign of forty-eight years. From his successor a constitution was extorted just before his death in 1907. Both Russia and England are interested in Persia: the former because of Persia's power over the Caspian Sea; the latter because Persia lies on the way to the English possessions in India. By the Anglo-Russian agreement of 1907, the Russian "sphere of influence" was limited to the northern part of the country, the British to the southeastern. Both powers agreed not to seek either political or commercial concessions beyond these districts, and to respect the independence of the country.

POE'S TALES AT THE PERSIAN COURT
[Nineteenth century]
BY WILFRID SPARROY

UNLIKE his brothers, who are nothing if not volatile in their attitude to study, Bahram Mirza possesses powers of concentration which, savoring, as they do, of the uncanny, have been the means of developing in him a memory of remarkable tenacity. The first novel he ever read was a French translation of "The Captain of the *Vulture*," by Miss Braddon. This book had been given him by the Zillu's-Sultan in order that the lad might while away his leisure hours in the harem by putting the gist of it into Persian, and be the means of hastening his father's post-prandial nap by reading the translation aloud after tiffin. To that blessed consummation, in fact, each boy had been made the present of a book; Feridun Mirza, being the most backward, receiving the most difficult work — Baudelaire's admirable translation of Edgar Allan Poe's "Tales," of which more anon. When Bahram Mirza had finished his holiday task, I called in doubt the thoroughness of his work, in order to test his knowledge of Miss Braddon's closely woven plot.

"Ah," cried Bahram triumphantly, cocking his head over the left shoulder and closing the right eye, "there I waited for you, monsieur! It is true that this is the first Firango story I ever read, but it shall not be the last. His Highness is very pleased with Miss Braddon's work. Would you believe it, monsieur, His Highness could not sleep after *nahar* (lunch) to-day! and as for me, she kept me awake all night; I was reading, reading, reading!"

"Ah," I retorted, "there I waited for you, my boy! What can you possibly know about the book?"

"I will tell you the tale, monsieur, if you will listen."

"All right," I replied, forearming myself against disappointment by expecting nothing save a blunt, bare outline of the plot; "begin."

Bahram Mirza was on his mettle. He made an excellent start. First he told me the title of the opening chapter, then he related the incidents in an interesting narrative style.

"That is the end of chapter I," he said. "Shall I go on, monsieur?"

"If you can," I replied.

He repeated the performance; after which he waited for the applause.

"Did you skip chapter III?" I asked.

The story took a third jump forward.

"Not so bad!" This from his tutor.

Bahram Mirza was nettled.

"Am I boring monsieur?" said he.

"Get along — get along!" I replied, feigning impatience.

Chapter IV contributed its quota to the plot.

"I lay odds that the next chapter is a blank!" I cried.

Not a bit of it! The contents of every single chapter in the book had been as it were pigeon-holed in the recesses of that tenacious memory of his: a *tour de force* all the more remarkable because no such task had been set him either by the prince or by me.

POE'S TALES AT THE PERSIAN COURT

"Are you pleased with me, sir?" he asked in English, after telling the story from beginning to end.

"You have paid Miss Braddon a marked compliment," I replied.

"She deserved it," was Bahram's courteous rejoinder.

I next turned to Feridun Mirza. "How are you getting on with Baudelaire's translation of Poe?" I asked.

"I cannot understand his French, monsieur," he replied; "it is too difficult for me."

"If I put 'The Fall of the House of Usher' into simple French, could you translate the tale into Persian?"

"Mais oui, monsieur!" cried Feridun Mirza, who is a born story-teller, and would make an entertaining dervish. His interest in the subject encouraged me to do my best to cheat the Zill of his customary siesta after tiffin. After I had put the story into simple words, paragraph by paragraph, and had pointed out the writer's skill in kindling in the reader an ever-increasing dread of the approaching doom, Feridun lending both his ears to my remarks, I made him sit down and throw off his impression at a heat under "an instinctive rather than technical guidance." His version of the story was an unqualified success. The siesta over, he came rushing into my study, followed by his special attendant.

"Ten *tumans!*" he cried. "His Highness gave me ten *tumans* for the story, and did not close an eye! Thank you, monsieur, thank you!"

"To-morrow," I returned, "you shall tell His Highness the tale of 'The Black Cat.' I am busy. Good-bye."

"Thank you, monsieur. I will do even better work to-morrow, that His Highness may make me a present of fifteen *tumans*." And the lad, so saying, went back to the harem, dreaming, no doubt, of the coveted reward.

The reward, however, remained a dream.

"What!" I said, two days later, "do you mean to say that His Highness gave you nothing? How was that?"

"Well, monsieur," replied Feridun Mirza, "when I was in the middle of the story, His Highness, who had eaten a bowl of *pilaw*, and a dish of *chilaw*, and had drunk a lot of cold tea, gave a loud snore. . . . How he snores, monsieur . . . it is terrible to hear!"

"*Cold* tea!" I exclaimed.

"Mais oui, monsieur!" Feridun was delighted at my bewilderment. "Cold tea is better for the teeth!"

Akbar Mirza, flinging back his head, burst into a sudden roar of laughter, and I cuffed his head for him.

"When a Persian takes upon himself the shame of wine," he explained, rubbing his impudent face, "he says he has been eating 'nightingale's flesh' or drinking 'cold tea' — you see now; yes, sair?"

"'The Murder in the Rue Morgue,' then, *versus* 'cold tea' — that shall be our next match. I lay odds on the 'cold tea' as a soporific."

"And so do I, monsieur," said Feridun Mirza, in a voice of funereal depression. It was plain that his heart, dashed by his recent disappointment, was no longer in the work.

"It is fortunate," he said, upon our translating the third story, "that His Highness is very sleepy now after his *nahar*."

"Why 'fortunate'?" I asked.

Feridun Mirza looked uncommonly knowing. "Because," he replied significantly.

I had to content myself with the explanation.

The next day came. "Did you have any success with your recital of 'The Murder in the Rue Morgue'?" I said to him.

"None at all, monsieur."

"I am sorry, my boy."

"Oh, it does n't matter so much now, monsieur."

"Shall I help you with a fourth story?"

"No, thank you, monsieur. I think I can manage by myself now."

"You are getting more used to the style, I suppose."

"That is one reason, monsieur; but I hope His Highness is n't!"

"Is n't what?"

"Getting used to the style also, monsieur."

The second reason was long in revealing itself, and in the end it was an accident that enlightened my fatuous obtuseness.

Many days wore away. Whenever it occurred to me to ask Feridun Mirza how he was getting on with his stories, I received the same reply —

"Very well, thank you, monsieur. His Highness always falls asleep as soon as I begin."

"Do you need any help in your work?" I would ask.

"No, thank you, monsieur," he would reply. "I can get along now all by myself, and His Highness is always very sleepy after eating."

But at the end of the month, much to my surprise, he came into class and begged me to lend him my assistance. His face wore a crestfallen expression. When I asked him, in all innocence, which of the tales remained to be translated, his face took on a more dejected look than ever.

"His Highness is very wide-awake now," he remarked at last.

"Don't parry the question. Frankness is the best policy."

"Well, monsieur, I have done 'The Fall of the House of Usher,' . . . and 'The Black Cat,' monsieur, . . . and 'The Murder in the Rue Morgue,' . . . and —"

He raised his eyes to mine, taking the measure of my mood, then turned a trifle pale as to the gills.

"And what else?"

Feridun's eyes fell. "And His Highness is tired of them, sir, and wants something new," he replied at last, all in a breath.

Akbar Mirza, chucking back his head, burst into that characteristic laugh of his, guileless, fresh, and hearty.

"'His Highness is very wide-awake'!" he cried in a convulsion of mirth. "'His Highness wants something new'!"

What I said was "Ah!" What I did was to reach out for the whip.

"Monsieur," said Feridun Mirza in a plaintive voice, "I will tell you the truth. When I told His Highness the story of 'The Fall of the House of Usher,' he was very pleased, and gave me ten *tumans*. But when I told him the tale of 'The Black Cat,' which I had translated ever so much better, he fell asleep, and so I lost my present. But notwithstanding my disappointment, I persevered, thank Allah, and next day I recited 'The Murder in the Rue Morgue.' Then, when His Highness fell asleep yet a second time, the Devil came and tempted me, saying,

POE'S TALES AT THE PERSIAN COURT

'You have translated three stories, two of which His Highness has not heard, all through his falling asleep. Why should you translate any more? All you need to do will be to repeat the stories over and over again in turn.' And that is what I did do, sir, keeping 'The Fall of the House of Usher' for Mondays and Thursdays, and 'The Black Cat' for Tuesdays and Fridays, and 'The Murder in the Rue Morgue' for Wednesdays and Saturdays. And that is the whole truth, monsieur, and it was the Devil who told me to do it. . . ."

"Then you must be the Devil's whipping-boy," I replied. "Come and receive your punishment like a man."

"But, monsieur, His Highness gave me the sticks when he found me out."

Feridun's voice pleaded that enough was as good as a feast.

I laid aside the whip. "And how did His Highness find you out?" I asked.

"Well, monsieur," said Feridun, returning my forbearance by telling the truth. "I made a little mistake. When I was in the middle of 'The Black Cat,' His Highness, who had every appearance of being asleep, opened his eyes all on a sudden, and said to me, 'You read that story yesterday.' Then I knew that I had put the wrong story into my pocket. It was a Wednesday, the most unlucky day in the week; so I begged pardon of His Highness, and went and fetched 'The Murder in the Rue Morgue,' which I began to translate, when His Highness woke up again and said, 'I want something new!' Then, the Devil tempting me yet a second time — for was it not a Wednesday? — I fell to reading the story of 'The

PERSIA

Fall of the House of Usher,' and this I did to pacify His Highness, who had been much pleased with the story. Monsieur will judge of my consternation when I tell him that His Highness, now wide-awake, seized me by the ankle and gave me six strokes of his cane on the soles of my feet, saying that the story had given him the *kabus* (nightmare) half a dozen times at least."

The unexpected climax threw Akbar Mirza into a second fit of laughter.

"Feridun Mirza, Prince Fortunate, is not an angel after all!" he cried, ready to burst his sides with merriment.

"Neither is he made of musk and of amber!" said Humayun Mirza, in a stage recitative.

"He is famous because he is liberal and just," said Bahram Mirza, smiling a grave, ironic smile.

"Let us practice justice and liberality, then," sang out Akbar Mirza, "to the end that we may become even as Feridun Mirza."

"And that was the advice that I was about to give you," said the impenitent sinner. "In fact, I should have used the selfsame words."

Then the two lads, having brought the tips of their fingers together, raised them to their lips, and from the lips to their foreheads, as a token that their thoughts had jumped together.

THE PRINCE WHO LOST HIS BOOK

BY WILFRID SPARROY

"And now give me your mark-books."

Bahram Mirza, Feridun Mirza, and Humayun Mirza brought me theirs at once; but Akbar Mirza, glancing at me furtively out of the tail of his eye, began to make excuse, saying —

"I cannot find my mark-book anywhere, sir. It must be lost, I think."

"There is no denying the fact that your marks have been mostly *minus* qualities of late," I said dryly.

Akbar Mirza's cheeks took on a nectarine flush. "May I eat dirt, if I was afraid of your showing the book to His Highness," he said all in a breath, replying to the tone of my remark, as is the way of boys in the East as in the West.

"That being the case, I must insist upon your finding it. If it is not here, it might be in the *andarun*. Go and look."

"It is not in this room, sir."

"Is it in the *andarun*?"

"I don't know, sir."

"Go and look."

"Sir, His Highness will be angry with me, if —"

"My dear boy, I cannot possibly take the prince's anger into consideration. The book must be found. I will not have you in the class until it is forthcoming. Off you go."

In half an hour's time he came back.

"The book?"

"I have sought, but I have not found it, sir."

"Begone."

"Sir, His Highness will be in the *andarun* now. Please excuse me, sir."

"Akbar Mirza, you have not told me a single untruth in all the months we have worked together. I believe you to be absolutely truthful. Be frank now. Have you destroyed the book?"

"No, sir, by the head of His Highness."

"Then the mark-book must be somewhere. Go and look for it again."

The next day, I asked him the same questions, and received the same replies, with this result for Akbar Mirza, that he was again banished from the precincts of *Chahil Sutun*. The light dawned upon the third day, but not upon the whereabouts of the missing book, nor upon the release of the prisoner on parole. On the fourth morning, however, he entered the classroom, and flung himself upon my mercy with characteristic frankness.

"Sahib," he said, "you are the master; my ear is in your hand; I am your slave; may I be also your sacrifice! The mark-book is not lost; it is destroyed. It was I who tore it in pieces."

"The giving of alms, Akbar Mirza, is, as you know, specially recommended by Muhammad. I am glad that you have appeased your conscience at last. Humayun Mirza was right when he said that 'to tell the truth is to give alms to one's conscience.' Sit down."

He obeyed, looking extremely crestfallen.

THE PRINCE WHO LOST HIS BOOK

"Don't be downhearted, my boy. Cheer up. All is forgiven and forgotten."

"I am your sacrifice, sir," he replied.

"Upon my life, that is exactly what you look like," said I. "For goodness' sake, try and wear a more cheerful expression. Is it my fault that you have n't a single mark to your name?"

"That is not the reason that I am sad, sir."

"Is it not? What is the reason, then?"

"God knows," he replied.

"Undoubtedly. But won't you enlighten me?"

"I like better not to say, sir."

"Of course, I cannot insist upon your confiding your trouble to me. But I do not like to see you so woebegone. Have you forgotten how to smile?"

Akbar Mirza, making a manful effort, summoned so livid a smile from the depths of his misery, that I implored him to weep outright and have done with it. Much to my surprise, he took me at my word, and burst into tears. I went home, meditating. The next time I saw him, he was his own man again, and so I dismissed the whole matter from my mind. But one day, some three or four months afterwards, when I was setting the book-shelves in order, I came across Akbar Mirza's mark-book hidden behind a row of the "Student's Modern Europe." I turned round and faced the class.

"What is the matter, sir?" asked Bahram Mirza. "You look as if you had seen a ghost."

"Precisely," I replied; "I have just seen the ghost of a book that departed this life some three — or was it four? — months ago. The strange thing is that it is not in bits, as the ghost of a book should be, but has every appearance of being fit to serve a useful purpose for some months to come. I wonder whether Akbar Mirza will recognize it or not. Here it is"; and I set it on the desk in front of him.

"It is my mark-book," said he.

"Which you destroyed," I added.

"It is —" He paused, overcome by prescience.

"A miracle, Akbar Mirza?"

"No, sir; it is the first lie I ever told you. That is why I was sad when I told it. Did I not weep, sir?"

Then I recalled his expression of unutterable misery.

"Yes, I remember now. But why, having told the truth in the first instance, did you not stick to it?"

"I will tell you, sir. It was like this. I had lost the book, and could not find it anywhere, and you would not give me any lessons until I had found it. All this I told to His Highness, when he asked me why I was absent from school. And my mother, who was present, said to me, 'You have told the truth, but the sahib will not teach you, until you have found the book. The truth has served you ill, beyond a doubt. Now, if you would say that you had destroyed the book, the sahib might give you the sticks, perhaps, but he would certainly give you your lessons.' And His Highness said, 'By my eyes, it would be wise to take your mother's advice.' And I replied, saying, 'But the sahib likes me to tell the truth. Since the book is not destroyed, he might find it. Would it be wise, therefore, to say that I had torn it in pieces?' And this I said on the second day. And His Highness said to me, 'Are you telling the truth now?' And I said, 'Yes; may I be your sacrifice!' And His Highness said, 'I hope you will find the book soon.' But

THE PRINCE WHO LOST HIS BOOK

I could not find it, try as I would. And then, on the third day, all the ladies of the *andarun* said to me, 'Why don't you tell the sahib that you destroyed the book? You must be a very silly boy to persevere in the truth when it serves you so ill. Be wiser to-morrow than you have been to-day.' And so I came to you next morning and told you the lie. I was sad then, and I am sorry now."

There was a pause, and a silence so deep that one could hear Akbar's heart beating, like a clock.

Said Bahram Mirza, "I wonder what the sahib will do. It is a very interesting situation."

"Akbar Mirza is not so much to blame as the women — is he, mosie mon ami?" said Humayun Mirza.

"And the sahib cannot give them the sticks," Feridun Mirza added.

"Silence, boys. Let me think"; and so saying, I struck a match.

"He is going to smoke," Humayun Mirza whispered. His voice was pitched in the key of a Gregorian chant.

He was right. When I had finished my pipe, I unburdened my completed reflection in the matter by saying —

"There is no thoroughfare; the incident is closed. There is nothing more to be said. To business now. . . . Bahram Mirza, stand up. I will tell you when you may sit down again."

Bahram Mirza smiled.

But my conscience would not keep silent, and well he knew it too!

"Sit down, boy," said I at last, tired of the unequal struggle; whereat the rogue smiled more eloquently than ever.

THE FOOD OF THE ROYAL TUTOR

BY WILFRID SPARROY

WHEN I was in Persia the most frequent question that came to my hand by post was: "What are you having to eat at your end of the world?" and I was rated soundly by my friends because of my remissness in not making epistolary capital out of my culinary experiences. I excused myself then by pleading the impossibility of paying a literary tribute to my food, since I had fallen into the Persian habit of taking a nap after tiffin, and of going to bed as soon as I had discussed my supper; "and surely," I added, "you would not expect me to wax eloquent on an aftertaste?" But the excuse was flung indignantly back to me.

The truth is, when we Firangis are grown accustomed to the Persian life, we do not think it worth the effort to give shape and color to our impressions by putting pen to paper. It is more comfortable to rejoice inwardly that our balance, amid the topsy-turveydom of our surroundings, has been restored by the kindly hand of custom; we prefer to chew the cud of meditation as the Persians do, and we will until the end of our stay be warned to evade the enthusiasm that would spur us into correspondence; for when a Firangi catches the Oriental fever, his gusto for writing is speedily swallowed by "a yawning figure of interrogation leaping over its own full stop."

Now the daily round, so long as I was content to abide

THE FOOD OF THE ROYAL TUTOR

within the court circle, kept pace with the sun. I would rise at six, take a header into the tank, drink a cup of tea without milk, and be ready at seven to saunter to school in the *Divan-Khane*, preceded by my two soldiers bearing the books and writing materials. These would be laid aside at midday, when the Persians take to themselves the *nahar*, the first substantial meal of the day. Mine, during the six weeks in which I was the Zillu's-Sultan's guest, was brought over to me from his cooking-house, on an immense tray of brass covered over with a cloth of brilliant design in purple and gold. The average number of courses (all served at once) was fifteen. Among these there were always a dozen poached eggs on a china dish; a basin of *ab-gusht*, or mutton broth under a layer of yellow oil; a platter containing a *pilaw* of boiled rice flavored with orange juice or mixed with currants; a more substantial *pilaw* mixed with stewed meat; and a lamb *kebab* on a wooden skewer, folded in a sheet of "pebble-bread" to keep it warm. The bread derives its name from the sloping back of pebbles (within the oven) on which are set the flat cakes of dough. The *entrées* consist of one rich *khoresh* (curry) of flesh and another of fowl, to be eaten with the *chilaw*, or plain boiled rice, of which there were two white pyramids on plates.

For dessert I had peaches as big as cocoanuts, grapes as big as English plums, several kinds of melon, for the growth of which Isfahan is famous, and delectable dates, from the Persian Gulf, stowed away in the rind of a melon. A bowl of delicious sherbet, composed of pomegranate juice split with iced sugar and water, and served with a beautifully carved pear-wood spoon from Abade, and an uncorked bottle of Shiraz wine, with a purple aster stuck in the neck by way of a stopper, were the beverages laid before me. Last of all, was a basin of *mast-khiyare*, curds and cucumbers, a favorite dish with the Persians, that should be eaten at the end of the repast, and digested in the arms of Morpheus; for the slight thirst it excites, as the uninitiated have learned from internal evidence, should not be made an excuse for the glass. The thirst will pass away in sleep, provided the sherbet and the wine be left alone: to quaff of the fragrant cups would be to set the curds and cucumbers a-squabbling and a-swelling to the visible discomfort of the inner man.

The Zillu's-Sultan's servant, having deposited the tray on the floor, would say to me, "Nush-i-jan-bad" ("May it be sweet to your soul!"), then he would withdraw, leaving my road-servant Sadik to lay the cloth. In the place of a table there was the floor; the five fingers of my right hand did duty for knives and forks; and as for the plates, behold a plentiful supply of "pebble-bread" in thin sheets, one on top of the other. First, Sadik would spread over the carpet a square of oilcloth, atop of which he would lay a gaudy strip of chintz, setting each dish where it belonged. The place of honor at the head of the tablecloth, facing the door, where the master of the house sits, is occupied by the two dishes of *pilaw;* opposite to them, at the other end, rise the two pyramids of white *chilaw;* the bowl of sherbet with the spoon floating in it stands in the middle; and the ragouts and fruits are placed at the extreme corners, facing one another diagonally. In the family circle, the father, having rolled up his sleeves and squatted himself

THE FOOD OF THE ROYAL TUTOR

on his knees and heels, helps himself first; then he passes the spoon (the dish remaining stationary) to his wife at his right hand, and she serves herself and her children in the order of seniority. The mode of consuming the rice, from time immemorial, is to get as much of it as possible in the fork of the forefinger and thumb pressed closely together, cramming it into the mouth by means of the latter; and the best way of eating the spicy ragout is to roll it up, bit by bit, in a morsel of pebble-bread, which, being as it is of the consistency of pancake, neither crumbles nor breaks in the process. The cooking of the rice is beyond all praise; the best Parisian *chef* could not prepare it half so well; the *chilaw*, in particular, is a triumph: every single grain of it is separate, so dry is it on the outside; but inside it is full of juice. The *pilaw* has a singularly sobering effect upon the diners, and can scarcely be said to be conducive to conversation — indeed, the Persians must do all their talking immediately before meals.

"The yellow weeping of the Shiraz vine" has the smack of old sherry, and at its prime is exceedingly dry, fruity, and inspiring. As everybody keeps silent, the meal, notwithstanding the enormous consumption of food, is all over within twenty minutes, and ends with the washing of hands by pouring water over them from a brass ewer into a brass bowl; after which mouths are rinsed, sleeves rolled down, then a pipe of tobacco is smoked, and slumber won, in summer-time, at least, without much wooing of the drowsy god.

I had no scruples about following the customs of the country in these particulars, and I persevered in the endeavor to gain proficiency in the Persian method of

PERSIA

dining, until I had wrung from the powers that be the necessaries of an English dinner-table. The desire to continue in the habit died with the necessity of doing so! After the post-prandial drowsiness had yielded to a siesta and a cold tub, I would dress myself in clean linen and white flannels, and while away the hours between three o'clock and sundown, first by drilling the young princes, and next by entertaining my guests, or by paying visits to my friends. The meal that brings the day to a close is called *sham:* it is served about two hours after sunset, and consists of the same viands as the *nahar* and in almost equal abundance. I owe it to my reputation to assure the reader that the food provided for me was not the measure of my appetite, but that of the prince's hospitality, on which a squad of soldiers might have fared not wisely, but too well.

A PERSIAN WEDDING
[1885]

BY CHARLES JAMES WILLS

LOVE at first sight is unusual in a country where the women are habitually veiled, and a glimpse even of a lady's face is seldom to be got, save by stratagem or by what is considered immodest — the raising of the corner of her veil by the lady herself. Shrouded as she is from head to foot in an immense sheet of blue, two yards square, a yet further precaution must be taken. Over all this is placed a *ruh-band* or veil — no transparent or flimsy device, as in our own lace "fall," or the thin and gauzy *yashmak* of the Turkish belle, serviceable alike to triumphant and to fading beauty. The *ruh-band* is a piece of white calico or cambric, a yard long, which hangs down like a long mask in front of the Persian woman's face, when clad in her hideous and purposely unbecoming outdoor costume: which costume, sad to say, is also an impenetrable disguise. In it all women are alike. An aperture four inches long, running transversely across the eyes, enables the Persian lady to see her way, and little more; for even this aperture is covered by elaborate and curious embroidery, between the threads of which she can only peep. But the Persian belle will yet find a way of rewarding an admirer with a glance; and thus the marriages so carefully brought about by parents and relatives are not infrequently the result of predilections slyly manifested. The outdoor dress, being a disguise, cuts both ways; and the *intrigante* amuses herself with impunity.

Certain marriages take place because in the eyes of the Orientals they are natural ones, such as the union of first cousins. The children have been like brother and sister from the cradle, and they are married as a matter of course; it is their fate, and they submit to it. But outside these marriages of custom, and far more numerous than the marriages of predilection to which we have referred, are the marriages usually arranged by "brokers." These brokers are old women, who always keep themselves in a position to quote the state of the marriage-market, which fluctuates. In hard times, even girls of good appearance are comparatively a drug. In time of plenty, they "rule firm." The marriage-broker is ever a welcome guest where there are daughters to marry, and also in houses where the sons wish to find a suitable bride. The young people are not consulted by the broker. She deals with the parents, and generally with the mothers. Crafty as a horse-dealer, she runs glibly over the various advantages, mental, physical, and pecuniary, of her *clientèle* of both sexes. So-and-so is a steady, quiet man. Such-an-one has brilliant prospects — has (important consideration!) no other wife. As for Yusuf, how good-looking he is! And Hassan, no man was ever so good-tempered. Of the other sex she sings the praises no less. The skill of Bebe as a housekeeper, the wealth of the ugly daughter of the banker, the dangerous charms of the portionless Zuleikha, she can never say too much about. Her main business is to bargain for the sum to be paid to the father for his daughter's hand; a sum which is usually expended

A PERSIAN WEDDING

by that father in pots and pans (all of copper) and other utensils, which he presents to his child as her separate property. The details being settled after much haggling, the young people are engaged, and the marriage-broker gets her commission from both the parents of the bride-groom and those of the bride-elect. Among the poor and laboring classes the bargain is arranged on other grounds. The peasant takes a wife for her thews and sinews, or her skill at weaving carpets or making cheese; while the bridegroom is or is not eligible according as he may be capable of hard work, or may hold some small office, or have a bit of land or a shop. Here the marriage-broker is generally an amateur, who conducts the negotiations purely from that love of match-making which *is* such a blessing to the world.

The *akd*, or marriage contract, is simply a legal form; but it is marriage and not betrothal. A few friends are invited; the bride — perhaps a child of ten — is seated in a room with her parents and relations; over the door hangs the usual curtain. Or, if the ceremony takes place in one room or in the open air, the women are all veiled. At the other side of the curtain, in an outer room or in the open air, are the male guests; and here squats the mullah or priest of the quarter, who now drones out in a monotonous voice the marriage contract, which has been previously drawn up by him. "It is agreed between Hassan the draper, who is *vakeel* (agent) for Houssein the son of the baker, that he, Houssein, hereby acknowledges the receipt of the portion of Nissa the daughter of Achmet the grocer." Here follows a list of the property of the bride in lands, money, houses, cattle, dresses, furniture, carpets, pots, pans, and so on. Always a copy of the Koran and a certain weight of sewing-silk are mentioned. This detailed account of her property, constituting the woman's separate estate, her husband merely holds in trust during their life together. At death or divorce it goes back again to herself or her heirs. And it is this *mehr*, or separate estate, that renders secure the otherwise precarious position of the Eastern wife in a polygamous country; for the various things enumerated, though acknowledged by the husband as received, may only exist on paper. Still, he has acknowledged them; and if he wish to put away his wife, or if they separate by consent, he is bound to refund the *mehr* of which he has legally acknowledged the receipt, or to obtain her legal discharge for the same. "And," continues the mullah, "he acknowledges the receipt of the aforesaid *mehr*." Then follows a hum of delight at the extent of the lady's property. "You, Hassan, how do you say as *vakeel* for Houssein — is this so?" — "Yes, yes, I agree," mumbles Hassan. "And you, Achmet, do you give your daughter, Lady Nissa, to be the wife of Lord Houssein?" "Yes, yes, I agree," replies Achmet the grocer. "And you, Lady Nissa, are you there?" "Yes, yes, she is here, mullah," replies a chorus of women from behind the curtain. "And you agree, Lady Nissa?" Here there is a giggle from the child-bride. "Yes, yes, she agrees," comes in a triumphant chorus from the women. "Then," says the mullah solemnly, "in the name of God the compassionate, the merciful, and of Mohammed the prophet of God, I declare you, Lord Houssein, and you, Lady Nissa, to be man and wife." Here the mullah puts his stamp of seal to the document: the various parties seal it too, it is carefully

A PERSIAN WEDDING

witnessed, and formally completed. The mullah receives his fee of a few shillings; and then, and not till then, he hands over the document — her settlement and "marriage-lines" in one — to the agent of the bride or to her father.

The legal ceremony is over; the young people are married fast, fast as the Mohammedan law can bind. And, theoretically, as yet they have never seen each other's face. But really Houssein has had many a glimpse of the fair Nissa: her mother has often allowed him to see her child from behind a curtain or a cupboard door. All this is understood. And the young people are now legally married. The wedding, as distinct from the espousals, may take place the same evening, in a week, a month, or not for years, according to the age, rank, or circumstances of the bride and bridegroom. Men and women feast separately; and after many water-pipes have been smoked, many pounds of sweetmeats consumed, and a plentiful banquet has been disposed of, the guests separate. All promise to be present at the actual wedding. No music, no rejoicings—nothing but what we have described is seen at the ceremony we have detailed.

From an early hour in the morning of an *arusee* or wedding — I speak of a wedding in the middle ranks of life — there has been considerable bustle in the house of the bride's father. The house has been literally swept and garnished. Carpets have been borrowed, and rooms that at other times are unused and empty are now furnished and decorated with flowers. The poor are standing in a crowd at the outer door, sure of being plentifully regaled. The outer court has been got ready for the men. Vases of flowers are placed in rows at all the open windows, and in every recess thirty or forty pounds of tobacco have been prepared by pounding and moistening for smoking; the courtyard is freshly watered. If it be a calm day — and spring and summer days in Persia are always free from wind — rose-leaves are sprinkled on the surface of the water of the raised tank in the center of the courtyard, so as to form the word "Bismillah" (in the name of God), the pious welcome of the Mussulman. Similar preparations, but on a larger scale, have been made in the *anderun*, that handsomer and larger courtyard which contains the women's quarters. In this courtyard the Negresses may be seen busily engaged in the kitchen preparing the breakfast for perhaps a hundred guests; and the visitors will stop all day, only leaving to escort the bride to the home of her new husband, whither she will go after dark. Large samovars, or Russian urns, which are in use in every Persian house, are hissing like small steam-engines, ready to furnish tea for the guests on their arrival: not our idea of tea, but a pale infusion sweetened to the consistency of syrup, from the center of each cup of which will project a little island of superfluous sugar. The sherbet-dar, too, is preparing in his own especial den immense quantities of ices and sherbets; and these ices will be served from china bowls, and each ice will be the size and shape of a fair-sized sugar-loaf. As for the sherbets (delicately scented and sweetened fruit-syrups dissolved in water, and with lumps of ice floating in the clear and various colored fluids), they will be supplied in gallons. Orange sherbet, lemon, pomegranate, rosewater, cherry, quince, and an endless further variety of these refreshing

A PERSIAN WEDDING

drinks will be offered to the thirsty guests. And now come the musicians in two bands, the Mussulmans', and the Jews'; the latter a ragged and motley crew, but more skillful than their better-clad rivals. They carry with them their strange Old-World instruments, and soon establish themselves in a corner of either courtyard. They, too, partake of tea, and then they prepare to strike up. Noticeable among the Mussulman musicians is the *dohol* player and his instrument. It is a species of big drum, only used at weddings; and, once heard, the awful resonant roar it makes can never be forgotten.

All is ready; the master of the house, dressed in his best, gives a last anxious glance at the preparations, and has an excited discussion with his wife or wives. He waves his hand to the musicians, and hurries to a seat near the door, to be ready to welcome his guests; the music strikes up a merry tune (it is really an air — barbaric, but inspiriting); the tremendous din of the *dohol* is heard at intervals. Then in a loud scream rises the voice of the principal solo singer, who commences one of the sad love-songs of Persia in a high falsetto voice. His face reddens with his exertions, which last through a dozen verses. His eyes nearly start from his head, the muscles of his neck stand out like ropes; but he keeps correct time on the big tambourine, which he plays with consummate skill. The rest of the musicians watch his every movement, and all join in the chorus of "Ah! Leila, Leila, you have made roast meat of my heart!" The music is the signal to the invited guests; they now commence to arrive in crowds. The music and singing proceed, and go on unceasingly till the bride leaves for her husband's home some ten hours after the artists begin. As the guests pour in, the host receives them with transports of pleasure — all the extravagant compliments of Eastern politeness pass between them. "May your wedding be fortunate!" "You are, indeed, welcome; this is a never-to-be-forgotten honor to me, your slave!" In they pour, the men in their best; the women, closely veiled, pass on unnoticed by the men into the *anderun*, where they unveil and appear to their delighted hostesses in their finest clothes and all their jewelry; and, we are sorry to add, in most cases with their faces carefully painted. As the dresses worn among Persian ladies for indoor use only reach to the knee and are very much *bouffé*, their wearers look like opera dancers. The ladies' feet and legs are bare, as a rule; a gauze shirt of gay color and a tiny zouave jacket daintily embroidered with gold lace on velvet or on satin are worn, while the head is decorated with a large kerchief of silk or gauze, elaborately embroidered with gold thread. From beneath this kerchief the hair falls in innumerable plaits behind, sometimes reaching almost to the ground. The colors of their clothes are of the brightest — pinks, greens, yellows, scarlets, crimsons, blues. The quantity of solid jewelry worn in honor of the bride is prodigious.

Every one takes tea, every one crunches the sweets of various kinds which are piled on china dishes in huge trays in the center of the rooms. Several hundredweight of confectionery — not food, but "sweets" — are thus consumed. Conversation goes on, pipes are smoked by both men and women. Messages pass between the two courtyards. But the men remain in their quarters, and

A PERSIAN WEDDING

the women in theirs. The musicians and buffoons are allowed, however, in the women's court on these occasions: they are supposed to be mere professional persons, and on this account are tolerated. At noon a heavy breakfast is served. If there be two hundred guests, there is meat for them and for, say, four hundred servants and hangers-on, while what remains, a still larger portion, is given to the poor.

Lutis or buffoons now bring their performing monkeys or bears — often a miserable and half-starved lion cowed by much beating. They dance, they sing songs, indecent enough in themselves, but tolerated in the East on such occasions. More tea, more ices, more sherbet, more sweets. Pipes without number pass from hand to hand, but no strong drink; that is never seen or tasted, save by the musicians and buffoons, who as the day wanes are freely supplied. The bride meanwhile goes to the bath, whither she is accompanied by many of the ladies, the friends and near relatives of the family. Dinner is served on the same lavish scale as the breakfast. Fowls by the hundred, boiled to rags, under piles of various-colored rice; lambs roasted whole, or boiled in fragments; mutton in savory stews; game and venison hot on the spit; *kababs* and *pilaws* of endless variety; soups, sweets, fruit in profusion: all this is served with the lavishness of true Oriental hospitality.

And now there is a hum of suspense. It is night; and the whole place is lighted up by lamps, candles in shades, and lanterns. A noise of a distant crowd is heard; alms in money are freely distributed among the crowd of beggars and poor at the door; horses are brought for the bride and her friends. The procession of the bride-

PERSIA

groom is approaching: and it must be understood that another grand party has been going on at *his* father's house. The musicians play and sing their loudest: the roofs (the flat roofs of the East) are thronged by all the women and children of the quarter. The bridegroom and his friends arrive, and are welcomed by the women with a peculiar echoing cry of "Kel lel lel," produced by tapping the cheeks. Then the bride appears, carefully veiled in a huge sheet of pink and spangled muslin. She goes to the door and mounts a gayly-caparisoned horse. All the male guests join the procession. Lighted cressets full of blazing embers are carried on high poles to lead and light the way. The lanterns of all the guests are lighted and borne in this procession, which joyfully wends its way through a cheering crowd. At the moment the bride leaves her father's house a shout of "Kel lel lel" announces the fact. Fireworks blaze, the music is deafening, above all is heard the monotonous banging of the wedding drum. And so, the buffoons and musicians leading the way, the procession slowly moves on. As it approaches the house of the bridegroom several sheep are sacrificed in honor of the bride; they are slain at her feet as she steps over her husband's threshold for the first time, accompanied by a female friend or two. Then, invoking blessings on the pair, all wend their way home, and the festival is over.

THE PERSIAN BAZAARS
[Twentieth century]
BY EUSTACHE DE LOREY AND DOUGLAS SLADEN

LIKE the bazaars in Constantinople and Cairo, those of Teheran consist of an immense labyrinth of streets covered with brick vaults, forming an uninterrupted row of little domes, in the middle of each of which a round hole is pierced to let in the light. Through this hole the sun darts its rays like the flash-lights of a man-of-war amid the half-lights of the vaults, which in summer keep the air so cool.

When you enter the great central artery, which starts from the south of the Sabz-Meidan, you are in the Bazaar of the Shoemakers. On both sides of the vault are stalls, from ten to fifteen feet square, with a floor about three feet above the ground. These are occupied by the makers of all sorts of shoes. Here are *pahboush*, yellow, or green for the mullahs; there are the tiny red slippers with turned-up toes and metal heels which the women wear. Farther on are the ugly boots of blacking leather or patent leather with elastic sides, which are intended for those who wish to enjoy the advantages of civilization. Then come the shops where you buy the *giveh*, the national shoes of Persia, made of very strong white linen, with soles of plaited thongs dyed green; and the yellow top-boots, with the red rolled-over tops and very turned-up toes and thick soles, like Tartar boots, which are worn by the Persians in the mountains.

PERSIA

Nothing used to amuse me more than the diversity of types we met in the bazaar. All the types and all the costumes of central and western Asia elbow each other here in the most extraordinary medley.

The first thing I saw in the bazaars, riding a mule, was a venerable mujtehid, in a close-rolled white turban of a thousand little folds, wound round and round a pointed conical cap. He was accompanied by a numerous suite of mullahs, who wore turbans too, but not with the same elaborate coils, because these are reserved for the highest ranks of the priesthood; of Seyyeds, with dark blue turbans, or green if they were *hadji* (pilgrims), as well as descendants of the Prophet, all of them wearing long flowing robes, belted in at the waist by a Cashmere shawl, in which the *calamdan* and the roll of paper appear which are the badge of men of letters. The crowd made deep bows to the mujtehid, and many of them kissed the hem of his garment. He looked at them with condescension, but with a distracted attention, for his eyes seemed to be regarding in the visionary distance the series of the Seven Heavens promised in the Koran. The Persian is very theatrical; he always likes to look his part. If he is a general, he is Bombastes; if he is a judge, he is Rhadamanthus.

Then came an Armenian in a low *kolah*, with clothes which he imagined to be European. He was careful not to brush the Mussulmans, knowing that they would curse him if he polluted them with his impure touch.

The men with flashing eyes and mustaches like a walrus's, wearing a sort of *bolero* made of plaited foals' hair, and a round white cap encircled with striped silk, whose fringe fell over their faces, were merchants from

THE PERSIAN BAZAARS

Kurdistan. Their rifles, slung over their right shoulders, and bandoliers full of cartridges, showed that even Mercury could not go out without being armed in their "charming" country.

The man with a square beard, with a blue-and-white striped cloth on his head, held in its place by a crown of camel's-hair cords with gold knobs, was a merchant of Baghdad; he was positively glittering in his sky-blue *abba* with golden stripes like sun-rays. As he passed by, the Orthodox Persians cursed him, for he was a Sunnite, and his dress was like the one that the assassins of Kassem wear in the religious procession of Moharrem. The young Negro who followed him was a Somali slave that he was probably going to sell.

Then came a water-carrier, dressed in nothing but a dirty shirt, bowed down by the weight of his goat-skin full of water, which swayed about on his back. He held in his left hand one of the legs of the skin, which is the tap through which he draws the water, and in his right, a brass cup engraved with sentences from the Koran and verses of poetry, reciting the praises of the liquid that he was selling. He was watering the front of a shop.

There were interminable files of black phantoms gliding from shop to shop, bargaining noiselessly, and disappearing like shadows. This is all that one sees of the fair sex, with the exception of a few Armenian women, half-veiled, with round caps of embroidered velvet on the tops of their heads, from which fall a quantity of plaits, concealed in the folds of the *chader*, which they wear like their Mussulman congeners.

Horsemen were riding about, and there were strings of little gray donkeys loaded with bricks for building, and interminable caravans of camels with deafening bells. Their heads, ornamented with tufts of red, green, and yellow, were balanced in a bored and supercilious sort of way on the top of their long swans' necks, encircled with collars of red leather ornamented with little white cowries. Their india-rubber-like feet flattened out as they touched the ground with the regularity of a clock; the loads hanging from each side of their humps, swaying and knocking against the walls, were a perpetual menace for the foot passenger. Suddenly there was a pandemonium: two caravans coming in opposite directions had met, the camel-drivers shouted to make their beasts give way to each other, but in vain; for the beasts were locked together as their loads caught, and dashed the foot passengers into the walls. The cries of fury and the oaths of the camel-drivers were blended with the growling of the camels, the yells of the people, and the howling of the dogs which were run over, and the screams of the frightened women.

The entire traffic was suspended, and it took more than half an hour to reëstablish order. This incident, during which the mirza and I took refuge in a shop in order not to be crushed, gave me the opportunity of bargaining for a pair of exquisite little *pahboush* of gazelle skin, embroidered with golden palms and mother-of-pearl dates. One of these was still in the hands of the workmen. The merchant asked a ridiculous price, as if the pearls had been real; and to give them more value in my eyes, he assured me that they belonged to one of those mysterious phantoms whom fear had driven into the corner of his shop, and who, he said, was a *khanoum* (i.e., lady) of importance. The

THE PERSIAN BAZAARS

mirza drew my attention to a *chader* of black silk fringed with gold lace in the middle of some cotton *chaders*. Who knows? it might have been a princess shopping with her maids. How exciting it would have been to have carried off the *pahboush* of the trembling phantom, who, seated in that corner, looked like a half-filled balloon in the middle of other half-filled balloons. All sorts of ideas passed through my mind: I had visions of a Cinderella of the "Thousand and One Nights," or else perhaps this mignon slipper that I was holding in my hand had been used by the lady to chastise her unfaithful husband, for the heel of the *pahboush* is a favorite weapon in the harem.

But the mirza frowned at me, and I understood that all this was the Eternal Persian Mirage, and must go the way of all mirages. . . . So I ran away laughing.

We passed through the bazaars of *kalyans*, *chibouks*, and other pipes, which were crowded with pilgrims from Kashgar, easily recognizable by their high cheek-bones and narrow eyes, laying in supplies for their journey to Mecca, and went to the Tobacco Bazaar.

It is a very quiet place, full of the fragrance of nicotine. On the counters were bricks of amber-colored tobacco, almost as closely pressed as wood — some a yard high and long and wide, some still sewn up in goatskins. There were also beautiful long leaves of tobacco of Shiraz for the *kalyans*, and tobacco of Kachan, shredded into fine flakes like curls of fair hair, for making into cigarettes.

Flint and steel are still much used, but are being driven out by Japanese and Russian imitations of Swedish matches — the Japanese being incomparably better.

PERSIA

There was an attempt to start a match factory in Persia, but it failed.

Seeing some very beautiful sheets of tobacco for the *kalyan*, I asked the price, and was told a price which came to about two francs — four *krans* [1] — the pound. I ordered two pounds.

"But you put your thumb on the scales!" I exclaimed, seeing that the merchant was cheating. He looked at me — there was a pause — and then he said, in the most unabashed way, "Do you imagine that I am going to give you tobacco of that fineness for four krans the pound if I did not put my thumb in the scale?"

I was so pleased to find a Persian so Persian that I could do nothing but take the tobacco and add a little backsheesh to the price he asked.

The bazaar into which one goes oftenest in Persia is the Bazaar of Carpets. This suggests much to the European mind, which at once thinks of a vast display of rich hangings and gorgeous colors. In Persia one sees nothing of the kind. The carpets are all piled up, one over the other, and when you want to buy a carpet, the men of the shop pull them out one after the other in front of you, and build them into fresh piles on the opposite side. It is very difficult to make up your mind, for you never see more than two displayed at the same time. It takes a very long time; for, carrying in your head as well as you can the remembrance of those you like best, you are always having another one pulled out, and before you manage to get the three or four you really like best all shown at the same time, several hours will have gone, and pounds of dust, coming from all parts of Persia, will

---

[1] About forty cents.

THE PERSIAN BAZAARS

have been swallowed. However, you need not regret the time expended, so many precious articles will have been exhibited before you, each more beautiful than the other.

The first carpet that struck me was one from Kerman, woven with extraordinary fineness. Its pattern represented a tree on which parrots in great profusion and every attitude ate extraordinary fruits. Under that tree, which took up nearly all the carpet, were some very small gazelles, a quarter of the size of the parrots, and round it was a very delicately drawn border. The next carpet was from Turkestan. On a background of Venetian red, dark blue geometrical drawings were repeated at regular intervals. But this one, which was made of very good material, had a hideous design. It was a bad copy of the Early Victorian carpet, representing a tiger eating an apple under a rosebush. Then the merchant brought out a beautiful dark blue carpet, decorated with narcissi, tulips, and hyacinths, white, red, yellow, and green, of a pre-Raphaelite pattern which came from Kurdistan. It was an old one; they are not made any more.

Directly after this, he showed me a carpet with a regular pattern of henna flowers, which was the modern representative of the same school. The next, of the same pattern, but with very crude colors, showed that in spite of the new laws forbidding aniline colors, these chemical dyes are spoiling the manufacture of modern carpets. Happily this was the exception, and it is to be hoped that the laws by which aniline dyes have recently been prohibited from entering Persia will be enforced with Draconian severity.

PERSIA

After many notable examples from Faraghan, Khorassan, Turkestan, Khoi, and Daghestan, I was shown one very curious carpet, with a white background, on which was drawn with black lines an Assyrian king with wings, copied from the bas-reliefs of Persepolis. His name, Nebuchadnezzar, was written under it in Roman letters. I regretted to see such good work and such fine materials wasted on such a miracle of bad taste. It was executed in one of the best workshops of Kerman.

Silk carpets are very much appreciated in Persia. They are generally of the type of prayer carpets, representing two columns, a vault, and in the middle a mosque lamp hanging down. Another usual pattern for the silk carpets is a vase of flowers with birds. The Persian weavers receive orders, especially from Cairo, for very large silk carpets.

The wily Persian has discovered the secret of making new carpets look ancient. He smokes them over a fire made with special herbs, and this gives the carpet a used appearance and fades the colors. It is nearly impossible, when this is well done, to distinguish between a genuine antique and a forgery.

A commoner way of aging a carpet (very common in the bazaars) is to spread it out on the street, in order that every passer-by and animal may trample on it.

In Tabriz, an Englishman, Mr. Stevens, conceived the happy idea of starting a carpet-weaving industry, where only old patterns are made. He tries to revive the old traditions, and has succeeded very well. I went to see his workrooms in the bazaars. They were established in a large sort of shed with mud walls and roof, lighted by mere holes of windows and skylights. The

THE PERSIAN BAZAARS

weaving was done on old-fashioned hand-looms, some of them eight or ten feet high. Little boys of ten to twelve were perched on planks in front of the looms; a man, holding in his hand the pattern of the carpet with all the colors marked in squares, like our Berlin wool-work patterns, sang to a popular tune the number and color of each thread — one blue, two red, one yellow, etc. — which was repeated in chorus by all the little boys, and accompanied by the noise of the bobbins which go through the warp threads, and the rhythmical swish with which the boys cut the thread after making the little knots.

These little apprentices, dressed in a variety of colors, perched on their planks and singing at the tops of their voices, were like love-birds sitting on a branch.

Interesting as it all was, the mirza and I were tired out before we made our escape, and nearly smothered by the dust we had to swallow.

NEW YEAR'S CALLS AND GIFTS

[1895]

BY SAMUEL G. WILSON

The Persians are eminently a social people. They are vivacious and entertaining; fond of jokes and story-telling, and ready in repartee. They are much given to visiting and feasting. This is remarkable, since the great bond of society with us is entirely wanting: the social intercourse of men and women is not permitted, and the idea of it shocks their sense of propriety. Men visit with men, women with women. Dancing amazes them beyond measure, and seems an immodest license and a perversion of liberty.

The Persians are a polite people. They have elaborate rules of etiquette, and many set phrases and compliments suitable for every occasion. Visits are made at the festivals, both for congratulation and condolence, and often for the transaction of business. The physician is honored with an hour's social chat before the ailments of the caller-in are mentioned. He is expected in return to make himself comfortable in the parlor for a prolonged tea-drinking before being inducted into the sick-room. Time is of little value. Social calls are often of three or four hours' duration.

The greatest social event in Persia is the festival of the New Year or Noruz. It commemorates the entrance of the sun into the sign of Aries at the vernal equinox. It is the most fitting and beautiful time for the New

NEW YEAR'S CALLS AND GIFTS

Year. Then the sacred year of the Jews and of some European nations began. March 25th was the first day of the year in Scotland until 1600, and in England until 1752. At this season, Persia, throughout most of its borders, begins to put on its robe of verdure, flowers begin to bloom, and the farmer takes up his work in the fields.

Some Persians affirm that the world began to move in its orbit on that day. Others place the origin of the festival in the time of Jemshid, the founder of Persepolis. He introduced the solar year, and celebrated its first day as a splendid festival. The sculptured procession on the great staircase at Persepolis is supposed to represent the bringing of presents from the various provinces at Noruz. This is the only festival of ancient Persia that has not been displaced by the sacred seasons of Mohammedanism. The Persians never fail to enter into its enjoyment, except when the movable lunar calendar of Islam brings some religious ceremony at the same time. From 1893 to 1896 Noruz falls in the great fast of Ramadan. The festivities with which ancient kings celebrated it are curiously described in the "Arabian Nights," in "The Enchanted Horse." In the introduction to this story it is said: "Noruz, or the new day, is a festival so solemn and so ancient throughout the whole extent of Persia, taking its origin even from the earliest period of idolatry, that the holy religion of the Prophet, pure and unsullied as it is, has been hitherto unable to abolish it; although it must be confessed that it is a custom completely pagan, and that the ceremonies observed in its solemnization are of the most superstitious nature. Not to mention large cities, there is no town, borough, village, or hamlet, however small, where the festival is not celebrated with extraordinary rejoicings. Those that take place at court surpass all others by the variety of new and surprising spectacles, so that nothing that is attempted in other parts of the world can approach or be compared with this sumptuous magnificence." A thousand years after Haroun-al-Raschid the festival still holds its place. To an outside observer its ceremonies do not seem as "pagan" as some of those connected with Shiahism.

Prior to the festival of Noruz the dervish pitches his white tent before the door of some nobleman, and sits there and yells, "Ya hak!" ("O truth!") until his claims to charity are satisfied. The letter-carrier presents himself to receive an *anam;* the cook expects a new coat; the mirza, and even the physician, are remembered by their patrons; and the alderman receives goodly donations from his constituents. During the last week of the old year the bazaars are profusely decorated. Gay cloths, carpets, and shawls are exhibited in the shops. Pictures, mirrors, mottoes, bunting, and embroideries are hung up. Arches are constructed, spanning the streets with pendent ornaments. Villagers crowd in front of the open shops, and groups of boys stroll about to see the sights. Every one buys a collection of nuts, raisins, figs, dates, dried apricots, grape-juice paste, etc. These fruits must be of seven kinds, the name of each beginning with the letter "S." The collection is called the *yeddi luvn.* Many send to their friends a plateful, with the compliments of the season. The last Wednesday, called Akhir Chahar-Shenba, is a gala day. It is the children's festival, but the whole population is ready for a frolic. Clowns in fantastic costumes and ludicrous masks, and

NEW YEAR'S CALLS AND GIFTS

strolling minstrels with tambourines and cymbals and leading a monkey, perform and collect shahis. Boys crowd the streets, and women gather on the housetops, to see the shows. School-boys enter into the spirit of the day and make a mock visit to their principal. One of them, arrayed like a Kurdish sheik, in long flowing robes, great turban, and a cotton beard, and with attendants armed like Kurds, but with canes for swords, presents himself and declares that a fine has been levied upon the school. He receives a present, and they all go off to expend it on some of the good things in the bazaars.

As the great day approaches, every man says to himself, "Well, to-morrow is Noruz. I must get my head shaved, go to the bath, dye my hands, nails, and beard with henna, put on a clean skull-cap, and see if the tailor has my new coat ready. I must buy some sugar and tea, tobacco and candy, and then I shall be ready for all comers."

In the capital the festival is ushered in and celebrated with elaborate ceremonies by the shah and his court. The crown prince in Tabriz keeps the day with similar rejoicings. At the astronomical termination of the year a tray of the seven fruits is brought before the prince. Some of these are eaten. Incense is burned, according to a custom of the fire-worshipers. One hundred and ten guns are fired off, with reference to Ali, who is said to have been named successor to Mohammed on this day. Consuls, nobles, and high officials, clothed in their uniforms and decorations, pay their salaam to His Highness, and partake of a feast. Luck-money, coined with the name of the shah, is distributed to all. Some of these gold and silver tokens are sent to the mujtehid and other ecclesiastics. They presage a fortunate year for the recipient, because the king thus indicates his royal favor. After the salaam there is a military review in the *medan* or public square. The trumpet is sounded; the officers on their gayly caparisoned horses present themselves with their companies. Each soldier receives a token of fourteen shahis in value. After the review, wrestling-contests and ram-fights enliven the scene. In some villages buffalo-fights are a part of the programme. These powerful animals, sometimes made ferocious by partial intoxication, make a rough contest. In other places, such as Hamadan, the day is ushered in with a display of pyrotechnics. From the housetops thousands of rockets and "fusing-jugs" are set off.

The festivities extend over two or three weeks. The bazaars are generally closed and business suspended. All are bent on pleasure. Merrymaking reigns supreme. Days are designated for visiting particular classes or wards of the city. On the first day the official class exchange visits, while the religiously inclined give the honor of precedence to the mujtehids. On succeeding days the crowd moves from ward to ward. Calls are often an hour long. About breakfast-time (noon) a group of friends may unexpectedly enter, and a new supply of pilaw must be served up quickly. Families that have suffered bereavement during the preceding year do not make visits, but receive them, serving to their guests bitter coffee and omitting all sweetmeats.

Noruz is a pleasant time to renew old acquaintances, make new ones, and to visit both rich and poor without interfering with their business engagements. I shall give an account of the visits made during one Noruz season,

NEW YEAR'S CALLS AND GIFTS

since they afford the best opportunity to become acquainted with the social customs of the people. According to a custom in visiting men of rank, we sent a request to the governor-general, the former Amir-i-Nizam, that His Excellency might appoint a convenient time to receive us. The governor's house, in a group of government buildings, was built in semi-European style, with windows on all sides and faced with red brick. He had two large reception-rooms, one furnished in Persian, the other in European style. The Persian room had portières over the doors, and was carpeted in the usual manner, with a larger center-piece, two *kenarehs* or side-strips, and a *kala* or head-piece, the four rugs neatly covering the entire floor. The *kenarehs* and *kala* were of soft *kecha* or felt, half an inch thick, and the color of camel's hair, with a simple figured border.[1] Over these was spread, for their protection, a breadth of cotton cloth, called *ru-farsh*. At the upper corners of the reception-room were divans, consisting of mattresses and pillows, and covered with the finest Senna rugs. On one of these divans the governor sat to receive Persian visitors; the other was reserved for men of high rank, while other guests sat on the carpets around the sides of the room.

We had removed our goloshes and hats on being ushered in. The governor, in stockinged feet and with hat on, received us cordially, rising and shaking our hands. To his "Salaam alakum!" ("Peace to you!") we responded, "To you peace! May Your Excellency's feast be blessed!" He replied, "May your favor be

[1] The best of these *kechas* are manufactured at Yezd and Hamadan. A traveler mentions one the dimensions of which were one hundred and twenty by eighty feet. It was transported from Yezd on a line of camels for the palace of the minister of justice at Teheran.

increased!" After being seated on chairs we inquired concerning His Excellency's "noble condition." He replied in the customary phrase, "Al hamd ul Ullah!" ("Praise God, I am well!"); but on second inquiry he declared that he was feeling ill, and most of his conversation in the midst of tea-drinking was about his ailments. He ended the interview by saying that he had a *peeshkesh* for the doctor, which proved to be ten imperials.

Afterward we called on the *beglar-begi* or mayor. He is of the Dumbli family, which have ruled in Azerbijan before the Kajar dynasty. He has great wealth, being lord of many villages. All the guests in the saloon rose and remained standing while he led us into a room furnished with tables and chairs. A special feature of the room was the great number of gilded and illuminated firmans and honorary degrees from the shah, framed and hung on the walls, or placed in the niches. According to custom, tea was brought in in tiny glasses having handles of silver, and placed on glass saucers. The cup-bearer served each person on an individual waiter of silver, and in the order of the rank of each one, as judged from the position of their seats. He first offered tea to his master, but he, with a wave of the hand, declined to be served until after his guests. The tea was piping hot, without cream, and as sweet as a syrup. On the waiters was a little bottle of Shiraz lemon-juice and sliced *naranj* (grape-fruit) for flavoring it. After a time the attendants reappeared. One bore a salver on which were tiny coffee-cups in holders. The latter resembled in shape an egg-cup. They are sometimes chinaware, and sometimes Zenjan-silver filigree, of exquisite workmanship.

NEW YEAR'S CALLS AND GIFTS

The other attendant bore a coffee-pot; he lifted one of the coffee-cups, placed it in the holder, and filled it about two thirds full of very thick, black, sweet coffee.[1]

The *kalean* or water-pipe was brought in and passed to us. We declined with the phrase, "It is not our custom." The host took a few whiffs and passed it to the guests in the saloon. Finally we said, in the customary form of adieu, "Will you command our dismissal?" He replied, "Do you withdraw your graciousness?" If the host wishes to shorten the visit he can hasten these courses.

A visit to the *kalantar*, the chief alderman, showed us some different phases of Persian life. An hour's ride on horseback brought us to his place in the suburbs. He had extensive grounds, beautifully laid out with fountains and flower-beds and shaded avenues. In his greenhouse were orange and lemon trees bearing fruit. One of his rooms was papered with chromos, another with cuts from the illustrated papers. He had a large household of retainers. The *kalantar* was fond of religious discussion and familiar with the Bible. He had written a book in defense of Islam against Christianity. His opinion was that Paul undermined and corrupted the religion of Jesus. He found in the prophecy of Habakkuk of the Holy One from Mount Paran, who drove asunder the nations, a prediction of Mohammed. Conversation on religion is habitual among the Persians.

Here there were set before us some choice sweetmeats. Among the favorite confections is *gaz*. It is made from

[1] Sometimes sherbets are substituted for the tea or coffee. These are drinks made of lemon, plum, cherry, rose, cucumber, or other fruit-syrups. Simpler forms are *skanjabi*, made of vinegar and honey, or *ayran*, a kind of buttermilk.

the juice of the tamarisk tree and has a delicious flavor, which is increased by being mixed with pistachios. Another favorite is fig-paste, called "ease of the throat." This is variously flavored and colored. Among the candies popular in Persia are sugared burned almond, pomegranate jelly cut in little squares, *khulva*, a taffy of molasses and nuts, rock-candy, and *peshmak*, which is made of sugar and butter, crystallized like snowflakes or thistledown, and formed into pyramids, cones, and other shapes. A very rich pastry sprinkled with sugar, but without fruit, is much prized. Their cakes, made of rice-flour and nuts, with sheep-tail fat and saffron flavor, are rarely agreeable to foreign taste. Year by year confections are being improved by contact with Tiflis and Constantinople. The best sweetmeats are now made in the houses of the wealthy, and some of their ladies are expert in the art. At Noruz and other festivals great *khonchas*[1] of candies are sent in by the clients of the great, and the center of the parlor is occupied by a large display of them. It has lately become the custom to rent a large amount of confections for an occasion, only those being paid for which are eaten, and the rest returned.

These visits, together with others to mollas, merchants, and physicians, gave us considerable knowledge of the life of well-to-do Persians. The impression was gained that their manner of living is very comfortable. Their wealth is not great, but they have the conveniences and luxuries which the country affords, or which they think it necessary to import. Their houses are

---

[1] A *khoncha* is a wooden tray, about two feet by four, which is carried on a man's head when a wedding-dowry or a present of sweetmeats is taken through the streets.

NEW YEAR'S CALLS AND GIFTS

neither of marble nor of cut stone, nor do they have many of the charms of beautiful architecture. But the wealthy class in the cities have pleasant rooms, excellent food, fruits and flowers in abundance, troops of servants waiting their every beck and call, stables full of valuable horses, incomes easily earned, plenty of leisure for an afternoon siesta and for social intercourse, many holidays and a disposition to enjoy them; and withal they have no reason to envy the far more opulent but possibly less contented plutocrats who under steam pressure and with lightning rapidity are "bulling and bearing" one another in the marts of civilization.

New-Year's calls on the poor of Persia revealed a striking contrast. We knocked at the outer door, that the women might have a chance to conceal themselves. Bending low, we stooped down and passed under a long arched way, and entered a little yard with mud-plastered walls. The *cahvakhana* or hall opened into a half-underground room, in one end of which was a poorly made window, covered with oiled paper, its cracks being similarly pasted over to keep out the wind. Its flopping, ill-fitting door was low, while the sill was very high, in order that the shoes may be taken off in the hall and not obstruct the opening and shutting of the door. The rafters overhead were unceiled. The furniture consisted of common carpets (*ghelim*), a mirror brought with the wedding-outfit, a copper basin and ewer, a small tea-urn and some glasses, and a *kalean* on the lower niches. On the upper niches were a few bottles, and on the once whitened walls had been pasted some cigarette-papers, caricature prints, and verses from the Koran. The host greeted us with a hearty "Welcome! You have done me a great favor." We replied, "May your festival be blessed, may your house be blessed!" He answered, "It is a present to you." The other guests rose, placed their right hands first on their hearts, then to their foreheads, and bowed low. We knelt on our knees on calico cushions, the weight of the body resting on the heels. The host, though his circumstances were straitened, was bright in conversation. A small boy dressed like a grown man entered, and we inquired, "Who is this?" "He is your slave," he replied; which meant, "He is my son." A dish of wheat was growing on the window-sill, a symbol of the renewal of the year. A fish was swimming in a pan, which called forth a remark from him that fish always look toward Mecca at Noruz. He placed before us a few candies, some boiled eggs, and pickled grapes. He had the samovar already boiling, and sat down beside it, washed the cups and saucers, and placed tea before us. We did not decline to drink, for the poor man would feel aggrieved. He honored us specially by almost filling our tea-glasses with sugar, though he himself sipped his tea through a small lump which he held between his teeth and retained to sweeten succeeding sups. What does a poor man have besides the things within sight? His goods consist of a few rude dishes of native pottery, a jar or two of pickled herbs and dried vegetables, a flour-bin, some copper pots, and a chest of clothing. With his wages of a dime a day as a laborer or servant he must provide for his Khadija and Ismiel, Husain and Fatima. He thanks God for the blessing of such a family; but how do they live on such a pittance? Most of it goes to buy bread, which, with some salty cheese to give it taste, or a glass of weak tea, constitutes

NEW YEAR'S CALLS AND GIFTS

his breakfast; his luncheon is bread and sour milk, garlic or onions or some cheap fruit; for dinner a stew of meat and vegetables, highly seasoned with red peppers and onions — a large quantity for a little meat — makes his bread palatable. Lack of employment or high prices reduce him to bread and water. In winter a few *shahis'* worth of charcoal lasts the family a long while under the *kurisee*.

In sleeping rich and poor alike lie on the floor. The bedding, which consists of a short mattress, a round pillow, and coverlets, is folded up and placed in a recess by day. In summer many of the people sleep on the roofs, rising when the sun disturbs them.

The social habit, which is so universally exemplified at Noruz, is a striking trait of the Persian character. One of the social institutions of great attraction is the tea-house. The tea-houses are of various grades. Some are rudely furnished, with merely a raised platform which surrounds the sides of the room, and is covered with matting or carpet. Others have an air of comfort imparted to them by divans, mirrors, chandeliers, etc. With tea at half a cent a glass, and one pipeful of tobacco sufficing for a crowd, it is no wonder loafers seek them and business men make appointments in them. The common pipe, cigarettes, and the *kalean* or water-pipe are much used. In the latter the smoke passes through the water and is drawn into the lungs. Lemon-juice and other flavors are sometimes mixed with the water.

The ordinary *kalean* is about two feet high. It consists of a vase capable of holding about a quart of water, a top about the size of a goblet, in which burning charcoal and dampened tobacco are placed, a wooden tube which supports the top on the vase, and a mouthpiece or stem about twenty inches long. The support and stem are turned on the lathe, in various ornamental designs. The vase and bowl are of glass, stone, china, brass, or silver, and are set with turquoises or other jewels, and carved, enameled, and decorated with pictures of the shah, flowers, and similar objects.

Another place of social resort and gossip is the bath-house. Custom and religion require frequent ablutions. For the men, with their dyeing of the hair and nails with henna, scraping the flesh with tufa, etc., the bath is a frequent necessity, and no less so for the women, whose hair-dressing, dyeing of eyelashes, etc., require so much time and attention. The bath-houses are below the level of the street, so as to be supplied with water. The arched domes are lighted through slabs of alabaster. One may know when he is near the bath-house by the long rows of colored towels hung on the street walls. The fuel used is weeds, thorn-bushes, straw, dried manure, bones, carcasses, or any other rubbish, and the odor inside and out is sometimes very offensive. The atmosphere of the vaulted room is very hot, as in the case of the Turkish bath. The water in the plunge-tank is changed only once in two or three months, and is consequently a prolific breeder of disease.

The Persian has few kinds of amusement. His theater is the "Takia" or passion-play of Muharram; his lyceum lecturers are the dervishes on the street corner, and the poets and marseyakhan in the residences of the rich. Singers, musicians, and dancers are adjuncts of weddings and other feasts. The Persian gentleman does not dance. A prince, seeing some European noblemen dancing,

NEW YEAR'S CALLS AND GIFTS

expressed his surprise, saying, "Why do you exert yourselves so much? In Persia we hire people to dance for us." No violent games of ball and no severe gymnastics are in vogue, except for the *pehlavans* or wrestlers. Horse-racing and hunting are favorite amusements; chess, checkers, and backgammon are old and standard games. Cards are being introduced throughout the entire country, and gambling is unhappily prevalent.

The custom of giving presents is universal. A person returning home brings a *sogat* or present to each of his relatives and friends. The custom is so binding that some men unwillingly go in debt to avoid a breach of it, and others stay away from home from inability to do what is expected of them. Gifts of dainties from the table, of the first-fruits from the orchard, and of loaves of fresh bread are sent from friend to friend. Formal tokens of commendation from a superior are greatly prized. The shah yearly sends a *khallat* or robe of honor to each governor on the renewal of his appointment. Its bearer is an important official. He is met by the governor at a villa called *khallat-pashan*, where the latter puts on his robe. Its style and elegance indicate the degree of appreciation intended to be shown. It is a high honor for a royal person to give another a robe which he himself has worn. When the crown prince wished to show his appreciation of Dr. Holmes by presenting him with a robe of honor, he first wore it himself a few days.

Certain other presents may be regarded as taxes. Such are the large amounts sent by the governors to the shah at Noruz. Of a similar nature are those sent to local officials by subjects and by foreign residents, as a recognition of obligation for civil protection. On the receipt of such a gift it is customary to give the bearer a sum of money, showing appreciation of the gift and its sender. Fees, tips, and *anams* are very common. *Peeshkesh* is a gift to a superior, and is generally made with the idea of procuring an equivalent in cash, favor, or influence. *Baksheesh* is a freewill offering to an inferior.

IV
HOW THINGS ARE DONE IN PERSIA

HISTORICAL NOTE

PERSIA is the land of ceremony, and serious offense is sometimes the result of transgressing some minute requirement of etiquette. For the rule of courtesy that demands promptness in meeting an engagement the Persians have no regard, and appear mildly surprised and aggrieved that it should be expected of them. On the other hand, they are generous and hospitable, and almost invariably kind to their servants and animals.

HOW THE PERSIANS BUILD A HOUSE
[About 1885]

BY S. G. W. BENJAMIN

It may be a surprise to learn that even the most costly mansions are constructed of sun-dried bricks, and that the flat roofs are of mud. But in a climate like this, these bricks are very durable. Some of the towers of Rhei, still standing after twelve centuries, are of this seemingly perishable material. Lightness, combined with strength, is often gained in Persia by ingeniously building a wall of square sun-dried bricks, arranged in hollow cubes as in a block-house. They are cemented by a layer of mud mixed with straw, over which in turn follows a coat of white plaster. Where great strength is required, the angles are fortified by a layer of burnt bricks. Such a wall will stand for ages. It is interesting to watch the builders at work. They wear long tunics, which are tucked into their girdles when working, displaying a length and muscular development of limb I have never seen equaled elsewhere. The one above sings out in musical tone, "Brother, in the name of God, toss me a brick!" The one below, as he throws the brick, sings in reply, "Oh, my brother! (or, 'Oh, son' of my uncle!') in the name of God, behold a brick!"

Less can be said, however, in favor of the roofs of mud. The only reason why they should be used is the rarity and costliness of wood in central Persia; perhaps, also, because a roof of great density better protects the

PERSIA

house from the long dry heat of summer. In that temperature, also, lies the safety of these roofs. Heavy undressed timbers are laid across the walls. Over these comes the lathing, or a layer of dry twigs. In the better houses, square, broad burnt bricks are laid on the lathing, and over these is put a layer of mud ten to twelve inches thick. But generally the bricks are dispensed with. During the summer such a roof becomes very hard; and when the surface is slightly inclined to allow the water to run off, long and heavy rains are required to penetrate it. After the wet season the surface is rolled again for the next winter. With these precautions such roofs last a long time in Persia. But there comes a time with most of them when a little seam appears in the ceiling; then follows a trickling stream, and the occupants, thus warned, remove the furniture without delay to the adjoining apartment. If the rain continues, the ceiling falls in. Occasionally one hears of fatal accidents, or very narrow escapes, from falling roofs in Teheran. But accidents may generally be avoided by proper precaution.

THE AUDIENCE CHAMBER OF THE SHAH
[About 1885]

BY S. G. W. BENJAMIN

THE most imposing portion of the palace of the Nasr-ed-Deen Shah is the grand audience chamber, which in dimensions and splendor of effect is one of the most imposing halls in the world. The ceiling and mural decorations are of stucco, but so were those in the Alhambra. The floor is paved with beautiful glazed tiles, arranged in the most exquisite mosaic. In the center of the hall is a large table overlaid with beaten gold, and a long row of armchairs are massively splendid with the same costly material covering every inch of space. At the end of the hall, facing the entrance, is the famous Peacock Throne, brought from Delhi by Nadir Shah, covered with gold and precious stones in a profusion that places the lowest estimate of its value at not less than thirteen millions of dollars.

The magnificence of the shah's audience hall is still further heightened by the fact that here also are stored many of the crown jewels. The reserve of coin and bullion which the shah has saved from his revenues, equal, it is said, to a sum of thirty millions of dollars, is safely locked up in the vaults of the palace. But one need only see the treasures in the audience hall to obtain an idea that Persia is still a land of wealth, and that the tales of splendor recounted in Oriental story were not wholly the fictions of a fancy steeped in opium or *b'hang*. Among

PERSIA

the spoils of ages gathered in the shah's treasury are superb crowns and jeweled coats-of-mail dating back four centuries, to the reign of Shah Ismael. In a glass case one sees a large heap of pearls dense as a pile of sand on the seashore. Diamonds, rubies, emeralds, and sapphires catch the eye at every turn, sometimes flashing forth like a crimson or a green fire on the boss of a buckler or a helmet worn at the front of battle ages ago. One ruby there is in that mine of splendor which, on being placed in water, radiates a red light that colors the water like the blood of the vine of Burgundy. There, too, is a globe of the world, twenty inches in diameter, turning on a frame of solid gold; the surface of the earth is represented by precious stones, different colors being used to indicate the divisions of land and sea. The ocean is entirely of turquoise, and Persia is represented by a compact mosaic of diamonds. The famous Dar-i-noor, or Sea of Light, the second of known diamonds in quality, size, and value, is kept carefully locked in a double iron chest, but is shown on rare occasions, and is worn by His Majesty on great state days.

HOW TO MAKE CALLS

[About 1885]

BY S. G. W. BENJAMIN

THE afternoon or the early morning is the time when the gentlemen of Teheran exchange calls; never in the evening. A Persian gentleman never calls on a Persian lady; he does not even venture to inquire after her health, or even to mention her to her husband. But after her death it is proper to call on the male relatives of the deceased, to express condolence. A father or a brother may visit a daughter or sister, unless forbidden by the husband. Notwithstanding these restrictions, the exchange of visits among the ladies, or among gentlemen, is a common custom at Teheran, and is a most formidable affair, affording a complete display of the elaborate etiquette for which Persia has always been famous. All the ceremonies attending such a visit are shaded down to the finest point, and form part of the education of every Persian, becoming in fact a second nature to him.

Before making a social call, a servant is sent (generally the previous day) to announce it. The rank of the servant who is sent is suited to the rank of the gentleman who is to receive the visit. If a person of very high degree is to call on one of similar position, it is considered eminently proper to announce and accept the visit in an autograph note. If the caller be of the higher rank, he simply states that he proposes to call at such an hour;

if of equal or lower rank, he asks permission to call. The call must be made on horseback or in a carriage, and the number of mounted attendants depends on the rank of the person visited.

On approaching the house, the visitor, if of high rank, is met by mounted heralds, who immediately return at full speed to announce the approach of the guest. If the host be of very high rank, he will try sometimes to see the effect on his guest of coming into the reception room after the arrival of the guest. Supposing he has not tried such a maneuver, a courteous skirmish occurs when the guest enters the door; each seeks to outdo the other in politeness, while each is exceedingly careful not to accept or allow a position to which he is not entitled by rank. The corner of the room the most remote from the entrance is the place of honor; the guest, if he outranks the host, while strenuously declining to take that seat, will be very careful that his host does not occupy it instead, and quite as careful not to accept it if inferior in rank, although urged, for to do so under such circumstances would be to affront the host, and invite an affront in return. The host, when in the apartment on the arrival of the guest, advances outside of the door of the reception room to receive one of superior rank; meets him at the door if of equal rank, and leads him by the hand to his seat; goes halfway the length of the apartment to meet one of slightly inferior rank, but does not condescend to advance a step for a guest far below in social or official position. When the host and guest are of equal rank, chairs or cushions are arranged in corresponding position opposite the refreshment table, — and so on through all the various social grades. Other

HOW TO MAKE CALLS

things being equal, the left hand, and not the right, is the place of honor.

The serving of refreshments is another important question regulated by undeviating custom. The *nazir*, or head steward of the household, enters in his stocking-feet, ushering a number of servants equal to the number to be served. If host and guest be of equal rank, the cup is presented to each at exactly the same moment; but if one outranks the other, he is first served. When there is present a member of the royal family, or one of the cabinet or council of the shah, or a foreign minister, the servants must always retire backward to the door. The number and character of the refreshments depend on the rank, the hour, and the season. In the morning tea is served once. In the afternoon, the guest being of equal or higher rank, he is first served with tea in dainty glasses. This is followed by the *kalean*, or water-pipe. When several persons of equal rank are to be served, it is the proper thing to bring an equal number of lighted pipes; but if one present outranks all the others, only one pipe is brought in, which is handed to him. Before smoking, he makes a feint of offering it in turn to all present; but woe to him who incautiously accepts before he of higher rank has smoked, for in that case he will be made to feel the withering scorn of which a Persian gentleman is capable.

After the first *kalean*, tea is served again, followed by a second pipe. After a proper interval, the length of which is regulated by the acceptability of the visit, coffee is served in tiny cups, followed in turn by the pipe. This is the signal that the limit of the entertainment has been reached, and soon the guest in honeyed words expresses his acknowledgment for the courtesy of the host, and requests permission to depart. When the Persian New Year begins, with the spring equinox, the season is indicated by the substitution of a cool sherbet for the first cup of tea, and sometimes of an ice in the place of coffee; but after the September equinoctial the tea and coffee are resumed. These may seem trivial matters, but in Persia they have great weight; and not only is the taste of the host indicated by the quality and style of the refreshments, but the *savoir-faire* and the rank of the guest are weighed by his bearing on such an occasion. It is of no slight importance that a European in Persia should understand the force of these laws of etiquette, otherwise he is liable to have his breeding as a gentleman misunderstood; while by strongly asserting his claim to all the privileges which he has the right to demand, suitable to his rank, he receives the respect which is his due, but which no Persian will give except when he sees him firm on these points.

MAKING A PRESENT TO AN OFFICIAL
[About 1885]

BY S. G. W. BENJAMIN

THE *mehmendar*, or entertainer of the guests of the shah, who received me on arriving in Persia, and accompanied me to the capital, was a man of agreeable disposition. He had lived many years in Europe; he spoke French with facility, and his manners were easy and gracious. On brief acquaintance, one would have set him down as a gentleman comparing favorably with gentlemen and men of affairs in Europe; and it was easy to believe that he would resent any attempt to present him with a trifling gift as a recompense for the services he rendered officially for his Government, and for which he had, presumably, been compensated by the shah. This would have been the conclusion reached by one unacquainted with Oriental character; but my experience in the East led me to think otherwise. I felt that it would be safer to venture to offer him an official tip than to risk offending him by showing too much delicacy in the matter. On arriving at Teheran, I therefore presented him with a new saddle and bridle I had brought with me. He showed not the slightest hesitation at the proposal of such a present, but returned the saddle after inspection, on the plea that it was shopworn, and that out of respect to me he would prefer not to show to his friends a gift that seemed to be unworthy of a Minister of the United States. As the saddle was entirely new and in perfectly good condition, I saw at once that his object was to receive a more valuable present, possibly in the shape of money. I therefore sent the saddle back to him with a message that I did not need instructions as to what kind of a present I should give, and that he ought to be thankful that I had remembered him at all. A European gentleman, who might have been consul for ten years, and held the rank of general and receiver of the royal guests, to whom such a message should be sent, would probably reply with a challenge; but I had not mistaken the Oriental character. The saddle was accepted with a profusion of thanks.

GETTING A GLASS OF MILK
[About 1885]
BY S. G. W. BENJAMIN

TOWARDS evening we were able to creep out of the tent; the cooler air suggested that a glass of milk would meet our wants better than anything else. But in Persia it would never do to send for the milk, for it would have been simply impossible to get it without water. Therefore, after much difficulty, we succeeded in having a cow brought to our tent. But even now the difficulties did not vanish. According to Persian notions, a cow may not be milked without the presence of its calf; it is a disgrace for a man to milk a cow, so a woman had also to come; her husband was obliged to come likewise to look after her. She was greatly embarrassed to conceal her face while milking, as the mantle would not remain in place; but she at last avoided the difficulty by sitting on the farther side of the cow, while we discreetly kept on the other side!

HOW A PERSIAN MOHAMMEDAN SAYS HIS PRAYERS

[About 1890]

BY REV. S. G. WILSON

FIVE times a day are appointed for prayer — dawn, middle of the morning, noon, middle of the afternoon, and sunset. Morning and evening the muezzin mounts a minaret or the roof of a mosque, and gives the *azan*, or call to prayer: "God is great! I testify that there is no God but God; I testify that Mohammed is the apostle of God, and Ali is the vicegerent of God. Come to prayer! Come to security! Prayer is better than sleep." The muezzin may be an educated mullah or an ignorant man. A wealthy neighbor had the call given from his housetop by an illiterate scavenger or porter, who had simply memorized the Arabic words, and was paid for his trouble with some loads of wheat. The preparations for prayer are somewhat elaborate. Certain ablutions are preparative. The ablutions are performed, not by dipping the hands in a basin, but by pouring water from a ewer or from the palm of the hand. The Sunnis and Shiah wash the hands differently. One rubs toward the elbow, the other downward. They can be distinguished from each other by the direction of the hair on the arm. The toes are also carefully rubbed with water, the ears moistened, and the teeth cleaned. A spot of ink, or other defilement, may invalidate the prayer.

When preliminaries have been finished, the worshiper

A PERSIAN MOHAMMEDAN AT PRAYER

takes his position on a prayer-rug, with head uncovered and shoes removed, faces toward the Kebla, the Kaaba at Mecca, and places a tablet of pressed earth from Kerbela before him, and holds a string of beads of the same earth in his hands. These beads number ninety-nine, according to the attributes of God. A long one at the end is called the molla; two double ones are called the caliphs. With the beads he keeps tally of his petitions. The tablet is placed before him because Mohammed enjoined that the worshipers should bow their heads to the earth. The prayer is said according to a fixed rote, every motion being prescribed. With the repetition of certain words the devotee raises his hands to heaven, with others his eyes; at one time he kneels, at another prostrates himself with his forehead on the earth; again he touches his knees, toes, palms of the hands, and forehead, to indicate his absolute submission. He must not look backward during the exercise. He may, however, keep an eye on those round about him, and on his goods lest they be stolen, or ejaculate a curse on his apprentice, or tell a passing customer to wait a little while and he will attend to him. He may interject a greeting to a guest or an order for tea, provided he proceeds without mistake. The prayer consists of certain suras of the Koran in Arabic, which are understood by few in Persia, the same words being repeated day after day.

All places are regarded as suitable for prayer. When the call sounds, the man stands up among his guests, or in his shop, in the midst of the noise of manufacturing, or on the housetop, or on the street-corner. The workmen throw aside the pick and shovel and begin their

PERSIA

devotions. The Gospel idea of closet prayer is unknown to them. At first acquaintance a Christian is an enigma to them, never being seen to engage in prayer. A native, describing a Christian lady, said, "She does not revile, she does not steal or lie, yet she has no religion."

MESOPOTAMIA

I
THE KINGDOMS OF CHALDÆA
AND ASSYRIA

HISTORICAL NOTE

THE history of the Tigris-Euphrates Valley begins with the Chaldæans of perhaps six thousand years ago. They were an intelligent people. They were skilled in astronomy, they knew how to write, and they collected large libraries of tablets of clay upon which inscriptions had been imprinted in cuneiform, or wedge-shaped characters. They built lofty temples, rising terrace above terrace, of sun-dried bricks, which crumbled in time and fell into shapeless masses.

About 1300 B.C. the Assyrians overcame the Chaldæans. The Assyrians were a proud, cruel people, and their kings delighted in recording the savageness with which they had treated their captives. They, too, were famous builders, but, unfortunately, they had no better material than the sun-dried brick. They were as interested as the Chaldæans in making collections of books, or tablets; and the Royal Library at Nineveh is thought to have contained ten thousand volumes, many of which were copies of the old Chaldæan writings. The best-known names among the Assyrian rulers are Sennacherib, who destroyed Babylon and besieged Jerusalem; and Asshur-bani-pal, whom the Greeks called Sardanapalus. The reign of the latter was marked by magnificence in his court and success in his military operations. This was the golden age of literature and a time of great prosperity.

THE CHALDÆANS AND THEIR WAYS

BY DIODORUS THE SICILIAN

[The northern part of Mesopotamia, or the country lying between the Tigris and the Euphrates Rivers, was ancient Assyria; the southern part was Chaldæa, or Babylonia. The supreme power in the valley was first held by the Chaldæans, then by the Assyrians, then by the Babylonians.
The Editor.]

Here it will not be amiss to say something of the Chaldæans (as the Babylonians call them), and of their antiquity, that nothing worth remark may be omitted.

They being the most ancient Babylonians, hold the same station and dignity in the commonwealth as the Egyptian priests do in Egypt; for, being deputed to divine offices, they spend all their time in the study of philosophy, and are especially famous for the art of astrology. They are mightily given to divination, and foretell future events and employ themselves either by purification, sacrifices, or other enchantments to avert evils or procure good fortune and success. They are skillful likewise in the art of divination by the flying of birds, and interpreting of dreams and prodigies; and are reputed as true oracles (in declaring what will come to pass) by their exact and diligent viewing the entrails of the sacrifices. But they attain not to this knowledge in the same manner as the Grecians do: for the Chaldæans learn it by tradition from their ancestors, the son from the father, who are all in the mean time free from all other public offices and attendances; and because their parents are their tutors, they both learn everything without envy, and rely with more confidence upon the truth of what is taught them; and being trained up in this learning from their very childhood, they become most famous philosophers (that age being most capable of learning wherein they spend much of their time).

They hold that the world is eternal, which had neither any certain beginning nor shall have any end; but all agree that all things are ordered, and this beautiful fabric is supported by a divine providence, and that the motions of the heavens are not performed by chance and of their own accord, but by a certain and determinate will and appointment of the gods. Therefore, from a long observation of the stars and an exact knowledge of the motions and influences of every one of them, wherein they excel all others, they foretell many things that are to come to pass.

They say that the five stars which some call planets, but which they call Interpreters, are most worthy of consideration, both for their motions and their remarkable influences, especially that which the Grecians call Saturn. The brightest of them all, and which often portends many and great events, they call Sol; the other four they name Mars, Venus, Mercury, and Jupiter, with our own country astrologers. They give the name of Interpreters to these stars, because these only, by a peculiar motion, portend things to come; and, instead of interpreters, do declare to men beforehand the good will of the gods; whereas the other stars (not being of the number of the planets) have a constant ordinary motion. Future events, they say, are pointed at some-

THE CHALDÆANS AND THEIR WAYS

times by their rising, and sometimes by their setting, and at other times by their color, as may be experienced by those that will diligently observe it; sometimes foreshowing hurricanes, at other times tempestuous rains, and then again exceeding droughts. By these, they say, are often portended the appearance of comets, eclipses of the sun and moon, earthquakes, and all the other various changes and remarkable effects in the air, boding good and bad, not only to nations in general, but to kings and private persons in particular. Under the course of these planets, they say, are thirty stars, which they call counseling gods, half of whom observe what is done under the earth and what is transacted in the heavens. Once every ten days' space, they say, one of the highest order of these stars descends to them that are of the lowest, like a messenger sent from them above; and then again another ascends from those below to them above, and that this is their constant natural motion to continue forever. The chief of these gods, they say, are twelve in number, to each of which they attribute a month and one sign of the twelve in the zodiac.

Through these twelve signs the sun, moon, and the other five planets run their course. The sun in a year's time, and the moon in the space of a month.

To every one of the planets they assign their own proper courses, where are performed variously in lesser or shorter time according as their several motions are quicker or slower. These stars, they say, have a great influence both as to good and bad, in men's nativities; and from the consideration of their several natures may be foreknown what will befall men afterwards. As they foretold things to come to other kings formerly, so they did to Alexander, who conquered Darius, and to his successors Antigonus and Seleucus Nicanor; and accordingly things fell out as they declared. They tell likewise private men their fortunes, so certainly that those who have found the thing true by experience have esteemed it a miracle and above the reach of man to perform. Out of the circle of the zodiac they describe four-and-twenty stars, twelve toward the North Pole and as many toward the South.

Those which we see they assign to the living; and the others, that do not appear, they conceive are constellations for the dead; and they term them judges of all things. The moon, they say, is in the lowest orb; and being therefore next to the earth (because she is so small) she finishes her course in a little time, not through the swiftness of her motion, but the shortness of her sphere. In that which they affirm, that she has but a borrowed light, and that when she is eclipsed, it is caused by the interposition of the shadow of the earth, they agree with the Grecians.

Their rules and notions concerning the eclipses of the sun are but weak and mean, which they dare not positively foretell, nor fix a certain time for them. They have likewise opinions concerning the earth, peculiar to themselves, affirming it to resemble a boat and to be hollow; to prove which, and other things relating to the frame of the world, they abound in arguments; but to give a particular account of them, we conceive would be a thing foreign to our history. But this any man may justly and truly say, that the Chaldæans far exceed all other men in the knowledge of astrology, and have

THE CHALDÆANS AND THEIR WAYS

studied it most of any art or science. But the number of years during which the Chaldæans say those of their profession have given themselves to the study of this natural philosophy is incredible; for when Alexander was in Asia, they reckoned up four hundred and seventy thousand years since they first began to observe the motions of the stars. But lest we should make too long a digression from our intended design, let this which we have said concerning the Chaldæans suffice.

HOW THE CHALDÆANS WROTE BOOKS

BY G. MASPERO

THE position of a scribe was an important one. We continually meet with it in all grades of society — in the palaces, in the temples, in the storehouses, in private dwellings; in fine, the scribe was ubiquitous, at court, in the town, in the country, in the army, managing affairs both small and great, and seeing that they were carried on regularly. His education differed but little from that given to the Egyptian scribe; he learned the routine of administration of judicial affairs, the formularies for correspondence either with nobles or with ordinary people, the art of writing, of calculating quickly, and of making out bills correctly. We may well ask whether he ever employed papyrus or prepared skins for these purposes. It would, indeed, seem strange that, after centuries of intercourse, no caravan should have brought into Chaldæa any of those materials which were in such constant use for literary purposes in Africa; yet the same clay which furnished the architect with such an abundant building material appears to have been the only medium for transmitting the language which the scribes possessed. They were always provided with slabs of a fine plastic clay, carefully mixed and kept sufficiently moist to take easily the impression of an object, but at the same time sufficiently firm to prevent the marks once made from becoming either blurred or effaced. When a scribe had a text to copy or a document

HOW THE CHALDÆANS WROTE BOOKS

to draw up, he chose out one of his slabs, which he placed flat upon his left palm, and taking in the right hand a triangular stylus of flint, copper, bronze, or bone, he at once set to work. The instrument in early times terminated in a fine point, and the marks made by it when it was gently pressed upon the clay were slender and of uniform thickness; in later times, the extremity of the stylus was cut with a bevel, and the impression then took the shape of a metal nail or a wedge. They wrote from left to right along the upper part of the tablet, and covered both sides of it with closely written lines, which sometimes ran over on to the edges. When the writing was finished, the scribe sent his work to the potter, who put it in the kiln and baked it, or the writer may have had a small oven at his own disposition, as a clerk with us would have his table or desk.

The shape of these documents varied, and sometimes strikes us as being peculiar: besides the tablets and the bricks, we find small solid cones, or hollow cylinders of considerable size, on which the kings related their exploits or recorded the history of their wars or the dedication of their buildings. This method had a few inconveniences, but many advantages. These clay books were heavy to hold and clumsy to handle, while the characters did not stand out well from the brown, yellow, and whitish background of the material; but, on the other hand, a poem, baked and incorporated into the page itself, ran less danger of destruction than if scribbled in ink on sheets of papyrus. Fire could make no impression on it; it could withstand water for a considerable length of time; even if broken, the pieces were still of use: as long as it was not pulverized, the entire document could be restored, with the exception, perhaps, of a few signs or some scraps of a sentence. The inscriptions which have been saved from the foundations of the most ancient temples, several of which date back forty or fifty centuries, are for the most part as clear and legible as when they left the hands of the writer who engraved them or of the workmen who baked them. It is owing to the material to which they were committed that we possess the principal works of Chaldæan literature which have come down to us — poems, annals, hymns, magical incantations; how few fragments of these would ever have reached us had their authors confided them to parchment or paper, after the manner of the Egyptian scribes! The greatest danger that they ran was that of being left forgotten in the corner of the chamber in which they had been kept, or buried under the rubbish of a building after a fire or some violent catastrophe; even then the débris was the means of preserving them, by falling over them and covering them up. Protected under the ruins, they would lie there for centuries, till the fortunate explorer should bring them to light and deliver them over to the patient study of the learned.

The cuneiform character in itself is neither picturesque nor decorative. It does not offer that delightful assemblage of birds and snakes, of men and quadrupeds, of heads and limbs, of tools, weapons, stars, trees, and boats, which succeed each other in perplexing order on the Egyptian monuments, to give permanence to the glory of Pharaoh and the greatness of his gods. Cuneiform writing is essentially composed of thin, short lines, placed in juxtaposition or crossing each other in a somewhat clumsy fashion; it has the appearance of numbers of nails scattered about at haphazard, and its angular configuration, and its stiff and spiny appearance, give the inscriptions a dull and forbidding aspect which no artifice of the engraver can overcome. Yet, in spite of their seemingly arbitrary character, this mass of strokes had its source in actual hieroglyphics. As in the origin of the Egyptian script, the earliest writers had begun by drawing on stone or clay the outline of the object which they desired to convey the idea. But, whereas in Egypt the artistic temperament of the race and the increasing skill of their sculptors had by degrees brought the drawing of each sign to such perfection that it became a miniature portrait of the being or object to be reproduced, in Chaldæa, on the contrary, the signs became degraded from their original forms on account of the difficulty experienced in copying them with the stylus on the clay tablets: they lost their original vertical position and were placed horizontally, retaining finally but the very faintest resemblance to the original model. For instance, the Chaldæan conception of the sky was that of a vault divided into eight segments by diameters running from the four cardinal points and from their principal subdivisions ⊕ ; the external circle was soon omitted, the transverse lines alone remaining ✷ which again was simplified into a kind of irregular cross ✚ . In later times, lists were made, in which

MESOPOTAMIA

the scribes strove to place beside each character the special hieroglyph from which it had been derived. Several fragments of these still exist, a study of which seems to show that the Assyrian scribes of a more recent period were at times as much puzzled as we are ourselves to get at the principles of their own script.

THE TOWER OF BABEL

BY SIR DAVID LYNDSAY

[THE story of the Tower of Babel is told in the eleventh chapter of the Book of Genesis. Sir David Lyndsay, or Lindsay, was a Scottish poet who lived in the first half of the sixteenth century.

The Editor.]

THEIR great fortress then did they found,
And cast till they gat sure ground.
All fell to work, both man and child,
Some howkit clay, some burnt the tyld.
Nimrod, that curious champion,
Deviser was of that dungeon.
Nathing they spared their labors,
Like busy bees upon the flowers,
Or emmets traveling into June;
Some under wrocht, and some aboon,
With strang ingenious masonry,
Upward their wark did fortify;
The land about was fair and plain,
And it rase like ane heich montane,
Those fulish people did intend,
That till the heaven it should ascend;
Sae great ane strength was never seen
Into the warld with men's een.
The wallis of that wark they made,
Twa and fifty fathom braid:
Ane fathom then, as some men says,
Micht been twa fathom in our days;
Ane man was then of mair stature

MESOPOTAMIA

Nor twa be now, of this be sure.
The translator of Orosius
Intil his chronicle writes thus;
That when the sun is at the hicht,
At noon, when it doth shine maist bricht,
The shadow of that hideous strength
Sax mile and mair it is of length:
Thus may ye judge into your thocht,
Gif Babylon be heich or nocht.

Then the great God omnipotent,
To whom all things been present,
He seeand the ambition,
And the prideful presumption,
How their proud people did pretend,
Up through the heavens till ascend,
Sic languages on them he laid,
That nane wist what ane other said;
Where was but ane language afore,
God send them languages three score;
Afore that time all spak Hebrew,
Then some began for to speak Grew,
Some Dutch, some language Saracen,
And some began to speak Latin.
The maister men gan to ga wild,
Cryand for trees, they brocht them tyld.
Some said, Bring mortar here at ance;
Then brocht they to them stocks and stanes;
And Nimrod, their great champion,
Ran ragand like ane wild lion,
Menacing them with words rude,
But never ane word they understood.

THE LION HUNT

THE LION HUNT

(*An Assyrian bas-relief*)

THE favorite art work of the Assyrians was a broad frieze of soft limestone whereon were large figures in bas-relief. These people had small notion of perspective, and they greatly preferred to present their subjects in profile. They had not the skill to indicate or suggest; each part must be brought forward and shown as nearly in full as possible. In the Lion Hunt, for instance, the moment is chosen when each of the four legs of the wounded lion are in view. It went beyond Assyrian skill to arrange the twelve legs of three horses in such wise as not to make them appear a mere wilderness; so here we are supposed to understand that the left legs of each animal are exactly behind the right legs, which are shown in the relief. Everything is clear and distinct. We know just how a driver held the reins, how an archer drew his bow, how many spokes were in the wheels, how his whip was made, indeed, we can almost count the arrows in the two quivers.

This is the fascination of Assyrian sculpture, that, little of art in the modern sense as it manifests, it does have the power to tell a story and to show how things were done. It reveals how the soldiers made their camp, crossed rivers, attacked cities, and tortured their enemies; how the king appeared sitting on his throne or offering up a sacrifice or eating his dinner with the queen in the palace gardens. In short, to study an Assyrian bas-relief is like taking a long look into the life that once dwelt between the Tigris and the Euphrates.

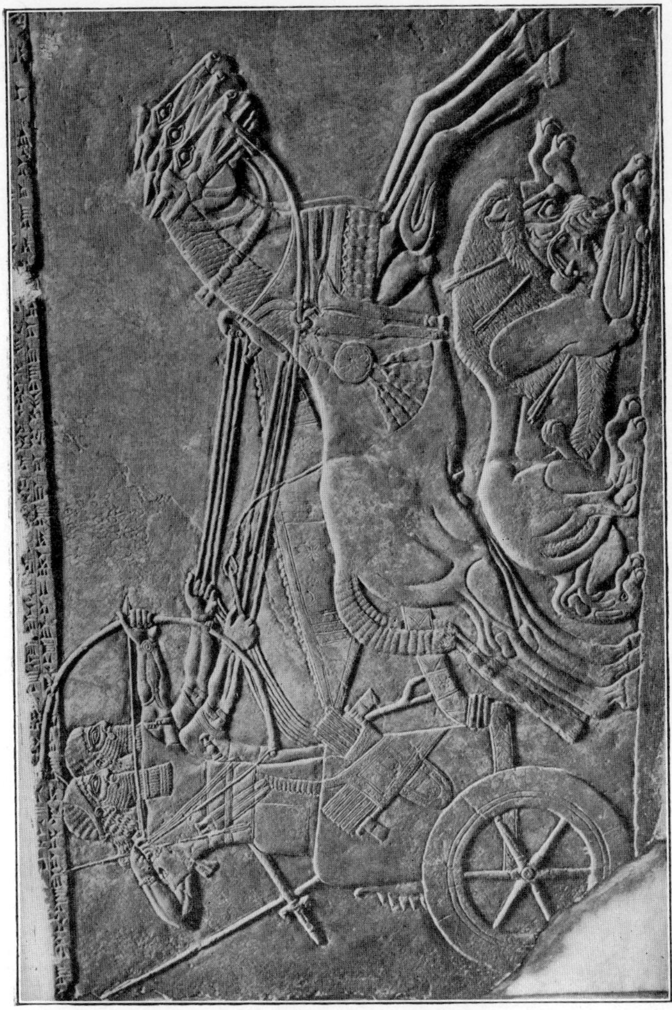

HOW THE ASSYRIANS AND BABYLONIANS LIVED

BY A. H. SAYCE

BABYLONIA was the land of bricks, Assyria of stone. It was in Babylonia that the great tower had been built of brick whose head, it was intended, should "reach to heaven." The bricks were merely dried in the sun; it was but rarely that they were baked in the kiln. When it was wished to give additional solidity to the walls of a building, lighted fuel was piled up against them, and their surfaces were thus vitrified into a solid mass. But usually the Babylonian builders were content with the ordinary sun-dried brick of the country. Naturally it crumbled away in the course of time, and the brick structure became a mound of shapeless mud. Nebuchadnezzar tells us how the great temple of the Seven Planets of Heaven and Earth at Borsippa, near Babylon, whose ruins are now known under the name of the Birs-i-Nimrud, and which has often been identified with the Tower of Babel, had been destroyed before his time by rain and storm, and neglect to repair its drains. In fact, the plain of Babylonia was covered with artificial hills formed of the débris of ancient temples which had been allowed to fall into decay. One of the earliest names given to it on the monuments is that of "the land of mounds."

No stone was found in the country. If stone was used, as, for instance, by Nebuchadnezzar in his construction

MESOPOTAMIA

of the quays of Babylon, it had to be brought from the distant mountains of Elam. Even the smallest stones and pebbles were highly prized. Hence it was that in Babylonia the art of engraving seems to have taken its rise. We learn from Herodotus that every Babylonian carried about with him an engraved seal attached to his wrist by a cord, and the statement is fully confirmed by the native monuments. The seal was of cylindrical shape, pierced longitudinally by a hole through which the cord was passed. When it was needed to be used, it was rolled over the wet clay which served the Babylonians as a writing material, and it was regarded as the necessary guaranty of the owner's identity. No legal deed or contract was valid without the impression of the seals belonging to the persons who took part in it; the engraved stone, in fact, was as indispensable to its owner as his name itself.

In Assyria, on the contrary, clay was comparatively scarce, and stone was plentiful. Hence, while the temples and palaces of Babylonia were built of brick, those of Assyria were, at all events in part, built of stone. The Assyrians, however, had originally migrated from Babylonia, and they carried with them the tradition of the art and architecture of their mother country. Accordingly, while making use of stone they nevertheless did not altogether forego the use of brick. The walls of Nineveh, in spite of their height, were constructed of brick, and it was only the basement of the palaces which was made of stone. We need not be surprised at this slavish imitation of a style of building which was out of place in the country to which it was transferred. In another respect the Assyrians imitated the architecture

HOW ASSYRIANS AND BABYLONIANS LIVED

of Babylonia even more slavishly and needlessly. This was in the construction of vast platforms of brick, upon which the temples of the gods and the palaces of the kings were erected. In Babylonia such platforms were necessary, in order to secure the edifices upon them from the danger of floods or the inconveniences of a marshy soil. But in Assyria similar precautions were not required. There the buildings could have been raised on a foundation of rock, without the intervention of an artificial platform.

The brick walls of the Babylonian houses were covered with stucco, which was then adorned with painting. Dadoes ran around them, whereon were depicted the figures of men and animals. In the Assyrian palaces the dado was formed of sculptured slabs of stone, and painted in imitation of the dadoes of painted stucco which were usual in Babylonia. The cornices and other portions of the walls were in the houses of the wealthy often ornamented with bronze and alabaster, and even gold. At times ivory was used for the same purpose, as in the ivory palaces of Samaria. The doors more especially were overlaid with bands of bronze, and were frequently double, the hinges revolving in sockets of bronze. The windows were protected from the weather by means of curtains of tapestry; and a flight of steps, open to the air, led to the upper stories of the house. The steps opened upon a court around which the sitting-rooms and bedchambers were built, the apartments assigned to the women being kept separate from those of the men.

All these luxuries, however, were confined to the rich and noble. The mass of the people lived, like their descendants to-day, in mud cabins, with conical roofs of clay. They had to be content to live on the ground floor, and to exclude the cold and rains of winter, not with costly tapestries, but by making the apertures in the walls which served as windows as small as possible. It is needless to say that the bronze and sculpture and painting which adorned the habitations of the wealthy were unknown in those of the poor.

Even in the houses of the wealthy the furniture was doubtless as scanty and simple as it is still to-day in the East. Rugs of variegated patterns were laid upon the floor, and chairs and stools of various shapes and sizes were used. The stools were generally lofty, so that the feet of the sitter had to be supported on a footstool. Some of the chairs were provided with arms.

At times, instead of chairs, couches or divans were employed. The luxurious Assyrian would even recline on a couch when eating, a habit which passed from the East to Greece, and from Greece to Rome, so that in the days of our Saviour it was more customary to "recline" than to sit at meat. One of the bas-reliefs in the British Museum represents the Assyrian King Assur-bani-pal lying on a couch while he drinks wine and feasts after the defeat and death of his Elamite enemy, though his wife, who participates in the banquet, is seated on a chair. The custom of reclining at meals was doubtless borrowed by the Assyrians from Babylonia, since the older native fashion was to seat the guests at a dinner party on lofty stools on either side of a small table. At night the wealthier classes slept on bedsteads covered with thick mattresses or rugs. Poorer people were satisfied with the mattress only, which was spread upon the ground, and rolled up when no longer needed for use. It

HOW ASSYRIANS AND BABYLONIANS LIVED

was a bed which could be taken up and carried away, like the "beds" we read of in the New Testament. All classes alike slept in their ordinary clothes.

The house of the well-to-do Assyrian or Babylonian was not considered complete unless it was provided with a garden or plantation, which, it would seem, was usually planted in front of it. It was well stocked with trees, among which the palm naturally held a chief place. In warm weather tables and seats were placed under the shade of the trees, and meals were thus taken in the open air. Those who could afford to keep slaves for the purpose employed one of them in waving a large fan, in order to drive insects away while the meal was being enjoyed. In taking the lease of a house, the tenant usually agreed to keep the garden in order, and to replace any trees that might die or be cut down.

The garden was irrigated from one of the numerous canals which intersected the whole of Babylonia. The rich employed hired laborers for the purpose; the poor had to irrigate their own plot of ground. The water was drawn up in buckets and then poured into a number of rivulets which ran through the garden. Vegetables of all kinds were grown along the edges of the rivulets, more especially onions and garlic. It would appear that flowers also were cultivated, at all events in the gardens of the wealthy, since vases of flowers were placed on the tables at a banquet.

The costume of the people was as varied as it is in the modern European world. Old lists of clothing have come down to us which contain as large an assortment of different dresses and their materials as could be found in a shop of to-day. Among the materials may be mentioned the *sindhu*, or muslin of "India," which is described as being composed of "vegetable wool," or cotton, and so bears testimony to an ancient trade between Chaldæa and the western coast of India. Most of the stuffs, however, were of home manufacture, and were exported into all parts of the civilized world. It will be remembered that among the Canaanitish spoil found in the tent of Achan was "a goodly Babylonish garment."

In spite of the changes of fashion and the varieties of dress worn by different classes of persons, the principal constituents of the Assyrian and Babylonian costume remained the same. These were a hat or head-dress, a tunic or shirt, and a long outer robe which reached to the ankles. In early Babylonian times the hat was ornamented with ribbons which projected before and behind like horns; at a later period it assumed the shape of a tiara or peaked helmet. The material of which it was composed was thick and sometimes quilted; the upper classes further protected their heads from the sun by a parasol, which in Assyria became the symbol of royal or semi-royal authority. The tunic was of linen or wool, the latter material being much employed, particularly in cold weather; it reached halfway down the thigh, and was fastened round the waist by a girdle. A second tunic was often worn under the first, doubtless during the winter season.

The long robe or cloak was specially characteristic of the Babylonians. It opened in front, was usually sleeveless, and was ornamented at the edge with fringes. In walking it allowed the inner side of the left leg to be exposed. Not unfrequently the girdle was fastened round it instead of round the tunic. In Assyria the king sometimes wore over his robe a sort of chasuble, richly ornamented like the robe itself.

The Babylonian priest was characterized by a curious kind of flounced dress which descended to the feet, and perhaps was made of muslin. From immemorial times a goat-skin was also flung over his shoulders, the goat being accounted an animal of peculiar sanctity. On Babylonian cylinders and seals a priest may always be at once distinguished by the flounces of his dress.

The costume of the women differed externally but little from that of the men — at least when the latter were dressed in their outer robe. The queen of Assurbani-pal is depicted in a long unsleeved robe, over which comes a fringed frock reaching below the knees, and over that again a light cape, also fringed and patterned with rosettes. On her feet are boots, and around her head is a crown or fillet representing a castellated wall, and thus resembling the mural crown of Greek sculpture. Earrings, bracelets, and a necklace complete her costume.

Earrings, bracelets, and necklaces were also worn by the men. Anklets are referred to in the inscriptions as well as finger-rings, though the usual substitute for a finger-ring was the cylinder, which, as has already been stated, was attached by a string or chain to the wrist.

The Babylonian, at any rate in earlier times, seems ordinarily to have gone bare footed. Already in the twelfth century B.C., however, we find the king [1] wear-

---

[1] Merodach-nadin-akhi, B.C. 1106. He has on his head a tall square cap, ornamented in front with a band of rosettes immediately above the forehead, while a row of feathers in an upright position runs round the top. It is curious that a similar head-dress was worn

ing a pair of soft leather shoes, and in Assyria sandals were in use from an early period, the sandal being furnished with a cap for protecting the heel. The northern conquests of Tiglath-pileser III and Sargon introduced the laced boot of the inhabitants of the colder regions in the north. The cavalry, who had hitherto ridden with bare legs, now adopted high boots, laced in front, and worn over tightly-fitting breeches of plaited leather. Certain of the foot-soldiers were also clothed in the same way; while others of them wore the boots without the trousers. Sennacherib was the first of the Assyrian kings who discarded the sandal in his own person and substituted for it a shoe, which like the military boot was laced in front.

It must not be imagined that the robe or even the tunic was always worn. In fact, the light-armed troops in the Assyrian army were contented with a simple kilt, which, together with a felt skull-cap, constituted the whole of their dress. This was also the costume of the Babylonian laborer when working in the fields, and both Assyrians and Babylonians, while engaged in manual work or military operations, discarded the long and inconvenient outer robe. It was only the upper classes who could afford the luxury of wearing it in everyday life. So, too, the use of a hat or cap was not universal. Numbers of people were satisfied with tying up their hair with a fillet or string, even when exposed to the heat of the sun. At times even the fillet was dispensed with.

The hair of the head was worn long, and the Assyrians distinguished themselves from their neighbors by

by the Zakkur, who are usually identified with the Teukrians, and are among the foreign enemies depicted upon the Egyptian monuments.

dressing and curling both it and their beards. The fashion must have been derived from the early Semitic population of Babylonia, since the hero of the great Chaldæan epic is represented on ancient engraved seals with a curled beard. On the other hand, the practice was unknown to the non-Semitic population of the country; the sculptured heads, for instance, found at Tel-loth, which belong to the Accado-Sumerian epoch, are either beardless or else provided with long uncurled beards which terminate in a point, "the musked and curled Assyrian bull," spoken of by Lord Tennyson, being a Semitic creation. Here, as elsewhere, fashion was determined by physical characteristics, and it was only among a Semitic people distinguished by its thick growth of black hair that the art of the hair-dresser could develop as it did in Semitic Babylonia and Assyria. The comparatively beardless Sumerians rather encouraged the barber, who accordingly occupies a conspicuous place in early Babylonian literature.

THE DESTRUCTION OF SENNACHERIB

BY LORD BYRON

[SENNACHERIB was an Assyrian king who lived during the seventh century, B.C. He was a famous builder and also a great warrior. On an expedition against the King of Judah, he laid siege to Jerusalem. The Egyptian forces drew near, coming to the aid of the Jews. Then Sennacherib and his men turned away from the city and went forth to meet the Egyptians. The following account of the result is taken from the nineteenth chapter of Second Kings: "And it came to pass that night, that the angel of the Lord went out, and smote in the camp of the Assyrians a hundred fourscore and five thousand: and when they arose early in the morning, behold, they were all dead corpses. So Sennacherib, king of Assyria, departed, and went and returned, and dwelt at Nineveh."

The Editor.]

THE Assyrian came down like a wolf on the fold,
And his cohorts were gleaming in purple and gold;
And the sheen of their spears was like stars on the sea,
When the blue wave rolls nightly on deep Galilee.

Like the leaves of the forest when summer is green,
That host with their banners at sunset were seen:
Like the leaves of the forest when Autumn hath blown
That host on the morrow lay wither'd and strown.

For the Angel of Death spread his wings on the blast,
And breathed in the face of the foe as he pass'd;

THE DESTRUCTION OF SENNACHERIB

And the eyes of the sleepers wax'd deadly and chill,
And their hearts but once heaved, and forever grew still!

And there lay the steed with his nostril all wide,
But through it there roll'd not the breath of his pride:
And the foam of his gasping lay white on the turf,
And cold as the spray of the rock-beating surf.

And there lay the rider distorted and pale,
With the dew on his brow, and the rust on his mail;
And the tents were all silent, the banners alone,
The lances unlifted, the trumpet unblown.

And the widows of Ashur are loud in their wail,
And the idols are broke in the temple of Baal;
And the might of the Gentile, unsmote by the sword,
Hath melted like snow in the glance of the Lord.

II
BABYLON THE MAGNIFICENT

HISTORICAL NOTE

In spite of the greatness and power of Sardanapalus, there were many revolts and conspiracies against him. These increased as the years passed, and in the time of his successor, Saracus, Nineveh was overthrown, and the kingdom of Babylon rose into supreme power.

Nebuchadnezzar, the second king of this new monarchy, captured and destroyed Jerusalem. He was so successful in his warfare that he could command the labor of thousands of captives, and so carry on the enormous amount of building with which his name is associated. He built and rebuilt temples and palaces and cities; he raised the wonderful Hanging Gardens; and he dug a complicated network of canals which carried water into every corner of his land.

Babylonia was a mighty kingdom, but lying to the eastward was the land of the Medes and Persians. They, too, were powerful, and their power was rapidly increasing. King Crœsus of Lydia and the joint kings of Babylon, Nabonius and his son Belshazzar, formed a league against them; but the Persian King Cyrus was more than equal to their combined strength, and Babylon fell into his hands. He spared the city, but his successors were not so forbearing, and in later years it was destroyed and the vast amount of treasure in the temples was carried away. Alexander the Great planned to rebuild the city, but his early death prevented this, and now hardly a vestige of even its mighty walls can be traced.

HOW SEMIRAMIS BUILT BABYLON

BY DIODORUS THE SICILIAN

[THE King of Assyria, being attacked by hordes from the north and the east, entrusted the southern part of his kingdom to his viceroy, Nabopolassar. The viceroy proved to be a traitor. He held the lands for himself, and with the help of the Medes and his son Nebuchadnezzar he captured Nineveh, the capital of the Assyrian kingdom, which Sennacherib boasted he had made "a city shining like the sun." This was the beginning of the Babylonian monarchy. According to Greek tradition, its capital, Babylon, was founded by Queen Semiramis, daughter of a goddess and wife of King Ninus.

The Editor.]

SEMIRAMIS was naturally of a high aspiring spirit, ambitious to excel all her predecessors in glorious actions, and therefore employed all her thoughts about the building of a city in the province of Babylon; and to this end having provided architects, artists, and all other necessaries for the work, she got together two millions of men out of all parts of the empire, to be employed in the building of the city. It was so built that the river Euphrates ran through the middle of it; and she compassed it round with a wall of three turrets; and such was the state and grandeur of the work that the walls were of that breadth as that six chariots might be driven together upon them. Their height was such as exceeded all men's belief that heard of it. But Clitarchus and those who afterwards went over with Alexander into

Asia have written, that the walls were in circuit three hundred and sixty-five furlongs;[1] the queen making them of that compass, to the end that the furlongs should be as many in number as the days of the year. They were of brick cemented with brimstone; in height, as Ctesias says, fifty orgyas; but as some of the later writers report, but fifty cubits only, and that the breadth was but a little more than what would allow two chariots to be driven in front. There were two hundred and fifty turrets, in height and thickness proportionable to the largeness of the wall. It is not to be wondered at that there were so few towers upon a wall of so great circuit, being that in many places round the city there were deep morasses; so that it was judged to no purpose to raise turrets there, where they were so naturally fortified. Between the wall and the houses there was a space left around the city of two hundred feet.

That the work might be the more speedily dispatched, to each of her friends was allotted a furlong, with an allowance of all expenses necessary for their several parts, and commanded that all should be finished in a year's time; which being diligently perfected with the queen's approbation, she then made a bridge over the narrowest part of the river, five furlongs in length, laying the supports and pillars of the arches with great art and skill at the bottom of the water, twelve feet distant from each other. That the stones might be the more firmly joined, they were bound together with hooks of iron, and the joints filled up with melted lead. And before the pillars she made and placed defenses, with sharp-pointed

[1] A furlong is one eighth of a mile; an orgyas is about six feet; a cubit is about eighteen inches.

HOW SEMIRAMIS BUILT BABYLON

angles, to receive the water before it beat upon the flat sides of the pillars; which caused the course of the water to run round by degrees gently and moderately, as far as to the broad sides of the pillars, so that the sharp points of the angles cut the stream, and gave a check to its violence, and the roundness of them by little and little giving way abated the force of the current. This bridge was floored with great joists and planks of cedar, cypress, and palm trees, and was thirty feet in breadth, and for art and curiosity yielded to none of the works of Semiramis.

On either side of the river she raised a bank, as broad as the wall, and with great cost drew it out in length a hundred furlongs. She built likewise two palaces at each end of the bridge upon the bank of the river, whence she might have a prospect over the whole city, and make her passage as by keys to the most convenient places in it as she had occasion. And whereas the Euphrates runs through the middle of Babylon, making its course to the south, the palaces lie the one on the east, and the other on the west side of the river; both built at exceeding costs and expense. For that on the west had a high and stately wall, made of well-burnt bricks, sixty furlongs in compass; within this was drawn another of a round circumference, upon which were portrayed in the bricks before they were burnt, all sorts of living creatures, as if it were to the life, laid with great art in curious colors. This wall was in circuit forty furlongs, three hundred bricks thick, and in height a hundred yards, upon which were turrets a hundred and forty yards high. The third and most inward wall immediately surrounded the palace, thirty furlongs in compass,

and far surmounted the middle wall both in height and
thickness, and on this wall and the towers were represented the shapes of all sorts of living creatures, artifi-
cially expressed in most lively colors. Especially was
represented a general hunting of all sorts of wild beasts,
each four cubits high and upwards. Amongst these was
to be seen Semiramis on horseback, striking a leopard
through with a dart; and next to her, her husband Ninus
in close fight with a lion, piercing him with his lance.
To this palace she built likewise three gates, under
which were apartments of brass for entertainments,
into which passages were opened by a certain engine.
This palace far excelled that on the other side of the
river both in greatness and adornments. For the outermost wall of that (made of well-burnt brick) was but
thirty furlongs in compass. Instead of the curious portraiture of beasts, there were the brazen statues of Ninus
and Semiramis, the great officers, and of Jupiter, whom
the Babylonians call Belus; and likewise armies drawn
up in battalia, and divers sorts of hunting were there
represented, to the great diversion and pleasure of the
beholders.

After all these in a low ground in Babylon she sank
a place for a pond, four-square, every square being three
hundred furlongs in length, lined with brick and cemented with brimstone, and the whole five and thirty
feet in depth. Into this having first turned the river, she
then made a passage in form of a vault, from one palace
to another, whose arches were built of firm and strong
brick, and plastered all over on both sides with bitumen,
four cubits thick. The walls of this vault were twenty
bricks in thickness and twelve feet high, beside and

HOW SEMIRAMIS BUILT BABYLON

above the arches; and the breadth was fifteen feet. This piece of work being finished in two hundred and sixty days, the river was turned into its ancient channel again, so that the river flowing over the whole work, Semiramis could go from one palace to the other without passing over the river. She made likewise two brazen gates at either end of the vault, which continued to the time of the Persian Empire.

In the middle of the city she built a temple to Jupiter, whom the Babylonians call Belus, as we have before said, of which, since writers differ amongst themselves, and the work is now wholly decayed through length of time, there is nothing that can with certainty be related concerning it; yet it is apparent it was of an exceeding great height, and that by the advantage of it the Chaldæan astrologers exactly observed the setting and rising of the stars. The whole was built of brick, cemented with brimstone with great art and cost. Upon the top she placed three statues of beaten gold, of Jupiter, Juno, and Rhea. That of Jupiter stood upright in the posture as if he were walking; he was forty feet in height and weighed a thousand Babylonish talents.[1] The statue of Rhea was of the same weight, sitting on a golden throne, having two lions standing on either side, one at her knees; and near to them two exceeding great serpents of silver weighing thirty talents each. Here likewise the image of Juno stood upright, and weighed eight hundred talents, grasping a serpent by the head in her right hand and holding a scepter adorned with precious stones in her left. For all these deities there was placed a com-

[1] The heavy Babylonian talent weighed about seventy-five pounds; the light talent, about fifty-two.

mon table made of beaten gold, forty feet long, and fifteen broad, weighing five hundred talents; upon which stood two cups, weighing thirty talents, and near to them as many censers, weighing three hundred talents. There were there likewise placed three drinking-bowls of gold, one of which, dedicated to Jupiter, weighed twelve hundred Babylonish talents, but the other two six hundred each; but all those the Persian kings sacrilegiously carried away. And length of time has either altogether consumed or much defaced the palaces and the other structures; so that at this day but a small part of this Babylon is inhabited, and the greatest part which lay within the walls is turned into tillage and pasture.

THE MAKE-BELIEVE ELEPHANTS OF SEMIRAMIS

BY DIODORUS THE SICILIAN

SEMIRAMIS, having settled her affairs in Egypt and Ethiopia, returned with her army into Asia to Bactria; and now having a great army and enjoying a long peace, she had a longing desire to perform some notable exploit by her arms. Hearing, therefore, that the Indians were the greatest nation in the whole world and had the largest and richest tract of land of all, she resolved to make war upon them. Stabrobates was at that time king, who had innumerable forces and many elephants bravely accoutered and fitted to strike terror into the hearts of his enemies. For India, because of the pleasantness of the country, excelled all others, being watered in every place with many rivers, so that the land yielded every year a double crop; and by that means was so rich and so abounded with plenty of all things necessary for the sustenance of man's life that it supplied the inhabitants continually with such things as made them excessively rich, insomuch as it was never known that there was ever any famine amongst them, the climate being so happy and favorable; and upon that account likewise there is an incredible number of elephants, which for courage and strength of body far excel those in Africa. Moreover, this country abounds in gold, silver, brass, iron, and precious stones of all sorts, both for profit and pleasure. All which being noised abroad, so stirred up the spirit of Semiramis that, though she had no provocation given her, yet she was resolved upon the war against the Indians. But knowing that she had need of great forces, she sent dispatches to all the provinces with command to the governors to list the choicest young men they could find, ordering the proportion of soldiers every province and country should send forth, according to the largeness of it; and commanded that all should furnish themselves with new arms and armor, and all appear in three years' time at a general rendezvous in Bactria, bravely armed and accoutered in all points. And having sent for shipwrights out of Phœnicia, Syria, Cyprus, and other places bordering upon the seacoast, she prepared timber for them fit for the purpose, and ordered them to build vessels that might be taken asunder and conveyed from place to place wherever she pleased. For the river Indus bordering upon that kingdom, being the greatest in those parts, she stood in need of many river boats to pass it in order to repress the Indians. But there being no timber near the river, she was compelled to convey the boats thither by land from Bactria. She further considered that she was much inferior to the Indians in elephants (which it was absolutely necessary for her to make use of). She therefore contrived to have beasts that should resemble them, hoping by this means to strike a terror into the Indians, who believed there were no elephants in any place but in India.

To this end she provided three hundred thousand black oxen, and distributed the flesh among a company of ordinary mechanics and such fellows as she had to play the cobblers for her, and ordered them, by stitching the

SEMIRAMIS'S MAKE-BELIEVE ELEPHANTS

skins together and stuffing them with straw, to imitate the shape of an elephant, and in every one of them she put a man to govern them and a camel to carry them, so that at a distance they appeared to all that saw them as if they were really such beasts.

They that were employed in this work wrought at it night and day in a place which was walled round for the purpose, and guards set at every gate, that none might be admitted either to go in or out, to the end that none might see what they were doing lest it should be noised abroad and come to the ears of the Indians.

Having therefore provided shipping and elephants in the space of two years, in the third she rendezvoused all her forces in Bactria. Her army consisted of three millions of foot, two hundred thousand horse, a hundred thousand chariots, and mounted upon camels a hundred thousand men with swords four cubits long. The boats that might be taken asunder were two thousand; which the camels carried by land as they did the mock-elephants, as we have before declared. The soldiers made their horses familiar with these feigned beasts by bringing them often to them, lest they should be terrified at the sight of them; which Perseus imitated many ages after when he was to fight with the Romans, who had elephants in their army out of Africa. However, this contrivance proved to be of no advantage either to him or her, as will appear in the issue herein a little after related.

When Stabrobates the Indian king heard of these great armies and the mighty preparations made against him, he did all he could to excel Semiramis in everything. And first he built of great canes four thousand river boats; for abundance of these canes grow in India about the rivers and fens, so thick as a man can scarce fathom; and vessels made of these reeds, they say, are exceedingly useful, because they will never rot or be worm-eaten. He was very diligent likewise in preparing of arms and going from place to place throughout all India, and so raised a far greater army than that of Semiramis. To his former number of elephants he added more, which he took by hunting, and furnished them all with everything that might make them look terrible in the face of their enemies; so that by their multitude and the completeness of their armor in all points it seemed above the strength and power of man to bear up against the violent shock of these creatures.

Having therefore made all these preparations, he sent ambassadors to Semiramis (as she was on her march towards him), to complain and upbraid her for beginning a war without any provocation or injury offered her; and by his private letters taxed her with her course of life, and vowed (calling the gods to witness) that if he conquered her he would nail her to the cross. When she read the letter, she smiled, and said the Indian should presently have a trial of her valor by her actions. When she came up with her army to the river Indus, she found the enemy's fleet drawn up in a line of battle; whereupon she forthwith drew up her own, and having manned it with the stoutest soldiers, joined battle, yet so ordering the matter as to have her land forces ready upon the shore, to be assisting as there should be occasion. After a long and sharp fight, with marks of valor on both sides, Semiramis was at length victorious, and sunk a thousand of the enemy's vessels, and took a great number of

SEMIRAMIS'S MAKE-BELIEVE ELEPHANTS

prisoners. Puffed up with this success, she took, in the cities and islands that lay in the river, and carried away, an hundred thousand captives. After this, the Indian king drew off his army (as if he fled for fear), but in truth to decoy his enemies to pass the river.

Semiramis, therefore (seeing things fall out according to her wish), laid a broad bridge of boats (at a vast charge) over the river, and thereby passed over all her forces, leaving only threescore thousand to guard the bridge, and with the rest of her army pursued the Indians. She placed the mock-elephants in the front, that the enemy's scouts might presently inform the king what multitudes of elephants she had in her army; and she was not deceived in her hopes, for when the spies gave an account to the Indians what a great multitude of these creatures were advancing towards them, they were all in amaze, inquiring among themselves whence the Assyrians should be supplied with such a vast number of elephants: but the cheat could not long be concealed, for some of Semiramis's soldiers being laid by the heels for their carelessness upon the guard, through fear of further punishment made their escape and fled to the enemy, and undeceived them as to the elephants; upon which the Indian king was mightily encouraged, and caused notice of the delusion to be spread through the whole army, and forthwith marched with all his force against the Assyrians; Semiramis, on the other hand, doing the like. When they approached near one another, Stabrobates, the Indian king, placed his horse and chariots in the vanguard, at a good distance before the main body of his army. The queen, having placed her mock-elephants at the like distance from her main body, valiantly received her enemy's charge; but the Indian horses were most strangely terrified; for in appearance the phantasms at a distance seemed to be real elephants, and the horses of the Indians (being inured to those creatures) pressed boldly and undauntedly forward; but when they came near and saw another kind of beast than usual, and the smell and almost everything else being strange and new to them, they broke in with great terror and confusion, one upon another, so that they cast some of their riders headlong to the ground, and ran away with others (as the lot happened) into the midst of their enemies: whereupon Semiramis, readily making use of her advantage, with a body of choice men fell in upon them and routed them, forcing them back to their main body. Though Stabrobates was something astonished at this unexpected defeat, yet he brought up his foot against the enemy with his elephants in the front. He himself was in the right wing, mounted upon a stately elephant, and made a fierce charge upon the queen herself, who happened then to be opposite him in the left. And though the mock-elephants in Semiramis's army did the like, yet they stood the violent shock of the other but a little while; for the Indian beasts being both exceeding strong and stout, easily bore down and destroyed all that opposed them, so that there was a great slaughter; for some they trampled under foot, others they rent in pieces with their teeth, and tossed up others with their trunks into the air. The ground therefore being covered with heaps of dead carcasses, and nothing but death and destruction to be seen on every hand, so that all were full of horror and amazement, none durst keep their order or ranks any

SEMIRAMIS'S MAKE-BELIEVE ELEPHANTS

longer. Upon which the whole Assyrian army fled outright, and the Indian king encountered Semiramis, and first wounded her with an arrow in the arm, and afterwards with a dart (in wheeling about) in the shoulder; whereupon the queen (her wounds not being mortal) fled, and by the swiftness of her horse (which far exceeded the other that pursued her) she got off. But all making one way to the bridge of boats, and such a vast multitude of men thronging together in one strait and narrow passage, the queen's soldiers miserably perished by treading down one another under foot, and (which was strange and unusual) horse and foot lay tumbling promiscuously one over another. When they at length came to the bridge, and the Indians at their heels, the consternation was so great that many on both sides the bridge were tumbled over into the river. But when the greatest part of those that remained had got over, Semiramis caused the cords and tenons of the bridge to be cut, which done, the boats (which were before joined together, and upon which was a great number of Indians not in the pursuit) being now divided into many parts, and carried here and there by the force of the current, multitudes of the Indians were drowned, and Semiramis was now safe and secure, having such a barrier as the river betwixt her and her enemies. Whereupon the Indian king, being forewarned by prodigies from heaven, and the opinions of the soothsayers, forbore all further pursuit. And Semiramis, making exchange of prisoners in Bactria, returned with scarce a third part of her army.

DANIEL THE FEARLESS

FROM THE OLD TESTAMENT

[Sixth century B.C.]

DANIEL IN THE FIERY FURNACE

NEBUCHADNEZZAR the king made an image of gold, whose height was threescore cubits,[1] and the breadth thereof six cubits: he set it up in the plain of Dura, in the province of Babylon. Then Nebuchadnezzar the king sent to gather together the princes, the governors, and the captains, the judges, the treasurers, the counsellors, the sheriffs, and all the rulers of the provinces, to come to the dedication of the image which Nebuchadnezzar the king had set up. Then the princes, the governors, and captains, the judges, the treasurers, the counsellors, the sheriffs, and all the rulers of the provinces, were gathered together unto the dedication of the image that Nebuchadnezzar the king had set up; and they stood before the image that Nebuchadnezzar had set up.

Then an herald cried aloud: "To you it is commanded O people, nations, and languages, That at what time ye hear the sound of the cornet, flute, harp, sackbut, psaltery, dulcimer, and all kinds of music, ye fall down and worship the golden image that Nebuchadnezzar the king hath set up: and whoso falleth not down and worshippeth shall the same hour be cast into the midst of a burning fiery furnace." Therefore at that time, when

[1] The cubit of the Hebrews was about seventeen and a half inches.

all the people heard the sound of the cornet, flute, harp, sackbut, psaltery, and all kinds of music, all the people, the nations, and the languages, fell down and worshipped the golden image that Nebuchadnezzar the king had set up.

Wherefore at that time certain Chaldeans came near, and accused the Jews. They spake and said to the king Nebuchadnezzar: "O king, live for ever. Thou, O king, hast made a decree, that every man that shall hear the sound of the cornet, flute, harp, sackbut, psaltery, and dulcimer, and all kinds of music, shall fall down and worship the golden image: and whoso falleth not down and worshippeth, that he should be cast into the midst of a burning fiery furnace. There are certain Jews whom thou hast set over the affairs of the province of Babylon, Shadrach, Meshach, and Abed-nego; these men, O king, have not regarded thee: they serve not thy gods, nor worship the golden image which thou hast set up."

Then Nebuchadnezzar in his rage and fury commanded to bring Shadrach, Meshach, and Abed-nego. Then they brought these men before the king. Nebuchadnezzar spake and said unto them: "Is it true, O Shadrach, Meshach, and Abed-nego, do not ye serve my gods, nor worship the golden image which I have set up? Now if ye be ready that at what time ye hear the sound of the cornet, flute, harp, sackbut, psaltery, and dulcimer, and all kinds of music, ye fall down and worship the image which I have made; well: but if ye worship not, ye shall be cast the same hour into the midst of a burning fiery furnace; and who is that God that shall deliver you out of my hands?"

MESOPOTAMIA

Shadrach, Meshach, and Abed-nego answered and said to the king: "O Nebuchadnezzar, we are not careful to answer thee in this matter. If it be so, our God whom we serve is able to deliver us from the burning fiery furnace, and he will deliver us out of thine hand, O king. But if not, be it known unto thee, O king, that we will not serve thy gods, nor worship the golden image which thou hast set up."

Then was Nebuchadnezzar full of fury, and the form of his visage was changed against Shadrach, Meshach, and Abed-nego: therefore he spake, and commanded that they should heat the furnace one seven times more than it was wont to be heated. And he commanded the most mighty men that were in his army to bind Shadrach, Meshach, and Abed-nego, and to cast them into the burning fiery furnace. Then these men were bound in their coats, their hosen, and their hats, and their other garments, and were cast into the midst of the burning fiery furnace. Therefore because the king's commandment was urgent, and the furnace exceeding hot, the flame of the fire slew those men that took up Shadrach, Meshach, and Abed-nego. And these three men, Shadrach, Meshach, and Abed-nego, fell down bound into the midst of the burning fiery furnace.

Then Nebuchadnezzar the king was astonished, and rose up in haste, and spake, and said unto his counsellors: "Did not we cast three men bound into the midst of the fire?"

They answered and said unto the king: "True, O king." He answered and said: "Lo, I see four men loose, walking in the midst of the fire, and they have no hurt; and the form of the fourth is like the Son of God."

DANIEL THE FEARLESS

Then Nebuchadnezzar came near to the mouth of the burning fiery furnace, and spake, and said: "Shadrach, Meshach, and Abed-nego, ye servants of the most high God, come forth, and come hither."

Then Shadrach, Meshach, and Abed-nego came forth of the midst of the fire. And the princes, governors, and captains, and the king's counsellors, being gathered together, saw these men, upon whose bodies the fire had no power, nor was an hair of their head singed, neither were their coats changed, nor the smell of fire had passed on them.

Then Nebuchadnezzar spake, and said: "Blessed be the God of Shadrach, Meshach, and Abed-nego, who hath sent his angel, and delivered his servants that trusted in him, and have changed the king's word, and yielded their bodies, that they might not serve nor worship any god, except their own God. Therefore I make a decree, That every people, nation, and language, which speak any thing amiss against the God of Shadrach, Meshach, and Abed-nego, shall be cut in pieces, and their houses shall be made a dunghill: because there is no other God that can deliver after this sort." Then the king promoted Shadrach, Meshach, and Abed-nego, in the province of Babylon.

DANIEL IN THE DEN OF LIONS

It pleased Darius to set over the kingdom an hundred and twenty princes, which should be over the whole kingdom; and over these three presidents; of whom Daniel was first: that the princes might give accounts unto them, and the king should have no damage. Then this Daniel was preferred above the presidents and princes, because an excellent spirit was in him; and the king thought to set him over the whole realm.

Then the presidents and princes sought to find occasion against Daniel concerning the kingdom; but they could find none occasion nor fault; forasmuch as he was faithful, neither was there any error or fault found in him. Then said these men, "We shall not find any occasion against this Daniel, except we find it against him concerning the law of his God." Then these presidents and princes assembled together to the king, and said thus unto him: "King Darius, live for ever. All the presidents of the kingdom, the governors, and the princes, the counsellors, and the captains, have consulted together to establish a royal statute, and to make a firm decree, that whosoever shall ask a petition of any God or man for thirty days, save of thee, O king, he shall be cast into the den of lions. Now, O king, establish the decree, and sign the writing, that it be not changed, according to the law of the Medes and Persians, which altereth not." Wherefore king Darius signed the writing and the decree.

Now when Daniel knew that the writing was signed, he went into his house; and his windows being open in his chamber toward Jerusalem, he kneeled upon his knees three times a day, and prayed, and gave thanks before his God, as he did aforetime. Then these men assembled, and found Daniel praying and making supplication before his God. Then they came near, and spake before the king concerning the king's decree: "Hast thou not signed a decree, that every man that shall ask a petition of any God or man within thirty days, save of thee, O king, shall be cast into the den of lions?"

DANIEL THE FEARLESS

The king answered and said: "The thing is true, according to the law of the Medes and Persians, which altereth not."

Then answered they and said before the king: "That Daniel, which is of the children of the captivity of Judah, regardeth not thee, O king, nor the decree that thou hast signed, but maketh his petition three times a day."

Then the king, when he heard these words, was sore displeased with himself, and set his heart on Daniel to deliver him: and he laboured till the going down of the sun to deliver him. Then these men assembled unto the king, and said unto the king: "Know, O king, that the law of the Medes and Persians is, That no decree nor statute which the king establisheth may be changed."

Then the king commanded, and they brought Daniel and cast him into the den of lions. Now the king spake and said unto Daniel: "Thy God whom thou servest continually, he will deliver thee." And a stone was brought, and laid upon the mouth of the den; and the king sealed it with his own signet, and with the signet of his lords; that the purpose might not be changed concerning Daniel.

Then the king went to his palace, and passed the night fasting: neither were instruments of music brought before him: and his sleep went from him. Then the king arose very early in the morning, and went in haste unto the den of lions. And when he came to the den, he cried with a lamentable voice unto Daniel: and the king spake and said to Daniel: "O Daniel, servant of the living God, is thy God, whom thou servest continually, able to deliver thee from the lions?"

Then said Daniel unto the king: "O king, live for

ever. My God hath sent his angel, and hath shut the lions' mouths, that they have not hurt me: forasmuch as before him innocency was found in me; and also before thee, O king, have I done no hurt."

Then was the king exceeding glad for him, and commanded that they should take Daniel up out of the den. So Daniel was taken up out of the den, and no manner of hurt was found upon him, because he believed in his God.

And the king commanded, and they brought those men which had accused Daniel, and they cast them into the den of lions, them, their children, and their wives; and the lions had the mastery of them, and brake all their bones in pieces or ever they came at the bottom of the den.

Then king Darius wrote unto all people, nations, and languages, that dwell in all the earth: "Peace be multiplied unto you. I make a decree, That in every dominion of my kingdom men tremble and fear before the God of Daniel: for he is the living God, and stedfast for ever, and his kingdom that which shall not be destroyed, and his dominion shall be even unto the end. He delivereth and rescueth, and he worketh signs and wonders in heaven and in earth, who hath delivered Daniel from the power of the lions."

BELSHAZZAR

[538 B.C.]

BY HEINRICH HEINE

Midnight came slowly sweeping on;
In silent rest lay Babylon.

But in the royal castle high
Red torches gleam and courtiers cry.

Belshazzar there in kingly hall
Is holding kingly festival.

The vassals sat in glittering line,
And emptied the goblets with glowing wine.

The goblets rattle, the choruses swell,
And it pleased the stiff-necked monarch well.

In the monarch's cheeks a wild fire glowed,
And the wine awoke his daring mood.

And, onward still by his madness spurred,
He blasphemes the Lord with a sinful word;

And he brazenly boasts, blaspheming wild,
While the servile courtiers cheered and smiled.

Quick the king spoke, while his proud glance burned,
Quickly the servant went and returned.

He bore on his head the vessels of gold,
Of Jehovah's temple the plunder bold.

MESOPOTAMIA

With daring hand, in his frenzy grim,
The king seized a beaker and filled to the brim,

And drained to the dregs the sacred cup,
And foaming he cried, as he drank it up,

"Jehovah, eternal scorn I own
To thee. I am monarch of Babylon."

Scarce had the terrible blasphemy rolled
From his lips ere the monarch at heart was cold.

The yelling laughter was hushed, and all
Was still as death in the royal hall.

And see! and see! on the white wall high
The form of a hand went slowly by,

And wrote, — and wrote, on the broad wall white,
Letters of fire, and vanished in night.

Pale as death, with a steady stare,
And with trembling knees, the king sat there;

The horde of slaves sat shuddering chill;
No word they spoke, but were deathlike still.

The magians came, but of them all,
None could read the flame-script on the wall.

But that same night, in all his pride,
By the hands of his servants Belshazzar died.

THE FALL OF BABYLON
[558 B.C.]

BY JACOB ABBOTT

[THE kingdom of the Medes and Persians, lying to the east of Mesopotamia, had been increasing in power so rapidly that the rulers of Lydia and of Babylonia became alarmed and formed a league against it. Cyrus, the Persian king, first overpowered Lydia, and then attacked the Babylonian king. In 538 B.C., Babylon fell into the hands of the Persians.
The Editor.]

IN his advance toward the dominions of Crœsus in Asia Minor, Cyrus had passed to the northward of the great and celebrated city of Babylon. Babylon was on the Euphrates, toward the southern part of Asia. It was the capital of a large and very fertile region, which extended on both sides of the Euphrates toward the Persian Gulf. The limits of the country, however, which was subject to Babylon, varied very much at different times, as they were extended or contracted by revolutions and wars.

The river Euphrates was the great source of fertility for the whole region through which it flowed. The country watered by this river was very densely populated, and the inhabitants were industrious and peaceable, cultivating their land, and living quietly and happily on its fruits. The surface was intersected with canals, which the people had made for conveying the water of the river over the land for the purpose of irrigating it. Some of these canals were navigable. There was one great trunk which passed from the Euphrates to the

Tigris, supplying many minor canals by the way, that was navigable for vessels of considerable burden.

The traffic of the country was, however, mainly conducted by means of boats of moderate size, the construction of which seemed to Herodotus very curious and remarkable. The city was enormously large, and required immense supplies of food, which were brought down in these boats from the agricultural country above. The boats were made in the following manner: first a frame was built, of the shape of the intended boat, broad and shallow and with the stem and stern of the same form. This frame was made of willows, like a basket, and, when finished, was covered with a sheathing of skins. A layer of reeds was then spread over the bottom of the boat to protect the frame, and to distribute evenly the pressure of the cargo. The boat, thus finished, was laden with the produce of the country, and was then floated down the river to Babylon. In this navigation, the boatmen were careful to protect the leather sheathing from injury by avoiding all contact with rocks, or even with the gravel of the shores. They kept their craft in the middle of the stream by means of two oars, or, rather, an oar and a paddle, which were worked, the first at the bows, and the second at the stern. The advance of the boat was in some measure accelerated by these boatmen, though their main function was to steer their vessel by keeping it out of eddies and away from projecting points of land, and directing its course to those parts of the stream where the current was swiftest, and where it would consequently be borne forward most rapidly to its destination.

These boats were generally of very considerable size,

THE FALL OF BABYLON

and they carried, in addition to their cargo and crew, one or more beasts of burden — generally asses or mules. These animals were allowed the pleasure, if any pleasure it was to them, of sailing thus idly down the stream, for the sake of having them at hand at the end of the voyage, to carry back again, up the country, the skins, which constituted the most valuable portion of the craft they sailed in. It was found that these skins, if carefully preserved, could be easily transported up the river, and would answer the purpose of a second voyage. Accordingly, when the boats arrived at Babylon, the cargo was sold, the boats were broken up, the skins were folded into packs, and in this form the mules carried them up the river again, the boatmen driving the mules as they walked by their side.

Babylon was a city of immense extent and magnitude. In fact, the accounts given of the space which it covered have often been considered incredible. These accounts make the space which was included within the walls four or five times as large as London. A great deal of this space was, however, occupied by parks and gardens connected with the royal palaces, and by open squares. Then, besides, the houses occupied by the common people in the ancient cities were of fewer stories in height, and consequently more extended on the ground, than those built in modern times. In fact, it is probable that, in many instances, they were mere ranges of huts and hovels, as is the case, indeed, to a considerable extent, in Oriental cities, at the present day, so that it is not at all impossible that even so large an area as four or five times the size of London may have been included within the fortifications of the city.

In respect to the walls of the city, very extraordinary and apparently contradictory accounts are given by the various ancient authors who described them. Some make them seventy-five, and others two or three hundred feet high. There have been many discussions in respect to the comparative credibility of these several statements, and some ingenious attempts have been made to reconcile them. It is not, however, at all surprising that there should be such a diversity in the dimensions given, for the walling of an ancient city was seldom of the same height in all places. The structure necessarily varied according to the nature of the ground, being high wherever the ground without was such as to give the enemy an advantage in an attack, and lower in other situations, where the conformation of the surface was such as to afford, of itself, a partial protection. It is not, perhaps, impossible that, at some particular points — as, for example, across glens and ravines, or along steep declivities — the walls of Babylon may have been raised even to the very extraordinary height which Herodotus ascribes to them.

The walls were made of bricks, and the bricks were formed of clay and earth, which was dug from a trench made outside of the lines. This trench served the purpose of a ditch, to strengthen the fortification when the wall was completed. The water from the river, and from streams flowing toward the river, was admitted to these ditches on every side, and kept them always full.

The sides of these ditches were lined with bricks too, which were made, like those of the walls, from the earth obtained from the excavations. They used for all this masonry a cement made from a species of bitumen, which was found in great quantities floating down one of the rivers which flowed into the Euphrates, in the neighborhood of Babylon.

The river Euphrates itself flowed through the city. There was a breastwork or low wall along the banks of it on either side, with openings at the terminations of the streets leading to the water, and flights of steps to go down. These openings were secured by gates of brass, which, when closed, would prevent an enemy from gaining access to the city from the river. The great streets, which terminated thus at the river on one side, extended to the walls of the city on the other, and they were crossed by other streets at right angles to them. In the outer walls of the city, at the extremities of all these streets, were massive gates of brass, with hinges and frames of the same metal. There were a hundred of these gates in all. They were guarded by watch-towers on the walls above. The watch-towers were built on both the inner and outer faces of the wall, and the wall itself was so broad that there was room between these watch-towers for a chariot and four to drive and turn.

The river, of course, divided the city into two parts. The king's palace was in the center of one of these divisions, within a vast circular inclosure, which contained the palace buildings, together with the spacious courts, and parks, and gardens pertaining to them. In the center of the other division was a corresponding inclosure, which contained the great temple of Belus. Here there was a very lofty tower, divided into eight separate towers, one above another, with a winding staircase to ascend to the summit. In the upper story was a sort of chapel, with a couch, and a table, and other furniture for use in the sacred ceremonies, all of gold. Above this, on the highest platform of all, was a grand observatory, where the Babylonian astrologers made their celestial observations.

There was a bridge across the river, connecting one section of the city with the other, and it is said that there was a subterranean passage under the river also, which was used as a private communication between two public edifices — palaces or citadels — which were situated near the extremities of the bridge. All these constructions were of the most grand and imposing character. In addition to the architectural magnificence of the buildings, the gates and walls were embellished with a great variety of sculptures: images of animals, of every form and in every attitude; and men, single and in groups, models of great sovereigns, and representations of hunting scenes, battle scenes, and great events in the Babylonian history.

The most remarkable, however, of all the wonders of Babylon — though perhaps not built till after Cyrus's time — were what were called the Hanging Gardens. Although called the Hanging Gardens, they were not suspended in any manner, as the name might denote, but were supported upon arches and walls. The arches and walls sustained a succession of terraces, rising one above another, with broad flights of steps for ascending to them, and on these terraces the gardens were made. The upper terrace, or platform, was several hundred feet from the ground; so high, that it was necessary to build arches upon arches within, in order to attain the requisite elevation. The lateral thrust of these arches was sustained by a wall twenty-five feet in thickness, which surrounded the garden on all sides, and rose as high as the lowermost tier of arches, upon which would, of course, be concentrated the pressure and weight of all the pile. The whole structure thus formed a sort of artificial hill, square in form, and rising, in a succession of terraces, to a broad and level area upon the top. The extent of this grand square upon the summit was four hundred feet upon each side.

The surface which served as the foundation for the gardens that adorned these successive terraces and the area above was formed in the following manner: Over the masonry of the arches there was laid a pavement of broad flat stones, sixteen feet long and four feet wide. Over these there was placed a stratum of reeds, laid in bitumen, and above them another flooring of bricks, cemented closely together, so as to be impervious to water. To make the security complete in this respect, the upper surface of this brick flooring was covered with sheets of lead, overlapping each other in such a manner as to convey all the water which might percolate through the mould away to the sides of the garden. The earth and mould were placed upon this surface, thus prepared, and the stratum was so deep as to allow large trees to take root and grow in it. There was an engine constructed in the middle of the upper terrace, by which water could be drawn up from the river, and distributed over every part of the vast pile.

The gardens, thus completed, were filled to profusion with every species of tree, and plant, and vine, which could produce fruit or flowers to enrich or adorn such a scene. Every country in communication with Babylon was made to contribute something to increase the endless variety of floral beauty which was here literally enthroned. Gardeners of great experience and skill were constantly employed in cultivating the parterres, pruning the fruit trees and the vines, preserving the walks, and introducing new varieties of vegetation. In a word, the Hanging Gardens of Babylon became one of the wonders of the world.

The country in the neighborhood of Babylon, extending from the river on either hand, was in general level and low, and subject to inundations. One of the sovereigns of the country, a queen named Nitocris, had formed the grand design of constructing an immense lake, to take off the superfluous water in case of a flood, and thus prevent an overflow. She also opened a great number of lateral and winding channels for the river, wherever the natural disposition of the surface afforded facilities for doing so, and the earth which was taken out in the course of these excavations was employed in raising the banks by artificial terraces, such as are made to confine the Mississippi at New Orleans, and are there called "levees."[1] The object of Nitocris in these measures was twofold. She wished, in the first place, to open all practicable channels for the flow of the water, and then to confine the current within the channels thus made. She also wished to make the navigation of the stream as intricate and complicated as possible, so that, while the natives of the country might easily find their way, in boats, to the capital, a foreign enemy, if he should make the attempt, might be confused and lost. These were the rivers of Babylon on the banks of which the captive Jews sat down and wept when they remembered Zion.

[1] From the French word *levée*, raised.

THE FALL OF BABYLON

This queen Nitocris seems to have been quite distinguished for her engineering and architectural plans. It was she that built the bridge across the Euphrates, within the city; and as there was a feeling of jealousy and ill-will, as usual in such a case, between the two divisions of the town which the river formed, she caused the bridge to be constructed with a movable platform or draw, by means of which the communication might be cut off at pleasure. This draw was generally up at night and down by day.

Herodotus relates a curious anecdote of this queen, which, if true, evinces in another way the peculiar originality of mind and the ingenuity which characterized all her operations. She caused her tomb to be built, before her death, over one of the principal gates of the city. Upon the façade of this monument was a very conspicuous inscription to this effect: "If any one of the sovereigns, my successors, shall be in extreme want of money, let him open my tomb and take what he may think proper; but let him not resort to this resource unless the urgency is extreme."

The tomb remained for some time after the queen's death quite undisturbed. In fact, the people of the city avoided this gate altogether, on account of the dead body deposited above it, and the spot became well-nigh deserted. At length, in process of time, a subsequent sovereign, being in want of money, ventured to open the tomb. He found, however, no money within. The gloomy vault contained nothing but the dead body of the queen, and a label with this inscription: "If your avarice were not as insatiable as it is base, you would not have intruded on the repose of the dead."

MESOPOTAMIA

It was not surprising that Cyrus, having been so successful in his enterprises thus far, should now begin to turn his thoughts toward this great Babylonian Empire, and to feel a desire to bring it under his sway. The first thing, however, was to confirm and secure his Lydian conquests. He spent some time, therefore, in organizing and arranging, at Sardis, the affairs of the new government which he was to substitute for that of Crœsus there. He designated certain portions of his army to be left for garrisons in the conquered cities. He appointed Persian officers, of course, to command these forces; but, as he wished to conciliate the Lydians, he appointed many of the municipal and civil officers of the country from among them. There would appear to be no danger in doing this, as, by giving the command of the army to Persians, he retained all the real power directly in his own hands.

One of these civil officers, the most important, in fact, of all, was the grand treasurer. To him Cyrus committed the charge of the stores of gold and silver which came into his possession at Sardis, and of the revenues which were afterward to accrue. Cyrus appointed a Lydian named Pactyas to this trust, hoping by such measures to conciliate the people of the country, and to make them more ready to submit to his sway. Things being thus arranged, Cyrus, taking Crœsus with him, set out with the main army to return toward the East.

As soon as he had left Lydia, Pactyas excited the Lydians to revolt. The name of the commander-in-chief of the military forces which Cyrus had left was Tabalus. Pactyas abandoned the city and retired toward the coast, where he contrived to raise a large army, formed

THE FALL OF BABYLON

partly of Lydians and partly of bodies of foreign troops, which he was enabled to hire by means of the treasures which Cyrus had put under his charge. He then advanced to Sardis, took possession of the town, and shut up Tabalus, with his Persian troops, in the citadel.

When the tidings of these events came to Cyrus, he was very much incensed, and determined to destroy the city. Crœsus, however, interceded very earnestly in its behalf. He recommended that Cyrus, instead of burning Sardis, should send a sufficient force to disarm the population, and that he should then enact such laws and make such arrangements as should turn the minds of the people to habits of luxury and pleasure. "By doing this," said Crœsus, "the people will, in a short time, become so enervated and so effeminate that you will have nothing to fear from them."

Cyrus decided on adopting this plan. He dispatched a Median named Mazares, an officer of his army, at the head of a strong force, with orders to go back to Sardis, to deliver Tabalus from his danger, to seize and put to death all the leaders in the Lydian rebellion excepting Pactyas. Pactyas was to be saved alive, and sent a prisoner to Cyrus in Persia.

Pactyas did not wait for the arrival of Mazares. As soon as he heard of his approach, he abandoned the ground, and fled northwardly to the city of Cyme, and sought refuge there. When Mazares had reached Sardis and reëstablished the government of Cyrus there, he sent messengers to Cyme, demanding the surrender of the fugitive.

The people of Cyme were uncertain whether they ought to comply. They said that they must first consult an oracle. There was a very ancient and celebrated oracle near Miletus. They sent messengers to this oracle, demanding to know whether it were according to the will of the gods or not that the fugitive should be surrendered. The answer brought back was, that they might surrender him.

They were accordingly making arrangements for doing this, when one of the citizens, a very prominent and influential man, named Aristodicus, expressed himself not satisfied with the reply. He did not think it possible, he said, that the oracle could really counsel them to deliver up a helpless fugitive to his enemies. The messengers must have misunderstood or misreported the answer which they had received. He finally persuaded his countrymen to send a second embassy: he himself was placed at the head of it. On their arrival, Aristodicus addressed the oracle as follows: —

"To avoid a cruel death from the Persians, Pactyas, a Lydian, fled to us for refuge. The Persians demanded that we should surrender him. Much as we are afraid of their power, we are still more afraid to deliver up a helpless suppliant for protection without clear and decided directions from you."

The embassy received to this demand the same reply as before.

Still Aristodicus was not satisfied; and, as if by way of bringing home to the oracle somewhat more forcibly a sense of the true character of such an action as it seemed to recommend, he began to make a circuit in the grove which was around the temple in which the oracle resided, and to rob and destroy the nests which the birds had built there, allured, apparently, by the sacred repose and quietude of the scene. This had the desired effect. A solemn voice was heard from the interior of the temple, saying, in a warning tone: —

"Impious man! how dost thou dare to molest those who have placed themselves under my protection?"

To this Aristodicus replied by asking the oracle how it was that it watched over and guarded those who sought its own protection, while it directed the people of Cyme to abandon and betray suppliants for theirs. To this the oracle answered: —

"I direct them to do it, in order that such impious men may the sooner bring down upon their heads the judgments of heaven for having dared to entertain even the thought of delivering up a helpless fugitive."

When this answer was reported to the people of Cyme they did not dare to give Pactyas up, nor, on the other hand, did they dare to incur the enmity of the Persians by retaining and protecting him. They accordingly sent him secretly away. The emissaries of Mazares, however, followed him. They kept constantly on his track, demanding him successively of every city where the hapless fugitive sought refuge, until, at length, partly by threats and partly by a reward, they induced a certain city to surrender him. Mazares sent him, a prisoner, to Cyrus. Soon after this Mazares himself died, and Harpagus was appointed governor of Lydia in his stead.

In the mean time, Cyrus went on with his conquests in the heart of Asia, and at length, in the course of a few years, he had completed his arrangements and preparations for the attack on Babylon. He advanced at the head of a large force to the vicinity of the city. The King of Babylon, whose name was Belshazzar, withdrew within the walls, shut the gates, and felt perfectly secure. A simple wall was in those days a very effectual protection against any armed force whatever, if it was only high enough not to be scaled, and thick enough to resist the blows of a battering-ram. The artillery of modern times would have speedily made a fatal breach in such structures; but there was nothing but the simple force of man, applied through brazen-headed beams of wood, in those days, and Belshazzar knew well that his walls would bid all such modes of demolition a complete defiance. He stationed his soldiers, therefore, on the walls, and his sentinels in the watch-towers, while he himself, and all the nobles of his court, feeling perfectly secure in their impregnable condition, and being abundantly supplied with all the means that the whole empire could furnish, both for sustenance and enjoyment, gave themselves up, in their spacious palaces and gardens, to gayety, festivity, and pleasure.

Cyrus advanced to the city. He stationed one large detachment of his troops at the opening in the main walls where the river entered into the city, and another one below, where it issued from it. These detachments were ordered to march into the city by the bed of the river, as soon as they should observe the water subsiding. He then employed a vast force of laborers to open new channels, and to widen and deepen those which had existed before, for the purpose of drawing off the waters from their usual bed. When these passages were thus prepared, the water was let into them one night, at a time previously designated, and it soon ceased to flow through the city. The detachments of soldiers marched in over the bed of the stream, carrying with them vast

THE FALL OF BABYLON

numbers of ladders. With these they easily scaled the low walls which lined the banks of the river, and Belshazzar was thunderstruck with the announcement made to him in the midst of one of his feasts that the Persians were in complete and full possession of the city.

PALESTINE

I
IN OLD TESTAMENT TIMES

HISTORICAL NOTE

FIFTEEN or sixteen centuries before Christ, Palestine was commonly known as the land of Canaan, and the people were called Canaanites. Into this country the Hebrews, after their deliverance from bondage in Egypt, forced their way; and about 1050 B.C. the Hebrew kingdom was formed, under Saul, who was succeeded by David and Solomon. This unity endured for little more than a century. Then the kingdom was divided. The northern kingdom was overcome by Assyria in the eighth century before Christ; and the southern fell into the hands of Nebuchadnezzar of Babylon in the sixth. Palestine was then ruled in turn by Persia, Macedonia, Egypt, and Syria. Antiochus IV of Syria did his best to destroy the Jewish religion. This brought about a war for independence, which resulted in Judæa's gaining control of southern Palestine, from the Jordan to the sea.

THE JOURNEY TO THE PROMISED LAND
[Thirteenth century B.C.]

AND [Pharaoh] called for Moses and Aaron by night, and said: "Rise up, and get you forth from among my people, both ye and the children of Israel; and go, serve the Lord, as ye have said. Also take your flocks and your herds, as ye have said, and be gone; and bless me also." And the Egyptians were urgent upon the people, that they might send them out of the land in haste; for they said, "We be all dead men." And the people took their dough before it was leavened, their kneading troughs being bound up in their clothes upon their shoulders. And the children of Israel did according to the word of Moses; and they borrowed of the Egyptians jewels of silver, and jewels of gold, and raiment. And the Lord gave the people favour in the sight of the Egyptians, so that they lent unto them such things as they required. And they spoiled the Egyptians.

And the children of Israel journeyed from Rameses to Succoth, about six hundred thousand on foot that were men, beside children. And a mixed multitude went up also with them; and flocks, and herds, even very much cattle. And they baked unleavened cakes of the dough which they brought forth out of Egypt, for it was not leavened; because they were thrust out of Egypt, and could not tarry, neither had they prepared for themselves any victual.

Now the sojourning of the children of Israel, who dwelt in Egypt, was four hundred and thirty years. And it came to pass at the end of the four hundred and thirty years, even the selfsame day it came to pass, that all the hosts of the Lord went out from the land of Egypt. It is a night to be much observed unto the Lord for bringing them out from the land of Egypt; this is that night of the Lord to be observed of all the children of Israel in their generations.

And it came to pass, when Pharaoh had let the people go, that God led them not through the way of the land of the Philistines, although that was near; for God said, "Lest peradventure the people repent when they see war, and they return to Egypt." But God led the people about, through the way of the wilderness of the Red Sea; and the children of Israel went up harnessed out of the land of Egypt. And Moses took the bones of Joseph with him; for he had straitly sworn the children of Israel, saying, "God will surely visit you; and ye shall carry up my bones away hence with you."

And they took their journey from Succoth, and encamped in Etham, in the edge of the wilderness. And the Lord went before them by day in a pillar of a cloud, to lead them the way; and by night in a pillar of fire, to give them light; to go by day and night. He took not away the pillar of the cloud by day, nor the pillar of fire by night, from before the people. And the Lord spake unto Moses, saying: "Speak unto the children of Israel, that they turn and encamp before Pi-hahiroth, between Migdol and the sea, over against Baal-zephon; before it shall ye encamp by the sea. For Pharaoh will say of the children of Israel, 'They are entangled in the land, the wilderness hath shut them in.' And I will harden Pharaoh's heart, that he shall follow after them; and I will

THE JOURNEY TO THE PROMISED LAND

be honoured upon Pharaoh, and upon all his host; that the Egyptians may know that I am the Lord." And they did so.

And it was told the king of Egypt that the people fled; and the heart of Pharaoh and of his servants was turned against the people, and they said, "Why have we done this, that we have let Israel go from serving us?" And he made ready his chariot, and took his people with him. And he took six hundred chosen chariots, and all the chariots of Egypt, and captains over every one of them.

THE PASSAGE ACROSS THE RED SEA

And the Lord hardened the heart of Pharaoh king of Egypt, and he pursued after the children of Israel; and the children of Israel went out with an high hand. But the Egyptians pursued after them, all the horses and chariots of Pharaoh, and his horsemen, and his army, and overtook them encamping by the sea, beside Pi-hahiroth, before Baal-zephon. And when Pharaoh drew nigh, the children of Israel lifted up their eyes, and, behold, the Egyptians marched after them; and they were sore afraid; and the children of Israel cried out unto the Lord. And they said unto Moses: "Because there were no graves in Egypt, hast thou taken us away to die in the wilderness? wherefore hast thou dealt thus with us, to carry us forth out of Egypt? Is not this the word that we did tell thee in Egypt, saying, 'Let us alone, that we may serve the Egyptians'? For it had been better for us to serve the Egyptians, than that we should die in the wilderness."

And Moses said unto the people: "Fear ye not, stand still, and see the salvation of the Lord, which he will shew to you to-day; for the Egyptians whom ye have seen to-day, ye shall see them again no more forever. The Lord shall fight for you, and ye shall hold your peace."

And the Lord said unto Moses: "Wherefore criest thou unto me? speak unto the children of Israel, that they go forward. But lift thou up thy rod, and stretch out thine hand over the sea, and divide it; and the children of Israel shall go on dry ground through the midst of the sea. And I, behold, I will harden the hearts of the Egyptians, and they shall follow them; and I will get me honour upon Pharaoh, and upon all his host, upon his chariots, and upon his horsemen. And the Egyptians shall know that I am the Lord, when I have gotten me honour upon Pharaoh, upon his chariots, and upon his horsemen." And the angel of God, which went before the camp of Israel, removed and went behind them; and the pillar of the cloud went from before their face, and stood behind them. And it came between the camp of the Egyptians and the camp of Israel; and it was a cloud and darkness to them, but it gave light by night to these; so that the one came not near the other all the night.

And Moses stretched out his hand over the sea; and the Lord caused the sea to go back by a strong east wind all that night, and made the sea dry land, and the waters were divided. And the children of Israel went into the midst of the sea upon the dry ground; and the waters were a wall unto them on their right hand, and on their left. And the Egyptians pursued, and went in after them to the midst of the sea, even all Pharaoh's horses, his chariots, and his horsemen. And it came to pass, that

THE JOURNEY TO THE PROMISED LAND

in the morning watch the Lord looked unto the host of the Egyptians through the pillar of fire and of the cloud, and troubled the host of the Egyptians, and took off their chariot wheels, that they drave them heavily; so that the Egyptians said, "Let us flee from the face of Israel; for the Lord fighteth for them against the Egyptians."

And the Lord said unto Moses: " Stretch out thine hand over the sea, that the waters may come again upon the Egyptians, upon their chariots, and upon their horsemen." And Moses stretched forth his hand over the sea, and the sea returned to his strength when the morning appeared; and the Egyptians fled against it; and the Lord overthrew the Egyptians in the midst of the sea. And the waters returned, and covered the chariots, and the horsemen, and all the host of Pharaoh that came into the sea after them; there remained not so much as one of them. But the children of Israel walked upon dry land in the midst of the sea; and the waters were a wall unto them on their right hand, and on their left.

Thus the Lord saved Israel that day out of the hand of the Egyptians; and Israel saw the Egyptians dead upon the sea shore. And Israel saw that great work which the Lord did upon the Egyptians; and the people feared the Lord, and believed the Lord, and his servant Moses.

GOD GIVES THE TEN COMMANDMENTS

And the Lord said unto Moses: " Go unto the people, and sanctify them to-day and to-morrow and let them wash their clothes, and be ready against the third day: for the third day the Lord will come down in the sight of all the people upon mount Sinai. And thou shalt set bounds unto the people round about, saying, 'Take heed to yourselves, that ye go not up into the mount, or touch the border of it: whosoever toucheth the mount shall be surely put to death: there shall not an hand touch it, but he shall surely be stoned, or shot through; whether it be beast or man, it shall not live': when the trumpet soundeth long, they shall come up to the mount."

And Moses went down from the mount unto the people, and sanctified the people; and they washed their clothes. And he said unto the people: "Be ready against the third day."

And it came to pass on the third day in the morning, that there were thunders and lightnings, and a thick cloud upon the mount, and the voice of the trumpet exceeding loud; so that all the people that was in the camp trembled. And Moses brought forth the people out of the camp to meet with God; and they stood at the nether part of the mount. And mount Sinai was altogether in a smoke, because the Lord descended upon it in fire: and the smoke thereof ascended as the smoke of a furnace, and the whole mount quaked greatly. And when the voice of the trumpet sounded long, and waxed louder and louder, Moses spake, and God answered him by a voice. And the Lord came down upon mount Sinai, on the top of the mount: and the Lord called Moses up to the top of the mount; and Moses went up.

And the Lord said unto Moses: "Go down, charge the people, lest they break through unto the Lord to gaze, and many of them perish. And let the priests also, which come near to the Lord, sanctify themselves, lest the Lord break forth upon them."

THE JOURNEY TO THE PROMISED LAND

And Moses said unto the Lord: "The people cannot come up to mount Sinai: for thou charged us, saying, 'Set bounds about the mount, and sanctify it.'"

And the Lord said unto him: "Away, get thee down, and thou shalt come up, thou, and Aaron with thee, but let not the priests and the people break through to come up unto the Lord, lest he break forth upon them." So Moses went down unto the people, and spake unto them.

And God spake all these words, saying: —

"I am the Lord thy God, which have brought thee out of the land of Egypt, out of the house of bondage.

"Thou shalt have no other gods before me.

"Thou shalt not make unto thee any graven image, or any likeness of any thing that is in heaven above, or that is in the earth beneath, or that is in the water under the earth: Thou shalt not bow down thyself to them, nor serve them: for I the Lord thy God am a jealous God, visiting the iniquity of the fathers upon the children unto the third and fourth generation of them that hate me; and shewing mercy unto thousands of them that love me, and keep my commandments.

"Thou shalt not take the name of the Lord thy God in vain; for the Lord will not hold him guiltless that taketh his name in vain.

"Remember the sabbath day, to keep it holy. Six days shalt thou labour, and do all thy work: but the seventh day is the sabbath of the Lord thy God: in it thou shalt not do any work, thou, nor thy son, nor thy daughter, thy manservant, nor thy maidservant, nor thy cattle, nor the stranger that is within thy gates: for in six days the Lord made heaven and earth, the sea, and all that in them is, and rested the seventh day: wherefore the Lord blessed the sabbath day, and hallowed it.

"Honour thy father and thy mother: that thy days may be long upon the land which the Lord thy God giveth thee.

"Thou shalt not kill.

"Thou shalt not commit adultery.

"Thou shalt not steal.

"Thou shalt not bear false witness against thy neighbour.

"Thou shalt not covet thy neighbour's house, thou shalt not covet thy neighbour's wife, nor his manservant, nor his maidservant, nor his ox, nor his ass, nor anything that is thy neighbour's."

And all the people saw the thunderings, and the lightnings, and the noise of the trumpet, and the mountain smoking: and when the people saw it, they removed, and stood afar off. And they said unto Moses: "Speak thou with us, and we will hear: but let not God speak with us, lest we die."

And Moses said unto the people: "Fear not: for God is come to prove you, and that his fear may be before their faces, that ye sin not." And the people stood afar off, and Moses drew near unto the thick darkness where God was.

THE WORSHIP OF THE GOLDEN CALF

And Moses went up into the mount, and a cloud covered the mount. And the glory of the Lord abode upon mount Sinai, and the cloud covered it six days: and the seventh day he called unto Moses out of the midst of the cloud. And the sight of the glory of the Lord was like

THE JOURNEY TO THE PROMISED LAND

devouring fire on the top of the mount in the eyes of the children of Israel. And Moses went into the midst of the cloud, and gat him up into the mount: and Moses was in the mount forty days and forty nights.

And when the people saw that Moses delayed to come down out of the mount, the people gathered themselves together unto Aaron, and said unto him: "Up, make us gods, which shall go before us; for as for this Moses, the man that brought us up out of the land of Egypt, we wot not what is become of him."

And Aaron said unto them: "Break off the golden earrings, which are in the ears of your wives, of your sons, and of your daughters, and bring them unto me." And all the people brake off the golden earrings which were in their ears, and brought them unto Aaron. And he received them at their hand, and fashioned it with a graving tool, after he had made it a molten calf; and they said: "These be thy gods, O Israel, which brought thee up out of the land of Egypt." And when Aaron saw it, he built an altar before it; and Aaron made proclamation, and said: "To-morrow is a feast to the Lord." And they rose up early on the morrow, and offered burnt offerings, and brought peace offerings; and the people sat down to eat and to drink, and rose up to play.

And the Lord said unto Moses: "Go, get thee down; for thy people, which thou broughtest out of the land of Egypt, have corrupted themselves. They have turned aside quickly out of the way which I commanded them; they have made them a molten calf, and have worshipped it, and have sacrificed thereunto, and said, 'These be thy gods, O Israel, which have brought thee up out of the land of Egypt.'" And the Lord said unto Moses:

"I have seen this people, and, behold, it is a stiffnecked people. Now therefore let me alone, that my wrath may wax hot against them, and that I may consume them; and I will make of thee a great nation."

And Moses besought the Lord his God, and said: "Lord, why doth thy wrath wax hot against thy people, which thou hast brought forth out of the land of Egypt with great power, and with a mighty hand? Wherefore should the Egyptians speak, and say, 'For mischief did he bring them out, to slay them in the mountains, and to consume them from the face of the earth'? Turn from thy fierce wrath, and repent of this evil against thy people. Remember Abraham, Isaac, and Israel, thy servants, to whom thou swarest by thine own self, and saidst unto them, 'I will multiply your seed as the stars of heaven, and all this land that I have spoken of will I give unto your seed, and they shall inherit it forever.'"

And the Lord repented of the evil which he thought to do unto his people. And Moses turned, and went down from the mount, and the two tables of the testimony were in his hand; the tables were written on both their sides; on the one side and on the other were they written. And the tables were the work of God, and the writing was the writing of God, graven upon the tables.

And when Joshua heard the noise of the people as they shouted, he said unto Moses: "There is a noise of war in the camp."

And he said: "It is not the voice of them that shout for mastery, neither is it the voice of them that cry for being overcome; but the noise of them that sing do I hear." And it came to pass, as soon as he came nigh unto the camp, that he saw the calf, and the dancing;

THE JOURNEY TO THE PROMISED LAND

and Moses' anger waxed hot, and he cast the tables out of his hands, and brake them beneath the mount. And he took the calf which they had made, and burnt it in the fire, and ground it to powder, and strewed it upon the water, and made the children of Israel drink of it.

And Moses said unto Aaron: "What did this people unto thee, that thou hast brought so great a sin upon them?"

And Aaron said: "Let not the anger of my lord wax hot. Thou knowest the people, that they are set on mischief. For they said unto me, 'Make us gods, which shall go before us; for as for this Moses, the man that brought us up out of the land of Egypt, we wot not what is become of him.' And I said unto them, 'Whosoever hath any gold, let them break it off.' So they gave it me; then I cast it into the fire and there came out this calf."

Then Moses stood in the gate of the camp, and said: "Who is on the Lord's side? let him come unto me." And all the sons of Levi gathered themselves together unto him. And he said unto them, "Thus saith the Lord God of Israel, 'Put every man his sword by his side, and go in and out from gate to gate throughout the camp, and slay every man his brother, and every man his companion, and every man his neighbour.'" And the children of Levi did according to the word of Moses; and there fell of the people that day about three thousand men. For Moses had said, "Consecrate yourselves to-day to the Lord, even every man upon his son, and upon his brother; that he may bestow upon you a blessing this day."

And it came to pass on the morrow, that Moses said unto the people: "Ye have sinned a great sin, and now I will go up unto the Lord; peradventure I shall make an atonement for your sin." And Moses returned unto the Lord, and said, "Oh, this people have sinned a great sin, and have made them gods of gold. Yet now, if thou wilt forgive their sin —; and if not, blot me, I pray thee, out of thy book which thou hast written."

And the Lord said unto Moses: "Whosoever hath sinned against me, him will I blot out of my book. Therefore now go, lead the people unto the place of which I have spoken unto thee: behold, mine Angel shall go before thee; nevertheless in the day when I visit I will visit their sin upon them." And the Lord plagued the people, because they made the calf, which Aaron made.

THE BUILDING OF THE TABERNACLE

And Moses spake unto all the congregation of the children of Israel, saying: "This is the thing which the Lord commanded, saying: 'Take ye from among you an offering unto the Lord: whosoever is of a willing heart, let him bring it, an offering of the Lord; gold, and silver, and brass, and blue, and purple, and scarlet, and fine linen, and goats' hair, and rams' skins dyed red, and badgers' skins, and shittim wood, and oil for the light, and spices for anointing oil, and for the sweet incense, and onyx stones, and stones to be set for the ephod, and for the breastplate. And every wise-hearted among you shall come, and make all that the Lord hath commanded; the tabernacle, his tent, and his covering, his taches, and his boards, his bars, his pillars, and his sockets, the ark, and the staves thereof, with the mercy seat, and the vail of the covering, the table, and his staves, and all his

THE JOURNEY TO THE PROMISED LAND

vessels, and the shewbread, the candlestick also for the light, and his furniture, and his lamps, with the oil for the light, and the incense altar, and his staves, and the anointing oil, and the sweet incense, and the hanging for the door at the entering in of the tabernacle, the altar of burnt offering, with his brasen grate, his staves, and all his vessels, the laver and his foot, the hangings of the court, his pillars, and their sockets, and the hanging for the door of the court, the pins of the tabernacle, and the pins of the court, and their cords, the cloths of service, to do service in the holy place, the holy garments for Aaron the priest, and the garments of his sons, to minister in the priest's office.'"

And all the congregation of the children of Israel departed from the presence of Moses. And they came, every one whose heart stirred him up, and every one whom his spirit made willing, and they brought the Lord's offering to the work of the tabernacle of the congregation, and for all his service, and for the holy garments. And they came, both men and women, as many as were willing-hearted, and brought bracelets, and earrings, and rings, and tablets, all jewels of gold: and every man that offered offered an offering of gold unto the Lord. And every man, with whom was found blue, and purple, and scarlet, and fine linen, and goats' hair, and red skins of rams, and badgers' skins, brought them. Every one that did offer an offering of silver and brass brought the Lord's offering: and every man, with whom was found shittim wood for any work of the service, brought it. And all the women that were wise-hearted did spin with their hands, and brought that which they had spun, both of blue, and of purple, and of scarlet, and of fine linen. And all the women whose heart stirred them up in wisdom spun goats' hair. And the rulers brought onyx stones, and stones to be set, for the ephod, and for the breastplate; and spice, and oil for the light, and for the anointing oil, and for the sweet incense. The children of Israel brought a willing offering unto the Lord, every man and woman, whose heart made them willing to bring for all manner of work, which the Lord had commanded to be made by the hand of Moses.

And Moses said unto the children of Israel: "See, the Lord hath called by name Bezaleel the son of Uri, the son of Hur, of the tribe of Judah; and he hath filled him with the spirit of God, in wisdom, in understanding, and in knowledge, and in all manner of workmanship; and to devise curious works, to work in gold, and in silver, and in brass, and in the cutting of stones, to set them, and in carving of wood, to make any manner of cunning work. And he hath put in his heart that he may teach, both he, and Aholiab, the son of Ahisamach, of the tribe of Dan. Them hath he filled with wisdom of heart, to work all manner of work, of the engraver, and of the cunning workman, and of the embroiderer, in blue, and in purple, in scarlet, and in fine linen, and of the weaver, even of them that do any work, and of those that devise cunning work."

Then wrought Bezaleel and Aholiab, and every wise-hearted man, in whom the Lord put wisdom and understanding to know how to work all manner of work for the service of the sanctuary, according to all that the Lord had commanded. And Moses called Bezaleel and Aholiab, and every wise-hearted man, in whose heart the Lord had put wisdom, even every one whose heart stirred him up to come unto the work to do it: and they received of Moses all the offering, which the children of Israel had brought for the work of the service of the sanctuary, to make it withal. And they brought yet unto him free offerings every morning. And all the wise men, that wrought all the work of the sanctuary, came every man from his work which they made; and they spake unto Moses, saying: "The people bring much more than enough for the service of the work, which the Lord commanded to make."

And Moses gave commandment, and they caused it to be proclaimed throughout the camp, saying: "Let neither man nor woman make any more work for the offering of the sanctuary." So the people were restrained from bringing. For the stuff they had was sufficient for all the work to make it, and too much. According to all that the Lord commanded Moses, so the children of Israel made all the work. And Moses did look upon all the work, and, behold, they had done it as the Lord had commanded, even so had they done it: and Moses blessed them.

And Moses reared up the tabernacle, and fastened his sockets, and set up the boards thereof, and put in the bars thereof, and reared up his pillars. And he spread abroad the tent over the tabernacle, and put the covering of the tent above upon it; as the Lord commanded Moses. And he took and put the testimony into the ark, and set the staves on the ark, and put the mercy seat above upon the ark: and he brought the ark into the tabernacle, and set up the vail of the covering, and covered the ark of the testimony; as the Lord commanded Moses. And he put the table in the tent of the congregation, upon the side of the tabernacle northward, without the vail. And he set the bread in order upon it before the Lord; as the Lord had commanded Moses. And he put the candlestick in the tent of the congregation, over against the table, on the side of the tabernacle southward. And he lighted the lamps before the Lord; as the Lord commanded Moses. And he put the golden altar in the tent of the congregation before the vail: and he burnt sweet incense thereon; as the Lord commanded Moses. And he set up the hanging at the door of the tabernacle. And he put the altar of burnt offering by the door of the tabernacle of the tent of the congregation, and offered upon it the burnt offering and the meat offering; as the Lord commanded Moses. And he set the laver between the tent of the congregation and the altar, and put water there, to wash withal. And Moses and Aaron and his sons washed their hands and their feet thereat. When they went into the tent of the congregation, and when they came near unto the altar, they washed; as the Lord commanded Moses. And he reared up the court round about the tabernacle and the altar, and set up the hanging of the court gate. So Moses finished the work.

Then a cloud covered the tent of the congregation, and the glory of the Lord filled the tabernacle. And Moses was not able to enter into the tent of the congregation, because the cloud abode thereon, and the glory of the Lord filled the tabernacle. And when the cloud was taken up from over the tabernacle, the children of Israel went onward in all their journeys: but if the cloud were not taken up, then they journeyed not till the day that it was taken up. For the cloud of the Lord was upon the tabernacle by day, and fire was on it by night, in the sight of all the house of Israel; throughout all their journeys.

THE DEATH OF MOSES

And Moses went up from the plains of Moab unto the mountain of Nebo, to the top of Pisgah, that is over against Jericho. And the Lord shewed him all the land of Gilead, unto Dan. And all Naphtali, and the land of Ephraim, and Manasseh, and all the land of Judah, unto the utmost sea, and the south, and the plain of the valley of Jericho, the city of palm trees, unto Zoar. And the Lord said unto him: "This is the land which I sware unto Abraham, unto Isaac, and unto Jacob, saying, I will give it unto thy seed: I have caused thee to see it with thine eyes, but thou shalt not go over thither."

So Moses the servant of the Lord died there in the land of Moab, according to the word of the Lord. And he buried him in a valley in the land of Moab, over against Beth-peor: but no man knoweth of his sepulchre unto this day. And Moses was an hundred and twenty years old when he died: his eye was not dim, nor his natural force abated. And the children of Israel wept for Moses in the plains of Moab thirty days: so the days of weeping and mourning for Moses were ended.

And there arose not a prophet since in Israel like unto Moses, whom the Lord knew face to face, in all the signs and the wonders, which the Lord sent him to do in the land of Egypt to Pharaoh, and to all his servants, and to all his land, and in all that mighty band, and in all the great terror which Moses shewed in the sight of all Israel.

THE SHEPHERD BOY WHO BECAME KING

[Eleventh century B.C.]

DAVID PLAYS ON THE HARP BEFORE SAUL

But the spirit of the Lord departed from Saul, and an evil spirit from the Lord troubled him. And Saul's servants said unto him:

"Behold now, an evil spirit from God troubleth thee. Let our lord now command thy servants, which are before thee, to seek out a man, who is a cunning player on an harp: and it shall come to pass, when the evil spirit from God is upon thee, that he shall play with his hand, and thou shalt be well." And Saul said unto his servants:

"Provide me now a man that can play well, and bring him to me." Then answered one of the servants, and said:

"Behold, I have seen a son of Jesse the Beth-lehemite, that is cunning in playing, and a mighty valiant man, and a man of war, and prudent in matters, and a comely person, and the Lord is with him." Wherefore Saul sent messengers unto Jesse, and said:

"Send me David thy son, which is with the sheep." And Jesse took an ass laden with bread, and a bottle of wine, and a kid, and sent them by David his son unto Saul.

And David came to Saul, and stood before him: and he loved him greatly; and he became his armourbearer. And Saul sent to Jesse, saying, "Let David, I pray thee, stand before me; for he hath found favour in my sight." And it came to pass, when the evil spirit from

THE SHEPHERD BOY WHO BECAME KING

God was upon Saul, that David took an harp, and played with his hand: so Saul was refreshed, and was well, and the evil spirit departed from him.

DAVID KILLS THE GIANT GOLIATH OF GATH

Now the Philistines gathered together their armies to battle. And Saul and the men of Israel were gathered together, and pitched by the valley of Elah, and set the battle in array against the Philistines. And the Philistines stood on a mountain on the one side, and Israel stood on a mountain on the other side: and there was a valley between them. And there went out a champion out of the camp of the Philistines, named Goliath, of Gath, whose height was six cubits and a span.[1] And he had an helmet of brass upon his head, and he was armed with a coat of mail; and the weight of the coat was five thousand shekels of brass.[2] And he had greaves of brass upon his legs, and a target of brass between his shoulders. And the staff of his spear was like a weaver's beam; and his spear's head weighed six hundred shekels of iron: and one bearing a shield went before him. And he stood and cried unto the armies of Israel, and said unto them: "Why are ye come out to set your battle in array? am not I a Philistine, and ye servants to Saul? choose you a man for you, and let him come down to me. If he be able to fight with me, and to kill me, then will we be your servants: but if I prevail against him, and kill him, then shall ye be our servants, and serve us."

And the Philistine said: "I defy the armies of Israel this day; give me a man, that we may fight together."

---

[1] About nine feet, six inches.
[2] A Hebrew shekel was equal to about half an ounce.

PALESTINE

When Saul and all Israel heard those words of the Philistine, they were dismayed, and greatly afraid.

Now David was the son of Jesse; and he had eight sons: and the man went among men for an old man in the days of Saul. And the three eldest sons of Jesse went and followed Saul to the battle: and David was the youngest: and the three eldest followed Saul. But David went and returned from Saul to feed his father's sheep at Beth-lehem. And the Philistine drew near morning and evening, and presented himself forty days. And Jesse said unto David his son: "Take now for thy brethren an ephah of this parched corn, and these ten loaves, and run to the camp to thy brethren; and carry these ten cheeses unto the captain of their thousand, and look how thy brethren fare, and take their pledge." Now Saul, and they, and all the men of Israel, were in the valley of Elah, fighting with the Philistines.

And David rose up early in the morning, and left the sheep with a keeper, and took, and went, as Jesse had commanded him; and he came to the trench, as the host was going forth to the fight, and shouted for the battle. For Israel and the Philistines had put the battle in array, army against army. And David left his carriage in the hand of the keeper of the carriage, and ran into the army, and came and saluted his brethren. And as he talked with them, behold, there came up the champion, the Philistine of Gath, Goliath by name, out of the armies of the Philistines, and spake according to the same words: and David heard them. And all the men of Israel, when they saw the man, fled from him, and were sore afraid. And the men of Israel said: "Have ye seen this man that is come up? surely to defy Israel is he

THE SHEPHERD BOY WHO BECAME KING

come up: and it shall be, that the man who killeth him, the king will enrich him with great riches, and will give him his daughter, and make his father's house free in Israel."

And David spake to the men that stood by him, saying: "What shall be done to the man that killeth this Philistine, and taketh away the reproach from Israel? for who is this Philistine, that he should defy the armies of the living God?"

And the people answered him after this manner, saying: "So shall it be done to the man that killeth him."

And Eliab his eldest brother heard when he spake unto the men; and Eliab's anger was kindled against David, and he said: "Why camest thou down hither? and with whom hast thou left those few sheep in the wilderness? I know thy pride, and the naughtiness of thine heart; for thou art come down that thou mightest see the battle."

And David said: "What have I now done? Is there not a cause?" And he turned from him toward another, and spake after the same manner: and the people answered him again after the former manner.

And when the words were heard which David spake, they rehearsed them before Saul: and he sent for him. And David said to Saul: "Let no man's heart fail because of him; thy servant will go and fight with this Philistine."

And Saul said to David: "Thou art not able to go against this Philistine to fight with him: for thou art but a youth, and he a man of war from his youth."

And David said unto Saul: "Thy servant kept his father's sheep, and there came a lion, and a bear, and took a lamb out of the flock: and I went out after him, and smote him, and delivered it out of his mouth: and when he arose against me, I caught him by his beard, and smote him, and slew him. Thy servant slew both the lion and the bear: and this Philistine shall be as one of them, seeing he hath defied the armies of the living God." David said moreover, "The Lord that delivered me out of the paw of the lion, and out of the paw of the bear, he will deliver me out of the hand of this Philistine."

And Saul said unto David: "Go, and the Lord be with thee."

And Saul armed David with his armour, and he put an helmet of brass upon his head; also he armed him with a coat of mail. And David girded his sword upon his armour, and he assayed to go; for he had not proved it. And David said unto Saul, "I cannot go with these; for I have not proved them." And David put them off him. And he took his staff in his hand, and chose him five smooth stones out of the brook, and put them in a shepherd's bag which he had, even in a scrip; and his sling was in his hand; and he drew near to the Philistine. And the Philistine came on and drew near unto David; and the man that bare the shield went before him. And when the Philistine looked about, and saw David, he disdained him: for he was but a youth, and ruddy, and of a fair countenance.

And the Philistine said unto David: "Am I a dog, that thou comest to me with staves?" And the Philistine cursed David by his gods. And the Philistine said to David, "Come to me, and I will give thy flesh unto the fowls of the air, and to the beasts of the field."

THE SHEPHERD BOY WHO BECAME KING

Then said David to the Philistine: "Thou comest to me with a sword, and with a spear, and with a shield: but I come to thee in the name of the Lord of hosts, the God of the armies of Israel, whom thou hast defied. This day will the Lord deliver thee into mine hand; and I will smite thee, and take thine head from thee; and I will give the carcases of the host of the Philistines this day unto the fowls of the air, and to the wild beasts of the earth; that all the earth may know that there is a God in Israel. And all this assembly shall know that the Lord saveth not with sword and spear: for the battle is the Lord's, and he will give you into our hands."

And it came to pass, when the Philistine arose and came and drew nigh to meet David, that David hasted, and ran toward the army to meet the Philistine. And David put his hand in his bag, and took thence a stone, and slang it, and smote the Philistine in his forehead, that the stone sunk into his forehead; and he fell upon his face to the earth. So David prevailed over the Philistine with a sling and with a stone, and smote the Philistine, and slew him; but there was no sword in the hand of David. Therefore David ran, and stood upon the Philistine, and took his sword, and drew it out of the sheath thereof, and slew him, and cut off his head therewith. And when the Philistines saw their champion was dead, they fled. And the men of Israel and of Judah arose, and shouted, and pursued the Philistines, until thou come to the valley, and to the gates of Ekron. And the wounded of the Philistines fell down by the way. And the children of Israel returned from chasing after the Philistines, and they spoiled their tents. And David took the head of the Philistine, and brought it to Jerusalem, but he put his armour in his tent.

SAUL'S JEALOUSY AND JONATHAN'S AFFECTION

And when Saul saw David go forth against the Philistine, he said unto Abner, the captain of the host: "Abner, whose son is this youth?"

And Abner said: "As thy soul liveth, O king, I cannot tell."

And the king said: "Enquire thou whose son the stripling is." And as David returned from the slaughter of the Philistine, Abner took him, and brought him before Saul, with the head of the Philistine in his hand. And Saul said to him: "Whose son art thou, thou young man?"

And David answered: "I am the son of thy servant Jesse the Beth-lehemite."

And it came to pass, when he had made an end of speaking unto Saul, that the soul of Jonathan [son of Saul], was knit with the soul of David, and Jonathan loved him as his own soul. And Saul took him that day, and would let him go no more home to his father's house. Then Jonathan and David made a covenant, because he loved him as his own soul. And Jonathan stripped himself of the robe that was upon him, and gave it to David, and his garments, even to his sword, and to his bow, and to his girdle.

And David went out whithersoever Saul sent him, and behaved himself wisely: and Saul set him over the men of war, and he was accepted in the sight of all the people, and also in the sight of Saul's servants. And it came to pass as they came, when David was returned from the

THE SHEPHERD BOY WHO BECAME KING

slaughter of the Philistine, that the women came out of all cities of Israel, singing and dancing, to meet king Saul, with tabrets, with joy, and with instruments of music. And the women answered one another as they played, and said, "Saul hath slain his thousands, and David his ten thousands." And Saul was very wroth, and the saying displeased him; and he said, "They have ascribed unto David ten thousands, and to me they have ascribed but thousands: and what can he have more but the kingdom?" And Saul eyed David from that day forward.

And it came to pass on the morrow, that the evil spirit from God came upon Saul, and he prophesied in the midst of the house: and David played with his hand, as at other times: and there was a javelin in Saul's hand. And Saul cast the javelin; for he said, "I will smite David even to the wall with it." And David avoided out of his presence twice.

And Saul was afraid of David, because the Lord was with him, and was departed from Saul. Therefore Saul removed him from him, and made him his captain over a thousand; and he went out and came in before the people. And David behaved himself wisely in all his ways; and the Lord was with him. Wherefore when Saul saw that he behaved himself very wisely, he was afraid of him. But all Israel and Judah loved David, because he went out and came in before them.

DAVID'S ESCAPE FROM SAUL

And Saul spake to Jonathan his son, and to all his servants, that they should kill David. But Jonathan, Saul's son, delighted much in David: and Jonathan told

David, saying, "Saul my father seeketh to kill thee: now therefore, I pray thee, take heed to thyself until the morning, and abide in a secret place, and hide thyself: and I will go out and stand beside my father in the field where thou art, and I will commune with my father of thee; and what I see, that I will tell thee."

And Jonathan spake good of David unto Saul his father, and said unto him, "Let not the king sin against his servant, against David; because he hath not sinned against thee, and because his works have been to thee-ward very good: for he did put his life in his hand, and slew the Philistine, and the Lord wrought a great salvation for all Israel: thou sawest it, and didst rejoice: wherefore then wilt thou sin against innocent blood, to slay David without a cause?" And Saul hearkened unto the voice of Jonathan: and Saul sware, "As the Lord liveth, he shall not be slain." And Jonathan called David, and Jonathan shewed him all those things. And Jonathan brought David to Saul, and he was in his presence, as in times past.

And there was war again: and David went out, and fought with the Philistines, and slew them with a great slaughter; and they fled from him. And the evil spirit from the Lord was upon Saul, as he sat in his house with his javelin in his hand: and David played with his hand. And Saul sought to smite David even to the wall with the javelin; but he slipped away out of Saul's presence, and he smote the javelin into the wall: and David fled, and escaped that night.

Saul also sent messengers unto David's house, to watch him, and to slay him in the morning: and Michal, David's wife, told him, saying, "If thou save not thy

THE SHEPHERD BOY WHO BECAME KING

life to-night, to-morrow thou shalt be slain." So Michal let David down through a window: and he went, and fled, and escaped. And Michal took an image, and laid it in the bed, and put a pillow of goats' hair for his bolster, and covered it with a cloth. And when Saul sent messengers to take David, she said, "He is sick." And Saul sent the messengers again to see David, saying, "Bring him up to me in the bed, that I may slay him." And when the messengers were come in, behold, there was an image in the bed, with a pillow of goats' hair for his bolster. And Saul said unto Michal, "Why hast thou deceived me so, and sent away mine enemy, that he is escaped?" And Michal answered Saul, "He said unto me, Let me go; why should I kill thee?" So David fled, and escaped, and came to Samuel to Ramah, and told him all that Saul had done to him. And he and Samuel went and dwelt in Naioth.

THE FRIENDSHIP OF JONATHAN

And it was told Saul, saying, "Behold, David is at Naioth in Ramah." And Saul sent messengers to take David: and David fled from Naioth in Ramah, and came and said before Jonathan: "What have I done? what is mine iniquity? and what is my sin before thy father, that he seeketh my life?"

And he said unto him: "God forbid; thou shalt not die; behold, my father will do nothing either great or small, but that he will shew it me: and why should my father hide this thing from me? it is not so."

And David sware moreover, and said: "Thy father certainly knoweth that I have found grace in thine eyes; and he saith, 'Let not Jonathan know this, lest he be grieved': but truly as the Lord liveth, and as thy soul liveth, there is but a step between me and death."

Then said Jonathan unto David: "Whatsoever thy soul desireth, I will even do it for thee."

And David said unto Jonathan: "Behold, to-morrow is the new moon, and I should not fail to sit with the king at meat: but let me go, that I may hide myself in the field unto the third day at even. If thy father at all miss me, then say, David earnestly asked leave of me that he might run to Beth-lehem his city: for there is a yearly sacrifice there for all the family. If he say thus, It is well; thy servant shall have peace: but if he be very wroth, then be sure that evil is determined by him. Therefore thou shalt deal kindly with thy servant; for thou hast brought thy servant into a covenant of the Lord with thee: notwithstanding, if there be in me iniquity, slay me thyself; for why shouldest thou bring me to thy father?"

And Jonathan said: "Far be it from thee: for if I knew certainly that evil were determined by my father to come upon thee, then would not I tell it thee?"

Then said David to Jonathan: "Who shall tell me? or what if thy father answer thee roughly?"

And Jonathan said unto David: "Come, and let us go out into the field." And they went out both of them into the field.

And Jonathan said unto David: "O Lord God of Israel, when I have sounded my father about to-morrow any time, or the third day, and, behold, if there be good toward David, and then send I not unto thee, and shew it thee; the Lord do so and much more to Jonathan: but if it please my father to do thee evil, then I will shew

THE SHEPHERD BOY WHO BECAME KING

it thee, and send thee away, that thou mayest go in peace: and the Lord be with thee, as he hath been with my father. And thou shalt not only while yet I live shew me the kindness of the Lord, that I die not: but also thou shalt not cut off thy kindness from my house for ever: no, not when the Lord hath cut off the enemies of David every one from the face of the earth."

So Jonathan made a covenant with the house of David, saying, "Let the Lord even require it at the hand of David's enemies." And Jonathan caused David to swear again, because he loved him: for he loved him as he loved his own soul.

Then Jonathan said to David: "To-morrow is the new moon: and thou shalt be missed, because thy seat will be empty. And when thou hast stayed three days, then thou shalt go down quickly, and come to the place where thou didst hide thyself when the business was in hand, and shalt remain by the stone Ezel. And I will shoot three arrows on the side thereof, as though I shot at a mark. And, behold, I will send a lad, saying, Go, find out the arrows. If I expressly say unto the lad, Behold, the arrows are on this side of thee, take them; then come thou: for there is peace to thee, and no hurt; as the Lord liveth. But if I say thus unto the young man, Behold, the arrows are beyond thee; go thy way: for the Lord hath sent thee away. And as touching the matter which thou and I have spoken of, behold, the Lord be between thee and me for ever."

So David hid himself in the field: and when the new moon was come, the king sat him down to eat meat. And the king sat upon his seat, as at other times, even upon a seat by the wall: and Jonathan arose, and

Abner sat by Saul's side, and David's place was empty. Nevertheless Saul spake not any thing that day: for he thought, Something hath befallen him. And it came to pass on the morrow, which was the second day of the month, that David's place was empty: and Saul said unto Jonathan his son: "Wherefore cometh not the son of Jesse to meat, neither yesterday, nor to-day?"

And Jonathan answered Saul: "David earnestly asked leave of me to go to Beth-lehem: and he said, Let me go, I pray thee; for our family hath a sacrifice in the city; and my brother, he hath commanded me to be there: and now, if I have found favour in thine eyes, let me get away, I pray thee, and see my brethren. Therefore he cometh not unto the king's table."

Then Saul's anger was kindled against Jonathan, and he said unto him: "Thou son of the perverse rebellious woman, do not I know that thou hast chosen the son of Jesse to thine own confusion? For as long as the son of Jesse liveth upon the ground, thou shalt not be established, nor thy kingdom. Wherefore now send and fetch him unto me, for he shall surely die."

And Jonathan answered Saul his father, and said unto him: "Wherefore shall he be slain? what hath he done?"

And Saul cast a javelin at him to smite him: whereby Jonathan knew that it was determined of his father to slay David. So Jonathan arose from the table in fierce anger, and did eat no meat the second day of the month: for he was grieved for David, because his father had done him shame.

And it came to pass in the morning, that Jonathan went out into the field at the time appointed with David,

THE SHEPHERD BOY WHO BECAME KING

and a little lad with him. And he said unto his lad, "Run, find out now the arrows which I shoot." And as the lad ran, he shot an arrow beyond him. And when the lad was come to the place of the arrow which Jonathan had shot, Jonathan cried after the lad, and said," Is not the arrow beyond thee?" And Jonathan cried after the lad, "Make speed, haste, stay not." And Jonathan's lad gathered up the arrows, and came to his master. But the lad knew not any thing: only Jonathan and David knew the matter. And Jonathan gave his artillery unto his lad, and said unto him, "Go, carry them to the city."

And as soon as the lad was gone, David arose out of a place toward the south, and fell on his face to the ground, and bowed himself three times: and they kissed one another, and wept one with another, until David exceeded. And Jonathan said to David, "Go in peace, forasmuch as we have sworn both of us in the name of the Lord, saying, 'The Lord be between me and thee, and between my seed and thy seed for ever.'" And he arose and departed: and Jonathan went into the city.

THE STORY OF KING SOLOMON

[Tenth century B.C.]

SOLOMON'S CHOICE

Now the days of David drew nigh that he should die; and he charged Solomon his son, saying, "I go the way of all the earth: be thou strong therefore, and shew thyself a man; and keep the charge of the Lord thy God, to walk in his ways, to keep his statutes, and his commandments, and his judgments, and his testimonies, as it is written in the law of Moses, that thou mayest prosper in all that thou doest, and whithersoever thou turnest thyself: that the Lord may continue his word which he spake concerning me, saying, If thy children take heed to their way, to walk before me in truth with all their heart and with all their soul, there shall not fail thee (said he) a man on the throne of Israel." So David slept with his fathers, and was buried in the city of David. And the days that David reigned over Israel were forty years: seven years reigned he in Hebron, and thirty and three years reigned he in Jerusalem.

Then sat Solomon upon the throne of David his father; and his kingdom was established greatly. And Solomon loved the Lord, walking in the statutes of David his father: only he sacrificed and burnt incense in high places. And the king went to Gibeon to sacrifice there; for that was the great high place: a thousand burnt offerings did Solomon offer upon that altar. In Gibeon the Lord appeared to Solomon in a dream by night: and God said: "Ask what I shall give thee."

THE STORY OF KING SOLOMON

And Solomon said: "Thou hast shewed unto thy servant David my father great mercy, according as he walked before thee in truth, and in righteousness, and in uprightness of heart with thee; and thou hast kept for him this great kindness, that thou hast given him a son to sit on his throne, as it is this day. And now, O Lord my God, thou hast made thy servant king instead of David my father: and I am but a little child: I know not how to go out or come in. And thy servant is in the midst of thy people which thou hast chosen, a great people, that cannot be numbered nor counted for multitude. Give therefore thy servant an understanding heart to judge thy people, that I may discern between good and bad: for who is able to judge this thy so great a people?"

And the speech pleased the Lord, that Solomon had asked this thing. And God said unto him: "Because thou hast asked this thing, and hast not asked for thyself long life; neither hast asked riches for thyself, nor hast asked the life of thine enemies; but hast asked for thyself understanding to discern judgment, behold, I have done according to thy words: lo, I have given thee a wise and an understanding heart; so that there was none like thee before thee, neither after thee shall any arise like unto thee. And I have also given thee that which thou hast not asked, both riches, and honour: so that there shall not be any among the kings like unto thee all thy days. And if thou wilt walk in my ways, to keep my statutes and my commandments, as thy father David did walk, then I will lengthen thy days." And Solomon awoke; and, behold, it was a dream. And he came to Jerusalem, and stood before the ark of the covenant of the Lord, and offered up burnt offerings, and offered peace offerings, and made a feast to all his servants.

A WISE JUDGE

Then came there two women unto the king, and stood before him.

And the one woman said: "O my Lord, I and this woman dwell in one house; and we were together; there was no stranger with us in the house, save we two in the house. And this woman's child died in the night; because she overlaid it. And she arose at midnight, and took my son from beside me, while thine handmaid slept, and laid it in her bosom, and laid her dead child in my bosom. And when I rose in the morning to give my child suck, behold, it was dead: but when I had considered it in the morning, behold, it was not my son, which I did bear."

And the other woman said: "Nay: but the living is my son, and the dead is thy son."

And this said: "No; but the dead is thy son, and the living is my son." Thus they spake before the king.

Then said the king: "The one saith, This is my son that liveth, and thy son is the dead: and the other saith, Nay; but thy son is the dead, and my son is the living." And the king said, "Bring me a sword." And they brought a sword before the king. And the king said, "Divide the living child in two, and give half to the one, and half to the other."

Then spake the woman whose the living child was unto the king, for her bowels yearned upon her son, and she

THE STORY OF KING SOLOMON

said: "O my lord, give her the living child, and in no wise slay it."

But the other said: "Let it be neither mine nor thine, but divide it."

Then the king answered and said: "Give her the living child, and in no wise slay it: she is the mother thereof." And all Israel heard of the judgment which the king had judged; and they feared the king: for they saw that the wisdom of God was in him, to do judgment.

SOLOMON BUILDS A HOUSE FOR THE LORD

And Hiram king of Tyre sent his servants unto Solomon; for he had heard that they had anointed him king in the room of his father: for Hiram was ever a lover of David. And Solomon sent to Hiram, saying, "Thou knowest how that David my father could not build an house unto the name of the Lord his God for the wars which were about him on every side, until the Lord put them under the soles of his feet. But now the Lord my God hath given me rest on every side, so that there is neither adversary nor evil occurrent. And, behold, I purpose to build an house unto the name of the Lord my God, as the Lord spake unto David my father, saying, Thy son, whom I will set upon thy throne in thy room, he shall build an house unto my name. Now therefore command thou that they hew me cedar trees out of Lebanon; and my servants shall be with thy servants: and unto thee will I give hire for thy servants according to all that thou shalt appoint: for thou knowest that there is not among us any that can skill to hew timber like unto the Sidonians."

PALESTINE

And it came to pass, when Hiram heard the words of Solomon, that he rejoiced greatly, and said, "Blessed be the Lord this day, which hath given unto David a wise son over this great people." And Hiram sent to Solomon, saying: "I have considered the things which thou sentest to me for: and I will do all thy desire concerning timber of cedar, and concerning timber of fir. My servants shall bring them down from Lebanon unto the sea: and I will convey them by sea in floats unto the place that thou shalt appoint me, and will cause them to be discharged there, and thou shalt receive them: and thou shalt accomplish my desire, in giving food for my household."

So Hiram gave Solomon cedar trees and fir trees according to all his desire. And Solomon gave Hiram twenty thousand measures of wheat for food to his household, and twenty measures of pure oil: thus gave Solomon to Hiram year by year. And the Lord gave Solomon wisdom, as he promised him: and there was peace between Hiram and Solomon; and they two made a league together.

And king Solomon raised a levy out of all Israel; and the levy was thirty thousand men. And he sent them to Lebanon, ten thousand a month by courses: a month they were in Lebanon, and two months at home: and Adoniram was over the levy. And Solomon had threescore and ten thousand that bare burdens, and fourscore thousand hewers in the mountains; besides the chief of Solomon's officers which were over the work, three thousand and three hundred, which ruled over the people that wrought in the work.

And the king commanded, and they brought great

stones, costly stones, and hewed stones, to lay the foundation of the house. And Solomon's builders and Hiram's builders did hew them, and the stonesquarers: so they prepared timber and stones to build the house.

And the word of the Lord came to Solomon, saying, "Concerning this house which thou art in building, if thou wilt walk in my statutes, and execute my judgments, and keep all my commandments to walk in them; then will I perform my word with thee, which I spake unto David thy father: and will dwell among the children of Israel, and will not forsake my people Israel."

So Solomon built the house, and finished it. And he built the walls of the house within with boards of cedar, both the floor of the house, and the walls of the ceiling: and he covered them on the inside with wood, and covered the floor of the house with planks of fir. And he built twenty cubits on the sides of the house, both the floor and the walls with boards of cedar: he even built them for it within, even for the oracle, even for the most holy place. And the house, that is, the temple before it, was forty cubits long. And the cedar of the house within was carved with knops and open flowers: all was cedar; there was no stone seen. And the oracle he prepared in the house within, to set there the ark of the covenant of the Lord. And the oracle in the forepart was twenty cubits in length, and twenty cubits in breadth, and twenty cubits in the height thereof: and he overlaid it with pure gold; and so covered the altar which was of cedar. So Solomon overlaid the house within with pure gold: and he made a partition by the chains of gold before the oracle; and he overlaid it with gold. And the

PALESTINE

whole house he overlaid with gold, until he had finished all the house: also the whole altar that was by the oracle he overlaid with gold. And within the oracle he made two cherubim of olive tree, each ten cubits high. And five cubits was the one wing of the cherub, and five cubits the other wing of the cherub: from the uttermost part of the one wing unto the uttermost part of the other were ten cubits. And the other cherub was ten cubits: both the cherubim were of one measure and one size. The height of the one cherub was ten cubits, and so was it of the other cherub. And he set the cherubim within the inner house: and they stretched forth the wings of the cherubim, so that the wing of the one touched the one wall, and the wing of the other cherub touched the other wall; and their wings touched one another in the midst of the house. And he overlaid the cherubim with gold. And he carved all the walls of the house round about with carved figures of cherubim and palm trees and open flowers, within and without. And the floor of the house he overlaid with gold, within and without. And for the entering of the oracle he made doors of olive tree: the lintel and side posts were a fifth part of the wall. The two doors also were of olive tree; and he carved upon them carvings of cherubim and palm trees and open flowers, and overlaid them with gold, and spread gold upon the cherubim, and upon the palm trees. So also made he for the door of the temple posts of olive tree, a fourth part of the wall. And the two doors were of fir tree: the two leaves of the one door were folding, and the two leaves of the other door were folding. And he carved thereon cherubim and palm trees and open flowers: and covered them with

THE STORY OF KING SOLOMON

gold fitted upon the carved work. And he built the inner court with three rows of hewed stone, and a row of cedar beams. In the fourth year was the foundation of the house of the Lord laid, in the month Zif: and in the eleventh year, in the month Bul, which is the eighth month, was the house finished throughout all the parts thereof, and according to all the fashion of it. So was he seven years in building it.

THE QUEEN OF SHEBA VISITS SOLOMON

And when the queen of Sheba heard of the fame of Solomon concerning the name of the Lord, she came to prove him with hard questions. And she came to Jerusalem with a very great train, with camels that bare spices, and very much gold, and precious stones: and when she was come to Solomon, she communed with him of all that was in her heart. And Solomon told her all her questions: there was not anything hid from the king, which he told her not. And when the queen of Sheba had seen all Solomon's wisdom, and the house that he had built, and the meat of his table, and the sitting of his servants, and the attendance of his ministers, and their apparel, and his cupbearers, and his ascent by which he went up unto the house of the Lord; there was no more spirit in her. And she said to the king, "It was a true report that I heard in mine own land of thy acts and of thy wisdom. Howbeit I believed not the words, until I came, and mine eyes had seen it; and, behold, the half was not told me: thy wisdom and prosperity exceedeth the fame which I heard. Happy are thy men, happy are these thy servants, which stand continually before thee, and that hear thy wisdom. Blessed be the Lord thy

God, which delighted in thee, to set thee on the throne of Israel: because the Lord loved Israel for ever, therefore made he thee king, to do judgment and justice." And she gave the king an hundred and twenty talents [1] of gold, and of spices very great store, and precious stones: there came no more such abundance of spices as these which the queen of Sheba gave to king Solomon. And the navy also of Hiram, that brought gold from Ophir, brought in from Ophir great plenty of almug trees, and precious stones. And the king made of the almug trees pillars for the house of the Lord, and for the king's house, harps also and psalteries for singers: there came no such almug trees, nor were seen unto this day. And king Solomon gave unto the queen of Sheba all her desire, whatsoever she asked, besides that which Solomon gave her of his royal bounty. So she turned and went to her own country, she and her servants.

SOME OF THE PROVERBS OF SOLOMON

The tongue of the just is as choice silver: the heart of the wicked is little worth.

The blessing of the Lord, it maketh rich, and he addeth no sorrow with it.

A righteous man regardeth the life of his beast: but the tender mercies of the wicked are cruel.

He that despiseth his neighbour sinneth: but he that hath mercy on the poor, happy is he.

In the fear of the Lord is strong confidence: and his children shall have a place of refuge.

All the days of the afflicted are evil: but he that is of a merry heart hath a continual feast.

[1] A talent of the Hebrews was equal to about $2000.

THE STORY OF KING SOLOMON

Better is little with the fear of the Lord, than great treasure and trouble therewith.

A soft answer turneth away wrath: but grievous words stir up anger.

Pride goeth before destruction, and an haughty spirit before a fall.

When a man's ways please the Lord, he maketh even his enemies to be at peace with him.

Pleasant words are as an honeycomb, sweet to the soul, and health to the bones.

He that is slow to anger is better than the mighty; and he that ruleth his spirit than he that taketh a city.

A friend loveth at all times, and a brother is born for adversity.

He that answereth a matter before he heareth it, it is folly and shame unto him.

A man that hath friends must shew himself friendly: and there is a friend that sticketh closer than a brother.

He that hath pity upon the poor lendeth unto the Lord; and that which he hath given will he pay him again.

Even a child is known by his doings, whether his work be pure, and whether it be right.

Whoso stoppeth his ears at the cry of the poor, he also shall cry himself, but shall not be heard.

Whoso keepeth his mouth and his tongue keepeth his soul from troubles.

He that oppresseth the poor to increase his riches, and he that giveth to the rich, shall surely come to want.

Seest thou a man diligent in his business? he shall stand before kings; he shall not stand before mean men.

PALESTINE

Rejoice not when thine enemy falleth, and let not thine heart be glad when he stumbleth:

Say not, I will do so to him as he hath done to me: I will render to the man according to his work.

He that hath no rule over his own spirit is like a city that is broken down, and without walls.

If thine enemy be hungry, give him bread to eat; and if he be thirsty, give him water to drink:

For thou shalt heap coals of fire upon his head, and the Lord shall reward thee.

Whoso diggeth a pit shall fall therein: and he that rolleth a stone, it will return upon him.

Boast not thyself of to-morrow; for thou knowest not what a day may bring forth.

Let another man praise thee, and not thine own mouth; a stranger, and not thine own lips.

Thine own friend, and thy father's friend, forsake not; neither go into thy brother's house in the day of thy calamity: for better is a neighbour that is near than a brother far off.

The wicked flee when no man pursueth: but the righteous are bold as a lion.

STORIES FROM THE TALMUD

[THE TALMUD, or "instruction," is a famous compilation of the traditional ceremonial laws of the Jews and of the rabbinical discussions thereon. Mingled with these are stories, bits of history and folklore, allegories and parables.
The Editor.]

PROVING A CLAIM

A CITIZEN of Jerusalem traveling through the country was taken very sick at an inn. Feeling that he would not recover, he sent for the landlord and said to him, "I am going the way of all flesh. If after my death any party should come from Jerusalem and claim my effects, do not deliver them until he shall prove to thee by three wise acts that he is entitled to them; for I charged my son before starting on my way, that if death befell me he would be obliged to prove his wisdom before obtaining my possessions."

The man died and was buried according to Jewish rites, and his death was made public that his heirs might appear. When his son learned of his father's decease, he started from Jerusalem for the place where he had died. Near the gates of the city he met a man who had a load of wood for sale. This he purchased and ordered it to be delivered at the inn towards which he was traveling. The man from whom he bought it went at once to the inn and said, "Here is the wood."

"What wood?" returned the proprietor, "I ordered no wood."

"No," answered the woodcutter, "but the man who follows me did; I will enter and wait for him."

Thus the son had provided for himself a welcome when he should reach the inn, which was his first wise act.

The landlord said to him, "Who art thou?"

"The son of the merchant who died in thy house," he replied.

They prepared for him a dinner and placed upon the table five pigeons and a chicken. The master of the house, his wife, two sons, and two daughters sat with him at the table.

"Serve the food," said the landlord.

"Nay," answered the young man; "thou art master, it is thy privilege."

"I desire thee to do this thing; thou art my guest, the merchant's son; pray help the food."

The young man, thus entreated, divided one pigeon between the sons, another between the two daughters, gave the third to the man and his wife, and kept the other two for himself. This was his second wise act.

The landlord looked somewhat perplexed at this mode of distribution, but said nothing.

Then the merchant's son divided the chicken. He gave to the landlord and his wife the head, to the two sons the legs, to the two daughters the wings, and took the body for himself. This was his third wise act.

The landlord said, "Is this the way they do things in thy country? I noticed the manner in which thou didst apportion the pigeons, but said nothing; but the chicken, my dear sir! I must really ask thee thy meaning."

Then the young man answered, "I told thee that it was not my place to serve thee; nevertheless when thou didst insist I did the best I could, and I think I have succeeded. Thyself, thy wife, and one pigeon make three; thy two sons and one pigeon make three; thy two daughters and one pigeon make three, and myself and two pigeons make three also; therefore is it fairly done. As regards the chicken, I gave to thee and thy wife the head, because ye are the heads of the family; I gave to each of thy sons a leg, because they are the pillars of the family, preserving always the family name; I gave to each of thy daughters a wing, because in the natural course of events they will marry, take wing, and fly away from the home-nest. I took the body of the chicken because it looks like a ship, and in a ship I came here and in a ship I hope to return. I am the son of the merchant who died in thy house; give me the property of my dead father."

"Take it and go," said the landlord. And giving him his father's possessions the young man departed in peace.

NOTHING IN THE WORLD WITHOUT ITS USE

David, King of Israel, was once lying upon his couch and many thoughts were passing through his mind.

"Of what use in the world is this spider?" thought he; "it but increases the dust and dirt of the world, making places unsightly and causing great annoyance."

Then he thought of an insane man: "How unfortunate is such a being. I know that all things are ordained by God with reason and purpose, yet this is beyond my comprehension; why should men be born idiots, or grow insane?"

Then the mosquitoes annoyed him, and the king

thought, "What can the mosquito be good for? Why was it created in the world? It but disturbs our comfort, and the world profits not by its existence."

Yet King David lived to discover that these very insects, and the very condition of life, the being of which he deplored, were ordained even to his own benefit.

When he fled from before Saul, David was captured in the land of the Philistines by the brothers of Goliath, who carried him before the king of Gath, and it was only by pretending idiocy that he escaped death, the king deeming it impossible that such a man could be the kingly David; as it is written, "And he disguised his reason before their eyes, and played the madman in their hands, and scribbled on the doors of the gate."

Upon another occasion David hid himself in the cave of Adullam, and after he had entered the cave it chanced that a spider spun a web over the opening thereto. His pursuers passed that way, but thinking that no one could have entered the cave protected by the spider's web without destroying it, they continued on their way.

The mosquito also was of service to David when he entered the camp of Saul to secure the latter's weapon. While stooping near Abner, the sleeping man moved and placed his leg upon David's body. If he moved, he would awake Abner and meet with death, if he remained in that position morning would dawn and bring him death; he knew not what to do, when a mosquito alighted upon Abner's leg; he moved it quickly, and David escaped.

Therefore sang David, "All my bones shall say, 'O Lord, who is like unto Thee.'"

STORIES FROM THE TALMUD

TRUST IN GOD

Rabbi Jochanan, the son of Levi, fasted and prayed to the Lord that he might be permitted to gaze on the angel Elijah, he who had ascended alive to heaven. God granted his prayer, and in the semblance of a man Elijah appeared before him.

"Let me journey with thee in thy travels through the world," prayed the Rabbi to Elijah; "let me observe thy doings, and gain in wisdom and understanding."

"Nay," answered Elijah; "my actions thou couldst not understand; my doings would trouble thee, being beyond thy comprehension."

But still the Rabbi entreated.

"I will neither trouble nor question thee," he said; "only let me accompany thee on thy way."

"Come, then," said Elijah; "but let thy tongue be mute. With thy first question, thy first expression of astonishment, we must part company."

So the two journeyed through the world together. They approached the house of a poor man, whose only treasure and means of support was a cow. As they came near, the man and his wife hastened to meet them, begged them to enter their cot, and eat and drink of the best they could afford, and to pass the night under their roof. This they did, receiving every attention from their poor but hospitable host and hostess. In the morning Elijah rose up early and prayed to God, and when he had finished his prayer, behold the cow belonging to the poor people dropped dead. Then the travelers continued on their journey.

Much was Rabbi Jochanan perplexed. "Not only did

we neglect to pay them for their hospitality and generous services, but his cow we have killed"; and he said to Elijah, "Why didst thou kill the cow of this good man, who —"

"Peace," interrupted Elijah; "hear, see, and be silent! If I answer thy questions we must part."

And they continued on their way together.

Towards evening they arrived at a large and imposing mansion, the residence of a haughty and wealthy man. They were coldly received; a piece of bread and a glass of water were placed before them, but the master of the house did not welcome or speak to them, and they remained there during the night unnoticed. In the morning Elijah remarked that a wall of the house required repairing, and sending for a carpenter, he himself paid the money for the repair, as a return, he said, for the hospitality they had received.

Again was Rabbi Jochanan filled with wonder, but he said naught, and they proceeded on their journey.

As the shades of night were falling they entered a city which contained a large and imposing synagogue. As it was the time of the evening service they entered and were much pleased with the rich adornments, the velvet cushions, and gilded carvings of the interior. After the completion of the service, Elijah arose and called out aloud, "Who is here willing to feed and lodge two poor men this night?" None answered, and no respect was shown to the traveling strangers. In the morning, however, Elijah reëntered the synagogue, and shaking its members by the hands, he said, "I hope that you may all become presidents."

Next evening the two entered another city, when the

Shamas (sexton) of the synagogue came to meet them, and notifying the members of his congregation of the coming of two strangers, the best hotel of the place was opened to them, and all vied in showing them attention and honor.

In the morning, on parting with them, Elijah said, "May the Lord appoint over you but one president."

Jochanan could resist his curiosity no longer. "Tell me," said he to Elijah, "tell me the meaning of all these actions which I have witnessed. To those who have treated us coldly thou hast uttered good wishes; to those who have been gracious to us thou hast made no suitable return. Even though we must part, I pray thee explain to me the meaning of thy acts."

"Listen," said Elijah, "and learn to trust in God, even though thou canst not understand his ways. We first entered the house of the poor man, who treated us so kindly. Know that it had been decreed that on that very day his wife should die. I prayed unto the Lord that the cow might prove a redemption for her; God granted my prayers, and the woman was preserved unto her husband. The rich man, whom next we called up, treated us coldly, and I repaired his wall. I repaired it without a new foundation, without digging to the old one. Had he repaired it himself he would have dug, and thus discovered a treasure which lies there buried, but which is now forever lost to him. To the members of the synagogue who were inhospitable, I said, 'May you all be presidents,' and where many rule there can be no peace; but to the others I said, 'May you have but one president'; with one leader no misunderstanding may arise. Now if thou seest the wicked prospering, be not envious; if thou seest the righteous in poverty and trouble, be not provoked or doubtful of God's justice. The Lord is righteous, his judgments are all true; his eyes note all mankind, and none can say, 'What dost thou?'"

With these words Elijah disappeared, and Jochanan was left alone.

PROVERBS FROM THE TALMUD

To be patient is sometimes better than to have much wealth.

The birds of the air despise a miser.

Thy friend has a friend, and thy friend's friend has a friend; be discreet.

The wine belongs to the master, but the waiter receives the thanks.

No man is impatient with his creditors.

When wine enters the head the secret flies out.

Into the well which supplies thee with water cast no stones.

Say little and do much.

He who is loved by man is loved by God.

The sun will set without thy assistance.

He who curbs his wrath merits forgiveness for his sins.

The thief who finds no opportunity to steal, considers himself an honest man.

When the shepherd is angry with his flock, he appoints for its leader a blind bell wether.

The man who sins is foolish as well as wicked.

There is a great difference between one who can feel ashamed before his own soul and one who is only ashamed before his fellow-man.

THE DESTRUCTION OF JERUSALEM
[Sixth century B.C.]

BY FLAVIUS JOSEPHUS; SIMPLIFIED BY WILLIAM SHEPARD

AFTER Jehoiakim had been king for four years, Nebuchadnezzar, the king of Babylon, marched against him with a great army, and threatened to destroy the country unless Jehoiakim would pay him a large sum of money every year. Jehoiakim was frightened, and agreed to do this. But the third year afterwards he heard that Nebuchadnezzar was about to fight with the Egyptians, so he did not pay his tribute that year, hoping the Egyptians would be victorious.

In vain did the prophet Jeremiah warn him against putting his trust in the Egyptians, and foretell that Jerusalem would be overthrown by the king of Babylon, who would take Jehoiakim captive. Jeremiah wrote down all his prophecies in a book, and read them to the people in the temple. When the rulers heard of this, they took the book from him and brought it to the king. And the king ordered that it should be read to him. But he was angry when he found what the book contained, and tore it up and threw it into the fire.

Nebuchadnezzar came against the city, as the prophet had foretold, and took it, and slew the king, Jehoiakim, and made his son Jehoiachin king in his place. But afterwards Nebuchadnezzar repented of having put Jehoiachin on the throne, fearing that he would endeavor to avenge his father's death; so he displaced him and made Zedekiah king instead, having first made him promise that he would always be faithful to him. Zedekiah was a brother of Jehoiakim. He was not a bad man naturally, but was weak, and could easily be persuaded to do evil. He allowed his courtiers and his people to sin against the laws of Moses, and he worshiped false gods himself. Jeremiah came often to him and warned him that if he did not leave off his transgressions great calamities would fall upon him and his people, and the king of Babylon would destroy their cities and carry their people into bondage. And another prophet, named Ezekiel, also prophesied that God would punish him. Now, Zedekiah did not believe these prophets, because, although they agreed in all other points, they seemed to disagree in one thing, for Jeremiah said that Zedekiah "would be carried a captive to Babylon," while Ezekiel said that "he would not see Babylon." So Zedekiah flattered himself that neither prophet spoke the truth.

After Zedekiah had been king eight years he broke his promise to Nebuchadnezzar, and allied himself with the king of Egypt, who was fighting against Babylon. Nebuchadnezzar gathered up an army, and, having defeated the Egyptians, marched against Jerusalem.

The prophet Jeremiah had been thrown into prison by his enemies, but he did not cease to exhort the multitude to open their gates to the king of Babylon and trust to his mercy; for if they resisted, the city would surely be taken, and they would suffer the worst at the hands of their conquerors. Then his enemies came to Zedekiah and accused the prophet of giving evil counsel to the people, and they persuaded the king to deliver

THE DESTRUCTION OF JERUSALEM

him into their hands. And they came into the prison and took him and let him down into a pit full of mire, that he might be suffocated there. And he stood up to his neck in the mire, and would surely have perished if one of the king's servants had not obtained permission to draw him out again. For the king was so weak and good-natured that it was easy to make him change his mind.

For eighteen months Nebuchadnezzar besieged Jerusalem, and then the city could no longer hold out against him. And when Zedekiah saw that all was lost, he took his wives and his children and his captains and his friends, and with them fled out of Jerusalem by night. But at daybreak the Babylonians overtook the fugitives near Jericho, and they seized the king and his wives and children, but let the rest escape. So Zedekiah was brought before Nebuchadnezzar. And Nebuchadnezzar reproached Zedekiah for having broken his promises to him who had made him ruler over Judæa. Then he ordered the children of Zedekiah to be slain in the presence of their father, and he put out the eyes of Zedekiah, and bound him, and carried him to Babylon. Thus the prophecies both of Jeremiah and of Ezekiel were fulfilled, for the king of Judæa was brought captive to Babylon, yet he did not see that city.

The general of Nebuchadnezzar's army was ordered to pillage the temple and the royal palace, and afterwards to set fire to them, and to overthrow the whole city to its foundations. And he did as he was told, so that not a stone remained in its place. He also carried away captive all the people of Jerusalem who were not slain, except a few of the poor of the land, who were left to work in the fields and vineyards. The gold and silver and all the treasures of the temple and the royal palace were taken to Babylon, and Nebuchadnezzar dedicated the holy vessels to the service of his own gods.

And thus the kingdom of Judah came to an end.

Nebuchadnezzar made a man named Gedaliah ruler over the handful of people who were left in Judæa. He was a good man, and ruled justly. He took Jeremiah out of prison, and treated him kindly, and suffered him to live in the city of Mizpah, as he wished to do. Now, there were a certain number of the Jews who had fled from Jerusalem when it was taken. Hearing that the Babylonians had gone, they returned to their own country and submitted to the rule of Gedaliah. But there was among them a man named Ishmael, who was of the royal family of David, and he determined to wrest the government from Gedaliah. So he came with ten men to the house of Gedaliah, and Gedaliah, suspecting nothing, invited him and his men to dinner. But after they had eaten they rose up and slew the governor, and Ishmael fled to the land of the Ammonites.

The Jews were angry at what Ishmael had done, and were also greatly afraid, thinking the king of Babylon would avenge the death of his governor. They came in their distress to Jeremiah, and asked him what they should do. Jeremiah advised them to remain in Judæa. But though they had asked his counsel, they would not accept it after he had given it, and they all removed into Egypt, carrying Jeremiah with them. So the land of Judah was left desolate and without any inhabitants.

JEREMIAH AT THE FALL OF JERUSALEM

JEREMIAH AT THE FALL OF JERUSALEM

BY EDUARD FRIEDRICH BENDEMANN

(Germany, 1811–1889)

THE prophet Jeremiah strove for forty years to arouse the Jews to the fear of the Lord; but his only reward was abuse and imprisonment. In 586 B.C., they were overcome by the Chaldean King Nebuchadnezzar, and the city was razed to the ground. Many of its people were taken to Babylon as captives, but Nebuchadnezzar had such respect for Jeremiah that he allowed the old prophet to go wherever he might choose. Jeremiah chose to remain among the ruins of his city. The Book of Lamentations is an expression of his grief at the fall of Jerusalem. It begins: —

"How doth the city stand solitary, that was full of people: how is she become as a widow! she that was great among the nations, and princess among the provinces, how is she become tributary!

"She weepeth sore in the night, and her tears are on her cheeks: among all her lovers she hath none to comfort her: all her friends have dealt treacherously with her, they are become her enemies.

"Judah is gone into captivity because of affliction, and because of great servitude: she dwelleth among the heathen, she findeth no rest; all her persecutors overtook her between the straits."

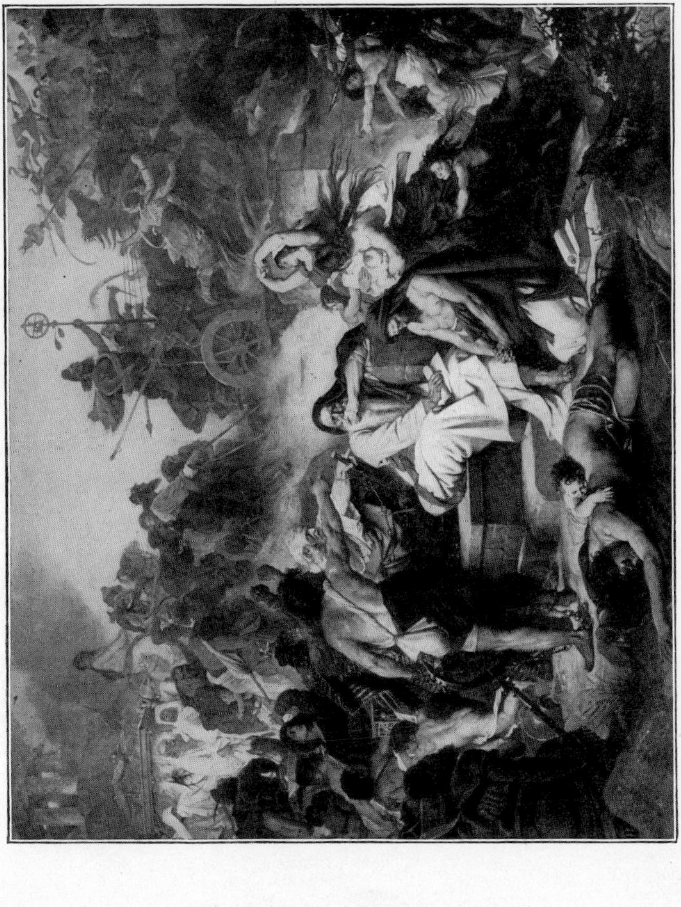

II
A ROMAN PROVINCE

HISTORICAL NOTE

DURING the last century before Christ, Pompey captured Jerusalem, and Palestine became a part of the Roman Empire. While Augustus was on the throne, in the most splendid period of Roman history, and during a time when, as Milton says, —

> "No war or battle's sound
> Was heard the world around," —

Jesus Christ was born in Bethlehem of Judæa.

The Jews were by no means quiet under the rule of Rome; but their fierce rebellions were crushed by their conquerors, and Jerusalem was leveled with the ground. Hadrian rebuilt the city, but changed its name to Ælia Capitolina, and forbade that any Jew should make it his home.

ON THE MORNING OF CHRIST'S NATIVITY

BY JOHN MILTON

I

THIS is the month, and this the happy morn,
Wherein the Son of Heaven's eternal King,
Of wedded maid and Virgin Mother born,
Our great redemption from above did bring;
For so the holy sages once did sing,
   That he our deadly forfeit should release,
And with his Father work us a perpetual peace.

II

That glorious Form, that Light unsufferable,
And that far-beaming blaze of majesty,
Wherewith he wont at Heaven's high council-table
To sit the midst of Trinal Unity,
He laid aside, and, here with us to be,
   Forsook the Courts of everlasting Day,
And chose with us a darksome house of mortal clay.

III

Say, Heavenly Muse, shall not thy sacred vein
Afford a present to the Infant God?
Hast thou no verse, no hymn, or solemn strain,
To welcome him to this his new abode,
Now while the heaven, by the Sun's team untrod,

PALESTINE

    Hath took no print of the approaching light,
And all the spangled host keep watch in squadrons
       bright?

IV

See how from far upon the Eastern road
The star-led Wisards haste with odours sweet!
Oh! run; prevent them with thy humble ode,
And lay it lowly at his blessèd feet;
Have thou the honour first thy Lord to greet,
    And join thy voice unto the Angel Quire,
From out his secret altar touched with hallowed fire.

THE HYMN

I

    It was the winter wild,
    While the heaven-born child
All meanly wrapt in the rude manger lies;
    Nature, in awe to him,
    Had doffed her gaudy trim,
With her great Master so to sympathize:
It was no season then for her
To wanton with the Sun, her lusty Paramour.

II

    Only with speeches fair
    She woos the gentle air
To hide her guilty front with innocent snow,
    And on her naked shame,
    Pollute with sinful blame,
The saintly veil of maiden white to throw;

ON THE MORNING OF CHRIST'S NATIVITY

Confounded, that her Maker's eyes
Should look so near upon her foul deformities.

III

But he, her fears to cease,
Sent down the meek-eyed Peace:
She, crowned with olive green, came softly sliding
Down through the turning sphere,
His ready Harbinger,
With turtle wing the amorous clouds dividing;
And, waving wide her myrtle wand,
She strikes a universal peace through sea and land.

IV

No war, or battail's sound,
Was heard the world around;
The idle spear and shield were high up-hung;
The hookèd chariot stood,
Unstained with hostile blood;
The trumpet spake not to the armèd throng;
And Kings sat still with awful eye,
As if they surely knew their sovran Lord was by.

V

But peaceful was the night
Wherein the Prince of Light
His reign of peace upon the earth began.
The winds, with wonder whist,
Smoothly the waters kissed,
Whispering new joys to the mild Ocean,
Who now hath quite forgot to rave,
While birds of calm sit brooding on the charmèd wave.

PALESTINE

VI

    The stars, with deep amaze,
    Stand fixed in steadfast gaze,
Bending one way their precious influence,
    And will not take their flight,
    For all the morning light,
Or Lucifer that often warned them thence;
But in their glimmering orbs did glow,
Until their Lord himself bespake, and bid them go.

VII

    And, though the shady gloom
    Had given day her room,
The Sun himself withheld his wonted speed,
    And hid his head for shame,
    As his inferior flame
The new-enlightened world no more should need:
He saw a greater Sun appear
Than his bright Throne or burning axletree could bear.

VIII

    The Shepherds on the lawn,
    Or ere the point of dawn,
Sat simply chatting in a rustic row;
    Full little thought they than
    That the mighty Pan
Was kindly come to live with them below:
Perhaps their loves, or else their sheep,
Was all that did their silly thoughts so busy keep.

ON THE MORNING OF CHRIST'S NATIVITY

IX

When such music sweet
Their hearts and ears did greet
As never was by mortal finger strook,
Divinely-warbled voice
Answering the stringèd noise,
As all their souls in blissful rapture took:
The air, such pleasure loth to lose,
With thousand echoes still prolongs each heavenly close.

X

Nature, that heard such sound
Beneath the hollow round
Of Cynthia's seat the airy Region thrilling,
Now was almost won
To think her part was done,
And that her reign had here its last fulfilling:
She knew such harmony alone
Could hold all Heaven and Earth in happier union.

XI

At last surrounds their sight
A globe of circular light,
That with long beams the shamefaced Night arrayed;
The helmèd Cherubim
And sworded Seraphim
Are seen in glittering ranks with wings displayed,
Harping in loud and solemn quire,
With unexpressive notes, to Heaven's new-born Heir.

PALESTINE

XII

Such music (as 't is said)
Before was never made,
But when of old the Sons of Morning sung,
While the Creator great
His constellations set,
And the well-balanced World on hinges hung,
And cast the dark foundations deep,
And bid the weltering waves their oozy channel keep.

XIII

Ring out, ye crystal spheres!
Once bless our human ears,
If ye have power to touch our senses so;
And let your silver chime
Move in melodious time;
And let the bass of heaven's deep organ blow;
And with your ninefold harmony
Make up full consort to the angelic symphony.

XIV

For, if such holy song
Enwrap our fancy long,
Time will run back and fetch the Age of Gold;
And speckled Vanity
Will sicken soon and die,
And leprous Sin will melt from earthly mould;
And Hell itself will pass away,
And leave her dolorous mansions to the peering day.

ON THE MORNING OF CHRIST'S NATIVITY

XV

    Yea, Truth and Justice then
    Will down return to men,
The enameled arras of the rainbow wearing;
    And Mercy set between,
    Throned in celestial sheen,
With radiant feet the tissued clouds down steering;
And Heaven, as at some festival,
Will open wide the gates of her high palace-hall.

XVI

    But wisest Fate says No,
    This must not yet be so;
The Babe lies yet in smiling infancy
    That on the bitter cross
    Must redeem our loss,
So both himself and us to glorify:
Yet first, to those ychained in sleep,
The wakeful trump of doom must thunder through the deep,

XVII

    With such a horrid clang
    As on Mount Sinai rang,
While the red fire and smouldering clouds outbrake:
    The aged Earth, aghast
    With terror of that blast,
Shall from the surface to the center shake,
When, at the world's last sessiön,
The dreadful Judge in middle air shall spread his throne.

PALESTINE

XVIII

And then at last our bliss
Full and perfect is,
But now begins; for from this happy day
The Old Dragon under ground,
In straiter limits bound,
Not half so far casts his usurpèd sway,
And, wroth to see his Kingdom fail,
Swindges the scaly horror of his folded tail.

XIX

The Oracles are dumb;
No voice or hideous hum
Runs through the archèd roof in words deceiving.
Apollo from his shrine
Can no more divine,
With hollow shriek the steep of Delphos leaving.
No nightly trance, or breathèd spell,
Inspires the pale-eyed Priest from the prophetic cell.

XX

The lonely mountains o'er,
And the resounding shore,
A voice of weeping heard and loud lament;
From haunted spring, and dale
Edgèd with poplar pale,
The parting Genius is with sighing sent;
With flower-inwoven tresses torn
The Nymphs in twilight shade of tangled thickets mourn.

ON THE MORNING OF CHRIST'S NATIVITY

XXI

    In consecrated earth,
    And on the holy hearth,
The Lars and Lemures moan with midnight plaint;
    In urns, and altars round,
    A drear and dying sound
Affrights the Flamens at their service quaint;
And the chill marble seems to sweat,
While each peculiar power forgoes his wonted seat.

XXII

    Peor and Baälim
    Forsake their temples dim,
With that twice-battered god of Palestine;
    And moonèd Ashtaroth,
    Heaven's Queen and Mother both,
Now sits not girt with tapers' holy shine:
The Libyc Hammon shrinks his horn;
In vain the Tyrian maids their wounded Thammuz mourn.

XXIII

    And sullen Moloch, fled,
    Hath left in shadows dread
His burning idol all of blackest hue;
    In vain with cymbals' ring
    They call the grisly king,
In dismal dance about the furnace blue;
The brutish gods of Nile as fast,
Isis, and Orus, and the dog Anubis, haste.

PALESTINE

XXIV

Nor is Osiris seen
In Memphian grove or green,
Trampling the unshowered grass with lowings loud;
Nor can he be at rest
Within his sacred chest;
Nought but profoundest Hell can be his shroud;
In vain, with timbreled anthems dark,
The sable-stolèd Sorcerers bear his worshiped ark.

XXV

He feels from Juda's land
The dreaded Infant's hand;
The rays of Bethlehem blind his dusky eyn;
Nor all the gods beside
Longer dare abide,
Not Typhon huge ending in snaky twine:
Our Babe, to show his Godhead true,
Can in his swaddling bands control the damnèd crew.

XXVI

So, when the Sun in bed,
Curtained with cloudy red,
Pillows his chin upon an orient wave,
The flocking shadows pale
Troop to the infernal jail,
Each fettered ghost slips to his several grave,
And the yellow-skirted Fays
Fly after the night-steeds, leaving their moon-loved maze.

ON THE MORNING OF CHRIST'S NATIVITY

XXVII
But see! the Virgin blest
Hath laid her Babe to rest,
Time is our tedious song should here have ending:
Heaven's youngest-teemèd star
Hath fixed her polished car,
Her sleeping Lord with handmaid lamp attending;
And all about the courtly stable
Bright-harnessed Angels sit in order serviceable.

THE BURNING OF THE TEMPLE
[70 A.D.]

BY FLAVIUS JOSEPHUS; SIMPLIFIED BY WILLIAM SHEPARD

[THE governors who were sent by the Romans to rule the province of Judæa treated the people so harshly that they rebelled. During the reign of Vespasian, his son Titus was sent against them. After a long siege, Jerusalem was captured in 70 A.D. Titus had intended that the Temple should be spared; but by the wanton act of a soldier it was burned. *The Editor.*]

IN order to destroy as many of their enemies as possible, the Jews made use of a stratagem. Along the western cloisters they filled the space between the rafters and the ceiling with dry wood, bitumen, and pitch, and then, as if worn out, they retreated from the cloisters. On this a number of Romans put up their scaling-ladders and mounted to the roof, without waiting for orders. But the more prudent suspected that a trap had been laid for them, and did not follow their comrades.

When the roof was filled with those who had clambered up, the Jews set fire to the whole range of cloisters from below. The flames rushed roaring upwards among the besiegers. They were thrown into a terrible fright. Some of them jumped down into the city, others into the very midst of the enemy. There they lay bruised to death or with broken limbs. Most of them, in trying to escape, perished in the flames, while many fell upon their own swords when they saw they could not save themselves.

THE BURNING OF THE TEMPLE

Titus, though very angry at all who had mounted the roof without waiting for orders, still was touched with pity when he beheld them burning up and dying before his eyes. He sprang forward and exhorted those around him to make every effort for their rescue. But nothing could be done to save them. A few of those who had mounted retired to a broader part of the roof, out of reach of the flames; but they were surrounded by the Jews and killed to a man, after having made a valiant resistance.

Towards the close of the struggle one of them, called Longus, was called upon by the Jews below, who said they would spare his life if he would come down and surrender. But his brother from among the Romans called out to him not to tarnish the honor of the family or that of the Roman arms by surrendering to the Jews. Longus then raised his sword in view of both armies and stabbed himself to the heart.

Among those who were entangled among the flames, one Artorius saved himself by his cunning. He called aloud to one of his fellow-soldiers below, "I say, Lucius! I will leave you heir to my property if you will come near and catch me."

Lucius ran up, and Artorius threw himself upon him, and was saved. But poor Lucius was dashed by the weight of his friend upon the pavement, and killed upon the spot.

The Roman soldiers were much cast down in spirits by the death of so many of their comrades, but still it made them all the more cautious and wary against the wily stratagems of the Jews. As the western gallery or cloister had been destroyed, they themselves set fire to the northern one, and laid it in ashes as far as the northeast corner, which was built over the ravine called Cedron.

In the mean time the famine raged with such fierceness that countless thousands died of hunger. In every house where there was the least morsel of food the inmates fought over it like dogs. The dearest friends fought for the most miserable little scraps. Gaping with hunger, the insurgents prowled about, and gnawed at anything that might seem like food. They chewed their belts and shoes, and tore off the leather from their shields. They ate up wisps of hay, and all sorts of nasty things, — in fact, anything that might help to sustain life.

When some of the mounds were finished, Titus ordered the battering-rams to be brought up at the western wing of the inner temple. For six days before, the largest of the rams had battered against the wall without effect. A part of the army tried to undermine the foundations of the northern gate. After a great deal of labor, they at last rolled out the front stones, but the gate itself, supported by the inner stones, still remained firm, so that the Romans gave up trying to force an entrance to the temple in this manner, and instead fixed their scaling-ladders to the galleries.

The Jews allowed the Romans to mount, but as soon as they reached the top, they hurled them down headlong, or slew them before they could cover themselves with their shields. Several ladders filled with armed men coming up to the attack they pushed aside from above, and thus hurled all the soldiers to the ground. All who had mounted fell by the swords of the Jews, and some of the Roman ensigns were captured. As Titus saw he

THE BURNING OF THE TEMPLE

could not force an entrance in this way, he ordered the gates to be set on fire.

At this time two of the insurgents belonging to Simon's body-guard deserted to Titus. They hoped for pardon because they surrendered in a moment of success. Titus had a great mind to put them both to death, because he thought that they had only surrendered through necessity, to save themselves from that ruin which they had helped to bring upon their native city. However, as he had promised protection to all who came to him, he kept his word, and allowed the deserters to depart without punishment.

The soldiers had already set the gates on fire, and the flames spread quickly to the galleries. When the Jews saw the circle of fire hem them in on every side, they lost courage, and stood gaping at the flames, without trying to put them out. Through the whole day and the following night the fire continued to burn the range of cloisters.

The next morning Titus gave orders that the fire should be put out and the gates thrown down, so as to admit the troops. He then called his generals together and held a council of war. Some of them wished to destroy the Temple at once, because they said as long as the Jews had the Temple to take refuge in they would continue to be rebellious. Others advised that if the Jews would leave the Temple at once it should be spared, but if they would continue to fight from it as if it were a fortress, it should be burned to the ground.

But Titus declared that, whatever happened, so magnificent a work as the Temple ought to be spared, because it would always be an ornament to the Roman

Empire. Three of his principal generals agreed with him in this view, and the council was dissolved. Some of the cohorts were immediately ordered to open a way through the ruins and put out the flames, while the rest of the army were allowed to repose, that they might be the more vigorous for action.

Upon the next day the Jews made a furious sally upon the guards who were posted in the outer court. The Romans closed up their ranks, locked their shields together in front like a wall, and bravely withstood the attack. But the Jews came pouring forth in such tremendous numbers that Titus was afraid the guards would be defeated, and hurried with his picked body of cavalry to assist them. The Jews could not withstand his charge, and retreated. But when he turned to go, they rallied and rushed again to the attack. The cavalry then charged, and the Jews were driven back, and shut up in the inner court of the Temple.

Titus then withdrew into Antonia, intending the next morning to make an attack with his entire force upon the Temple. But the beautiful edifice was upon that day doomed to destruction. The fated day had come, the 10th of August, the very day on which the former Temple had been destroyed by the King of Babylon.

When Titus retired, the insurgents again charged the Romans. A conflict took place between the Jewish guards of the sanctuary and the Roman troops who were trying to put out the flames in the inner court. The Jews were routed, and pursued even to the sanctuary.

At this moment a soldier, neither waiting for orders nor awed by so dread a deed, snatched up a burning brand, and, lifted by one of his comrades, he threw the

THE BURNING OF THE TEMPLE

brand through a small golden door on the north side which opened on the apartments around the sanctuary. As the flames caught, a fearful cry was raised by the Jews. They rushed to the rescue, caring nothing for their lives, now that their Temple was burning.

Titus was lying down in his tent, when some one rushed in and told him that the Temple was in flames. Starting up as he was, he at once ran to the spot in order to stop the flames. But there was such a noise and confusion that the soldiers either could not or would not hear the commands of their general, or heed the waving of his hand. Nothing could check the headlong fury of the soldiers. Many were trampled down by their own comrades about the entrances, and falling among the burning ruins of the outside galleries, they shared the fate of their enemies.

Mad with rage, and pretending not to hear the orders of their general, the soldiers rushed on, and hurled their torches into the sanctuary. The insurgents now were helpless, and made no attempt at defense. On every side was slaughter and flight. Numbers of feeble and unarmed citizens were butchered. Around the altar were heaps of slain; down its steps flowed a stream of blood which washed down the bodies that lay about.

As Titus could not restrain the fury of his soldiers, he entered with some of his generals into the holy place of the sanctuary, and looked upon all the splendors that it contained. As the flames had not yet reached the interior, but were still feeding upon the apartments around the Temple, Titus made one last effort to save the beautiful structure.

He hurried out, and again exhorted the soldiers to put

out the flames. At the same time he ordered one of his centurions to beat with his staff those who would not obey him. But neither respect for their general nor fear of punishment could check the soldiers. The din of battle, their rage, and hatred of the Jews, and hope of rich plunder, all combined to make the Romans ungovernable. For they saw that all about the Temple was made of gold, and they believed that within it they would find immense treasures.

Though Titus rushed out to restrain the soldiers, one even of those who had entered with him thrust fire amid the darkness between the hinges of the gate that opened into the inner temple. The whole building was in flames in an instant. Titus and his generals withdrew, and the beautiful building was left to its fate.

III
THE CRUSADES

HISTORICAL NOTE

IN 635, the Mohammedan Saracens gained possession of Palestine. They had no objection to the visits of pious pilgrims to Jerusalem; but after the capture of the land by the Seljukian Turks in the eleventh century, these visits became a dangerous matter, for the pilgrims were robbed and tortured and sometimes put to death. The indignation aroused in Christian nations resulted in the Crusades. At first these met with success, and what was called the Latin Kingdom of Jerusalem was founded. Less than a century later, however, the land was recaptured by the Saracen commander Saladin; and in the hands of the Mohammedans it has since remained. Among the Jews, however, the Zionist movement, a plan for their return to Palestine, is arousing much enthusiasm. This and the opening of the country to railroads give hope of progress and improvement.

"GOD WILLETH IT!"

[1095]

BY FRANÇOIS PIERRE GUILLAUME GUIZOT

HAKEM, Caliph of Egypt from 996 to 1021, persecuted the Christians, especially at Jerusalem, with all the violence of a fanatic and all the capriciousness of a despot. He ordered them to wear upon their necks a wooden cross five pounds in weight; he forbade them to ride on any animals but mules or asses; and, without assigning any motive for his acts, he confiscated their goods and carried off their children. It was told to him one day that, when the Christians assembled in the temple at Jerusalem to celebrate Easter, the priests of the church rubbed balsam-oil upon the iron chain which held up the lamp over the tomb of Christ, and afterwards set fire, from the roof, to the end of the chain; the fire stole down to the wick of the lamp and lighted it; then they shouted with admiration, as if fire from heaven had come down upon the tomb, and they glorified their faith. Hakem ordered the instant demolition of the church of the Holy Sepulchre, and it was accordingly demolished. Another time a dead dog had been laid at the door of a mosque; and the multitude accused the Christians of this insult. Hakem ordered them all to be put to death. The soldiers were preparing to execute the order when a young Christian said to his friends, "It were too grievous that the whole Church should perish; it were better that one should die for all; only promise to bless my memory year by year." He proclaimed himself alone to blame for the insult, and was accordingly alone put to death.

[Meanwhile, interest in the Holy Land was growing stronger every year. Rich and poor, nobles and peasants, were making pilgrimages to Jerusalem, sometimes several thousand in a company. When they returned, often with their numbers sadly diminished, they had terrible tales to tell of the sufferings that they had undergone while trying to fulfill a pious duty. Matters grew worse and worse, for the most barbarous tribe of the Turks now ruled the Holy Land, and the savage cruelty shown to both pilgrims and Christian inhabitants became intolerable. The ardor of the Christians of the West was all ready to burst into flame. Peter the Hermit was the man who applied the torch.

The Editor.]

Peter the Hermit, who was born in the neighborhood of Amiens about 1050, had gone, as so many others had, to Jerusalem, " to say his prayers there." Struck disconsolate at the sight of the sufferings and insults undergone by the Christians, he had an interview with Simeon, patriarch of Jerusalem, who "recognizing in him a man of discretion and full of experience in affairs of the world, set before him in detail all the evils with which the people of God, in the holy city, were afflicted.

"'Holy father,' said Peter to him, 'if the Roman Church and the princes of the West were informed, by a man of energy and worthy of belief, of all your calamities, of a surety they would essay to apply some remedy thereto by word and deed. Write, then, to our lord the Pope and to the Roman Church, and to the kings and princes of the West, and strengthen your written testimony by the authority of your seal. As for me, I shrink not from taking upon me a task for the salvation of my soul: and with the help of the Lord I am ready to go and seek out all of them, solicit them, show them the immensity of your troubles, and pray them all to hasten on the day of your relief.'"

The patriarch eagerly accepted the pilgrim's offer; and Peter set out, going first of all to Rome, where he handed to Pope Urban II the patriarch's letters, and commenced in that quarter his mission of zeal. The pope promised him not only support, but active coöperation when the propitious moment for it should arrive. Peter set to work, being still the pilgrim everywhere, in Europe, as well as at Jerusalem. "He was a man of very small stature, and his outside made but a very poor appearance; yet superior powers swayed this miserable body; he had a quick intellect and a penetrating eye, and he spoke with ease and fluency. . . . We saw him at that time," says his contemporary Guibert de Nogent, "scouring city and town, and preaching everywhere; the people crowded round him, heaped presents upon him, and celebrated his sanctity by such great praises that I remember not that like honor was ever rendered to any other person. He displayed great generosity in the disposal of all things that were given him. He restored wives to their husbands, not without the addition of gifts from himself, and he reëstablished, with marvelous authority, peace and good understanding between those who had been at variance. In all that he did or said he seemed to have in him something divine, insomuch that people went so far as to pluck hairs from his mule to keep as relics. In the open air he wore a woolen tunic, and over it a serge cloak which came down to his heels;

he had his arms and feet bare; he ate little or no bread, and lived chiefly on wine and fish."

In 1095, after the preaching errantry of Peter the Hermit, Pope Urban II was at Clermont, in Auvergne, presiding at the grand council, at which thirteen archbishops and two hundred and five bishops or abbots were met together, with so many princes and lay-lords that "about the middle of the month of November the towns and the villages of the neighborhood were full of people, and divers were constrained to have their tents and pavilions set up amidst the fields and meadows, notwithstanding that the season and the country were cold to an extreme." The first nine sessions of the council were devoted to the affairs of the Church in the West; but at the tenth Jerusalem and the Christians of the East became the subject of deliberation. The Pope went out of the church wherein the council was assembled, and mounted a platform erected upon a vast open space in the midst of the throng. Peter the Hermit, standing at his side, spoke first, and told the story of his sojourn at Jerusalem, all he had seen of the miseries and humiliations of the Christians, and all he himself had suffered there; for he had been made to pay tribute for admission into the Holy City, and for gazing upon the spectacle of the exactions, insults, and tortures he was recounting. After him, Pope Urban II spoke, in the French tongue, no doubt, as Peter had spoken, for he was himself a Frenchman, as the majority of those present were, grandees and populace. He made a long speech, entering upon the most painful details connected with the sufferings of the Christians of Jerusalem, "that royal city which the Redeemer of the human race had made

GOD WILLETH IT

illustrious by his coming, had honored by his residence, had hallowed by his passion, had purchased by his death, had distinguished by his burial. She now demands of you her deliverance; ... men of France, men from beyond the mountains, nations chosen and beloved of God, right valiant knights, recall the virtues of your ancestors, the virtue and greatness of King Charlemagne and your other kings; it is from you above all that Jerusalem awaits the help she invokes, for you above all nations, God has vouchsafed signal glory in arms. Take ye, then, the road to Jerusalem for the remission of your sins, and depart assured of the imperishable glory which awaits you in the kingdom of heaven."

From the midst of the throng arose one prolonged and general shout, "God willeth it! God willeth it!" The Pope paused for a moment; and then making a sign with his hand as if to ask for silence, he continued, "If the Lord God were not in your souls, ye would not all have uttered the same words. In the battle, then, be those your war-cry, those words that came from God; in the army of the Lord let naught be heard but that one shout, 'God willeth it! God willeth it!' We ordain not, and we advise not that the journey be undertaken by the old or the weak, or such as be not suited for arms, and let not women set out without their husbands or their brothers: let the rich help the poor; nor priests nor clerks may go without the leave of their bishops; and no layman shall commence the march save with the blessing of his pastor. Whosoever hath a wish to enter upon this pilgrimage, let him wear upon his brow or his breast the cross of the Lord, and let him, who in accomplishment of his desire, shall be willing to march away, place the cross behind him, between his shoulders; for thus he will fulfill the precept of the Lord, who said, 'He that doth not take up his cross and follow Me, is not worthy of Me.'"

The enthusiasm was general and contagious, as the first shout of the crowd had been; and a pious prelate, Adhemar, Bishop of Puy, was the first to receive the cross from the Pope's hands. It was of red cloth or silk, sewn upon the right shoulder of the coat or cloak, or fastened on the front of the helmet. The crowd dispersed to assume it and spread it.

THE CRUSADERS BEFORE JERUSALEM

THE CRUSADERS BEFORE JERUSALEM

BY WILHELM VON KAULBACH

(*Germany*, 1805-1874)

IN the center of the picture, but far away, stand the temple domes of Jerusalem. Directly over this is a vision in the heavens, the Christ, the Virgin Mary, and a group of saints and martyrs. The arms of the Christ are extended as if to bless all those who are yet upon the earth, represented by a multitude of figures. Among them there is in the foreground Peter the Hermit, cross in hand. Near him are the psalmists and also penitents, some of whom are scourging themselves for their sins. At his left is Armida with her knight Rinaldo, characters from Tasso's "Jerusalem Delivered." Between them and Jerusalem are bishops, knights, and preachers gazing eagerly at the Holy City. On a hill at the right Godfrey of Bouillon sits on a charger which is plainly wild and fiery, but now stands with head meekly bowed. Godfrey upholds in his hand the crown, which he offers to the Saviour as the real King of Jerusalem. Near him are many crusaders. The eyes of all are turned either upon Jerusalem or upon the vision in the clouds.

The artist's idea was to express symbolically the thought that the religion of Christ has become the faith of the world.

THE TEARING DOWN OF ENGLAND'S FLAG
[1191]

BY SIR WALTER SCOTT

[RICHARD I of England had barely been crowned when he set off on a crusade. With him were Philip of France and Leopold of Austria. Jealousy of Richard soon arose, and the two princes abandoned him and sought their own domains. In the following story, Scott has pictured one of their disagreements.

The Editor.]

THE king was soon at the foot of St. George's Mount, the sides as well as platform of which were now surrounded and crowded, partly by those belonging to the Duke of Austria's retinue, who were celebrating, with shouts of jubilee, the act which they considered as an assertion of national honor; partly by bystanders of different nations, whom dislike to the English, or mere curiosity, had assembled together, to witness the end of these extraordinary proceedings. Through this disorderly troop Richard burst his way, like a goodly ship under full sail, which cleaves her forcible passage through the rolling billows, and heeds not that they unite after her passage, and roar upon her stern.

The summit of the eminence was a small level space on which were pitched the rival banners, surrounded still by the Archduke's friends and retinue. In the midst of the circle was Leopold himself, still contemplating with self-satisfaction the deed he had done, and still listening to the shouts of applause which his partisans bestowed with no sparing breath. While he was in this state of self-gratulation, Richard burst into the circle, attended, indeed, only by two men, but in his own headlong energies an irresistible host.

"Who has dared," he said, laying his hands upon the Austrian standard, and speaking in a voice like the sound which precedes an earthquake; "who has dared to place this paltry rag beside the banner of England?"

The Archduke wanted not personal courage, and it was impossible he could hear this question without reply. Yet, so much was he troubled and surprised by the unexpected arrival of Richard, and affected by the general awe inspired by his ardent and unyielding character, that the demand was twice repeated, in a tone which seemed to challenge heaven and earth, ere the Archduke replied with such firmness as he could command, "It was I, Leopold of Austria."

"Then shall Leopold of Austria," replied Richard, "presently see the rate at which his banner and his pretensions are held by Richard of England."

So saying, he pulled up the standard-spear, splintered it to pieces, threw the banner itself on the ground, and placed his foot upon it.

"Thus," said he, "I trample on the banner of Austria — is there a knight among your Teutonic chivalry dare impeach my deed?"

There was a momentary silence; but there are no braver men than the Germans.

"I," and "I," and "I," was heard from several knights of the Duke's followers; and he himself added his voice to those which accepted the King of England's defiance.

THE TEARING DOWN OF ENGLAND'S FLAG

"Why do we dally thus?" said the Earl Wallenrode, a gigantic warrior from the frontiers of Hungary: "brethren, and noble gentlemen, this man's foot is on the honor of your country; let us rescue it from violation, and down with the pride of England!"

So saying, he drew his sword, and struck at the King a blow which might have proved fatal, had not the Scot intercepted and caught it upon his shield.

"I have sworn," said King Richard, — and his voice was heard above all the tumult, which now waxed wild and loud, — "never to strike one whose shoulder bears the cross; therefore live, Wallenrode, — but live to remember Richard of England."

As he spoke, he grasped the tall Hungarian round the waist, and, unmatched in wrestling, as in other military exercises, hurled him backwards with such violence that the mass flew as if discharged from a military engine, not only through the ring of spectators who witnessed the extraordinary scene, but over the edge of the mount itself, down the steep side of which Wallenrode rolled headlong, until, pitching at length upon his shoulder, he dislocated the bone, and lay like one dead. This almost supernatural display of strength did not encourage either the Duke or any of his followers, to renew a personal contest so inauspiciously commenced. Those who stood farthest back did, indeed, clash their swords, and cry out, "Cut the island mastiff to pieces!" but those who were nearer, veiled, perhaps, their personal fears under an affected regard for order, and cried, for the most part, "Peace! peace! the peace of the Cross — the peace of Holy Church, and our Father the Pope!"

These various cries of the assailants, contradicting each

other, showed their irresolution; while Richard, his foot still on the archducal banner, glared round him, with an eye that seemed to seek an enemy, and from which the angry nobles shrunk appalled, as from the threatened grasp of a lion. De Vaux and the Knight of the Leopard kept their places beside him; and though the swords which they held were still sheathed, it was plain that they were prompt to protect Richard's person to the very last, and their size and remarkable strength plainly showed the defense would be a desperate one.

Salisbury and his attendants were also now drawing near, with bills and partisans brandished, and bows already bended.

At this moment, King Philip of France, attended by one or two of his nobles, came on the platform to inquire the cause of the disturbance, and made gestures of surprise at finding the King of England raised from his sick-bed, and confronting their common ally the Duke of Austria, in such a menacing and insulting posture. Richard himself blushed at being discovered by Philip, whose sagacity he respected as much as he disliked his person, in an attitude neither becoming his character as a monarch, nor as a Crusader; and it was observed that he withdrew his foot, as if accidentally, from the dishonored banner, and exchanged his look of violent emotion for one of affected composure and indifference. Leopold also struggled to attain some degree of calmness, mortified as he was by having been seen by Philip in the act of passively submitting to the insults of the fiery King of England.

Possessed of many of those royal qualities for which he was termed by his subjects the August, Philip might

THE TEARING DOWN OF ENGLAND'S FLAG

be termed the Ulysses, as Richard was indisputably the Achilles, of the Crusade. The King of France was sagacious, wise, deliberate in council, steady and calm in action, seeing clearly, and steadily pursuing, the measures most for the interest of his kingdom — dignified and royal in his deportment, brave in person, but a politician rather than a warrior. The Crusade would have been no choice of his own, but the spirit was contagious, and the expedition was enforced upon him by the Church, and by the unanimous wish of his nobility. In any other situation, or in a milder age, his character might have stood higher than that of the adventurous Cœur-de-Lion. But in the Crusade itself, an undertaking wholly irrational, sound reason was the quality, of all others, least estimated, and the chivalric valor which both the age and the enterprise demanded, was considered as debased, if mingled with the least touch of discretion. So that the merit of Philip, compared with that of his haughty rival, showed like the clear but minute flame of a lamp, placed near the glare of a huge blazing torch, which, not possessing half the utility, makes ten times more impression on the eye. Philip felt his inferiority in public opinion, with the pain natural to a high-spirited prince; and it cannot be wondered at if he took such opportunities as offered, for placing his own character in more advantageous contrast with that of his rival. The present seemed one of those occasions, in which prudence and calmness might reasonably expect to triumph over obstinacy and impetuous violence.

"What means this unseemly broil betwixt the sworn brethren of the Cross — the royal Majesty of England

and the princely Duke Leopold? How is it possible that those who are the chiefs and pillars of this holy expedition —"

"A truce with thy remonstrance, France," said Richard, enraged inwardly at finding himself placed on a sort of equality with Leopold, yet not knowing how to resent it, — "this duke, or prince, or pillar, if you will, hath been insolent, and I have chastised him — that is all. Here is a coil, forsooth, because of spurning a hound!"

"Majesty of France," said the Duke, "I appeal to you and every sovereign prince against the foul indignity which I have sustained. This King of England hath pulled down my banner — torn and trampled on it."

"Because he had the audacity to plant it beside mine," said Richard.

"My rank as thine equal entitled me," replied the Duke, emboldened by the presence of Philip.

"Assert such equality for thy person," said King Richard, "and, by St. George, I will treat thy person as I did thy broidered kerchief there, fit but for the meanest use to which kerchief may be put."

"Nay, but patience, brother of England," said Philip, "and I will presently show Austria that he is wrong in this matter. — Do not think, noble Duke," he continued, "that, in permitting the standard of England to occupy the highest point in our camp, we, the independent sovereigns of the Crusade, acknowledge any inferiority to the royal Richard. It were inconsistent to think so; since even the oriflamme itself — the great banner of France, to which the royal Richard himself, in respect of his French possessions, is but a vassal — holds

THE TEARING DOWN OF ENGLAND'S FLAG

for the present an inferior place to the Lions of England. But as sworn brethren of the Cross, military pilgrims, who, laying aside the pomp and pride of this world, are hewing with our swords the way to the Holy Sepulchre, I myself, and the other princes, have renounced to King Richard, from respect to his high renown and great feats of arms, that precedence, which elsewhere, and upon other motives, would not have been yielded. I am satisfied, that when your royal grace of Austria shall have considered this, you will express sorrow for having placed your banner on this spot, and that the royal Majesty of England will then give satisfaction for the insult he has offered."

The *spruch-sprecher* and the jester had both retired to a safe distance when matters seemed coming to blows, but returned when words, their own commodity, seemed again about to become the order of the day.

The man of proverbs was so delighted with Philip's politic speech, that he clashed his baton at the conclusion by way of emphasis, and forgot the presence in which he was, so far as to say aloud, that he himself had never said a wiser thing in his life.

"It may be so," whispered Jonas Schwanker, "but we shall be whipt if you speak so loud."

The Duke answered, sullenly, that he would refer his quarrel to the general Council of the Crusade — a motion which Philip highly applauded, as qualified to take away a scandal most harmful to Christendom.

Richard, retaining the same careless attitude, listened to Philip until his oratory seemed exhausted, and then said aloud, "I am drowsy — this fever hangs about me still. Brother of France, thou art acquainted with my humor, and that I have at all times but few words to spare; know, therefore, at once, I will submit a matter touching the honor of England neither to Prince, Pope, nor Council. Here stands my banner — whatsoever pennon shall be reared within three butts' length of it — aye, were it the oriflamme, of which you were, I think, but now speaking, shall be treated as that dishonored rag; nor will I yield other satisfaction than that which these poor limbs can render in the lists to any bold challenge — aye, were it against five champions instead of one."

"Now," said the jester, whispering his companion, "that is as complete a piece of folly, as if I myself had said it; but yet, I think, there may be in this matter a greater fool than Richard yet."

"And who may that be?" asked the man of wisdom.

"Philip," said the jester, "or our own Royal Duke, should either accept the challenge — But oh, most sage *spruch-sprecher*, what excellent kings would thou and I have made, since those on whose heads these crowns have fallen, can play the proverb-monger and the fool as completely as ourselves!"

While these worthies plied their offices apart, Philip answered calmly to the almost injurious defiance of Richard, — "I came not hither to awaken fresh quarrels, contrary to the oath we have sworn, and the holy cause in which we have engaged. I part from my brother of England as brother should part, and the only strife between the Lions of England and the Lilies of France shall be, which shall be carried deepest into the ranks of the infidels."

"It is a bargain, my royal brother," said Richard,

THE TEARING DOWN OF ENGLAND'S FLAG

stretching out his hand with all the frankness which belonged to his rash but generous disposition; "and soon may we have the opportunity to try this gallant and fraternal wager!"

"Let this noble Duke also partake in the friendship of this happy moment," said Philip; and the Duke approached half sullenly, half willing to enter into some accommodation.

"I think not of fools, nor of their folly," said Richard, carelessly; and the Archduke, turning his back on him, withdrew from the ground.

THE CHILDREN'S CRUSADE

[1212]

BY EVA MARCH TAPPAN

A MARVELOUS thing now came to pass, for the children of France and Germany went on a crusade. Stephen, a French shepherd boy twelve years old, declared that Jesus had appeared to him and bidden him lead a company of children to rescue the Holy Sepulcher from the infidels. Other children joined him, and they went about from village to village, bearing crosses and candles, swinging censers, singing hymns, and crying, "God wills it! God wills it!" Soon a great army of boys and girls, including the humblest shepherd lads and the children of wealthy nobles, started on a march for the Holy Land. No one could stop them. The king bade them return to their homes, but they only cried the more, "God wills it!" They broke away from their friends, from the very arms of their parents. The older folk knew not what to think. Some said this was a work of Satan to destroy the children. Others believed that it was the will of God that where armed men had failed, innocent children should succeed; and they dared not hold them back lest they should be fighting against God.

In Germany, too, there was a boy preacher, one Nicholas; and he aroused the German children as Stephen aroused the French. The little German boys and girls set out, twenty thousand strong, many of them wearing long gray coats upon which crosses were sewn.

THE CHILDREN'S CRUSADE

They had broad-brimmed hats, and they carried the staffs of pilgrims. As they marched, they sang hymns. One of these has come down to us. It begins, —

> "Fairest Lord Jesus,
> Ruler of all nature."

But the way grew rougher and rougher. The air of the mountains was cold. They came to desert places where there was no food. Thousands died, and when the others reached the city of Genoa, they were only seven thousand. Still the children did not lose courage. God would open a way for them through the sea, they believed, and soon they would be in the Holy Land. They would tell the story of the good Jesus. The infidels would listen and would become his followers.

The morning came. They waited patiently on the shore at Genoa, but no path was opened through the sea. There is a tradition that part of the children sailed for Syria, but what became of them is not known. Some pressed on to Rome. They told the Pope about their journey and their sufferings. He said that it was of no use for them to try to reach Syria, but, as they were bound by their vows, they must go on a crusade when they were older.

By this time only a few children were left. Many had died, as has been said; some had been stolen or sold as slaves, and still others had stopped in one place or another. Nothing now remained but to suffer the long, hard journey home; and at last this, too, was ended. "Tell us of your wanderings. Where have you been?" begged their parents and friends; but all that the tired little crusaders could answer was, "We do not know."

Meanwhile, the French children, thirty thousand in

PALESTINE

all, had set out for Marseilles. Their way was less rough, but the heat of the summer was terrible. Many of the little ones had never been farther from their homes than some neighboring village, and whenever they came in sight of a city wall or a castle, they would ask piteously, "Is n't that Jerusalem?" After a journey of three hundred miles, about twenty thousand of them came to Marseilles. "Let us stay here to-night," they begged, "and to-morrow God will open a way for us through the sea." No path was opened, and many started to return to their homes. At length two merchants offered to provide vessels for all who wished to go to the Holy Land. "We do it for the cause of God," they said, "and we ask no reward but your prayers." Then the children were happy. "This is the path through the sea," they cried joyfully. "This is what God promised us." Seven vessels full of the bravest of the children set sail to cross the blue Mediterranean. Eighteen years later, an old priest came to Europe and told the sad ending of the story. Two of the seven vessels had been wrecked; but the hundreds of children on board the others had been carried to the coast of Africa and sold to the Mohammedans as slaves; for the generous men of Marseilles who had so kindly offered to carry them across the sea were slave-traders. Of the seven shiploads of children, not one ever saw his home again.

THE CHILDREN'S CRUSADE
[1212]

BY HENRY WADSWORTH LONGFELLOW

WHAT is this I read in history,
Full of marvel, full of mystery,
Difficult to understand?
Is it fiction, is it truth?
Children in the flower of youth,
Heart in heart, and hand in hand,
Ignorant of what helps or harms,
Without armor, without arms,
Journeying to the Holy Land!

Who shall answer or divine?
Never since the world was made
Such a wonderful crusade
Started forth for Palestine.
Never while the world shall last
Will it reproduce the past;
Never will it see again
Such an army, such a band,
Over mountain, over main,
Journeying to the Holy Land.

Like a shower of blossoms blown
From the parent trees were they;
Like a flock of birds that fly

PALESTINE

Through the unfrequented sky,
Holding nothing as their own,
Passed they into lands unknown,
Passed to suffer and to die.

ST. LOUIS AS A PRISONER
[1250]

BY JOSEPH FRANÇOIS MICHAUD

[IN 1248, Louis IX of France (St. Louis) went on a crusade. He invaded Egypt and captured Damietta, but was taken prisoner by the Mussulmans.
The Editor.]

HE [Louis] had no covering at night but a coarse cassock, which he owed to the charity of another prisoner. In this state, he never addressed one petition to his enemies, nor did the tone of his language announce either fear or submission. One of his almoners afterwards attested upon oath that Louis never suffered a word of despair or a movement of impatience to escape from him. The Mussulmans were astonished at this resignation, and said among themselves that if ever their prophet should leave them a prey to such great adversities, they would abandon his faith and his worship. Of all his riches, Louis had saved only his book of psalms, too sterile a spoil to be worth the attention of the Saracens; and when all the world seemed to have abandoned him, this book alone consoled him in his misfortune. He every day recited those hymns of the prophets in which God himself speaks of his justice and his mercy, reassures virtue which suffers in his name, and threatens with his anger those whom prosperity intoxicates, and who abuse their triumph.

Thus religious sentiments and remembrances sustained the courage of Louis even in fetters; and the pious monarch, surrounded every day by fresh perils, amidst a Mussulman army that he had irritated by his victories, might still cry out with the prophet-king, "Supported by the living God, who is my buckler and my glory, I will not fear the crowd of enemies encamped around me."

The Sultan of Cairo, appearing inclined to soften his rigorous policy, sent Louis fifty magnificent dresses for himself and the lords of his train. Louis refused to clothe himself in them, saying that he was the sovereign of a greater kingdom than Egypt, and that he would never wear the livery of a foreign prince. Almoadam ordered a great feast to be prepared, to which he invited the king. But Louis would not accept of this invitation, as he was persuaded it was meant only to exhibit him as a spectacle to the Mussulman army. At length the sultan sent his most skillful physicians to him, and did all he could to preserve a prince whom he destined to adorn his triumph, and by whose means he hoped to obtain the advantages attached to his last victory. Before long he proposed to the king to break his chains upon condition of his giving up Damietta and the cities of Palestine that were still under the power of the Franks. Louis replied that the Christian cities of Palestine did not belong to him; that God had recently replaced Damietta in the hands of the Christians, and that no human power had the right to dispose of it. The sultan, irritated by this refusal, resolved to employ violence. At one time he threatened Louis to send him to the Caliph of Bagdad, who would closely imprison him till death; at another, he announced the project of leading

ST. LOUIS AS A PRISONER

his illustrious captive throughout the East, and of exhibiting to all Asia a king of the Christians reduced to slavery. At length he went so far as to threaten to have him placed in the barnacles, a frightful punishment reserved for the greatest criminals. Louis still showed himself firm, and as the only reply to all these menaces, said, "I am the sultan's prisoner, he can do with me what he pleases."

The King of France suffered, though he did not complain; he feared nothing on his own account, but when he thought of his faithful army, and of the fate of the other captives, his heart was a prey to the deepest sorrow. The Christian prisoners were crowded into one open court; some sick, others wounded, the greater part naked, and all exposed to hunger, the injuries of the elements, and the ill-treatment of their pitiless guards. A Mussulman was commanded to write the names of all these wretched captives, whose number amounted to more than ten thousand. They led all that could purchase their liberty into a vast tent; the others remained in the place into which they had been driven like a flock of animals, destined to perish miserably. Every day an emir, by the sultan's orders, entered this abode of despair, and caused two or three hundred prisoners to be dragged out of the inclosure. They were asked if they would abjure the religion of Christ; and those whom the fear of death induced to desert their faith received their liberty; the others were put to the sword, and their bodies were cast into the Nile. They were slaughtered during the night; silence and darkness adding to the horrors of the execution. During several days the steel of the executioner thus decimated the unhappy prisoners.

None were ever seen to return who went out of the inclosure. Their sad companions, on bidding them farewell, wept beforehand over their tragical end, and lived in certain expectation of a similar fate. At length the lassitude of slaughter caused those that remained to be spared. They were led away to Cairo; and the capital of Egypt, into which they had flattered themselves they should enter in triumph, beheld them arrive covered with rags and loaded with chains. They were thrown into dungeons, where many died of hunger and grief; the others, condemned to slavery in a foreign land, deprived of all assistance and of all communication with their leaders, without knowing what was become of their king, were hopeless of ever recovering their liberty, or of revisiting the West.

The Oriental historians relate the scenes we have just described with indifference; many even seem to consider the massacre of prisoners of war as a second victory; and, as if the misfortune and murder of a disarmed enemy could heighten the glory of a conqueror, they exaggerate in their accounts the misery of the vanquished, and particularly the number of the victims immolated to Islamism.

The barons and knights that were shut up in the pavilion were not ignorant of the fate of their companions in arms; they passed their days and nights in continual terrors. The sultan wished to obtain from them that which he had not been able to obtain from Louis IX. He sent an emir to inform them that he would set them at liberty if Damietta and the Christian cities of Palestine were restored to the Mussulmans. The Count of Brittany replied, in the name of all the prisoners, that

that which was asked of them was not in their power, and that French warriors had no other will than that of their king. "It is plainly to be perceived," said the messenger of Almoadam, "that you care very little for liberty or life. *You shall see some men accustomed to sword-playing.*" The emir retired, leaving the prisoners in expectation of an early death. The apparatus of punishment was exhibited before them. The sword remained several days suspended over their heads; but Almoadam could make no impression upon their firmness. Thus, neither the captivity of an entire army, nor the death of so many warriors, had been able to deprive the Christians of a single one of their conquests, and one of the bulwarks of Egypt was still in their hands. The conquerors prayed and threatened by turns; the conquered resisted all their endeavors, and always appeared masters.

In the mean time several French nobles offered to pay their own ransom. Louis was informed of this; and as he feared that many, not having the means to redeem themselves, would remain in chains, he forbade any particular treaty. The barons and knights, but lately so intractable, did not persist in opposing the will of an unfortunate king, and instantly gave up all idea of a separate negotiation. The king said he would pay for everybody, and that he would never think about his own liberty till after he had assured that of all others.

While the Sultan of Cairo was thus making useless attempts to overcome the pride and lower the courage of Louis and his knights, the favorites he had brought with him from Mesopotamia pressed their master to conclude the peace quickly. "You have," said they to him, "enemies much more dangerous than the Christians; they are the emirs, who wish to reign in your place, and who never cease to boast of their victories, as if you had not yourself conquered the Franks, as if the God of Mahomet had not sent pestilence and famine to aid you in triumphing over the defenders of Christ: hasten, then, to terminate the war, in order that you may strengthen your power within, and begin to reign." These speeches, which flattered the pride of Almoadam, induced him to make rather more reasonable proposals to his enemies. The sultan limited his demand to a ransom of a million of golden byzants, and the restitution of Damietta. Louis, aware that the city of Damietta could not resist, consented to the proposals that were made to him, *if the queen approved of them.* As the Mussulmans expressed some surprise at this, the king added, "*The queen is my lady; I can do nothing without her consent.*" The ministers of the sultan returned a second time, and told the French monarch that if the queen would pay the sum agreed upon, he should be free. "A King of France," answered he, "is not to be redeemed by money; the city of Damietta shall be given up for my deliverance, and a million of golden byzants paid for that of my army." The sultan agreed to all; and, whether he was pleased at having terminated the negotiations, or whether he was touched by the noble character the captive monarch had displayed, he reduced the sum fixed upon as the ransom of the Christian army a fifth.

The knights and barons were still ignorant of the conclusion of the treaty, and were revolving in their minds their customary melancholy reflections, when they saw an old Saracen enter their pavilion. His venerable figure

ST. LOUIS AS A PRISONER

and the gravity of his carriage inspired respect. His train, composed of men-at-arms, inspired fear. The old man, without any preliminary discourse, asked the prisoners by means of an interpreter if it was true that they believed in a God, born of a woman, crucified for the salvation of the human race, and resuscitated the third day. All having answered at once that that was their belief: "In that case," added he, "congratulate yourselves at suffering for your God; you are yet far from having suffered as much for Him as He suffered for you. Place your hopes in Him, and if He has been able to recall Himself to life, He will not want power to put an end to the evils that afflict you now."

On finishing these words, the old Mussulman retired, leaving the crusaders divided between surprise, fear, and hope. On the next day it was announced to them that the king had concluded a truce, and wished to take counsel of his barons. John of Vallery, Philip de Montfort, and Guy and Baldwin d'Ibelin were deputed to wait upon the king. It was not long before the crusaders learned that their captivity was about to end, and that the king had paid the ransom of the poor as well as the rich. When these brave knights turned their thoughts towards their victories, they never could conceive how it was possible for them to have fallen into the hands of the infidels; and when they reflected on their late misfortunes, their deliverance appeared equally miraculous to them. All raised their voices in praises to God, and benedictions to the King of France.

END OF VOLUME II

The Riverside Press
CAMBRIDGE · MASSACHUSETTS
U · S · A

RET'D NOV 15 1986

FEB 25 1990